PIERCING THE REICH

PIERCING THE REICH

THE PENETRATION OF NAZI GERMANY BY AMERICAN SECRET AGENTS DURING WORLD WAR II

JOSEPH E. PERSICO

BARNES
&NOBLE
BOOKS
NEW YORK

To my mother and the memory of my father

And Moses sent them to spy out the land of Canaan, and said unto them, Get you up this way southward, and go up into the mountain:

And see the land, what it is; and the people that dwelleth therein, whether they be strong or weak, few or many;

And what the land is that they dwell in, whether it be good or bad; and what cities they be that they dwell in, whether in tents, or in strong holds. . . .

NUMBERS 13:17–19

Preface

✣ ✣ ✣

This story could not be told for over thirty years. Prior to 1976, the record of the penetration of Nazi Germany by American intelligence agents was locked in the archives of the Central Intelligence Agency, classified "Secret" and "Top Secret." Then, in February 1976, the first official revelation of these operations appeared when the CIA declassified *The War Report of the OSS, Volume II.* This history had been prepared in 1947 and kept under a security wrap ever since. The report summarized OSS operations worldwide during the war, including a brief but tantalizing account of the largely undisclosed infiltration of the Third Reich by nearly two hundred American spies. I was fortunate enough to obtain an early Xerox copy of the *War Report* within days of its declassification.

The idea of secret agents of the United States infiltrating as thoroughgoing a police state as Nazi Germany was immediately compelling. Under the Freedom of Information Act, I requested that the CIA declassify its files on these OSS operations. As this material was made available to me, it became apparent that beneath the tip of the iceberg revealed by the *War Report* loomed a dramatic, significant, and largely unexplored intelligence triumph of World War II. I presented the possibilities to my publishers, who immediately encouraged me to proceed.

My plan was to research the work on two levels: to use the CIA files and to interview personally those who planned the missions and those who actually served as America's secret agents inside the Reich. From the CIA, I eventually acquired 520 previously classified documents and thus became the first private citizen to see this material since it had been locked away over three decades before.

The second research approach, the interviews with participants, proved a more difficult undertaking. Even after the passage of so many years, the CIA still felt compelled to conceal the identity of all foreigners (the bulk of OSS agents) who had served as secret operatives of the United States inside Germany. Thus, in the material provided to me, these names had been excised. The problem of locating someone, thirty-two or thirty-three years after the event, presumably living somewhere in Germany, Austria, Belgium, or France, with nothing to go on but a code name, seemed insurmountable.

Locating Americans whose names appeared in OSS documents proved no minor task, either. The best that the CIA could provide was a person's address at the time of entry into OSS. Few Americans in this mobile society, it seemed, still live in the 1970s where they lived in the 1940s. Finding these people was complicated by the fact that the logical sources of assistance, the Department of Defense or the Veterans Administration, will not provide last-known addresses of former servicemen; providing this information is regarded as a violation of the Privacy Act of 1974.

The breakthrough came when I was able to acquire a ten-year-old mailing list of a private organization, the Veterans of OSS. Finding one participant in the German missions through this list led to finding others. Some of these American intelligence officers had actually served as agents within the Reich. Others had maintained contact with foreign agents whom they had infiltrated into Germany, or recalled these agents' names and, in some cases, old addresses. In the course of nearly two years of searching, on both sides of the Atlantic, I was ultimately able to reach almost everyone I sought who was still alive, 122 persons in all.

Through these personal meetings, supplemented by telephone and written interviews, together with the documents declassified at my request by the CIA, the full account of American espionage inside Nazi Germany emerged. Most of the missions described in *Piercing the Reich* are thus revealed for the first time. To those few accounts of operations inside the Reich which have previously been published, I have been able to add much original material from the written record and the first-hand recollections of participants.

In some cases I have been asked by persons interviewed to use pseudonyms. Even at this late date, several Europeans were concerned about possible repercussions should it become known that they had performed as secret agents of a foreign and, in some cases, an enemy power. Pseudonyms have also been employed where no other identification was provided in OSS records. All such instances have been noted in supplemental material at the back of the book.

The penetration of Germany was a long-postponed decision, one that OSS had avoided and hoped would not be necessary until the prolongation of the war after the autumn of 1944 made it unavoidable. The British, mentors of the inexperienced Americans in affairs of intelligence, had no great faith that the Reich could be penetrated and made little effort in that direction themselves. Their experiences had left them dubious of any espionage operations within enemy territory not supported by a reasonably strong local resistance organization. But the United States did succeed on a significant scale and reaped an abundant harvest of intelligence. OSS, in fact, reached its fullest maturation as an intelligence service in the penetration of Nazi Germany. The United States, essentially without such a service at the war's beginning, had, by the end of the German operations, an espionage apparatus to rival any nation's. Of all the clandestine battles of World War II, this piercing of the Nazi heartland emerges as one of the most daring, and it was carried off by some of the boldest combatants in the secret war.

JOSEPH E. PERSICO

Washington, D.C.
July 19, 1978

Acknowledgments

✣ ✣ ✣

Among all authors, the writer of history recognizes most clearly his debt to the expertise and assistance of others. The story of OSS operations inside Germany, for example, was first suggested to me in conversations with William Cunliffe, assistant chief of the Modern Military Branch at the National Archives. I am also indebted to his associates, particularly John Taylor, for further research assistance and to Mr. Cunliffe for careful reading of the final manuscript.

The great mass of written documentation with which I worked was acquired from the archives of the Central Intelligence Agency. There, I received valued assistance from Gene Wilson and his staff, particularly Bernard Drell, who was unfailingly helpful. Also at the CIA, William Flippen and Robert Owen were most cooperative. Above all, I am grateful to Joseph Gigliotti, who treated my requests to the CIA with good judgment and as much speed as possible. I also had the good fortune of having access to the private library of Mr. Walter Pforzheimer, of the CIA, who has gathered a unique collection of works on intelligence.

I was generously assisted by the military-service historians. I particularly want to thank, at the Department of the Army, Charles B. MacDonald and Hannah M. Zeidlik. Kenneth Adelman, formerly of the secretary of defense's staff, was invaluable in helping to locate people essential to the story.

The nature of the operations on which I wrote required considerable research at the air force archives, and here I am deeply grateful to the able staff of General John W. Huston, particularly George Watson, Max Rosenberg, and David Schoem. Dana Bell, of the air force's 1361st Audio-Visual Squadron, kindly provided me with not only photographs but highly useful documents.

At the Library of Congress, Margrit Krewson was invaluable not only in facilitating the use of reference works essential to the project but for her research advice and indispensable help with documents in German. Mrs. Krewson, because of her family's personal wartime experience in Germany, had a special perception of the work. I am grateful as well for the thoughtful assistance at the library of Sybil Pike.

Many of the former OSS personnel whom I interviewed went well beyond providing information on the German operations and took great pains to help me locate colleagues important to the story. William J. Casey was generous with his time and a good friend throughout the project. Henry B. Hyde opened many useful doors for me. John Shaheen provided me with a treasure of early material published on the OSS. John Howley, of the Veterans of OSS, kindly opened his membership files to me, which proved invaluable. Ray Cline ran a story in the Veterans' newsletter, which led to several participants in the story. Similarly, John J. Coakly, executive director of the Association of Former Intelligence Officers, enabled me to locate people through the columns of the AFIO newsletter. Two OSS veterans to whom I could always turn for informed guidance were Gary Van Arkel and Otto C. Doering.

In preparing for my research abroad I was dependent on several foreign embassies in Washington. I will forever be indebted to the press secretary of the Austrian embassy, Franz Cyrus, who not only did so much to make my Austrian interviews succeed but provided guidance on numerous substantive matters and proved a good friend. I also appreciate the highly helpful letters of introduction provided to me by James Preuschen, chargé d'affaires of the Austrian embassy. Equally valuable letters were prepared for me by His Excellency Berndt von Staden, ambassador of the Federal Republic of Germany, and his Excellency Willy Van Cauwenberg, ambassador of Belgium.

My interviews in Europe succeeded, in great measure, because I had the aid of officials of the U.S. Information Agency. My former USIA colleague, Jody Lewinsohn, graciously paved the way. At USIS Austria,

Arthur Bardos and his associate, Ingrid Hirt, did a great deal to assist me, as did James McIntosh and Patricia Baker in Belgium. In Strasbourg, I benefited immeasurably from the energies and talents of Gilbert Hadey of the American consular staff.

My work in Europe was also importantly aided by Herbert Steiner of the Austrian Resistance Archives Center in Vienna, Martin Dolp, who translated for me in Innsbruck, and Dr. Jean Vanwelkenhuysen of the World War II Historic Research and Study Center in Brussels.

The gifted historian John Toland was good enough to share some of his research materials and his wisdom with me. My good friend Ann Whitman made, through her vast knowledge of Washington, valuable introductions for me. William Buchanan, publisher of the Carrollton Press, kindly opened the OSS files of his unique Declassified Documents Reference Service to me, which proved significant.

My editor, Alan Williams, encouraged me as much by his shared enthusiasm for this period of history as by his wise editing counsel.

I was fortunate enough to have three conscientious and capable friends help prepare the manuscript: Deborah McPherson, Henrietta Wexler, and Gladys Shimasaki.

There were two young people at home who share my love of history and who helped with the endless clerical and research tasks which the book generated—my daughters Vanya and Andrea. And finally my gratitude to my wife, Sylvia, without whose unfailing support the project would not have been possible.

Contents

✠ ✠ ✠

CONTENTS

Illustration section follows page 152

PIERCING
THE REICH

✠ ✠ ✠

I

The Delayed Decision

✠ ✠ ✠

It was a cloudless evening in the English autumn of 1944. A small knot of men, their collars turned up against the chill, approached a Lancaster bomber silhouetted against a far corner of an airfield outside London. In the center of the party a figure lumbered along in a cavernous jump suit under a huge helmet and parachute pack.

When they reached the aircraft, the man in the group with an American accent hurriedly introduced the party to the waiting RAF crew. He pumped the hand of the parachutist and helped boost him through the belly hatch of the plane. The British pilot acknowledged his passenger with a bare nod as he continued to complete his departure ritual. He checked the plane's tires and tested the ailerons, elevators, trim tab, and rudder for loose play. He scanned the ship's skin lengthwise looking for breaks and wrinkles from turbulence and hard landings. Then the pilot disappeared into the aircraft.

The engines began to turn and the propellers cut fitfully into the night air. The men remaining on the ground retreated from the swirling dust kicked up by the backwash. As the pilot pushed forward on the throttle, the propellers picked up speed and the engines rose to a full-throated roar. The pilot released the brakes, the plane jerked forward, and rolled onto the runway. The lights on the wing tips bobbed gently as the plane accelerated. Flares bordering its path shot past the cockpit window in red blurs. The thick-waisted, graceless craft pulled itself into the air. The first attempt by the United States to parachute a secret agent into Nazi Germany was under way.

The parachutist who boarded the bomber was Jupp Kappius, a German by nationality, a structural engineer by training, and a political radical by conviction. Kappius, in his early thirties, was a wiry, sharp-featured, intense man, with an untrimmed mustache of the style favored by working-class Englishmen, among whom he had lived for the past seven years.

As a youth, in his native Germany, Jupp Kappius had been caught in the roiling political torrents which convulsed that nation after World War I. He had abandoned engineering and committed his life to a militant, purist Socialist sect. By 1937, Kappius was on the Gestapo's wanted list for offenses punishable by death, and he had fled to England.

He was recruited into espionage by the same American who had escorted him to the airfield this September night, George O. Pratt, chief of the London Labor Division of the U.S. Office of Strategic Services. Kappius's mission, once inside Germany, was to organize a campaign of sabotage aimed at crippling war production in the industrial Ruhr.

Before they left London, Pratt, an older, fatherly man and an unlikely spymaster, had spoken with unvarnished honesty of the risks. OSS had never parachuted an agent into Germany. They did not know the strength of the false documents Kappius carried or the credibility of his cover story. He would land in the Reich alone and unaided. Quite possibly he would not return. Pratt had seemed to be testing the man's resolution.

The plane now carrying Kappius toward Sögel, Germany, was in the air for two hours when a red light in the forward part of the aircraft switched to yellow. The dispatcher shook Kappius, who had fallen into a fretful sleep almost immediately after takeoff. The crewman cupped his hands to his mouth: "Over target in ten minutes." He went to the jump hole and released the catches on the cover. Kappius reflexively moved his hands to his shoulders to test the straps on the parachute. One of his instructors had said that the first thing the Gestapo did to suspected spies was check for strap bruises across the chest and thighs.

Kappius lowered himself to the rim of the jump hole. His legs were buffeted by a powerful airstream. Above him, the dispatcher checked the static line which would automatically trip open the parachute when Kappius jumped. A full moon shone, and he could see the outlines of the earth in surprising detail. With the hatch open, the roar of the engines seemed to engulf him. He forced his mind to the mechanics of the task. He must jump straight, holding his legs together, with his chin on his chest. He remembered the dubious advantage of jumping at night that his instructor had described: "You jump better when you can't see anything. In daytime, you see a big rock and you say, 'Oh God, I hope I don't hit it.' "

The plane banked into a shallow arc, then leveled off at low altitude. "Running in," the dispatcher shouted. Kappius heard the engines throttled back. The plane shuddered and he felt it lose speed. The amber glow went off, replaced by a green light. The dispatcher pounded his shoulder: "Go!"

For all his determination to remain straight, the prop wash flipped him about helplessly. Then he felt a faint tug at his thighs and armpits. Overhead the chute billowed out, section by section, opening like the petals of a gigantic blossom. After the roar of the engines and the shouts of the dispatcher, it was suddenly incredibly still. Kappius floated in a moon-bathed sea of silence, utterly alone. America's first agent to parachute into the Reich touched enemy soil on a remote, plowed field shortly after midnight on September 2, 1944.

The mission upon which Jupp Kappius had embarked traced its roots to the earliest actions which OSS officers had engaged in three years before. On the day after Christmas in 1941, a black-hulled liner cleared quarantine in the Narrows and steamed toward her berth in New York Harbor. Along the sides, tall, rust-streaked white letters proclaimed her to be the *Serpa Pinto*, a neutral vessel, out of Lisbon.

Nineteen days before the *Serpa Pinto*'s arrival, America had been blasted into war at Pearl Harbor. The Japanese were driving on Manila from four directions. Hong Kong had fallen. The nation's attention was then riveted on the Pacific. Eclipsed for the moment was the war in Europe and refugees from it escaping on ships like this dreary Portuguese steamer.

It was a Friday, a wet, stone-gray winter day in Manhattan. In an obscure office on Madison Avenue, Peter Karlow combed the *Serpa Pinto*'s passenger list. The navy had provided it to him under an arrangement with the organization for which young Karlow worked, an ambiguous new government entity called the "Coordinator of Information." It was a light manifest this trip, only 178 passengers. Still, the potential was there. All but a handful were Jewish refugees out of France, Czechoslovakia, Poland, and, most promising, several dozen German-Jewish nationals.

Karlow, fresh out of college, multilingual, son of a distinguished voice coach, worked in a subsection of COI, the Oral Intelligence section. His colleagues included a former assistant district attorney, a labor leader, a Red Cross official, a writer. Trial, error, and intuition had taught them how to mine a ship's manifest. Passenger's place of birth? Did it have military or industrial significance? If it did, the passenger may have lived there or visited recently and might possess useful information. Date of birth? People in early middle age proved better informed than the young, and not as rigid or frightened as the old. They looked for educated people —doctors, lawyers, engineers. They particularly valued manifests, like the *Serpa Pinto*'s, heavy with Jewish surnames, people with a powerful motive to cooperate.

Passengers were given time to settle down at their new addresses, which the manifest also provided. Then, the Oral Intelligence section moved. Direct phone calls in German, French, or other native languages had proved to be too sudden, too intimidating. They aroused the fear, "My God, they've tracked us here." A letter was preferable, something brief, simply worded, explaining that the Coordinator of Information, an undefined organization, was interested in researching conditions inside occupied Europe. Would the new arrivals help by stopping by the Madison Avenue office?

Responses were usually positive. They were fearful of not cooperating in this new, unknown land. Most of them wanted to help. The refugees had lived a harrowing adventure and were bursting to speak of it. The Americans who sent these letters genuinely did seek information on economic, social, and military conditions in Nazi-held Europe. But they wanted more. They wanted the clothes off the refugees' backs. They wanted their wristwatches, pens, razors, wallets, luggage, their underwear. They paid for everything and had faintly plausible explanations for this odd acquisitiveness. The quality, fabric, and workmanship of a suit, they said, could indicate the state of the German economy. The kind of steel in a razor might reveal something of German industrial processes European watches and rings? The Americans said they wanted them as souvenirs.

Karlow, a navy lieutenant who wore civilian clothes for this work, had a talent for drawing out his visitors. This handsome, open-faced young American, with European graces, speaking their languages so comfortably, invited confidence. Gladly, they reminisced about life in Wiesbaden or Nuremberg before the war, the neighborhoods where they had lived, who their neighbors were, the location of prominent landmarks, the railroad station, major industries, the telephone and telegraph offices. And if for some strange reason this American wanted to buy one's old hat or weathered valise, why not? A refugee could always use the money.

The Oral Intelligence section was not COI's sole scavenger. Other agents were cultivating exiled European trade unionists, interviewing merchant seamen who had recently been in Nazi-controlled ports. This quest for facts and artifacts had made something of a rag merchant of a scion of one of America's great fortunes. Henry S. Morgan, grandson of J. Pierpont Morgan, had been asked to head COI's Office of Censorship and Documentation in Washington. Morgan enlisted a Jewish banker friend back in New York to find refugees through agencies such as the Hebrew Immigration Aid Society. Morgan's man quietly bought up battered suitcases and cast-off clothing from the refugees and from the secondhand shops that they frequented on the Lower East Side.

Piles of suits, hats, dresses, valises, shaving brushes, belts, and shoes began to accumulate in a warehouse in Washington. What was to be done with it all was then uncertain. But it seemed the sort of inventory which a fledgling espionage service ought to be accumulating if one day it intended to put its secret agents into an enemy nation. It was from this rummage heap, nearly three years later and thirty-five hundred miles away, that Jupp Kappius was outfitted for OSS's penetration of Nazi Germany.

Alone among the great powers, the United States had lacked a real intelligence service at the outbreak of the war. The function, until 1939, is said to have been discharged by six elderly maiden ladies jealously standing watch over a few secret file cabinets at the War Department. That this intelligence void was filled as America went to war is explained largely by an enigmatic and charismatic figure, William J. Donovan.

"Wild Bill" Donovan had led the storybook Fighting Sixty-ninth Regiment during World War I and emerged—with three wounds, the Congressional Medal of Honor, and other awards—as one of the most decorated soldiers in American history. After the war, he served for a time as deputy attorney general, then developed a spectacularly successful Wall Street law firm whose clients included Standard Oil of New Jersey, large New York banks, and leading international companies. His law practice made him a rich man and gave Donovan entry to powerful and influential figures.

On July 11, 1941, President Franklin D. Roosevelt named Donovan to a post without precedent in American history. Under the unilluminating title of "Coordinator of Information," redesignated a year later to the equally opaque "Office of Strategic Services," Roosevelt created America's first central intelligence system, less than five months before the country went to war.

America's first spy chief was a silver-haired, rather dumpy man of fifty-eight, an indifferent dresser who looked out at the world from mild, pale-blue eyes, and habitually spoke in a subdued voice. Physically unprepossessing perhaps, but Donovan had magnetism. In the quiet voice was unmistakable authority. The pale-blue eyes had an unexpected power to transfix. When he was a young OSS counterintelligence officer, James Angleton used to brief Donovan, and recalled: "He would grasp a man's hand, fix you with those eyes, and say, softly, 'I'm counting on you.' And people believed him." Another colleague remembered: "He was softspoken, but determined. He would persuade you with logic, charm, and presence, but always persuade you."

Donovan had a restless, devouring mind that leaped from enthusiasm to enthusiasm, giving the brilliant and the crack-brained an equal hearing. He seemed to have adapted, from the realm of American jurisprudence, a generous intellectual standard that every new idea had merit until proven faulty. In a perhaps overly kind interpretation of this trait, David Bruce described Donovan as a "universal man" in that "nothing human was alien to him."

Donovan was uninhibited by conventional patterns of thinking. His viewpoint could be highly original, not to say odd. Milton Katz, one of the nation's most brilliant legal scholars, went to work for Donovan and was astonished by the man's blend of brilliant insight and occasional intellectual nonsense. When General Douglas MacArthur was resisting Donovan's desire to place OSS agents in the Far East, Donovan explained to the baffled Katz, "You know, intelligence is like the weather. Weather comes from the east and good intelligence comes from the east." Katz, like most people whom Donovan touched, stood in awe of the man.

The old war hero was apparently without physical fear and assumed that others shared his fatalism. David Bruce recalled going ashore with Donovan after the Normandy landings. They soon found themselves pinned down behind a hedgerow by German machine guns. As they hugged the earth, Donovan said, "David, we cannot be captured. We know too much." Drawing his pistol, he said, "I'll shoot first."

"Yes, sir, but how much can we do with our pistols against a machine gun?"

"No, no. You don't understand. If we are going to get captured, I'll shoot you first. Then myself. After all, I'm the commanding officer."

Given the secret information he possessed, exposing himself to capture

—in Normandy, earlier in Sicily, and later in Burma—amounted to negligent bravado. There was in this man an enduring streak of the exuberant boy.

Donovan's OSS eventually comprised five major components. Secret Intelligence (SI) was charged with what the layman thinks of as spying, the procurement of information by clandestine means.

Secret Operations (SO) was the stuff of high adventure. SO operatives parachuted behind the lines into France, or slipped ashore from small craft and nourished resistance movements with arms, money, and their own morale-building presence.

A Research and Analysis branch (R and A), studded with Ph.D.'s, produced mundane, and possibly the most consistently useful intelligence of the war. One R and A officer could estimate bomb damage to railways in the south of France by monitoring the price of oranges on the Paris produce market. When orange prices dropped, it was time to start bombing these lines again.

Morale Operations (MO), or "black propaganda," preyed on the minds, hopes, and hearts of the enemy. The MO ran phony "resistance" radio stations, purportedly operated from inside Germany by anti-Nazis. MO would air-drop innocent-appearing songbooks near German troops. Along with the music and lyrics to "Hänschen klein" the war-weary could find instructions in these books for feigning illness in order to gain a welcome stay in the hospital or possibly an early discharge.

"X-2" was the counterintelligence branch, charged with protecting American intelligence from infestation by enemy spies and with trying to place American agents inside the enemy's espionage nest. X-2, in effect, spied on spies.

By 1944, this child of Donovan's energy and imagination had grown to a strength of fifteen thousand men and women. OSS was headed toward an expenditure of $57 million that year, for most of which no accounting was required. It was neck-deep in both the European and Asian conflicts, and had won mixed, though on the whole favorable, notices.

The undeniable resentment which this brash newcomer generated was caused by its often arrogant, unbridled style. OSS was ostensibly part of the military. But where the sheer size and complexity of conventional services required operating strictly by the book, OSS threw out the book. In the rank-ridden military world, lieutenants deferred to captains, and captains to majors, and so on up. Yet, bespectacled OSS privates with Ph.D.'s flashed special orders which left them virtually untouchable. OSS personnel assigned to Supreme Headquarters Allied Expeditionary Forces (SHAEF) carried a blue-covered pass—signed by General Dwight D. Eisenhower—which said, in effect, that the bearer was subject virtually to no restrictions.

Most annoying to regular military personnel was the suspicion, grounded partly in fact, that OSS was a place where the well connected could play at war. Donovan used the old-boy network to staff his fledgling agency. With its personnel recruited from prestigious law firms, old-line banks, the academic elite, from those who had been educated abroad and spoke foreign languages, and from friends of friends with these connections, OSS's appearance as a privileged caste became inevitable. Far preferable for a young fellow with influence to wrangle an OSS commission and comment smugly at fashionable parties, "I'm simply not in a position to discuss what I do," than to crouch in a foxhole with the infantry at Anzio.

In a no doubt overly harsh judgment, one veteran commented: "In half of my OSS comrades, I knew the bravest, finest men I would ever meet. The rest were phonies." In any balanced appraisal, OSS emerged as an organization of largely courageous, exceptional people, possessed of an amazing range of talents, who within less than three years of existence had compiled an impressive record of achievement and acceptance on European and Asian battlegrounds.

On September 11, 1944, western Allied troops stood on German soil for the first time since the world had plunged into war five years before. The American First Army halted before the ancient capital of Aachen, in a moment rich with symbolism. In Adolf Hitler's rendering of history, his Third Reich traced its lineage to Aachen. Charlemagne was presumably born there, and his Holy Roman Empire was the First Reich, Bismarck's rule launched the second, and Nazi Germany was the third. Now, Hitler's Reich, proclaimed to last a millennium, seemed about to be obliterated between converging Allied armies.

On the eastern front, Red divisions had driven the Germans out of Mother Russia back through Poland and onto German soil in East Prussia. On the western front, the Allies had stormed across the northern half of France and had driven the enemy back to the Siegfried Line along the German border. On August 15, a joint American and French force landed on the Riviera, raced up the Rhone Valley, and linked with General George S. Patton's Third Army near Dijon. Their union signaled the effective liberation of France.

World War I had demonstrated that the Germans had no desire to fight on their own soil. Now, with defeat again inevitable, they were surely too wise to carry the destruction they had wreaked on the rest of Europe to their homeland. Final victory seemed within the Allies' grasp. For the men in the ranks, home by Christmas of 1944 became a possible dream.

And then it fell apart. The headlong advance through France literally ran out of gas and stopped short of the German border. The Germans refused to play the role—assigned them by the Allies—of vanquished but reasonable men. They stiffened their defenses and lashed back. From Metz in the south to Arnhem in the north, the Allies felt the unspent sting of the Wehrmacht. Field Marshal Karl von Rundstedt halted Patton along the Moselle River and a fierce battle raged over Metz. By mid-October, nearly a month after the First Army initially had menaced Aachen, that German city was still not conquered.

Most shattering to Allied hopes for an early peace was the failure of Field Marshal Bernard Montgomery's gamble to circumvent the Siegfried Line, Operation MARKET GARDEN. The line began at Holland and followed the German border along Belgium and France south to Switzerland. Montgomery had persuaded Eisenhower that the Siegfried Line could be outflanked by a massive airborne assault through Holland. From there, Allied troops would knife into the Ruhr, drive on to Berlin, and finish off the Germans. Operation MARKET GARDEN collapsed when British troops were unable to hold the critical bridge over the Rhine at Arnhem in Holland. Montgomery's end run around the Siegfried Line had failed.

In the Mediterranean theater, the situation continued grim. By the fall of 1944, the long, bloody crawl up the rugged spine of Italy had stalled south of Bologna.

By the end of November, Winston Churchill was telling war-worn Britons, "The truth is no one knows when the German war will be finished." He advised the House of Commons to "keep our pugnacity, as far as possible, for export purposes." President Roosevelt sent a confidential message to military and civilian officials to refrain from statements suggesting an early end of the war, which might tend to relax arms production.

In five years of war, Hitler had never really squeezed the German home front. Losses of men in the field had been heavy, 3.5 million. But Hitler had insisted on continued production of consumer goods to maintain high civilian morale. The number of German families able to keep servants had remained constant throughout the war. Despite incessant day and night pounding by Allied bombers, German industry sustained a remarkable output and actually reached its zenith when the Allies had approached the German border in the fall of 1944.

Hitler then began to pump out remaining reservoirs of German manpower. They might never equal the fighting prowess of crack Panzer divisions and Waffen SS, but Germany still had millions of bodies to pour into battle, and millions more to provide the matériel of war. Between September and October another half a million men were added to the Wehrmacht. Twenty-five new infantry divisions and ten new Panzer brigades were formed. As the end of 1944 approached, Germany had 10 million men under arms.

Hitler was also counting on the genius of German science to reverse his fortunes. He would regain control of the skies through secret planes then beginning to roll off German production lines. Conventional Allied aircraft had been unable to touch these new jet-powered German models.

Monthly casualty reports out of SHAEF also told the story of a war hardly over. Men killed, wounded, and missing on the western front in September had been a relatively light 2529. In October, there were 44,535 casualties; in November, 61,724; and in December, 153,250, including 24,291 killed in that first month of the Battle of the Bulge.

Even before the Bulge, another specter had risen to dash hopes for an early peace. On September 22, 1944, OSS Washington headquarters issued a scholarly study on the southern region of the Reich. Because of Allied bombing, German government agencies were being relocated south, this report claimed. The study predicted that as the Allies advanced on Germany's borders, this movement would accelerate.

In the same month America's intelligence source closest to Germany, OSS in Bern, Switzerland, echoed the theme in a report expressing concern that the Nazis planned to withdraw to an alpine fortress.

The heart of this "National Redoubt" was expected to be the Salzkammergut, a mountainous area in northern Austria, rugged and inaccessible. There, "vast underground factories, invulnerable in their rocky depths" were supposedly being hewn from the mountainsides. Preparations were said to be under way for the retreat of Nazi rulers to this impenetrable mountain fastness, where they would carry on the fight, defended by elite troops and sustained by huge stores of food, fuel, arms, and ammunition buried underground. The capital of the Redoubt was said to be Hitler's mountain retreat, near Berchtesgaden in the Obersalzberg.

American intelligence officials in Switzerland predicted that subjugation of the Redoubt could extend the war from six months to two years and exact more casualties than all the previous fighting on the western front.

Was the Redoubt a chimera, a fancy fed by military romantics? The superheated rhetoric of an alpine rampart "defended by nature and by the most efficient secret weapons yet invented" had the ring of pulp fiction. Yet the Allied Supreme Commander, General Eisenhower, did not dismiss this threat. "If the German was permitted to establish the Redoubt, he might possibly force us to engage in a long, drawn-out guerrilla type of warfare, or a costly siege. Thus, he could keep alive his desperate hope that through disagreement among the Allies, he might yet be able to secure terms more favorable than those of unconditional surrender." Eisenhower concluded: "The evidence was clear that the Nazi intended to make the attempt. . . ."

With the Germans stoutly defending their borders, with the added prospect that they intended to hole up in an impregnable alpine retreat if the front collapsed, Allied military commanders reconciled themselves to a protracted war. They now hungered for military intelligence from the next battlefield, from the Reich itself. They wanted, out of Germany, the same fruits of espionage which had aided their conquest of the occupied countries.

OSS had successfully penetrated these earlier battlegrounds. It had fed, armed, even mid-wived European resistance movements. With British intelligence, OSS had parachuted one hundred agent teams into France prior to the invasion of Normandy to coordinate the fight of the French underground with the invaders. Throughout virtually all the conquered empire of the Third Reich—Norway, Denmark, Holland, Belgium, France, Italy, Yugoslavia, Greece—agents of the OSS had been in place fostering resistance and acquiring enemy secrets.

By May 1944, OSS had over fourteen hundred agents and subagents operating in the south of France who provided the majority of strategic intelligence from the area. By the time that French and American invaders arrived off the Riviera on August 15, they were aware of virtually all transportation and troop movements, coastal defenses, battle order, and the precise location of minefields, roadblocks, artillery, even searchlights. OSS's richly detailed anatomy of the enemy defenses won this campaign the designation "the best-briefed invasion in history."

Now Allied armies needed this depth of information from the German heartland. What was happening inside the Reich? How was this unexpected tenacity of the Germans possible? How long could it go on? Was this stiff resistance a brittle shell or did it have depth? What kind of defenses had been erected against Allied invasion? Where were they located? Where were German troops moving? How many and what kind? Where were the arsenals of the Reich, the factories producing the tanks, planes, cannon, and shells? Where were the hidden airdromes harboring the new jet aircraft? Where were the principal rail junctions? What were Germany's remaining reserves of manpower, munitions, fuel, food? What was the political and economic climate in Germany, the state of morale, with the war now brought home? And how likely was the National Redoubt to prolong the war?

Allied expectations of an early end to the war had been based on an assumption that the German General Staff would seek peace when casualties became prohibitive and before Germany was destroyed. Neither the Allies nor the German generals had reckoned on Adolf Hitler's willingness to pull the Reich down around German heads. In the early fall of 1944, with France liberated and the war still raging, OSS strategists made a long-postponed decision. They would have to penetrate the German heartland.

The commanding officer of European operations for OSS was a lean and patrician American, Colonel David K. E. Bruce. His staff was headquartered in London and spread over several addresses on Grosvenor Street. Bruce was the son of a U.S. senator, former husband of one of the world's richest women, the kind of man British aristocrats considered a proper American cousin. With Bruce, the British felt none of the discomfort they sometimes experienced when dealing with Americans from middle- and southern-European backgrounds, many foreign-born, often with strange accents, and, they feared, questionable loyalties. A veteran British diplomat described Bruce as "a perfect example of all that was best in U.S. intelligence." Along with impeccable social credentials, Bruce was an unusually able man, who had been a lawyer of wide experience, a legislator, diplomat, and gentleman farmer by the time he took command of OSS in Europe in 1943 at the age of forty-five.

Bill Donovan had met Bruce before the war and had filed him away in the talent bank he maintained in his head. When Bruce returned from a European mission for the Red Cross after the fall of France, Donovan said simply, "David, you have to join my organization." By 1943, Bruce was commanding two thousand spies, saboteurs, propagandists, and supporting staff at the OSS European headquarters in London.

In the fall of 1944, Bruce's top aides faced their new priority, the penetration of Germany. William J. Casey, recently named as the chief of Secret Intelligence in Europe with the express responsibility for infiltrating the Reich, remembered their deliberations: "The big thing for OSS London until then had been, how do you get onto that beach? How do you pull off an invasion of France without being thrown back into the sea? We were thinking only of that coast of France and just a little beyond it. We didn't have the time or the people to think beyond that. Then, all of a sudden, that phase of the war was over. We had exploded out of France and had overrun all our agents. We had this big organization and practically nothing inside Germany."

OSS had placed agents behind enemy territory in the occupied countries. But these missions, for all the courage demanded, risks posed, and lives lost, were less formidable than penetrating the Reich. Agents who parachuted into occupied countries were aided by people who shared their hatred of the Nazis. Signal lights, bonfires, and flashlights in friendly hands guided Allied aircraft to drop zones secured by resistance fighters who rushed forward to help bury chutes, carry equipment, and provide warm food. Safe houses were made available where agents could live and set up their clandestine radios. Spies who were natives of the occupied nations could melt among their countrymen without a trace. They became members of a herd, protected by their own from alien beasts of prey. The agent penetrating Germany, instead, was asked to parachute amid the predators, to jump blind, with no reception committees, no safe houses, no friends, into a hostile world.

By the fall of 1944, no serious anti-Nazi movement remained in the Reich. The plot against Hitler's life had failed that summer, followed by the ruthless and thorough extermination of its perpetrators. The security which OSS had to penetrate was far tighter inside Germany than in the occupied nations. In the Redoubt area, security was tightest of all. There, the Germans had gone to ingenious lengths to discourage potential cooperation with Allied spies. In Austria, the Gestapo infiltrated its own phony Allied agents who would pretend to look for safe houses as a ruse for flushing out disloyal Austrians.

Whom could OSS recruit for the penetration of Germany? German-speaking Americans, even those German-born, would be hopelessly ignorant of daily life in Germany under Nazi rule. Could dissident German POWs and political refugees be trusted? The apostate, however sincere, is always suspect. German Communists in exile possessed unquestionable anti-Nazi credentials but lacked political reliability and were initially ruled out. So, at first, were young, able-bodied Germans, since they would be liable for induction into the Wehrmacht. The pool of anti-Nazi, anti-

Communist Germans who were not POWs, not subject to conscription, yet not too old or unfit to parachute was discouragingly small.

The British were pessimistic from the outset about operations within Germany and gave the Americans scant encouragement. They had strong doubts about sustaining agents without the support of a native resistance movement. The British also had their own good reasons for not wanting the Yanks to muck up a good thing which they had carefully cultivated since 1941. British counterintelligence had caught and doubled virtually the entire German spy apparatus in England. These agents remained in the pay of the Germans, but acted in the interests of the British. British intelligence feared that agents sent from England into Germany could, if captured, blow this masterful web of double deception. Initially, the British had refused outright to allow the Americans to use England as a launchpad for any operations into Germany, but later they relented.

British lack of enthusiasm to infiltrate the Reich was perhaps best explained by a feeling that it was unnecessary. The western Allies had, after all, Ultra, the operation through which the British had managed to break the presumably unbreakable German wireless communications encoded on the "Enigma" machine. Thus, they already had remarkable foreknowledge of German intentions, from military actions to the highest levels of Nazi diplomacy.

OSS was still determined to plunge ahead, perhaps motivated in part by an unspoken, even unconscious drive to outdo the master. OSS had shown its mettle in France. But British intelligence had still clearly dominated the field, while the Americans remained junior partners. Now, a chance had arisen for OSS to succeed in a formidable challenge, and one for which their British mentors had shown little enthusiasm.

From the outset, the attitudes of British intelligence professionals toward their American colleagues had been a thoroughly human mélange of contradictions. Top British leaders, beginning with Churchill, had welcomed and indeed encouraged America's entry into secret warfare. But at the working level, the old pros of the British secret service, while they recognized that they needed to have the Americans in the game, nevertheless resented the need.

British intelligence traced its origins back nearly four hundred years to Queen Elizabeth's Joint Secretary of State, Sir Francis Walsingham, who honeycombed Europe with his agents, and whose first triumph was to obtain minute details of the impending attack by the Spanish Armada. During World War II, British intelligence had become a two-track affair. MI-6, for "Military Intelligence," the traditional service, with MI-6(v) its counterintelligence wing, was the lineal descendant of Walsingham. MI-6, known also as SIS, for Secret Intelligence Service, functioned under the Foreign Office. SOE, Special Operations, Executive, was an offshoot of MI-6, created in 1940 to carry out subversion and sabotage, to instigate and assist guerrilla movements. SOE operated under the Ministry of Economic Warfare. The two systems got along naturally for intelligence services under the same flag. They were mutually deprecating rivals.

The British believed that the Americans, few generations removed from the wilderness, were hardly prepared for the subtle profession of deception, which was virtually bred into the British soul. A perceptive MI-6 officer noted: "They [the Americans] work better as a group and are not natural 'lone wolves' . . . the British were quite good at clandestine life because their boarding-school education was a constant battle against authority from the age of seven on."

Though General Donovan had opened a London office before Pearl Harbor, the Americans were still often treated as novices. An American officer, sent as liaison to SOE, late in 1944, learned that Maurice Buckmaster, head of the SOE French section, had instructed his secretary not to show "that OSS fellow" anything except old files, nothing current.

OSS London had largely accepted its protégé status as inevitable in the beginning. SO, Special Operations, tagged after SOE. X-2 was the contented child of British counterespionage. The OSS designation of counterintelligence as X-2 was, in fact, a variation of the British counterintelligence XX Committee. In London, SO and X-2 were actually formal partners of SOE and MI-6 (v), respectively, with little doubt as to who was senior.

SI, Secret Intelligence, labored under the shadow of MI-6, though it was not organizationally integrated with the British service. SI had developed independent operations in North Africa, Italy, and the neutral countries, but had carried out only two wholly independent missions during the campaign in France.

Donovan was respectful but unawed by Britain's seniority in secret warfare. Britain's domination of intelligence, he believed, was essentially an accident of geography. "The habit of control has grown up with them, through their relations with refugee governments and refugee intelligence services. . . . We are not a refugee government."

With the emphasis now shifting from guerrilla warfare and sabotage in occupied Europe to intelligence from inside Germany, the intuitive Donovan sensed a subtle distinction. Subordination to British experience in paramilitary operations had been tolerable. When the war ended, those exercises would end with it. But Donovan saw secret intelligence as a permanent necessity of government, as natural as taxing and spending. The United States was caught without an intelligence service by World War II, but it should never happen again.

In October 1943, Donovan had won from the U.S. Joint Chiefs of Staff the authority to conduct independent secret intelligence. In the penetration of Germany, on a grand scale, directed out of England, OSS was to exercise this declaration of independence from the British.

The British writer Malcolm Muggeridge archly signaled the American service's maturation: "Ah, those first OSS arrivals in London! How well I remember them, arriving like *jeunes filles en fleur* straight from a finishing school, all fresh and innocent, to start work in our frowsty old intelligence brothel, . . . all too soon they were ravished and corrupted, becoming indistinguishable from seasoned pros who had been in the game for a quarter of a century more."

II

The Manufacture of Illusion

✠ ✠ ✠

Bill Casey, the newly named London SI chief responsible for organizing the German operations, was a thirty-two-year-old New York attorney who had made a fortune before the war writing "how-to" handbooks for other lawyers. He was a large man whose casual manner disguised boundless energy and confidence. His machine-gun speech accurately reflected the speed of Casey's mind.

Casey had joined the navy after Pearl Harbor, but bad eyesight had doomed him to examining procurement contracts in a Washington office. As a man who had learned early how power functions, Casey knew that in OSS most power lines led back to the Donovan law partnership in New York. Through a former law partner, Casey arranged to meet Otto C. Doering, General Donovan's executive officer in New York City, and a former member of the Donovan law firm. Casey was soon transferred to OSS. In Washington, he organized a secretariat to impose some semblance of order on the administrative shambles in which General Donovan operated. He was sent to London initially to set up a similar secretariat for David Bruce.

In Casey, OSS had a man with an analytical mind, tenacious will, and a capacity to generate high morale among his staff. He delegated authority easily to trusted subordinates and set a simple standard—results. He had no patience with the well-born effete who had flocked to OSS, people he dubbed the "white-shoe boys."

Casey's new mission would require the relatively young naval lieutenant to deal on an equal footing with generals and admirals. His superiors in London, believing that the rank of civilian would serve best in this situation, placed Casey on inactive duty and sent him out to buy some appropriate gray business suits.

In describing his new duties, Casey noted: "We recognized that, compared to France, it was a different proposition. Much more hazardous. More difficult. More uncertain. We thought we would lose far more men. But what we would lose would be quantitatively small compared to the loss that was being incurred in the foot-slogging fighting on the Siegfried Line."

David Bruce instructed Bill Casey to turn a then-foundering SI division into the single most important operation in OSS. SI London then had no capability for processing agents beyond looking after their day-to-day wants, seeing that their teeth were fixed and inoculations given. Casey had a free hand to conscript whomever and whatever he needed from all other branches of OSS London.

The place to begin planning the penetration of Germany, Casey knew, was upstairs, over his office at 72 Grosvenor Street. Here were located the cluttered quarters of the OSS London Labor Division.

Instant legend had it that OSS was a preposterous fraternity of tycoons, scholars, safecrackers, football stars, scientists, pickpockets, financiers, playboys, and playwrights which somehow worked. Rarely mentioned in this roll of the prestigious and picaresque was the unglamorous figure of the trade unionist. But the pragmatic General Donovan had felt none of the discomfort of some of his Wasp elitists in welcoming the agents of organized labor into his organization. He had immediately seized upon an idea suggested to him three years before by Heber Blankenhorn.

Blankenhorn moved in several worlds. In World War I, he had served as an intelligence officer. Later, during the New Deal era, Blankenhorn was on the staff of those two labor champions, senators Robert Wagner and Robert La Follette. Blankenhorn saw an Allied opportunity in the Nazi determination to destroy the trade-union movement in Germany and the conquered countries. In pursuing this objective, the Nazis had created a dangerous enemy for themselves, the beast who has been wounded, but not killed.

Blankenhorn saw, in the surviving remnants of European trade unionism, an anti-Nazi network that touched every economic vein and artery of the Third Reich. Donovan quickly grasped the potential. James Murphy, Donovan's former law clerk, whom he had placed in charge of X-2, suggested that they recruit George Bowden, a former Chicago legal associate, to help develop a labor operation.

Bowden had in his early manhood been a professional football player and an organizer for the "Wobblies," the radical Industrial Workers of the World. He later wedded a successful tax practice to continuing leadership in leftist causes, particularly the National Lawyers Guild. Late in 1941, Bowden brought with him to Washington to set up the OSS Labor Branch the thirty-four-year-old chief counsel of the CIO and a stalwart of the union's anti-Communist wing, Arthur J. Goldberg.

They began working a virtually untapped mine of intelligence. Goldberg expressed the potential in a memorandum to Donovan: ". . . the working people of Europe have unparalleled access to strategic information. We must remember that they man the ships and the trains which transport the men and matériel of war. They pour the steel, dig the coal, process the food and make the munitions which are the sinews of war." Not only did these workers supply and move their nations but, he pointed out, they were natural partners of the Allies. "We can take advantage of the hatred of Hitler by members of the European labor movement. They fought the rise of Fascism from its inception. They are its implacable enemy."

After February 1942, Goldberg was in and out of Donovan's operation on a consultant basis. New York City at that time offered rich possibilities for contact with European-refugee trade unionists who were eager to strike back at their oppressors. Donovan asked Goldberg to work with Allen Dulles, who was then running the OSS office in New York. By March, Goldberg was working full time as the OSS labor chief out of the Dulles offices in the International Building of Rockefeller Plaza.

Goldberg and the others who created the Labor Branch were rarely actual labor figures. Goldberg himself was a lawyer for labor and not a union leader. OSS also raided the ablest talents of the National Labor Relations Board, a New Deal agency that heard cases of anti-union corporate behavior. The board's general counsel, Gerhard ("Gary") Van Arkel, was recruited by OSS and sent to North Africa, a refuge for European Socialists and exiled trade unionists. The NLRB's chief trial counsel, George Pratt, went to work initially in the New York City office. These men, while not identified with any labor faction, knew the field well. By working through them, Donovan's organization thus avoided the harsh rivalries among leaders of the U.S. labor movement.

Labor's enlistment in the secret war was not universally applauded. The international trade-union movement was poorly understood by many politically conservative OSS officers who could not comprehend what a collection of Socialist pipefitters had to do with the grand game of espionage. Yet—until 1944, when the Germans held sway over most of Europe —when the outcome of the war was still far from certain, virtually the only American intelligence on conditions inside Germany came from the OSS Labor Branch in New York.

In the spring of 1942, George Bowden and Arthur Goldberg had an interesting caller. Omar Becu, a Belgian, was secretary of the International Transport Workers Federation (ITWF). He had continued his labor leadership as a refugee in London when the Nazis conquered his homeland and had proved enormously useful to British intelligence, especially in recruiting radio operators from among ITWF members.

During a New York visit, Becu confirmed to the Americans their wisdom in establishing a Labor Branch. He told Bowden and Goldberg that anti-Nazi cells of his federation were still persevering in Germany and the occupied countries. Becu urged the Americans to exploit particularly the refugee-labor community in England, and through it, to reach surviving trade unionists on the Continent.

A splendid opportunity was about to present itself. In May 1942, the ITWF was to hold its international congress in London. This assembly would offer a chance for OSS to recruit labor agents with ties throughout Europe. The Americans provided Becu with some funds and told him that the London office would be in touch with him. Becu threw out one final suggestion before leaving. There was a young diamond merchant who knew his way around European anti-Communist union movements. Becu believed that he was now somewhere in America. The labor office ought to look up Albert Jolis. "Bert's the sort of fellow you need."

In August 1942, Arthur Goldberg left the United States to organize a Labor Division within OSS London. Later, in the fall, George Pratt, the former NLRB lawyer, arrived from New York to take over the Labor Division, permitting Goldberg to return to New York.

Military rank posed a quandary for OSS labor officers. Arthur Goldberg had originally signed on with Donovan as a civilian. During his London service, he took a commission at General Donovan's urging, he said, as an army major. Goldberg was expected to enter combat zones and could stand up better to General Eisenhower's staff with some gold on his shoulders.

20

He wore the uniform briefly—only long enough for it to yield an unexpected dividend. He was unhappy with flea bag quarters near Marble Arch and had mentioned to an amused David Bruce that he would like to stay at Claridge's, then the posh residence of guests such as the exiled King Peter of Yugoslavia. Goldberg ran into the American secretary of the navy, Frank Knox, as both men were entering the hotel. Goldberg had known Knox before the war when they were professional adversaries. Goldberg had represented the Newspaper Guild in its negotiations with Knox's *Chicago Daily News*. Goldberg was assumed to be Knox's military aide by Claridge's and was immediately assigned a rent-controlled room at one pound one shilling per night, which allowed him to live in a style to which the American labor movement had yet to accustom him.

George Pratt refused a commission because the European labor leaders with whom he would be dealing were historically mistrustful of the military. He need not have concerned himself. To Europeans, the American military looked like civilians in uniform anyway.

In the summer of 1943, Arthur Goldberg and George Pratt visited Gary Van Arkel in Algiers, where the former NLRB general counsel was working with Socialist and labor exiles. Some of these people had fled directly from Germany during the 1930s. Others were veterans of the defeated Loyalist side in the Spanish civil war.

Van Arkel cultivated these sources, scoured prisoner-of-war cages, and recruited sixteen Germans with potential as future agents. It was an assignment by default. At that point, few officers in North Africa were thinking much beyond the next sand dune. Van Arkel was one of a handful of OSS people looking toward the eventual penetration of Germany.

When Goldberg and Pratt came to Algiers, Van Arkel described the talents of some of his recruits. He had instructed four German trainees to go from Algiers to Oran on a practice exercise in which they were to seek information on activities in the Allied-controlled port. The group spoke little English, and their sole resource was a modest sum of money.

They headed first to a supply center, where they bought American uniforms. The oldest of the group fixed his epaulettes with the stars of a general. They used OSS facilities to forge orders enabling them to fly from Algiers to Oran. In Oran, they checked into a hotel reserved for American military personnel. The group's radio operator had himself assigned a room on the top floor. The bogus general then took the agents to the port, where officers and enlisted men accorded his party smart salutes. They counted every ship and shipment in sight, then returned to the hotel and radioed back to Algiers a comprehensive report on activities in the Port of Oran.

Back in London, George Pratt continued to cultivate close relationships with virtually every German Socialist and labor refugee worth knowing. He understood the irony of their position. The British had given them asylum. But they were, nevertheless, Germans, and the British took no responsibility for their day-to-day well-being. Pratt found himself as much social worker as spymaster. Many of the refugees were destitute. He paid them small sums for research, two pounds, five pounds, rarely more than ten pounds a month. In return, they spent long hours in his office analyzing German-language papers, forming a nucleus for future German operations, and keeping warm.

Among the exiles Arthur Goldberg met during his journeys to London was Samuel Zygelbojm, a Socialist labor leader and a member of the Polish government-in-exile. Zygelbojm, who had escaped from the Warsaw ghetto in 1940, was the first to reveal to Goldberg the blackest secret of the Third Reich: that the Germans were embarked on the extermination of a whole people.

Zygelbojm pleaded with Goldberg to urge the Allies to demonstrate their awareness of the death camps, even if the only desperate gesture available were to bomb them. Hundreds of lives were already being lost in these camps every day anyway.

Goldberg agreed to raise the issue. He later reported to Zygelbojm that Allied commanders could do nothing about the concentration camps at that point; they had higher-priority targets. Goldberg had passed this information to the bitterly disappointed Zygelbojm over dinner at Claridge's. The next day, May 12, 1943, Samuel Zygelbojm killed himself. He had taken an overdose of pills to protest Allied indifference to the tragedy of Europe's Jews.

The London Labor Division did not deal in secret inks and sabotage but in the minutiae of commerce, in railroad bills of lading, and the cargoes of barges plying the Rhine. All of it would have been utterly uninspired, except that this accretion of humble facts revealed hidden factories, troop movements, ammunition dumps, some of the best strategic-bombing intelligence to come out of the war.

By 1943, Goldberg believed that labor agents dispatched from London could penetrate Germany. General Donovan was enthusiastic. But at that time, the idea died of inattention and skepticism. The occupied countries were the priority intelligence targets. It also seemed to Goldberg that the chief of OSS Europe, David Bruce, and other top London brass, were still uncomfortable with the idea of entrusting espionage to Germans, particularly German leftists. Thus, while SI and SO were caught up in the high drama of the invasion and liberation of Fortress Europa, the London labor office prepared trade unionists for a day that might never come, when they might have to penetrate Germany.

After D day, Goldberg again came to London. This time he roomed in a flat in Shepherd Market with Gary Van Arkel. Van Arkel had been sent to Italy with the labor agents he had originally recruited in North Africa. But no use had been made of his men there, and he was then transferred to England.

Goldberg stayed briefly in London and then went to visit the battle-fronts in France, leaving George Pratt still in charge of the London Labor Division. He had ridden in a jeep with General Jacques Leclerc's French Second Armored Division on its way to liberate Paris, in bumper-to-bumper traffic, with not a sign of enemy aircraft overhead. It looked then to Goldberg that the Allies could drive on, unresisted, all the way to Berlin. The efforts of the Labor Division to prepare for the eventual penetration of Germany seemed, happily, unnecessary. Soon after, Goldberg asked General Donovan if he might be placed on inactive status. By October 1944, Major Arthur Goldberg was out of the war.

Then, with France liberated and peace still nowhere in sight, the American military determined that intelligence had to be obtained from inside the Reich. Attention at OSS London focused on the Labor Division, as a spotlight might suddenly pick out an obscure dancer in the last row of a chorus. Bill Casey moved George Pratt's operation to center stage.

Willis Reddick was a trim man, with a pencil-line mustache, a jaunty smile, always fastidiously dressed, whether in civilian clothes or army khaki, the sort of fellow inevitably described as dapper. Reddick had taken a degree in journalism at the University of Illinois and later worked in advertising and printing. By the time he had entered the army, Reddick owned a thriving printing business in Springfield, Illinois.

Reddick was a reserve infantry officer, and, when the war came along, the printer, then thirty-eight, hoped to win command of a rifle company. Instead, Reddick found himself in April 1942 drawn into the vortex of chaos at early COI headquarters in Washington. He was wholly unaware of why this obscure new agency wanted him. Reddick was assigned to an empty basement and there learned his new métier. He was to organize a printshop and recruit, equip, and direct a team of counterfeiters and forgers. His true function was masked by making Reddick part of the "Office of Research and Development."

Reddick found the assignment enraging. He was to acquire machinery, buy paper, and recruit personnel without revealing the purpose of his actions and, initially, without funds. He attacked the problem by quietly arranging his transfer to infantry school at Fort Benning, but he was soon hauled back.

Reddick finally equipped his shop through the help of a man who ran a secondhand printing-machinery business in Washington. He also found an oasis of sanity in the confusion through an unexpected friendship with Henry Morgan, the grandson of J. Pierpont Morgan. As head of the Office of Censorship and Documentation, Morgan was to arrange false papers and cover stories for agents. Morgan had also been involved in the effort to acquire the clothing and personal effects of refugees in New York City.

Henry Morgan was a short man of affable manner and good sense, who easily won friendship and respect. The printer from Illinois and the scion of Wall Street hit it off from the outset. The friendship may have thrived in the soil of mutual frustration. One of Morgan's early assignments had been to procure false passports, an idea which horrified bureaucrats at the State Department. Finally, OSS won the reluctant cooperation of the Passport Office when Morgan presented his alternative. If State would not provide them, then OSS would counterfeit its own passports in Reddick's shop. Thereafter, Morgan was allowed to bring phony vital data to the State Department office, where the information was entered on genuine passports.

The lines of responsibility in the Washington office ran from tangled, to blurred, to nonexistent. Willis Reddick was unsure where Morgan's responsibilities ended and his own began. But they worked well together snatching personnel from the Federal Bureau of Engraving and Printing and from major commercial printers by using a simple argument: these highly skilled men could continue to work at their trade within the new intelligence agency, or else be drafted. The romantic notion that the best forgers and counterfeiters could be sprung from America's prisons amused Willis Reddick. "These people were a bunch of dilettantes, amateurs. If they were any good, they wouldn't have been caught. We wanted professionals."

As the work progressed, one conclusion became inescapable to Henry Morgan. Washington was too remote to produce the paraphernalia of deception needed in the war zones. To serve the European theater, a clothing and documentation operation would have to be set up in England. In April 1944, Willis Reddick arrived in London to build, all over again, another forging and counterfeiting shop, still under the cloak of "Research and Development."

British intelligence agents took the raw recruits of OSS under their wing almost too tenderly. Indeed, the British were quite willing to spare the Americans the chore of fabricating documents and offered to produce the papers for Reddick. The British were not eager to have foreign counterfeiters operating inside their country and outside of their control.

The preparation of these documents by the British would also reveal a good deal about the Americans' operations: who was working for them, what their agents were doing, and where they functioned. The Americans found their British cousins cloyingly close on this point. General Donovan was firm. OSS would produce its own documents. But an independent operation would still require close British cooperation.

Willis Reddick's practical Midwestern mind abhorred ostentation. On his arrival in England, he had been given a tour of British facilities where documents were produced and where the gadgetry of secret warfare was concocted. He had been much impressed by a display that he saw in a laboratory, a hammer was enclosed in a glass case with a sign reading "Why muck about on a silly invention when you can accomplish the same job with this."

Reddick found himself working closely with William Turnbull, another officer recently out of Washington. Turnbull, like their mutual friend Henry Morgan, came out of an investment family. He was a balding man of square, lean frame, whose face assumed a faintly pained smile whenever he spoke. His speech was quiet, understated, and precise, his background prototype OSS. The former financier had learned French as a child, even before speaking English, and he had been raided from naval intelligence by OSS.

Responsibilities between Reddick and Turnbull in London were divided along an arbitrary line. Reddick was to produce documents for agent cover; Turnbull was to see that those documents were filled out to match the cover story. They ignored this artificial allocation and set out to solve their real problem, which was to acquire skilled men and equipment to begin production. The machinery to equip a complete printing, lithography, and photoengraving plant was supposed to have been shipped from the United States to England. The shipment was either rusting on a Baltimore pier or resting on the ocean floor. It never arrived. American military forces in England had printing equipment but were not about to yield any of it to OSS. The London plant would have to be equipped locally, no simple feat in wartime England.

Reddick and Turnbull began searching for machinery through printing shops and used-equipment dealers. One firm loaned them an offset press. Another printer provided a photoengraving camera. But they were stymied in locating a lithographic press.

Reddick thought that a newcomer to his operation might be the man to find the press. Second Lieutenant Carl Strahle had been sent to London in response to Reddick's request for more personnel, and had also been sent, Reddick suspected, to remove a strong personality from the Washington office. But Willis Reddick liked Carl Strahle from the beginning, and there was no questioning Strahle's mastery of printing.

Carl Strahle had originally been commissioned in the Army Map Service, destined to fight the war from a stateside drafting board. OSS learned of his expertise and had him transferred to its printing operation. Strahle had expected to find in London a going concern. He found instead a plant whose equipment consisted of one ultraviolet light.

Reddick sent Carl Strahle to see one of England's largest printers in Birmingham. Strahle was warmly welcomed in this bomb-scarred industrial capital. He was invited to a Rotary luncheon where he delivered a rousing speech on British-American kinship. Strahle's British escort explained to the printing-plant manager that this American fellow needed a lithographic press, but he could not disclose why. The Americans would return it at the end of the war. Strahle apparently touched a universal Rotarian chord, since the press was rented to OSS for the equivalent of one dollar a year and delivered on the Fourth of July, 1944.

Reddick's operation still faced a formidable task. Procuring presses and cameras for counterfeiting posed problems in logistics. Producing paper for forged documents invaded the realm of art. Printing presses leave no identifying mark as to their origin. They are essentially neutral. But paper can almost be said to have nationality. Papers from mainland Europe have fibers from North Africa, easily distinguished from paper made elsewhere in the world. The color of paper also poses vexing problems. Identically colored sheets may look different under a fluorescent light. One white paper might fluoresce green, another orange. The Germans were known to use fluorescent lighting as a security check against counterfeit documents. Reddick and Turnbull took their problems in producing paper to an elderly colonel in the documents section of British intelligence. The old man shook his head. "But you are asking for the state secrets! Most irregular, gentlemen, most irregular."

They were advised to return in a few days. During this time the Britisher apparently was directed by his superiors to accommodate the Americans. A satisfactory arrangement was concluded and a small paper mill took on the job of manufacturing imitation foreign papers for OSS.

The counterfeiting operation was housed just behind OSS headquarters on Grosvenor Street. The building had reputedly been built as a country home by Christopher Wren. A wealthy Englishman had had the place dismantled and reassembled in London, and for a time it was the London residence of Charles de Gaulle. The heavy presses were placed on the concrete floor of the garage. The engraving plant was set up in the kitchen for easy access to water taps. Spread over three levels of the house was a staff of eighteen—engravers, offset cameramen, retouchers, and artists —who worked amid carved moldings, leaded windows, and tiled fireplaces disturbed only occasionally by the explosion of a buzz bomb.

Reddick had begun to build his staff before he left Washington. He again proceeded by finding out—from the Bureau of Engraving and Printing, the American Bank Note Company, the Curtis Publishing Company, and other quality printers—who had gone into military service. He then arranged to have transferred to England some of the ablest commercial artists and photoengravers from *Life* magazine, the *Saturday Evening Post*, and major advertising agencies.

Reddick particularly liked to draw on the American Bank Note Company, printers of currency for countries around the world. This firm paid the best salaries and usually employed the finest engravers. The firm's officials were not all that eager to cooperate. American Bank Note possessed secret processes which it preferred not to share with the U.S. government, even in wartime.

J.R. Work had graduated from the Chicago Art Institute in 1928, and for a time in the 1930s he and Willis Reddick were with the same printing company back in Springfield. Work had run into Reddick once when the latter returned home on leave. Willis Reddick was evidently into something unusual. This ordinarily direct man refused to reveal what he did in the army. Reddick did tell Work that if he ever went into the service, to let him know. Reddick said he was in a position to make interesting things happen.

Work was at the time advertising manager of a plant engaged in war contracts and, much to his surprise, was drafted. He contacted Reddick and soon found himself an army sergeant assigned to the OSS documents operation in London.

There, Work discovered a natural gift for forgery. He found himself signing "Adolf Hitler" to false commendations and orders, in an affected, vertical style, along with the signatures of "Heinrich Himmler" and "Joseph Goebbels." Work forged the handwriting of company adjutants, local police chiefs, and rationing officials. He was amused by the differences in the samples he studied—the strokes of Nazi warlords, bold, large, and illegible; those of minor officials, submissive, crabbed, apologetic. In forging the names of small cogs in the German war machinery, he would, if pressed for time, dash off something illegible, suffixed by ". . . mann." Bob Work forged Gestapo orders or ration cards with equal nonchalance. He could not read German and had not the faintest idea what he was signing.

When visitors came through the document printing plant now run by Carl Strahle, his pet tactic was to have them sign a "guest book." The forgers would then imitate the visitors' signatures. At the end of the visit, Strahle would ask, deadpan, if they had signed the book more than once. When they answered no, Strahle would ask, in mock puzzlement, "Then will you please tell us which of these is your signature?"

A staple in the repertory of the forgers was "William J. Donovan." Donovan's constant travels presented the problem of keeping him in one place long enough so that he could sign routine correspondence. With the establishment of the counterfeiting operation, the problem was solved for OSS London. Strahle's forgers signed Donovan's papers.

On one visit to London, when Donovan was to tour the printshop, the staff decided to give him a special demonstration of its prowess. Carl Strahle had conducted these tours frequently for Donovan, and came away each time convinced that the OSS chief would never grasp the mysteries of printing.

On this day, his crew had just finished reproducing its first Gestapo identification card without British aid. It had been an especially trying document requiring endless experiments to duplicate an elusive fluorescent match. They located a photograph of Donovan in uniform, airbrushed out the epaulettes and retouched the clothing to make it appear that he was wearing a civilian suit. They had the photograph reduced and affixed to one of the newly printed Gestapo passes. One of the forgers then signed it in Donovan's handwriting, "Wilhelm von Donovan." At the end of the general's tour, he was presented with the card.

He became visibly upset and demanded to know where they had obtained this photograph. Never, he said, had he posed for such a picture,

28

and in these clothes! Strahle sought to calm him. "Sir, you know what we do here—"

"But this signature. Where did you get my signature?"

Strahle explained patiently, "General, we probably have some of the best forgers in the world in this shop."

Donovan thought for a moment, then suddenly brightened. "This could be great. I can take this to Congress and show it to them when they want to know where all the money goes."

By the fall of 1944, the plant behind Grosvenor Street had become possibly the finest specialty printshop on earth. It produced a small, highly specialized product, sometimes only a single copy and sometimes a single sheet of paper had to be manufactured to make it. The mass-produced, journeyman work, such as food-rationing stamps, was left to the counterfeiting operation in Washington. But documents which demanded the highest printing skills and which had to be prepared under preposterous time pressures were produced in London.

Bill Turnbull, investment banker turned record falsifier, had gone to France on the heels of the advancing army to ransack abandoned enemy installations for sample documents. After Paris was liberated, the call came from London for Turnbull to intensify his search for papers usable within Germany—orders, forms, stamps, paper samples. Men on burial details were instructed to take paybooks, personal letters, copies of orders from the bodies of the German dead, any paper which could be used directly, altered, or copied for an agent's cover.

German Army regulations prohibited a soldier from carrying personal or other documents to the front, his paybook being almost the only exception. But the habit of carrying documents was so ingrained in the national character that these body searches invariably produced valuable items for Turnbull to send back to London.

The documents staff worked long, irregular hours. Carl Strahle curbed the habit of some of his men who were inclined to dart for the basement whenever air-raid warnings sounded. The unpredictability of V-weapons made it impractical to stop work at every warning. He had the windows blocked and curtained to block out light and flying glass, and the presses kept rolling.

Strahle was a conscientious craftsman and would sometimes wake up in the middle of the night wondering if he had permitted some potentially fatal detail on a document. He learned after the war that a team in Germany had been forced to change its itinerary because a critical umlaut was missing from a man's travel orders.

At one time the pigments for inks had presented discouraging problems. German pigments were difficult to match and virtually unreproducible. The matter was solved, quite simply, by ordering genuine German pigments. Carl Strahle was not sure where they came from, possibly through Sweden or Switzerland. It did not matter; he had only to submit a requisition to the supply people for German pigments, and the order was filled, usually within a month.

The shop had solved the problem of printing with German type by casting its own fonts. The printers would make a photoengraving of the specimen to be copied and, from the engraving, manufacture their own type. The copied model was scrupulously examined for flaws. If it contained a broken "P," then an identical flaw would be chipped into the newly cast type.

They mastered as well the most exacting challenge in paper manufacture, the counterfeiting of watermarks. The mysteries of the watermark had foiled the Germans for eighteen months in their attempts to forge a credible U.S. passport. When at last they succeeded, the U.S. Passport Office had already changed the design.

OSS put Jack M. Rudolph, an expert papermaker from the mills of the Kimberly-Clark Corporation, to work on the watermark. Watermarks were fiendishly tough because the device which produced the mark, the rubberized "dandy roll," became flattened in the manufacturing process to produce a watermark of a certain shape. The design on the dandy roll at rest was therefore different from its design when it pressed the paper. Through painstaking effort and enough money, Rudolph solved this problem.

The Germans had an evident passion for the reassuring thump of rubber against paper. An authentic German document invariably bore rubber stamps. Each civil jurisdiction and military unit had its own identifying stamp and wielded it liberally. Stamps were usually of identical size and similar design. The most common rubber stamp displayed an eagle over a swastika, with the local identification lettered around the perimeter. OSS experts devised a few basic stamps with interchangeable letters and numbers which could be set to replicate the stamp of any jurisdiction.

To give documents a convincing patina of age, they were treated with potassium permanganate, possibly stained with coffee, and baked in an oven. They might be rubbed with a powder of crushed rock and the corners frayed with sandpaper. On hot, humid days, rapid aging could be achieved by having someone carry a document in a hip or breast pocket.

Papers carried under the armpit obtained a swift and persuasive appearance of long use.

Handwritten entries on forms were plausibly executed by a fussy, dyspeptic second lieutenant, a German-born Jewish refugee who wrote in a fine bureaucratic script.

At times the talents of his printers made Carl Strahle uneasy. He had seen how effortlessly his men had solved the scarcity of cigarettes simply by counterfeiting extra ration stamps for themselves. He had examined the English £5 note with some trepidation. Producing the British bill would be a cinch for his printers. Strahle and his staff learned that anything which can be printed can be counterfeited. The essential elements were the human skills and enough money. OSS, by this stage, had both.

At OSS London there also served a celebrated private, Dr. Lazare Teper, a man who moved easily among the refugee Socialists and intellectuals gathered under George Pratt's Labor Division. Teper was a large, dark-haired, shambling man, with an off-center smile, and an easy, rolling laughter. He was rare among Americans in the Labor Division in that he actually came out of the American labor movement. Teper was, however —in the mold of European trade unionists—educated, cultivated, and had a strong pragmatic streak.

Lazare Teper had been born in Russia to a Jewish family comfortable enough to provide young Lazare with a German governess in preparation for his expected eventual education in Germany. The family, forced to leave Russia in 1924, detoured to Istanbul for several years before settling in France. Lazare Teper studied at the Sorbonne and won a scholarship to Johns Hopkins, where he discovered a talent for economics. In the 1930s, he became research director of the International Ladies' Garment Workers Union in New York City. Teper was drafted, but before he completed his basic training, OSS reached out for him.

In 1943, Lazare Teper reported to 70 Grosvenor Street and was assigned an office on the upper floor. The building had originally been the House of Worth, a famous couturier. In his new office, Teper found a three-seat toilet with an enameled sign over the middle position reading, "For Fitters Only."

Feeling inadequately prepared by his OSS training, Teper spent his free time in England educating himself by watching spy movies. He worked in the Labor Division doing research on the conditions of daily life inside Germany. What papers, ration cards, work permits, and travel passes were needed there? Which cover stories might succeed best? What were the details of ordinary living that an inhabitant of the Third Reich would know as well as his own name?

Teper's job was aided by some of the rather make-work tasks performed by the labor refugees under George Pratt. For over a year, they had been clipping German newspapers obtained mostly through neutral Portugal and Sweden. To the astute reader, these papers yielded a sharply defined X-ray of life inside Germany. Innocent-sounding items from the Berlin *Angriff,* the *Frankfurter Zeitung,* and the Munich party mouthpiece, the *Völkischer Beobachter* revealed much of everyday conditions on the other side of the war. News of curfew hours, rationing allowances, and new regulations provided rich ore for an intelligence operation planning to infiltrate the enemy's homeland.

Small-town journals, less rigidly censored, offered obscure treasures. A woman was reported fined for selling cigarettes to a French laborer working outside her town. Thus, OSS learned the location of a camp which could be fitted into the cover story of an agent posing as a conscript worker. Pratt's émigrés devoted nearly all of 1943 to this worm's-eye anatomization of the Third Reich.

In April 1944, Private Teper's duties were formalized and enlarged into a new unit which he was to head; it was specifically charged with devising cover stories for agents going into Germany. Teper was initially assigned one assistant, Private Henry Sutton. Sutton was a soft balloon of a man, thirty-seven years old, with apple cheeks and undisciplined tufts of thinning blond hair. He spoke in a pinch-nosed Viennese accent, which inevitably raised the question, whence the name "Henry Sutton"?

He had been born Heinrich Sofner to Viennese Catholic parents. Before the Anschluss, Sofner served as an officer in a white-collar workers' union. An Austrian court had sentenced him to five years for an inflammatory speech which he had delivered in defiance of a ban on labor activity. After serving eighteen months, he was released under a general amnesty, just as the Nazis annexed Austria. He then began a political hegira which led him to Switzerland, France, and, finally, the United States.

Sutton was drafted into the U.S. Army and took the opportunity to apply for early American citizenship. During the citizenship hearing a court officer asked Sutton if he had a criminal record. He admitted to the sentence in Austria. The OSS man who had accompanied him saw the reaction of the court official and feared that Sutton had destroyed his hopes of becoming an American. "Sutton," he whispered, "are you a

Communist?" "Of course not, I am a Social Democrat." "But, are you a Jew?" "I am a Catholic." How could someone, not a Communist and not a Jew, have possibly been sentenced for treason in Austria, the man wondered.

Sutton eventually attained U.S. citizenship. But European Socialists and trade unionists like him would continue to bother certain of their native American OSS colleagues.

Lazare Teper found Henry Sutton a tactless subordinate suffering from a severe case of middle-European pedantry. But the man possessed two virtues. He quickly absorbed an encyclopedic knowledge of conditions inside Germany and he spoke fluent European socio-politicalese, a valuable asset in dealing with the Labor Division's refugees.

Teper's new cover-story operation was assigned quarters in a building code-named "Milwaukee." He was asked what code designation he wanted for his unit. "Pabst," Teper said. "That's from Milwaukee." The choice was rejected as too frivolous. Teper then selected the name of his favorite composer. Thus the BACH Section was born.

Private Teper managed to magnify the meager powers of his military rank by dressing as a civilian. He often lunched with British counterparts in the rarefied atmosphere of their officers' mess where guests were seated in descending order of rank from the commandant at the head of the table on down. Teper, as a presumed civilian eminence, was usually seated next to the commandant. He made no effort to enlighten fellow OSS officers unaware of his actual station. On one occasion a major had fussed to Teper about another officer who had been prodding the major about the progress of his mission: "I do not intend to have my work checked by any damned captain." Teper had nodded sympathetically.

Lazare Teper possessed a flair for practical theatrics along with skills as a researcher. He once had difficulty convincing an agent that he could get away with carrying a pistol in a shoulder holster unnoticed. He called the man into his office. Teper talked to him from behind his desk, got up, paced the room, leaned into the man's face and argued his case. At one point, the man briefly averted his gaze and returned to find himself staring into the barrel of a .32-caliber pistol. Teper burst out laughing. He opened his suit coat and revealed the unobtrusive holster.

On one London visit, General Donovan wanted to meet these fabled privates, Teper and Sutton. He was particularly impressed by a flow chart which Henry Sutton had painstakingly constructed, tracing an OSS agent at every stage from recruitment to infiltration into enemy territory. "Have a copy of that thing made up for me. I want to show it to the Senate Armed Forces Committee." Sutton was horrified at this potential exposure of OSS's innermost secrets, and later conveyed his objections to Teper. Teper wanted to know how his assistant had registered this disapproval to Donovan. Sutton smiled. "I said, 'Why not, General?'"

III

Burglars with Morals

✠ ✠ ✠

George Pratt, the chief of the Labor Division, knew virtually everything about the exiled European labor leadership in London and nothing about putting agents into enemy territory. Pressure was now on him to use his knowledge of one to achieve the other. Pratt had headed the Labor Division since November 1942, after Arthur Goldberg had set down the early foundations. He was a low-key, able performer, a courteous man of winsome, understated humor, given to unexpectedly spirited renderings of labor songs at OSS parties.

In November 1944, Bill Casey created a new entity, the Division of Intelligence Procurement (DIP), specifically to carry out the German venture, absorbing the Labor Division as DIP's nucleus. He named George Pratt to head DIP.

Personnel were commandeered from offices of waning priority and assigned to Pratt's new division. DIP subsumed several existing SI offices, including the nationality desks—French, Belgian, Polish, Dutch, Czech, Scandinavian, and German. These desks were to work with counterpart governments-in-exile in recruiting prospective agents.

Recognizing his innocence of clandestine operations, Pratt went to Casey and David Bruce to ask for more experienced help. Bruce made the first delivery on Pratt's request in the person of Hans Tofte, a spirited

Danish-American with a handsome, open face, thinning blond hair, and the lilting cadence of his native land still in his speech.

Cooler heads bridled at Tofte's impetuosity, his disdain for conventional authority, extreme even in an organization as loose as OSS. But he had an unarguably impressive record. Hans Tofte had left Denmark at the age of nineteen to study Chinese in Peking. He stayed abroad eight years and had just returned home when the Nazis seized his homeland. He then fled to the United States. In New York City, he was recruited by the man called Intrepid, William Stephenson, who ran British Security Coordination, the MI-6 operation in the United States. The British wanted Tofte for his knowledge of Oriental languages and sent him on a mission to Singapore. When that city fell to the Japanese, the Dane returned to the United States with the unlikely rank of brevet major in the Indian Army. Tofte said good-bye to all that, and, in order to hasten his American citizenship, entered the American army as a private. There OSS found him.

Tofte went abroad first to Bari, and ran a highly successful operation supplying Yugoslav partisans across the Adriatic. Tofte's partner in Bari was a craggy OSS army captain, Robert E. S. Thompson, a son of missionary parents and a former reporter with the *Philadelphia Inquirer*, whose customary speech was a vigorous profanity.

Tofte and Thompson perfected a system for supplying the Yugoslavs by daring boat runs rather than the air drops employed earlier. They delivered 6,000 tons of water-borne supplies to the partisans, compared to 125 tons dropped earlier by air. Thompson and Tofte later were awarded Yugoslavia's highest military decoration for their Adriatic gunrunning.

The summer of 1944 found Hans Tofte chafing at a London desk job, working on OSS Scandinavian operations. When DIP was formed, Tofte became George Pratt's deputy. They arrived at a happy division of labor. In long days, often stretching deep into the night, Pratt buried himself in the administrative demands of his new function—memoranda, policy positions, and organizational plans. Tofte, impatient with paperwork, prodded people on the nationality desks for agent material. He also looked for American personnel with practical experience in handling agents to be transferred to England. One man he wanted was his old partner from Bari, Rob Thompson.

Rob Thompson was located in France, where he had been assigned to work with the U.S. First Army after his service in Bari. The First Army had never warmed to OSS-style operations. At the outbreak of the Battle of the Bulge, the First, in fact, had no OSS contingent; and as General Donovan wryly noted, this army had been caught completely off guard by the German thrust. The First Army's attitude toward OSS personnel had not changed much, and Rob Thompson was just as happy to leave for a new assignment.

David Bruce explained to Thompson why he had been brought to London. "We need people who can look these agents in the eye and say, 'I've done it, and I know it can be done.' We've got too many people who have never performed themselves."

"Colonel, you have another fellow wandering around the halls here with nothing to do," Thompson told Bruce. "He's parachuted himself and he's had plenty of experience behind the lines. If you'll turn us loose, we can get something done."

The man Thompson wanted was Lieutenant Junior Grade E. M. ("Mike") Burke, a dark-haired Irishman, twenty-six years old, and a former halfback at the University of Pennsylvania. General Donovan had once seen Burke make a spectacular kick-off return against Michigan. When he met the tall, lithe Burke at a Washington party, the OSS chief recruited him on the spot.

Burke spoke so quietly that one often had to strain to hear him, but the speech was colorful and articulate and the listener could detect the faintest trace of Galway clinging to his tongue from Burke's early youth in Ireland.

In 1943, the long-limbed, six-feet-two-inch Burke was slipped ashore into Italy from a PT boat disguised, in an abysmal piece of casting, as an Italian peasant. He and his team were to make contact with the anti-Fascist commander of the Italian Navy and persuade him to surrender his fleet to the Allies. Later, Burke parachuted into the Vosges Mountains to help organize the French resistance.

On February 17, 1945, Rob Thompson was named operations officer of the Division of Intelligence Procurement, and Mike Burke became his deputy. They took responsibility for coordinating the training, communications, air operations, and twelve other stages of agent preparation. Previously, every nationality desk had competed separately for these support services. The new team broke through bottlenecks, replenished scarce supplies, jolted the air force into reluctant action, and began to pump agents through the system.

The pieces were fitting into place. The nationality desks were providing spy recruits. The BACH operation was manufacturing cover stories. Bill Reddick's staff provided false documents and authentic clothing, and the operations staff knew how to get a trained and properly equipped agent onto a plane and into Germany.

An American officer described the OSS agent recruits: "We were dealing with an unusual type of individual. Many had natures that fed on danger and excitement. Their appetite for the unconventional and the spectacular was far beyond the ordinary. It was not unusual to find a good measure of temperament thrown in."

Some wanted to be heroes, others wanted to finish the war on the side of the Americans, who were clearly going to inherit the postwar earth. Many had long since forgotten the rhythms of normal life. In 1939, they had left home for military service, worked underground after defeat, fled their conquered homelands, and endured long separations from families. What OSS now proposed fell easily within the norms of their existence.

For veteran adventurers, the fear, tension, and pressures had become an addiction. Days spent in the safety of rear-echelon headquarters were a restless interlude before the high of the next mission.

General Donovan was aware of the unnatural moral environment that espionage operations produced, and he sought out social scientists for guidance. His chief of psychology, Dr. Henry Murray, warned of the pitfalls. "The whole nature of the functions of OSS was particularly inviting to psychopathic characters; it involved sensation, intrigue, the idea of being a mysterious man with secret knowledge."

For the many Jews who volunteered, the Nazis had supplied all the motivation necessary. To proud, good Germans, sickened by what had become of their country, Hitler and Nazism also provided the rationale for fighting against their own nation.

OSS screening officers found that vengeance and hatred were unreliable stimuli. Consuming passion could be an undependable partner under pressure. The obsessed man belonged behind a machine gun, not in espionage. An OSS manual on recruiting noted: "A man should not have too many ideals, should work with his intelligence rather than his heart." Stability was cardinal, with anger muted and fury cold. An agent undone by his own impetuosity risked not only his own life but endangered all those involved with him, along with the secrets he possessed. The ideal candidate was honest and devious, inconspicuous and audacious, quick and prudent, zealous and cool. One agent summed up his role: "I was a burglar with morals."

Some had been enticed by hints, even bald promises that an espionage stint for OSS would gain them entry into the United States after the war.

American official policy on this point seemed calculatedly confused. Some officers believed they were authorized to offer agents the prospect of United States citizenship. Word of these promises filtered back to Washington. Distressed OSS lawyers warned their colleagues abroad that under U.S. immigration laws such inducements were impossible to fulfill and dishonest to make. The final OSS policy on this point was candid, if brutal: "No agent should be recruited without serious thought being given to the means of disposing of him after his usefulness has ended." Still, emigration to the United States and American citizenship were dangled before prospective agents right to the end of the war.

There were legitimate inducements as well. OSS arranged for a German alien living in America to be recruited into the navy. The incentive offered was citizenship within a few months. In order to make the deal more attractive, OSS persuaded the navy to commission the man. He was sent to London, where the freshly minted naval officer refused to undertake a mission. OSS tried to get the navy to strip him of his rank. But by then, the navy had had its fill of OSS spy games and refused.

Along with qualities of character, OSS recruiters sought practical skills. Radio operators were prized. People with knowledge of the structure of German society—with postal, telegraph, telephone, rail, and shipping experience—were valued. Women were useful. Their cover stories were more easily contrived, and they could travel under less suspicion.

Prisoner-of-war cages, initially out-of-bounds to recruiters, were canvassed. The flow of volunteers from the cages followed the tides of battle. After the sweep through France, candidates were abundant. During the Battle of the Bulge, hard-core Nazis rioted and tried to seize control of some prison camps, and prospective recruits evaporated. In one cage in England, a prisoner was found dead. All signs pointed to his execution by a kangaroo-court as a suspected anti-Nazi. The commandant mustered the men from the victim's company and said, to spare punishing the entire group, that he wanted the guilty parties to step forward. Every man in the company stepped out.

Once selected, potential agents were checked by X-2 counterespionage to determine if OSS was dealing with a possible double agent. The precaution was well warranted. Henry Sutton, of the BACH operation, interviewed a prisoner from a German *Strafbataillon*, a punishment battalion. The man claimed he was a leftist and anti-Nazi. Sutton came away impressed. The prisoner clearly knew the underground world of surviving German trade unionists. He discussed key figures and factions knowledgeably. He had served, he said, in the German merchant fleet before the

war and had picked up his knowledge of English as a waiter at a Longchamps restaurant in New York. Now, he wanted to work for the Allies.
Sutton reported to his chief, Lazare Teper, who agreed that the man
looked promising. "But, let's have X-2 check him out."

The man's name appeared on no ship's manifest. Immigration and
Naturalization had no knowledge of him, nor did Longchamps. The truth
finally emerged. The man was an SS operative, originally assigned to the
punishment battalion as a phony anti-Nazi to keep an eye on his politically
unreliable comrades. When he, along with the rest of the *Strafbataillon,*
was captured, he surmised during his interrogation that the Americans
were looking for agents. He volunteered, reasoning that at best he could
infiltrate the enemy's intelligence system; and at the very least, he would
get back home.

After he was exposed, the German was thrown back into the POW
camp. Under the Geneva Convention, he had committed no offense.
Prisoners of war were allowed to lie. "But," Henry Sutton noted after the
near disaster, "we were not obliged to believe them."

The SS officer had gone aground on one point: the claim that he had
traveled to the United States, the only specific that OSS could check. He
had committed the sin of excessive detail, a lesson not lost on the BACH
Section in devising its own cover stories.

The files of the BACH Section were maintained in alphabetical order
by German cities. Henry Sutton savored certain items. Every city file had
to include the color of the local streetcar. It was, he had heard, a stock
question the Gestapo put to a suspected enemy agent.

Another fact which Sutton drilled into the heads of prospective agents
was the burial place of their parents. It was common to pose an agent as
an orphan to make it harder for Nazi authorities to check his past.
Consequently, BACH researchers routinely read obituaries in German
papers to learn the names of cemeteries. It was Sutton's patience, even
his pleasure in assembling these minutiae, that made him invaluable to
Lazare Teper.

Information flowed to the BACH files from numerous sources, most
profitably from OSS officers attached to field commands at the front. One
perceptive and productive field officer was Lieutenant Richard Watt, a
tall, boyish, recent law-school graduate. Watt worked the prisoner-of-war
cages from Luxembourg to Holland, directly behind the lines, gathering
fresh information to send to London. He spoke good German and had a
thoughtful, sympathetic manner that invited trust.

Watt would turn a casual conversation to the cost of living and black-marketing. How was the food supply, the latest ration allowances? Local transportation conditions? What neighborhoods had been bombed? What streets? What house numbers? Bombed-out residences would provide valuable home addresses for agents, since they could not be checked. And, always, of course, What was the color of the local streetcar? Watt assumed that the intent of his queries must have been evident to the shrewder prisoners. But POWs were a lonely lot, and most of them craved human contact. One thing amused and puzzled him. Whenever Watt entered the compound, the prisoners stiffened to attention and saluted him. Was he supposed to return the salute?

The BACH operation took the information which officers like Watt gathered and with it counterfeited human identities. The work demanded vivid imagination along with a passion for trifling detail. Minor ignorances and small inconsistencies could begin to unravel the most carefully woven fabric of deception.

The BACH staff began with the premise that the best cover was the least cover. If a former civil engineer could get by using his own identity and his own occupation, no further cover was necessary or wise. If the mission required that his identity be concealed, but not his occupation, then cover was provided for only the identity. The important point was to minimize the details that could be checked and to lighten the fictional baggage which the agent had to carry.

The character of the Nazi regime worked both for and against the construction of plausible cover stories. The efficiency of the security system, the pervasive surveillance by police over citizens and by citizens over their neighbors, the documents required to eat, work, dress, and travel, all formed an intimidating barrier to penetration. An ordinary civilian in the Reich would be expected to carry, besides his ID card, a police registration, labor registration, food and clothing ration stamps, travel permits, housing registration, and perhaps a driver's license, draft exemptions, and other specialized papers.

At the same time, the nature of the Nazi industrial economy offered an inviting side door into the Reich. Virtually the entire able-bodied male civilian population in Germany between the ages of sixteen and fifty was composed of foreigners impressed into the service of the war economy. In importing laborers from occupied lands, Germany had become a host to some 3 million foreigners.

Posing an agent as a foreign worker offered an ideal cover. He need not speak much German. He was not subject to the draft. His past was difficult to check. He could penetrate key war industries. The cover demanded some additional documentation, the *Fremdenpass*, or foreign worker's passport, the *Arbeitskarte*, the work permit, along with most of the papers a German would carry. But the documentation section could provide them all.

The next best cover was as a German or foreigner serving in the Wehrmacht. Military cover offered ease of movement and access to military installations. The disadvantage was in feigning a convincing knowledge of military life, unless the agent had actually served in the German armed services.

A somewhat more hazardous cover was to pass off an agent as a civilian deferred from military service, specialist craftsman, party official, or member of the police. If the latter were chosen, it was best to go first-class, and use the cover of a Gestapo official. The Gestapo was a fairly large organization. Its members generally wore civilian clothes, allowing the agent to blend easily into the populace. And few German officials had the stomach to challenge the secret police.

The operating premise in preparing false documents was similar to the approach employed in creating cover stories. A wholly genuine document was best; a partially genuine document, an actual passport for instance, with a faked identity, was next best. Wholly fabricated documents were the last resort. Broad-coverage documents were preferable to the narrow. It was better to supply agents with food-ration stamps issued for travel status—persons bombed out, moving, or changing jobs—rather than stamps valid only in one district.

A faked doctor's certificate stating that the bearer had a contagious disease was an especially valuable paper. It could get a conscript worker out of the barracks and into a better position to glean intelligence.

The document had also to be understood in its context. Sutton grilled prisoners of war, particularly those recently drafted or just back from home leave. Who issued a particular document? Under what circumstances? When and where was it likely to be checked? What did each entry mean? An agent's survival might well hinge on knowing the answers. Then, the BACH Section would place its orders with the printshop.

The work required a passion for the seemingly inconsequential. Did the completed documents have convincing minor mistakes? They could be too perfect. Had photographs on identification cards been properly aged? Was clothing authentic? Buttons on American-made clothing were sewn on with the threads parallel, but in European tailoring the thread was criss-crossed. A laborer's clothing should have a coarser-gauge thread than a tailored suit. Authentic German suspender buttons were marked "Elegant" or "For Gentlemen." American laundries used fluorescent marks. Did German cleaners? Where were the agent's eyeglasses ground? What kind of toothbrush did he use? Was his dental work customary for a European? If a man had suddenly to empty his pockets or a woman her purse, was the litter convincing—ticket stubs from the local opera, keys, coins, matches? With tobacco short in Germany, why would a man have heavy nicotine stains on his fingers? Stains had to be sanded off with a pumice stone.

The absorption in petty detail—gauge of thread, tobacco stains—was not exaggerated. The Gestapo checked these trivial matters with relentless thoroughness. One OSS agent had been exposed because entries on his work permit, supposedly filled out in two different cities, were clearly in the same handwriting.

When the paraphernalia of deception was good, it did more than deceive the enemy. Good papers, the right clothes, a credible cover story helped the agent to live his cover, to convince himself, and thus be convincing to others. Agents were wakened from a deep sleep to hear someone shouting, "What is your name? Where did you go to school? What is the newspaper in your town?"

In the end, the capricious, the absurd, the unanticipated might still undo the best-prepared spy. The British warned the Americans of an agent they had lost in Cairo. The fellow had failed to bend his knees in the Egyptian style when he urinated. After trying to clothe one agent, Lazare Teper lamented, "You show the fellow a nice plain suit. He says, 'No, it will make me look conspicuous.' Then he picks out something with chalk stripes an inch wide!"

Teper learned to accept the limitations of his work. No cover was foolproof. All could be pierced. The BACH Section wove the most plausible story possible with the materials at hand. Still, Teper often found it thin stuff, ten percent hard fact, the rest conjecture, intuition, deduction. A spy might be passed off as a Gestapo official, but under hard questioning, could not make the story stick.

The agents were never as aware of the fragility of their disguises as the men who concocted them. What was the point? They were all volunteers, eager to go. Nothing was to be gained by increasing their anxiety. War was risk. Some men would die on invasion beaches and others against a wall. The best Teper could hope for was that the cover story would hold up long enough to get the agent through a control point and save him from rigorous interrogation, where in the end his story must inevitably crack. The final defenses existed in a spy's mind, in the fear, the distrust, the loneliness that honed his senses and his vigilance.

IV

Back Door to the Reich

✛ ✛ ✛

Bern, the Swiss capital, is a medieval city with an air of bourgeois content-ment. Its arcaded streets suggest a mercantile cloister, a fourteenth-cen-tury fair become permanent. During the war, the capital offered little culture or entertainment, and the complacent Bernese did not mind. Zurich and Geneva could provide these diversions. Bern's principal pas-time seemed to be the consumption of heavy meals at rustic country inns. No dramatist would have cast the city for what it became—a nexus of global intrigue, a tiny mirror reflecting the machinations of great powers locked in battle. The city seemed too small, too self-satisfied, too unsophis-ticated to stage the intelligence rivalries of half a dozen great nations.

To this unlikely field of secret warfare, a forty-nine-year-old American, gray-haired and bespectacled, arrived on November 8, 1942. The man looked like the son of a Presbyterian parson, which he was. He also possessed the disarming charm of a country lawyer, and, happily for his mission, the instincts of a spy. His name was Allen Welsh Dulles, and he had come to Bern, ostensibly, as "Special Legal Assistant" to the Ameri-can minister, Leland Harrison. The Swiss newspapers had it wrong. They described Dulles as the "personal representative of President Roosevelt" in Bern. Dulles did not object. The conjecture could only serve his ends.

That he had arrived in Switzerland at all had been the purest luck.

Dulles had taken the last train from Annemasse, France, near the Swiss border, the day after Allied forces invaded North Africa. The Germans immediately seized unoccupied France, thus sealing off Switzerland from the outside world and completing its encirclement by the Nazis.

Long before OSS London had begun to mobilize for the penetration of Germany on a grand scale, Dulles had been working toward the same objective from Bern. He had in fact been transferred from the OSS New York Office to Switzerland in 1942 for that very purpose, because the British initially opposed letting OSS use England as a springboard for operations inside the Reich.

He arrived carrying letters of introduction to the prominent in every important area of Swiss life. He also knew the anti-Nazi German politicians, labor leaders, religious figures, scientists, professors, diplomats, and businessmen living in exile in Switzerland.

Dulles brought far more experience to the craft of espionage than most of his OSS colleagues. That experience had also begun in Bern twenty-five years before, when he had served as a young foreign-service officer collecting intelligence on Germany and the Austro-Hungarian Empire. After the war, Dulles worked at the Versailles Peace Conference with his older brother, John Foster. He went on to a meteoric career in the State Department capped, at the age of twenty-nine, by his appointment as chief of the Near East Division. The money in government was not good, so Allen Dulles left State to join his brother's prestigious international law firm in New York, Sullivan and Cromwell.

In the 1920s, during his State Department career, he had met and been much taken by another lawyer, William J. Donovan, then with the Justice Department. Barely a month after Pearl Harbor, Allen Dulles had heeded Donovan's appeal and joined OSS.

During the war, the Swiss guarded their neutrality zealously. They were well aware of how closely they had escaped Nazi occupation. In 1940, German armies had been poised to strike France, using Switzerland as a path. Only the quick French collapse had spared the Swiss from being swallowed whole. In subsequent years, German generals eyed Swiss rail lines as tempting corridors for supplying their armies in North Africa and Italy. Though democratic, benevolent, and tacit champions of Allied victory, the Swiss lived in fear of provoking the Germans. They enacted scrupulous prohibitions against any acts favoring the interests of a belligerent power. They maintained a special force, the Fremdenpolizei, the foreign police, to monitor embassy staffs and other foreigners in their country for violations of Swiss neutrality. Swiss counterintelligence was known for its sensitive antennae and swift arrest of offenders. To the Allies, the Swiss seemed to say, "Play your game, but play it well so that we need not catch you."

In this small, uneasy corner of Europe, Allen Dulles began to weave his net. He took up residence at Herrengasse 23 in the old section of Bern. Adjoining houses across the Aare River housed his OSS officers. These buildings also contained the U.S. Office of War Information, which offered a legitimate if thin legality, since, in the European lexicon, "information" was virtually synonymous with "intelligence." The cover did, however, provide OSS staff with vital diplomatic immunity.

On Dulles's arrival, his staff had consisted of two other persons. With the Swiss borders now sealed, he might have faced a serious manpower problem. Allen Dulles was undaunted. There was talent to be found elsewhere on the embassy staff and among American citizens living in Switzerland. People could be begged, borrowed, and induced to serve. It was only a matter of knowing how to use people, and Allen Dulles knew how.

A refugee Austrian journalist recalled his first meeting with the American. The young man had come to Dulles's attention because of anti-Nazi articles he had written in *Weltwoche* and other periodicals. His work revealed both acute political perception and obvious access to well-placed sources. "I loved him right away," the journalist said of Dulles. "He had this marvelous, low-key way of speaking, so different from a European of position."

Dulles brought up the journalist's pet obsession, postwar planning for Germany. The writer was flattered that Dulles knew of this concern, and poured out his views, at long last, to an important and interested listener. Dulles asked him if he would be willing to prepare some papers on various subjects of postwar planning.

The young journalist left Dulles's office entranced. He worked hard and soon completed studies on the future of the German university and the library system in postwar Europe. He looked forward eagerly to his audiences with Dulles. He knew it was silly, but he had lost his own father some years before, and Dulles seemed to fill a part of that void.

Dulles always praised the young man's work lavishly. At the close of their long conversations, he would ask casually, "By the way, Robert, what do you think of this talk of a plot against Hitler? Anything to it? Do you know Gisevius? Do you think he's reliable?" It was not until after a year of drafting postwar planning papers that the journalist grasped his true value to Allen Dulles.

Among the expatriate Americans who went to work for Allen Dulles was a woman named Mary Bancroft. She had been doing free-lance journalism when Dulles asked her to analyze the German press for the reports which he telephoned almost nightly to Washington. Digesting foreign newspapers was the least of Mary Bancroft's talents.

This daughter of the publisher of *The Wall Street Journal* was a hellfire Democrat and liberal. Mary Bancroft was attractive in a wholesome, athletic style and a woman of vivid opinions which she was rarely reluctant to express.

While living in Zurich, Mary was deeply influenced by the Swiss psychiatrist Carl Gustav Jung. She later wrote of Jung, "Although he was twenty-eight years older than I, I found him extremely attractive as a man. This was a shock. Until that moment I had never regarded men more than ten years older than myself as sex objects."

She attended Jung's seminars at the Psychological Club in Zurich, and eventually worked up the courage to approach the great man with her own problem: protracted bouts of sneezing in social situations, mostly, she found, when she was bored. Mary Bancroft saw Jung on and off for over four years as a student, collaborator, and friend. He developed a genuine affection for this candid American.

Jung's good opinion was not held unanimously. One of his colleagues, a woman psychiatrist, found dealing with Mary Bancroft "like wrestling with a boa constrictor."

Soon after her recruitment into espionage, Mary Bancroft began commuting almost weekly between her home in Zurich and Dulles's apartment in Bern. She had extensive connections throughout the country and eventually graduated from analyzing the press for him to helping Dulles meet useful people and avoid dry wells. Dulles discovered in Mary Bancroft a woman wielding an intuitive scalpel with an unerring instinct for laying bare a person's character.

One night, after dinner at his apartment, Dulles fixed Mary Bancroft with his Presbyterian minister's stare and said, "Contrary to general belief, I think you can keep your mouth shut." Mary Bancroft had never kept a secret in her life. She had, since a child, habitually blurted out everything she knew. She protested his opinion as absurd, but continued to listen.

Dulles had a job that had to be done, and there was no one else to do it. If she could not keep quiet about it, "Five thousand people will be dead," Dulles warned. The argument moved her, for this woman was, at heart, a profound moralist. "You will soon get a call," he told her in best spy fashion, "from a Dr. Bernhard."

The man who would use this name in dealing with Mary Bancroft was Hans Bernd Gisevius, an agent of the Abwehr, the German military's secret intelligence service. He was posted at the German consulate in Zurich under diplomatic cover as vice-consul. Gisevius typified the internal conflicts within the Abwehr, in which loyalty to Germany warred with disloyalty toward its present leaders. It was a struggle that assailed members of the Abwehr up to the very summit of the organization, including its enigmatic chief, Admiral Wilhelm Canaris.

Canaris was believed by one school of Allied intelligence officers to be anti-Nazi and to represent a valuable conduit for the conduct of peace negotiations. There was some speculation that Canaris had been reached by the British long ago through Juan March, a powerful Spanish Jew whom Canaris knew from his long involvement with Spain. March reported that Canaris's unhappiness with Hitler supposedly dated from well before the war. Others saw Canaris as the quintessential intriguer whose cold heart, in the end, belonged to the Third Reich.

Hans Bernd Gisevius had come to Dulles several months before, in February 1943, with astonishing information and Dulles was eager to keep this new freshet of intelligence flowing. The key to pleasing Gisevius lay in a book he was writing, his political testament. Gisevius desperately wanted it translated so that the book could come out in English the moment the war ended. Dulles assured him that he could arrange a translator. Mary Bancroft, Dulles had decided, was the one to do it.

While working on the book, she was also to draw Gisevius out and report to Dulles everything that the German said. She agreed, largely because Mary Bancroft was incapable of saying no to Allen Dulles. The man fascinated her. As a person of deep ethical principles, she wondered how men who seemed amoral in their professional conduct could be such believing Christians.

Mary Bancroft did not learn the real name of Dr. Bernhard until much later, and that Gisevius had come to Allen Dulles to tell him that he was part of a conspiracy to assassinate Adolf Hitler.

In June 1943, "Dr. Bernhard" called Mary Bancroft and made an appointment to come to her apartment in Zurich that same afternoon. She opened her door to a forty-year-old man whose shoulders virtually blotted out the doorway. The huge figure struck her at once as both Prussian and professorial, yet somehow vulnerable, too. Mary Bancroft was instantly fascinated.

Hans Bernd Gisevius had been born in Prussia into a family of traditional civil servants. He had joined the Gestapo almost at its creation, when the secret police was still under its founder, Hermann Göring. Gisevius was viewed in the Gestapo as a bumptious young man on the make, as he dueled with other in-fighters for power in the rising secret police organization.

Early in this disillusioning experience Gisevius asked a Gestapo colleague, "Tell me, please, am I in a police office, or in a robbers' cave?" "We did not dare step ten or twenty feet across the hall to wash our hands," he wrote later, "without telephoning a colleague and informing him of our intentions to embark on so perilous an expedition. . . . It was so usual for members of the Gestapo to arrest one another that we scarcely took notice of such incidents, unless we happened to come across a more detailed example of such an arrest by way of the hospital or morgue."

Gisevius was apparently out of his depth amid intriguers of this stripe and within five months was ousted in a purge. He later joined the Berlin police, but was dismissed for criticizing the SS. He eventually became a member of the Abwehr and was posted to Zurich.

Though the connection had been brief and many years had since passed, Gisevius could not entirely cleanse himself of the stain of early association with the Gestapo. The stigma was unfortunate. Gisevius was a committed anti-Nazi and one of a small band of Germans courageous enough to act on his convictions. As early as 1939, he had made overtures to the British in Switzerland and had acted briefly as an intelligence source for them. But he was eventually dropped by MI-6 as a self-seeking opportunist at best and a double agent at worst. The man, after all, had stayed on with the Nazis a bit long.

MI-6 had already been badly stung by supposed anti-Nazi Germans. Just two months into the war, on November 9, 1939, at Venlo on the Dutch-German border, the two senior MI-6 officers on the Continent, Major S. Payne Best and Captain R. Henry Stevens, had been lured to a meeting with phony anti-Nazi militarists. They had been abducted instead.

The British, thereafter, reacted coolly to professed German anti-Nazis, and a person like Gisevius personified their skepticism. Politically, he was a man of the right who blamed Hitler's rise on liberals and Communists of the Weimar Republic. The British tended to view anti-Nazi generals and people like Gisevius merely as rivals of Hitler in a German power struggle. If successful, they would only substitute the belligerence of the German officer class for that of the Nazis, and the war would go on. The British also had to consider the unhappiness of their Soviet allies, should they be found consorting with German militarists.

Gisevius, for his part, found the British depressingly narrow and blind to exploitable currents of unrest in Germany. The Americans, he hoped, might be more responsive. His initial contact was made through Gero von Gaevernitz, a German-born American, then managing family business interests in Switzerland.

Von Gaevernitz, in his early forties, a tall, suave aristocrat, had long wanted to bring together American officials and anti-Nazi Germans. Von Gaevernitz first approached the military attaché at the American embassy, Brigadier General Barnwell Legge. Legge demurred, believing that this undercover business lay outside his province. But the general did suggest, after Allen Dulles arrived, that Dulles might want to meet Gisevius.

At their first meeting, Gisevius told Dulles that the conspiracy, of which he was part, intended to overthrow Hitler and sign a separate peace with the western Allies, thus foreclosing a Soviet conquest of eastern Germany.

The hope of dividing the Allies had no prospects whatever, Dulles knew. Just the month before, in January 1943, Roosevelt and Churchill had declared at Casablanca that the only terms for peace were unconditional surrender. But the Gisevius visit did educate Dulles to the depth of anti-Nazi sentiment within certain important circles in the Reich. Thereafter, Gisevius, working through Allen Dulles, became the chief link between the German conspirators and the United States.

In one of his early meetings with Dulles, as a demonstration of good faith, Gisevius drew from his pocket several secret telegrams that had been sent by the American embassy in Bern. They had been intercepted and broken by the Germans. It was a code which Dulles occasionally used himself.

General Legge had employed a Swiss civilian in his office whom the Swiss police warned him had been a member of the outlawed Swiss Nazi Party. Legge, evidently a man of bottomless trust, resolved the problem by demoting the man to janitor, where he exploited the general's habit of throwing carbon copies of secret messages into the wastebasket. The janitor emptied Legge's trash in the office of a German intelligence agent in Bern, a service which had subsequently enabled the Germans to crack the State Department code. After Gisevius's revelation, the compromised cipher was replaced.

Gisevius was ever eager to please Dulles. To him, the American represented deliverance. He had become sadly accustomed to the cloud of suspicion he habitually raised. Finally, he seemed to have won the trust of someone worthwhile. He described Dulles as "The first intelligence officer who had the courage to extend his activities to the political aspects of the war. . . . Everyone breathed easier. At last a man had been found with whom it was possible to discuss the contradictory complex of problems emerging from Hitler's war."

Dulles reciprocated the esteem. He told a friend: "I have seen many men in my lifetime, but this one is extraordinary. I've never quite met anyone like him. My office is piled high with denunciations of him as a double agent. That doesn't bother me." Gisevius also evinced no interest in money, which Dulles noted appreciatively. His passion was his book. And that was where Mary Bancroft fitted in.

Mary Bancroft violated her pledge to keep secret the matter of Hans Bernd Gisevius almost immediately. It was to be her only breach, and one psychologically necessary for her in carrying out the mission. She confided in Dr. Jung. The psychiatrist also expressed his belief that she could keep quiet. He then told her something which she thought about long afterward: "Only after you have had to keep a secret can you learn the true outlines of the self."

To know, in the Europe of 1943, that a conspiracy was afoot to kill Hitler and that this man with whom she was to work was party to the plot thrilled Mary Bancroft. On his first visit, Gisevius brought fourteen hundred pages of his manuscript, a sight almost as overpowering as the man himself. Not only was Hans Gisevius huge—six feet four—and massively proportioned, but he had extremely poor eyesight, which caused him to hover over people, peering through thick glasses, thus enhancing an already monumental presence. His vision was so poor that Gisevius could not drive a car, use a typewriter, or serve in the military.

Mary Bancroft found the translation exhausting. Gisevius expressed himself in an abstruse Hochdeutsch which seemed to require deciphering as much as translation. Still, the two personalities fed off each other from the start, the impatient, self-absorbed Teuton and this outspoken American. His poor vision, she found, had given Gisevius some of the intuitive sense of a blind person, a power she appreciated and shared. Their relationship quickly fell into a pattern of sharp-edged debate, rambling philosophic discourse, mixed exasperation and affection.

They fought marvelously. Mary Bancroft even managed to unearth a deeply buried vein of humor in Gisevius, rarely detected by others. "You know," she said after a particularly jarring collision, "they say that man van der Lubbe, who burned down the Reichstag, was half-witted. Sometimes I think you're more half-witted than he was." Thereafter, he was "Lubber" to her. Gisevius called these her "Stuka" attacks, after the dread German dive bomber.

She confronted Gisevius directly with the question that nagged even those who wanted most to believe in him. What had he been doing in the Gestapo? He explained frankly that he was trying to gain control of his department and confessed himself a fool to think he could have ever beaten the likes of Heydrich and Himmler.

Dulles referred to the enormous German privately as "Tiny," a term quickly adopted by others of the staff. Mary Bancroft did not like it. She found the name demeaning and, worse, terribly unoriginal.

She accepted, in time, that Gisevius was a hopeless right-winger, but a sincere Christian and a man who could never have been a believing Nazi, or much of a success in the work of the Gestapo.

Though she came to care deeply for this lumbering, complex man, she continued her obligation to Allen Dulles. After her meetings with Gisevius, she dutifully journeyed to Bern to report. After the first session with Gisevius, Dulles had eagerly summoned her to relate her conversation with the German. As she was leaving, Dulles said, "But you haven't told me what you think of him."

"I don't think he would do anything that you wouldn't do."

"Well," Dulles answered, "I don't know if that's so good."

In time, Mary Bancroft had become aware of an extraordinary communion between herself and Hans Gisevius. She told Dr. Jung that whenever she wanted Gisevius to telephone, she had only to think about him for ten minutes. The phone would soon ring, and he would say, "Yes, I just got your message. What is it?" She had described the same phenomenon to Dulles, who told her that she was crazy. When she countered that Jung had been quite impressed by this experience, Dulles displayed rare irritation. He warned her to stop the nonsense. "I don't want to go down in history as a footnote to a case of Jung's!"

Jung had predicted to her from the outset that she was going to have an extraordinary experience with Gisevius because they were psychologically mated. But he had warned her that to keep Gisevius talking she must never ask him outright for hard facts. This approach would switch his mentality to a level of inferior perception, and she would lose the rewards of their freewheeling association.

When Gisevius learned that Mary Bancroft was an intimate of Jung, he too wanted to meet the famous man. Gisevius had been vastly impressed by the "Wotan" article Jung had written in 1936 in which he diagnosed Germany as suffering from an outbreak of demonic forces of the unconscious, personified by Hitler. This perception comfortably fit Gisevius's own explanation of the madness which had seized his homeland.

In discussing her work with Jung, Mary Bancroft found that even the renowned professor was eager to play at espionage. He asked Mary if she had ever heard that he supposedly flew regularly to the Führerhauptquartier to advise Hitler? Jung had found this "idiotic" rumor troubling. She had not heard it. The rumor had been launched, he assumed, by the famous Berlin physician Dr. Ernst Ferdinand Sauerbruch, who treated Hitler and who had met Jung several times in Switzerland.

Jung then gave Mary information from a "usually reliable source," that Hitler, who often railed against "the drunkard Churchill," had himself begun to drink heavily. He asked her if she had any confirmation. If so, he believed it could be psychologically revealing.

Among the people whom Allen Dulles had contacted within forty-eight hours of his arrival in Switzerland was an Austrian expatriate lawyer named Kurt Grimm. During the 1930s, Grimm's law firm had been the Vienna correspondent of Dulles's New York firm. The two men had met when Dulles had gone on business to Europe.

Dulles had left France for Switzerland so abruptly that he brought little clothing with him. Grimm's first service had been to take the American to his tailor to have him outfitted. Dulles soon put the important question to Grimm: Would the Austrian be willing to cooperate with American intelligence?

Long before Dulles's arrival, Grimm had already become a valued intelligence source of the British in Switzerland. Through a lawyer friend in Berlin, he had lines into the Abwehr and had given the British a fair estimation of the date of the German invasion of Yugoslavia. Through his financial contacts, he also learned well before the Nazi invasion of Russia that the Germans were planning to build a plant in the Ukraine for manufacturing agricultural equipment.

Kurt Grimm had left Austria in May 1938 convinced that war was inevitable and equally certain that he did not want to face it from the Nazi side. He brought with him far-ranging contacts in finance, industry, and the legal profession. He obtained a license from the Swiss government as a counselor in international law. He also headed something called the "Austrian Committee to Aid Refugees," and it was through this apparatus that Kurt Grimm conducted his major subsidiary interest: espionage against the Third Reich.

Kurt Grimm was a man in his late thirties, portly, grave in manner, wealthy, and respected. He spoke with spare precision in a labored, gravelly voice. If anti-Nazi Austrians in Switzerland had a headquarters, it was Grimm's well-appointed lakeside apartment in the Hotel Bellerive au Lac. If they needed money, he provided it. If they were arrested by the Swiss, he arranged to have them freed. If they needed papers, Grimm could get them. His apartment, with three separate entrances, was ideally suited to his secret life.

After having proved his worth to Dulles, Grimm went to the American with his own problem. His principal contact with the Abwehr, the lawyer from Berlin, was having difficulty justifying his frequent trips to Switzerland. He needed, he told Grimm, a bone to throw to the Germans. Dulles said that he would contact the State and War departments and see what he could provide.

In the spring of 1943, Grimm informed the German lawyer that he had important information dealing with American aircraft. The man came to his apartment with an Abwehr official connected with the German aviation industry. Grimm drew from his pocket a list of figures provided by Dulles, a projection of the expected number of planes the Americans would manufacture over the coming years. The figures were little more than refinements of what President Roosevelt had already promised in his state of the union address nearly eighteen months before, 100,000 combat aircraft and 125,000 total aircraft by the end of 1943. Grimm's figures merely extended the projections.

The Abwehr official examined the figures and said, "I don't believe it." Grimm turned to his lawyer friend: "You know that you can believe me." The lawyer nodded. The Abwehr man's face tightened. "Then Germany must lose the war."

In an auditorium in Zurich a pianist rose as the audience exploded in applause. The woman had performed the all-Chopin program with technical brilliance and rich color. On stage, Barbara Issikides appeared tall, darkly regal. Actually, she was a woman of ordinary height, possessed of extraordinary presence. She had a classic Grecian face, and an unexpected shock of white streaking through her black hair heightened an already striking appearance. As the audience filed out of the theater, Barbara Issikides made her way quickly to her dressing room. Soon afterward, she entered Kurt Grimm's apartment in the Hotel Bellerive au Lac.

Barbara Issikides was a Viennese in her late twenties, the daughter of a well-to-do Oriental rug merchant in Vienna, a leader in the city's Greek community. She had scant interest in politics but had come under the influence of two men who shared one of her few political sentiments, a deep detestation of the Nazis. They made an oddly cast trio—a pianist, a priest, and an industrialist.

The priest was Heinrich Maier, a forty-year-old intellectual, who held doctoral degrees in theology and law and whose leftist politics were markedly out of step with his church in post-Anschluss Austria. Maier was dark-skinned and dark-haired, a warm, gregarious man, fueled by a restless energy for which some of his friends called him "Hans Dampf," Hans Steam. Dr. Maier belonged to a fourteen-member anti-Nazi circle in Vienna and, like others in the group, had his own ring of subagents, among whom were Barbara Issikides and Franz Josef Messner.

Messner was a tall, imposing man, forty-eight years old, general director of the far-flung Semperit Rubber Company with plants from the Vistula to the Rhine. Though born in Brixlegg in the Tirol, Messner had later acquired Brazilian citizenship. His position in a critical wartime industry gave him access to key secrets of German military production and the freedom to travel widely on the business of the Semperit empire. He was an avid anti-Nazi and further motivated to hasten the regime's downfall to realize his own political ambitions after the war.

Barbara Issikides was drawn to the intelligent idealism of both men and had something of value to offer. As a beautiful and accomplished artist, she was much sought after by Viennese society and found herself on state and social occasions often thrust into the company of important Nazis. It is a weakness of vain and powerful men to try to impress beautiful women. Barbara Issikides thus learned much from these associations. Her concert tours provided relative freedom to travel widely, and Barbara Issikides passed along whatever she learned herself and intelligence provided to her by Messner and Dr. Maier to Kurt Grimm who, in turn, relayed the information to Allen Dulles. Grimm eventually presented Barbara Issikides and Franz Josef Messner to Dulles personally when the Semperit industrialist was in Switzerland.

Messner became one of the contributors to the mosaic of intelligence which led to a decisive air strike of the war. When, on August 17, 1943, six hundred British bombers dealt their savage blow to the German secret V-Weapons installation at Peenemünde on the Baltic, they were guided, in part, by information which Allen Dulles had pieced together from Hans

Bernd Gisevius, Franz Josef Messner, and a German businessman named Kraus.

Gisevius had informed Dulles in May 1943 that the Germans were developing a missile propelled by the rocket principle. Messner had provided Dulles with information on the speed and destructive power of this "V-2" rocket. Dr. Kraus, general manager of the Siemens branch plant in Austria, another informant recruited by Kurt Grimm, had revealed that his firm was delivering parts to a remote thumb of land called Peenemünde for a highly secret project.

Hitler had predicted to German leaders that with the V-Weapons "London would be leveled to the ground by the end of 1943," and that Britain would be "forced to capitulate."

British versions tend to slight or ignore the contribution of the Dulles operation to the Peenemünde strike. American accounts may exaggerate it. The salient fact is that the raid succeeded in decisively delaying the development of these weapons which, at one point, were projected to kill 108,000 Britons a month. The first V-1s struck England on June 13, 1944, too late to blunt the invasion of Normandy or to decimate the British populace.

Franz Josef Messner also provided other priceless strategic-bombing intelligence. He and the ring supplied the first information on synthetic-rubber production in the Reich. The ring notified OSS that the vast Messerschmitt aircraft complex at Wiener Neustadt, Austria, had been dispersed to Ebreichsdorf, Pottendorf, and Bad Vöslau, information subsequently exploited by Fifteenth Air Force bombers. Through the Semperit plant in Poland, Messner gave OSS Bern early confirmation of the existence of a vast extermination camp at Auschwitz.

Switzerland was not the ring's only outlet. It had contacts in Istanbul who were in touch with OSS Turkey. Allen Dulles warned Messner and Barbara Issikides to be careful of these Istanbul colleagues. His advice proved sound but belated.

Like Bern, Istanbul was an intelligence hothouse. Through the seven hills of this old city flowed a constant stream of refugees, businessmen, and officials. Seventeen foreign intelligence services competed in Istanbul, of which the most resolutely inept appears to have been the American.

The contacts which OSS Istanbul did have were monopolized by an arrogant and voluble Czech engineer, code-named DOGWOOD. DOGWOOD had been passed to OSS by British intelligence, which should have raised a skeptical eyebrow somewhere.

He did have connections with a mixed bag of people, some helpful, others quite useless. But they were undifferentiated, since DOGWOOD refused to disclose to the OSS Istanbul chief who his contacts were. This refusal denied OSS counterintelligence officers the opportunity of checking out the worth of members of DOGWOOD's net. It was consequently impossible to evaluate his information as good, bad, or planted.

The OSS Istanbul chief chose not to challenge DOGWOOD's crippling monopoly over his sources of intelligence. Thus, all contacts to OSS Istanbul were channeled through DOGWOOD, including Franz Josef Messner, who came occasionally to the city on the business of the Semperit Rubber Company. Through his plant operations, Messner was able to pass to DOGWOOD valuable industrial intelligence on targets in Poland, Hungary, and the rest of eastern Europe.

In 1943, a Hungarian, known to be an intelligence agent of his country, got in touch with DOGWOOD and suggested that they cooperate. Out of arrogance or ignorance, DOGWOOD assumed that he could handle this man and get more than he gave. What he got is unclear. What he gave was a fairly detailed knowledge of Austrian and Hungarian agents working with OSS through Istanbul.

On March 19, 1944, German forces occupied Hungary. German intelligence officials fell heir to Hungarian secret files and were thus able to identify several Hungarians and Austrians known to be working with OSS. Within twelve days, Franz Josef Messner, Dr. Heinrich Maier, and Barbara Issikides were arrested by the Gestapo in Vienna.

Hans Bernd Gisevius continued to brief Allen Dulles on the gathering momentum of the conspiracy within the Reich. The plotters, who at times had considered only toppling Hitler, were now bent on killing him. Gisevius's role was to win the support of the Allies for the conspirators' political objectives through his contacts in Switzerland. Prime among their aims remained the dogged hope to negotiate separately with the western powers.

Dulles was told that the assassination was set for March 13, 1943. The day came and passed without event. Undaunted, the conspirators plotted anew and continued to seek the support of the Allies. Dulles conveyed word to them, through Gisevius, that Washington's position remained adamant. There could be no overt assistance. If good Germans wanted to break the Nazi grip, they must first strike the blow against Hitler themselves. And, under no circumstances, would America break faith with her Russian ally through a separate peace.

BACK DOOR TO THE REICH

In April 1943, the Gestapo arrested several anti-Nazi leaders. The shadow of suspicion fell across Hans Gisevius as well. The Gestapo applied pressure to have him returned to Germany, but he successfully resisted. He could, however, no longer serve as the direct courier between the conspirators in Germany and the Allies. He now relied on Edward Waetjen, like himself a lawyer and Abwehr agent, also wearing the cloak of vice-consul in the Zurich consulate. Waetjen, a cultivated aristocrat whose mother was American, took over the duty as courier between the conspirators and Switzerland.

After their meeting in June 1943, Mary Bancroft continued to labor for nearly a year with Gisevius on his manuscript. They worked in furious bursts, four and five days at a time. He would disappear for weeks, then suddenly return with new pages.

She worked on the Gisevius book and held his hand as his anxiety grew with each delay in the coup against the Nazis. Her tolerance and understanding largely surpassed that of other Dulles people who described Gisevius, with curious consistency, as charming perhaps, in a heavy sort of way, but not particularly likable.

To Mary Bancroft, Gisevius confided that he would return to Germany the moment the signal was given for the strike on Hitler. She did not believe him. Knowing that the Gestapo suspected him, she did not think Gisevius would throw his life away in a gesture of empty bravado. The question was moot anyway. She had observed for nearly a year now the blunders and setbacks of the conspirators. All their schemes, she was convinced, would come to nothing.

In April 1944, fourteen months after his first meeting with Gisevius, Dulles was reporting to Washington the latest intentions of the conspirators: "The group is prepared to proceed, only if they can get some assurances from the western powers that upon the removal of the Nazis, they can enter into direct negotiations with the Anglo-Saxons. . . . The principal motive for their action is the ardent desire to prevent central Europe from coming ideologically and factually under the control of Russia."

In early May 1944, Gisevius passed on to Allen Dulles the latest plan from Berlin. The conspirators' strategy was daring, but not improbable. Strong German armies would hold off the Russians on the eastern front, while the way would be cleared for landing three Allied airborne divisions near Berlin, to be coordinated with other landings at Bremerhaven and Hamburg. Anti-Nazi troops, meanwhile, would isolate Hitler and his cohorts in his alpine retreat at Berchtesgaden. Critical to the plan was the neutralization of German armies then waiting to repel the expected invasion of France. This was a missing piece in an otherwise artfully crafted strategy. Field Marshal Erwin Rommel, the defender of the French coast, at this point, still remained loyal to Hitler.

In June, Gisevius told Dulles that another date had been set for an attempt on Hitler's life. Dulles kept Washington informed, and on July 12 reported, "Dramatic developments may be pending up north." If the plot succeeded, he said, the best German divisions would probably be sent to the Russian front, while in the west there would be an orderly withdrawal.

Gisevius's information at this point was a few beats behind that of his collaborators. The conspiracy's leaders in Berlin had accepted, as soon as Hitler was killed, that they would have to surrender unconditionally to the Russians as well as the Allies.

On the same day that Washington received Dulles's latest message, Hans Gisevius had secretly returned to Berlin. Though he was on Himmler's wanted list, he still had powerful protectors, among them Count Wolf Heinrich von Helldorf, the Berlin police chief, and Artur Nebe, chief of the Reich detective service, both co-conspirators. Gisevius had only to lie low in the basement of the house of a friend at Nürnbergerstrasse 31 until the fated day, July 20, 1944.

Mary Bancroft had taken a little house in the Tessin, where she was staying with her daughter. Her nerves were shot. The year with Gisevius had been emotionally exorbitant. At the same time, she had been having difficulties with her marriage. That evening, she heard the Swiss radio interrupt its regular broadcast to announce that an attempt had been made on Hitler's life. This news was followed, some time later, by a bulletin reporting that the coup had failed.

Initially, she had not believed that Gisevius would return to Germany, but he had. In the weeks that followed the assassination attempt, as reports reached Switzerland of the whirlwind of Nazi vengeance against the conspirators, she doubted that he could have survived.

Hans Gisevius became one of a rapidly vanishing species in Germany, a plotter who—at least for the moment—still lived. When it was learned that Hitler had miraculously escaped death in the bomb blast at Rastenburg, loyal Nazi forces in Berlin moved in on the conspirators' command post in the Wehrmacht headquarters on Bendlerstrasse. Gisevius had been in the building earlier with the other conspirators awaiting news from Rastenburg. He had left the headquarters temporarily, just before the Nazis surrounded it. Nearly all the conspirators trapped in the building were to die before the day was out and the rest soon after.

Gisevius's first impulse was to escape the city by train. But at the station he ran into a triple ring of security, the Gestapo already stalking the traitors, military police looking for deserters, and the criminal police hunting for conscript laborers and escaped prisoners of war. Through friends, Gisevius managed to be driven out to the countryside to look for a possible refuge. He was appalled by the secondary effects of Allied air raids. People in villages within a sixty-mile perimeter of Berlin were quartering bombed-out refugees. Every prefect and policeman was under orders to report immediately the presence of unidentified newcomers. Gisevius decided that the safest hiding place was back in the lion's mouth. He returned to Berlin, where a woman friend named Gerda took him in.

Several days after the plot, Gisevius managed to get off a message to Dulles through a courier to Switzerland. Despite the coup's failure, he still had hope that its momentum could be exploited. He wrote to Dulles, ". . . it is only necessary now for the Allies to strike hard and the entire German structure will collapse." Dulles did not get the message until over three weeks later, on August 17, when it seemed hopelessly out of date. Still Dulles agreed, in spite of the collapse of the plot, there continued to exist a "serious Allied overestimate of the German will to resist."

In September, Dulles met General Donovan in France and urged upon him new initiatives for tapping the remaining reservoir of anti-Hitler feeling. He sensed a golden moment to follow up the stunning Allied military advances by persuading anti-Nazi generals to arrange the surrender of their troops on the western front. The moment was ripe, Dulles believed, to drive a wedge between these old-line officers and the furiously loyal Nazi SS commanders.

Dulles sent a representative to General Omar Bradley and to Allied officials in London to ask them to consider using captured German generals as conduits to their brother officers who were still fighting in the west. The effort won Bradley's blessing and was making slow progress when, three months later, von Rundstedt unleashed the offensive in the Ardennes. Thereafter, the project was dropped. The offensive itself demonstrated the ascendancy of the SS breed of diehards over Junker traditionalists in the German Army. By then, those officers who might have considered surrender, Rommel, Kluge, Schwerin, and Stülpnagel, had already been killed, driven to suicide, or removed as suspected conspirators. Fanatic Nazi generals were now directing the German war machine. An opportunity for significantly shortening the war had been allowed to slip through Allied hands.

Dulles had never received any encouragement from Washington in his dealings with the German resistance. He assumed that the greatest objection had been President Roosevelt's fear of contaminating the purity of unconditional surrender. But Dulles never knew explicitly why he was pressured to cool his contacts with the conspirators. He once speculated to a colleague that the reaction may have grown out of President Roosevelt's respect for the opinions of Marshal Foch, the Allied supreme commander in World War I. According to Dulles, Foch had apparently once told Roosevelt that had that war been brought to German soil, the Germans would never again dare to start another.

With the fate of Hans Bernd Gisevius unknown, Allen Dulles had still, however, not lost all his lines into Germany, or even the best. There was still Fritz Kolbe.

Joachim von Ribbentrop found Karl Ritter invaluable. Ritter, a rough, forceful character, had been chosen by the German foreign minister to perform a task for which few of his diplomats had the stomach: to stand up to the generals. Ritter served as Ribbentrop's liaison with the OKW, the German Military High Command. He was one of a handful of aides with direct access to and some influence over the petulant, overbearing Ribbentrop.

The privilege was not particularly pleasant. Whenever Ribbentrop fell out with Hitler, he would plunge into despair and take to his bed for days on end. When he emerged, he vented his anger on his subordinates, with Ritter a handy target.

Into Karl Ritter's office flowed the key cables from German diplomatic outposts throughout the world, particularly matters bearing on the military—army plans, submarine warfare, Luftwaffe operations and developments in the occupied territories. These cables frequently totaled over one hundred a day.

To sort through this mass and sift out the consequential, Ritter employed an assistant, Fritz Kolbe, the perfect bureaucrat, small, gray, and competent. It was Kolbe's responsibility to arrive early in the morning, before the rest of the staff, and determine which incoming cables were worthy of Karl Ritter's attention. It was a position of trust but no particular eminence for a man who had already spent nearly twenty years in the diplomatic service.

Kolbe had, however, moved well above his humble origins. Fritz Kolbe was born in 1900, the son of a saddlemaker. He had gone originally into the civil service as an official of the German state railways. There, he had applied a compulsive diligence to become Germany's youngest stationmaster. At the age of twenty-five, Kolbe abandoned a promising railroad career to attempt the loftier realm of diplomacy. He studied at night school, went on to the university, and subsequently passed his foreign-service examinations.

Over the years, through a succession of posts abroad, Kolbe earned a reputation as an able eccentric, a quirky man, full of fussy energy, and utterly reliable. His services were always in demand by department heads looking for the ideal subordinate, one who could take over the drudgery in their careers.

For a bureaucratic drone, Fritz Kolbe could be astonishingly frank. He had once referred to Mussolini, in the presence of a Nazi party official, as a "pig," and he refused to back down upon being sternly reprimanded. His candor was tolerated as part of the man's eccentricity, in keeping, for example, with his refusal to join the Nazi party. All this was overlooked, since Fritz Kolbe for the most part kept his mouth shut, did his job, and did it well.

What he never revealed to any foreign-service colleagues was his incandescent hatred of the Nazis. Kolbe had flirted briefly with anti-Nazi circles in Berlin, but he found the people involved hopelessly ineffectual. He had concluded, ruefully, for he was a fierce patriot, that his country's only hope lay in the defeat of Germany in the war. He became increasingly obsessed with contributing to that end.

Kolbe had undergone an experience common among those who resisted the regime. Somehow, one intuitively sensed a kindred soul. A word, a gesture, a knowing expression at some Nazi excess, a knowledge of a person's background induced people to trust near strangers. Fritz Kolbe had this feeling about Fräulein Maria von Heimerdinger, the daughter of a Prussian aristocrat and an employee of the Foreign Office. Maria held an advantageous post. She was assistant chief of the courier section and exercised considerable authority in determining who went on courier runs abroad.

Their acquaintance had been passing in the most literal sense, in hallways, on elevators, in subways. They exchanged greetings, a comment on the weather, nothing more. Still, Kolbe took the chance. He told Maria von Heimerdinger that he had business interests in Switzerland, and that it would be helpful if she could assign him as a courier to Bern. She asked no questions and said only that she thought something might be arranged.

In the mid-1930s, while serving in the German embassy in Madrid, Fritz Kolbe had made a friend of Dr. Ernesto Kocherthaler, a German-born Jew who had become a Spanish citizen. The doctor's title had been earned in an area other than medicine; he was a businessman. After the Spanish civil war, Dr. Kocherthaler had settled in Switzerland. On August 23, 1943, when Kolbe made his first journey to Bern as a diplomatic courier, he immediately re-established contact with his friend and confided his intentions to Kocherthaler.

Through the businessman's intercession, Kolbe made an appointment with an attaché at the British embassy in Switzerland, a Colonel Cartwright. Kolbe was a disaster. His speech tumbled out in erratic bursts, his movements were awkward and unsettling. The British officer listened to this strange little man telling him that he was a sensitively placed official in the German Foreign Office, and that he was prepared to turn over German state secrets of the highest importance. Kolbe showed a sample of the kinds of documents he was prepared to deliver to the British. As Kolbe later recalled, the attaché looked at him and said stonily, "I don't believe you"; then added, "and if you are telling the truth, you are a cad."

The Englishman's reaction represented more than mocking British indignation at unfair play. Kolbe had run aground on the same shoals of British prejudice that had earlier stopped Hans Gisevius. Though it applied more to the generals than to a minor diplomat like Kolbe, the British still regarded the German anti-Nazis as a self-interested clique, motivated mainly by a desire to perpetuate their own class.

The head of the British secret service, Stewart Menzies, had ignored a peace overture from Admiral Canaris not long before, presumedly because it might arouse Russian suspicions. The British Foreign Office had directed MI-6 to dismiss any peace feelers from Germans, since they were invariably conditioned on separate peace negotiations, excluding the Soviet Union.

Kolbe found the experience at the British embassy shattering. He told Kocherthaler that never again would he enter another embassy cold. They pondered another approach.

Among the Americans in Bern whom Allen Dulles had absorbed into his service was Gerald Mayer of the Office of War Information. Mayer had spent much of his life in Europe, spoke fluent German, and was now in Switzerland to generate a psychological climate favorable to the Allies.

On the morning of August 24, Mayer got a telephone call from Paul Dreyfuss, a banker friend in Basel, asking him to receive Dr. Kocherthaler that same morning at nine. His visitor was stiff, formal, more than a little pompous, a caricature German, Mayer thought. Dr. Kocherthaler gave a too detailed account of his own life, explaining what had led him to leave Germany for Spain and then settle in Switzerland. Mayer listened with cold professional detachment. Sophisticated people in Bern knew what Dulles and his staff did, and the inevitable result was a parade to the OSS offices of self-seekers, adventurers, zealots, and, occasionally, a useful informant. Kocherthaler recognized that he would need more than words to penetrate the aloof Mayer.

He drew an envelope from his coat, removed three sheets of paper from it, and spread them before Mayer. Stamped across each page were the words *"Geheime Reichsache,"* Secret State Document. Mayer began to read and as he did it became increasingly difficult to maintain his indifferent pose. Each page summarized a cable to the German foreign minister, Joachim von Ribbentrop. One was signed by Franz von Papen, the German ambassador to Turkey, reporting British plans to infiltrate secret agents into the Balkans via Istanbul. Another, from Paris, described opportunities to ship German spies through the American and British lines in North Africa. The third reported progress in crushing the resistance in Czechoslovakia. Mayer asked Kocherthaler where he had obtained this information.

A man was at present in Bern, Kocherthaler explained, who spent his days handling precisely this kind of information at the Foreign Office in Berlin. "This man is willing, indeed eager, to provide this kind of material to you." Mayer excused himself and asked Kocherthaler to wait in his anteroom. He ran upstairs to Allen Dulles's office. Dulles, whose conversational German was poor, nevertheless read the language well enough to grasp the extraordinary possibilities of what he had been shown.

Dulles suggested to Mayer three explanations. It could be a scheme for breaking the American code; Dulles would be expected to encode and radio the messages back to Washington; German radio monitors then would have a basis for comparing the original and encoded versions. Or, their visitor might be an *agent provocateur;* he would tip off the Swiss police that the Americans possessed these messages as proof that they were engaged in espionage, and thereby might have Dulles and his crew kicked out of the country. There was a third possibility, that a dedicated anti-Nazi, with implausibly good connections, had somehow fallen out of the sky and into their laps.

Dulles, who had once passed up an opportunity to meet with an obscure émigré revolutionary named Vladimir Ilyich Lenin during his World War

I service in Bern, had long since learned to keep all his pores open. A meeting with Kolbe was arranged for that night in Gerald Mayer's apartment in the Kirchenfeld district.

To Allen Dulles, the key question was motivation. What had prompted this astounding offer, and how could the Americans verify the man's claims? At Gerald Mayer's apartment, Dulles was introduced to the Germans as Mayer's assistant, "Mr. Douglas." The atmosphere was strained. The Germans were in the uncomfortable position of having to prove themselves. The Americans were resolutely determined not to be duped.

But the desire to believe was strong, as Kolbe spread before them 186 documents that he had smuggled from the German Foreign office. One was an *aide-mémoire* of a visit the Japanese ambassador had made to Ribbentrop. He also had full-length dispatches from twenty German diplomatic missions, along with longhand notes from the top-secret files of the Nazi regime. Kolbe revealed to Dulles a detailed knowledge of Ribbentrop's office, the personalities, the intrigues and cliques. But why?

The man facing the two Americans was an undistinguished figure, forty-three years old, with broad, Slavic features and a halo of short blond hair framing a bald head. His furtive manner and excited speech initially made them uneasy. But as Fritz Kolbe explained the feelings that had motivated his desperate act, he became composed, more credible. He described his deep aversion to Nazism, his sad conclusion that defeat in the war was best for Germany's future. "It is not enough to clench one's fist and hide it in one's pocket," he said. "The fist must be used to strike."

Kolbe also candidly confessed that he had made his first overture that day to the British and been rebuffed. He anticipated the Americans' desire to run a check on him and freely gave his name, his dates of diplomatic service, the name of his late first wife and her date of birth, the address of a young son then living with friends in South Africa, and the name of his second wife, from Zurich. He ransomed his life to these strangers to win their trust. Kolbe said he hoped to make a second trip out of Germany soon and would contact them again. The men shook hands all around. Kolbe and Kocherthaler left.

Dulles and Mayer worked through the night on the thick sheaf of Kolbe's material. They transmitted the best of it to Washington. They requested X-2 in Washington and London to run a check on the man. And, as soon as it was a decent hour in the morning, Dulles contacted the officer whom Kolbe had first approached at the British embassy. "Oh, that weird little fellow?" Yes, he remembered the visit. Nothing to him.

The Englishman further took the opportunity to lecture the American not to be taken in too easily by German double agents in the appealing guise of anti-Nazis.

In Washington, General Donovan seized excitedly on his first potential penetration of the Reich. He took some of Kolbe's papers directly to President Roosevelt. Back in Bern, Fritz Kolbe received the sanction of a code name. Henceforth, he was to be known to OSS as "George Wood."

Fritz Kolbe made his second journey to Bern in October 1943, less than three months after the first trip. In the intervening period, he had chafed impatiently for another courier run as priceless intelligence passed through his hands daily. He had accumulated particularly valuable knowledge of disquieting developments in Ireland and Spain. He pressed Maria von Heimerdinger for another assignment.

Kolbe had suffered a bad scare after his first mission, but the game had become a passion stronger than his fears. After the August trip, he had returned to Berlin to find a message on his desk stamped "Urgent," ordering him to report at once to the security office. His heart pounded as he thought how mad he had been to imagine he could outplay the Nazis. The security chief wasted few words. There was, he noted, an unexplained absence during Kolbe's stay in Bern. Where had he been between midnight and nearly four o'clock in the morning on August 25?

He had gone, Kolbe explained, to a bar where he had picked up a woman. The security chief remained unconvinced. Kolbe then produced a certificate from a doctor's office in Bern stating that on that morning he had been given a prophylactic and a blood test. The officer lectured him on proper comportment abroad for a courier and dismissed him. Kolbe returned to his desk, outwardly composed, but faint with fear.

On his second trip to Bern, Kolbe refined some of the crudities of the first visit. The first time, he had strapped the illicit documents to his leg. Dangerous and undignified, he concluded. The second time, he took a ten-by-fifteen-inch envelope containing the material destined for Allen Dulles and stuffed it into a twelve-by-eighteen-inch envelope: seventy-six telegrams totaling over two hundred pages. He then sealed the outer envelope with an official stamp bearing the swastika.

On October 7, 1943, immediately after clearing both German and Swiss customs at Basel, Switzerland, Kolbe slipped into the railroad station men's room. He tore away the outer envelope of the pouch, ripped it into small pieces, and flushed it down the toilet. He stuffed the purloined messages into his coat pocket, carried the official pouch in hand, and proceeded by train to Bern.

He stopped at the German embassy first and disposed of his legitimate burden. He then called Dr. Kocherthaler. This time they all met at Herrengasse 23, Dulles's Bern apartment.

The chief of American intelligence was again astonished at the range and quality of Kolbe's material. One telegram from the German embassy in Madrid reported: "Shipments of oranges will continue to arrive on schedule." It meant that Generalissimo Franco, in violation of his pledge to the Allies, was shipping tungsten for tempering steel to Germany in orange crates. An Anglo-American petroleum embargo was thereafter imposed against Spain in retaliation.

Another cable from the German embassy in Buenos Aires reported the impending departure of a large Allied convoy from a port in the United States. The convoy's schedule was altered in time to escape a Nazi U-boat wolf pack.

The Germans had been operating a secret radio station out of Ireland to report on Allied ship movements. The Irish government had finally yielded to repeated protests by the U.S. State Department and silenced the station by removing an indispensable component. Kolbe produced a telegram showing that the German minister was planning to smuggle a duplicate part into Ireland.

Kolbe also had an idea for filling the information void between his visits. He had devised a means of sending material through a brother-in-law of Dr. Kocherthaler who lived in Zurich. The thorough Kolbe had also devised a signal for acknowledging that his messages had been received. Dr. Kochenthaler was to mail him a package containing canned sardines, chocolate, and coffee. The coffee was to be included only when they had received a report from Kolbe.

Before returning to Germany from his second trip, Kolbe made two requests of Dulles: he wanted a pistol and a camera to microfilm documents. The gun was denied, but he was given the camera. He then returned to Berlin.

The arrivals of Fritz Kolbe in Bern thereafter became a nightmare for Allen Dulles's communications staff. A typical spy might carry a page of information hidden in secret ink. Fritz Kolbe delivered full, uncoded texts by the pound. Fed by his success, he became more daring, more resourceful. He jotted down notes on conversations he overheard in the Foreign Office. He delivered sketches of the Wolfsschanze, Hitler's rustic headquarters near Rastenburg in East Prussia. In spite of the quantity, he continued to provide ore of a remarkably high assay. Allen Dulles cabled Washington, "Sincerely regret that you cannot see at this time Wood's

[Kolbe's code name] material as it stands without condensation or abridgment."

Fortunately for the overwhelmed staff, relief fell literally from the skies. Several U.S. fliers had brought their damaged aircraft to forced landings in Switzerland. The Swiss allowed some of them to be transferred to the staff of the American legation. OSS soon had the fliers trained and working around the clock transmitting Kolbe's information to Washington and London.

Since OSS had no direct sources of intelligence from inside Japan, Bern was beseeched by Washington to use its contacts to procure intelligence on Japanese naval strength. Kolbe was the obvious source. But how to reach him in Berlin before his next trip to Bern? Gerald Mayer struck on an idea.

One of Kolbe's alternate channels of communication had been through an anti-Nazi German living in Switzerland to whom he addressed phony love letters. Mayer had this contact send Kolbe a postcard, an alpine scene, which read, "Perhaps you remember my little son. His birthday is coming soon and I wanted to get him some of those clever Japanese toys with which the shops here used to be full, but I can't find any. I wonder if there might be some left in Berlin."

The opaque intent of this message was somehow clear to Kolbe. On his next delivery to Bern, he included a voluminous report on Japanese plans, including the battle order of the Imperial fleet, all secured from cables sent by the German military attaché in Tokyo to Ribbentrop.

When Kolbe could not come personally to Bern, the Americans still did not have long to wait for his secrets. He had pieced together a chain of collaborators who could get a priority message to Bern within four days of its arrival in Berlin.

The grossest Allied security leak of the war was uncovered by Fritz Kolbe. In the fall of 1943, while screening cables for his chief, Karl Ritter, Kolbe came across an astonishing communication. On November 4, Franz von Papen, the German ambassador to Turkey, informed Ribbentrop that he had "an important German agent" procuring documents of the most secret nature directly from the British embassy in Turkey.

On a subsequent trip to Bern, in about the second week of December, Kolbe provided Dulles with three copies of telegrams, dated early in November, from von Papen to Ribbentrop describing this intelligence bonanza. Dulles passed copies of the telegrams to a colleague on the British side who alerted London.

The "important German agent" was Cicero, born Elyesa Bazna, the

Albanian valet to the British ambassador to Ankara, Sir Hughe Montgomery Knatchbull-Hugessen. Bazna was later to be immortalized in the pantheon of espionage through best-selling books and a hit movie. For a stiff price, Cicero was photographing the contents of his master's safe and turning the information over to a man named L. C. Moyzisch, a Nazi intelligence agent under camouflage as a member of the German embassy staff. Through an information exchange, Bazna's material went to the SS intelligence branch, the Abwehr, and the German Foreign Office, where Fritz Kolbe saw the Cicero cables.

Though London was advised of the leak—rather, the hemorrhage—in British security by Dulles, Cicero remained for months afterward in the service of the British ambassador and continued to supply the Germans with the richest British secrets. Turkey, as a vital neutral crossroads and as a gateway to the East and Middle East, had vast strategic importance. As a result, Sir Hughe's safe bulged with vital information.

Yet, it was actually *after* Dulles warned the British that a spy had penetrated their Ankara embassy that Cicero delivered to the Germans his ultimate prize. He provided copies of messages revealing the Allies' plan for the invasion of Europe. In the very last roll of film he delivered to Moyzisch, Cicero disclosed the code name for the Normandy invasion, OVERLORD.

Cicero quit when he felt he was about to be exposed. He took his considerable bundle, £300,000, and, late in April 1944 resigned as the British ambassador's valet. He learned later that while he had delivered the Germans pure gold, they had rewarded him with worthless paper. The notes with which he was paid were brilliant forgeries, produced by the Nazis, under a project code-named "Bernhard."

Cicero/Bazna would leave in his oily wake an enduring controversy. Did the British know about him? Did they merely keep Cicero on to feed the Germans only what they wanted the enemy to know? This is a thesis later advanced, supposedly, by no less than the head of MI-6, Stewart Menzies.

That MI-6 controlled Cicero would provide a perfectly respectable defense for a spy service seemingly caught with its drawers down. But to believe that Cicero was controlled required one to believe that the British deliberately let the Germans know of OVERLORD, the most jealously guarded offensive in all military history. One also had to believe that the British let pass information on other military plans, major bombing raids intended, and the negotiations among Churchill, Stalin, and Roosevelt at the critical Cairo and Teheran conferences, about which Cicero also informed the Germans. Finally, to believe that the British were playing Cicero was to believe as well that they possessed a marvelous channel for deceiving the Germans, yet never used it. There is no evidence that any deliberately deceptive material was ever planted in the British ambassador's safe. Cicero's stuff was always good.

In the end, it did not matter. The jealousies were so vicious and suspicions so deep among rival German intelligence services that the value of Cicero's intelligence was debated into the ground. The RSHA chief, Ernst Kaltenbrunner, defended this extraordinary coup of his intelligence service. Ribbentrop argued that Cicero was obviously a British plant. Their mutual distrust made the gold that Cicero had given the Germans as worthless as the paper with which they had paid him for it.

Whether or not the British were on to Cicero or the Germans appreciated him, Fritz Kolbe had demonstrated, in unmasking the master spy, his strategic position inside Germany's most intimate councils.

Kolbe also enlarged his contacts in Berlin beyond the Foreign Office. By the beginning of 1944, he had two dozen well-connected informants in place, a group he designated his "Inner Circle." Besides the reliable Fräulein von Heimerdinger, the ring included industrialists, military officers, and clergymen, including Father Schreiber, abbot of the monastery at Ottobeuren near Munich, Kolbe's religious adviser.

The life he was leading required spiritual support. His fear of being exposed was constant, enervating, and wholly justified. Once, while photographing documents in the basement of a hospital, Kolbe had received word that Himmler was demanding of Ribbentrop to see the very file then under Kolbe's camera. He sped back to the Wilhelmstrasse and fumbled through cabinets pretending to pull out of his files what he was actually drawing from his coat pocket.

At OSS Bern, Fritz Kolbe came to be viewed with a disbelieving awe. To many on the staff, he was a divinely inspired fanatic. To Mary Bancroft, he remained a preposterous hero. She found it difficult to accept that this unimpressive little man could fully comprehend the magnitude of his acts and the significance of his material. He was to her like an aging holy child, entrusted to carry a sacred vessel without grasping fully the consequences of his mission.

The chief of OSS Bern had a more detached view of the Kolbe persona. The man's information was incomparable and invaluable. Nothing else mattered to Allen Dulles. In one dispatch to Washington, apparently drafted by a hyperbolic aide, since Dulles himself was incapable of a rhetorical excess, he reported:

. . . the final death-bed contortions of a putrefied Nazi diplomacy are pictured in these telegrams. The reader is carried from one extreme of emotion to the other as he examines these messages and sees the cruelty exhibited by the Germans in their final swan-song of brutality toward the peoples so irrevocably and pitifully enmeshed by the Gestapo after half a decade of futile struggles. . . .

On April 11, during Holy Week, Dulles cabled Washington that "Wood" had arrived "with more than two hundred highly valuable Easter eggs." Washington cabled back, "What a bunny!" The flow continued for the next three months. Then, after July 20, the golden circuit of Fritz Kolbe went silent.

V

The Invisible Invasion

✝ ✝ ✝

Among German labor refugees in England, the purest hearts belonged to the ISK. In 1928, a puritanical faction had been expelled from the German Socialist Party. The banished members thereafter formed their own organization, the Internationalen Sozialistischen Kampfbundes. Their falling out with the regular Socialists had occurred over the Marxist interpretation of capitalist society. Adherents of the ISK believed that capitalism was morally wrong and ultimately doomed for that reason. They rejected the Marxist expectation that capitalism would collapse from its own internal contradictions. They also disavowed the materialist economics of traditional socialism. Their vision was of a world ruled by ethical humanitarianism.

The ascetic politics of the ISK extended into the members' daily lives. They eschewed drinking, smoking, and eating meat. Before the war, they had organized vegetarian restaurants in Germany, which became the centers of their political activity. They limited their membership to full-time workers, and sought, rather than a mass following, to influence the leaders of other Socialist factions. ISK members shunned publicity and, in their oblique pursuit of power, had, in effect, mastered the techniques of infiltration and underground maneuver well before the Nazis took over and drove them from Germany.

Willi Eichler, a bear of a man, led the ISK exiles in England and dominated them by his physical and intellectual presence. He grudgingly admired the Nazis' brilliant manipulation of the German national character. Slavish obedience to authority was inbred in the German people, he ruefully concluded. "If a policeman says, 'Do it,' the German does it, no matter what." While Eichler lamented the docility of his countrymen, he exacted total obedience from his ISK subordinates.

It was from the ranks of this militant band that George Pratt, while still heading the Labor Division, had chosen the first OSS agent to be parachuted into Germany, Jupp Kappius, who bailed out of the British Lancaster bomber near Sögel the night of September 2, 1944. Kappius had been an ISK organizer since his early youth, forsaking his academic preparation as a structural architect. He and his wife, Anne, were wanted by the Gestapo for capital political crimes. In 1937, the couple escaped from Germany and ultimately made their way to England via Austria.

As early as March 1944, the London Labor Division had contemplated several related missions, under the code name DOWNEND, to infiltrate the Ruhr, the heart of German industry and the center of German trade unionism. Originally, the plan called for implanting four agents, two men and two women, all with labor backgrounds.

OSS London was at that stage still unprepared to mount missions into Germany by itself. The Americans had, therefore, proposed that British SOE join them in a common venture. The Americans would provide the agents and the financing. The British would train them and arrange the logistics.

Willi Eichler pressed George Pratt to use his people first. The Socialist movement in Germany, after more than a decade of suppression, had been bled almost to death. Eichler feared that unless he could get fresh leadership into Germany before the war ended, a resurgent capitalism would block the Socialist revolution.

The first three agents chosen included Jupp and Anne Kappius and Hilde Meisel, all from the ISK. The last was a quiet woman in her early thirties who reflected the resolute simplicity of this Socialist sect. Her brown hair was pulled back in a tight, severe bun. She wore no make up and dressed with no concession to style. The fourth agent was Willi Drucker, that rarity, a German policeman of liberal outlook. Drucker, who was not of the ISK, had been recruited earlier by Gary Van Arkel in North Africa, then sent to Italy and later England.

The original plan was to place the two men into Jupp Kappius's hometown of Bochum, an iron and steel center between Essen and Dortmund.

They were to parachute into Germany, and the women were to serve as their couriers, operating in and out of Switzerland. Throughout the spring and summer of 1944, the agents trained for the mission in London and in a remote area of Scotland.

Late in the summer, ISK members in Switzerland reported that they had arranged a safe house in Bochum, but only for one agent. A disappointed George Pratt suggested strongly to Willi Eichler that the placement of a single agent could hardly justify the joint investment of British and American intelligence services in the DOWNEND project. Eichler was adamant. He wanted an ISK foot in the door of the Reich, and one would be enough for a start. The other agent, he argued, could leave as soon as another safe house was available. The agent who must go, Eichler said, was Jupp Kappius.

During the training that summer, a strong friendship grew between Willi Drucker and Kappius, though Drucker found the abstemious habits of the ISK people so much nonsense. What had a beer, a smoke, or a wurst to do, Drucker wondered, with the struggle for social justice? Kappius, he found, nevertheless, was tough, intelligent, and fiercely committed. He once told Drucker that he was prepared to undergo a face lift, if it would improve his chances for success inside Germany. Kappius had refused to take a salary for his work and accepted only £5 a week for expenses.

Of Kappius his OSS evaluator wrote:

> He is well above the average in intelligence with a shrewd, calculating mind and well-balanced powers of judgment. He thinks and expresses his ideas clearly and logically. He is well able to look after himself. He has imagination and definite initiative. In character he is determined and self-confident and gives the general impression of physical and moral strength. He is dependable and trustworthy. He is serious-minded; he has a quiet sense of humor, and would certainly inspire confidence as a leader. He is keen and worked hard and genuinely benefited from his course. He is one of the most serious-minded, careful, and determined students we have had here and should do a first-class job.

The mission agreed to by OSS and SOE for Kappius seemed rather ambitious for one man:

> . . . you will create an underground organization for the purpose of (1) promoting internal resistance to the Nazi regime; (2) committing acts of sabotage against the war effort; (3) encouraging subversion in all its forms . . . you will cause rumors to be spread according to the following directions: (1) to create dissension between Wehrmacht troops and all political and semi-

political formations, e.g., Waffen SS, Gestapo, Hitler Jugend ... (2) to create financial panic on the German home front and among troops resulting in a run on the banks ... (3) to encourage surrender or desertion. ...."

Kappius was to communicate initially by courier and to notify OSS when he was ready to have a radio operator dropped to him. If he wanted to communicate by post-office box through Sweden, he was to do so through a rigidly set procedure:

> You must never try to write letters direct to the postbox address, but you will work through a trusted courier and in the following way: The letter, which will contain a coded message, you will address to your courier in Germany, preferably through the ordinary German post in a German envelope with a German postage stamp, so that it will seem quite normal for your courier to have such a letter on him. When the courier arrives in Sweden he will extract the letter from its German envelope and will insert it in a fresh envelope, which he will then address to the postbox in the neutral land. Should a reply to the message be required, then the courier will have to insert a suitable sender's address on the reverse of the envelope.

Lazare Teper's BACH unit devised a cover for Kappius using convenient elements of his past. He became "Wilhelm Leineweber," a structural architect and section leader in the Todt Organization, which carried out German military construction. He was coming from France via Holland to the city of Sögel to search for his mother, who had been bombed out, and then was proceeding on to Bochum for reassignment. Kappius was provided with nine forged documents, including the basic *Kennkarte*, the universal German ID, food-rationing coupons, and blank travel orders to cover contingencies.

Henry Sutton pulled his "Bochum" folder from the BACH file and briefed Kappius on latest known conditions in that city. OSS London's first agent destined for Germany was ready. Jupp Kappius was going home.

The DOWNEND flight had been a textbook exercise capped by touches of luck. Jupp Kappius had landed gently in a plowed field near convenient woods where he quickly concealed his parachute. Then, unaccountably, a powerful lethargy overcame him. Though he had dozed throughout virtually the entire plane ride, he again fell asleep in the woods.

Two hours later, he awoke and began burying his parachute and jump suit. Something was missing. He started looking, first carefully, then frantically for his metal identification tag. After a fruitless, hour-long search, he dropped to the ground overcome by despair. How, he wondered, would he survive in Germany as a spy if he could commit so gross a blunder at the outset. The audacity of what he had embarked on suddenly struck Kappius and engulfed him in self-doubt. He had no will to go on. He sat limply, feeling a coldness in the gray hours before sunrise which seemed to come from within himself rather than from the raw night air.

With the dawn, as the light began to give shape and color to his surroundings, he felt his strength return. He found a road and headed toward what he hoped was Sögel. The route was surprisingly alive in the early morning with farmers, schoolchildren, prisoners of war and their guards. He wondered at the greeting customary in this region, which was some distance north of his goal of Bochum. As he passed the first man, he made as if to greet him, then hesitated. "Good morning," the man said. Kappius returned the greeting. He had thought that it might be *"Heil Hitler."*

He boarded a train without difficulty at Sögel. En route, he committed another shattering blunder. As the conductor approached, Kappius handed him his ticket and said in English, "Do you want this?" The conductor took no notice.

At eleven-thirty that night, Jupp Kappius arrived in Bochum and found his way to Burgstrasse 15, a three-family house on the outskirts of the city. The safe address was the home of a young ISK couple, both of whom had already served prison terms at hard labor for anti-Nazi activities. The couple's identification as known dissidents posed risks for them and Kappius, but there had been no alternative.

The twenty-six-year-old husband ran a wholesale kitchen-supply business. He was tubercular and, therefore, exempt from military service. They had been alerted to expect a visitor, but did not know who. They were honored to shelter Jupp Kappius, who commanded considerable stature within the ISK.

The house on Burgstrasse proved a fortunate choice. The man's business gave him considerable freedom to move about and keep unusual hours. He would serve as Kappius's contact man, while the spy remained in the house. The man also maintained an office in his home, thus the arrival and departure of strangers would arouse little suspicion.

Jupp Kappius began a strangely disembodied existence. His life became days of monotony, scattered hours of accomplishment, and moments of terror. He obtained several sets of papers through his host identifying him alternatively as an employee of the Krupp works, a miner, and a worker in a Bochum factory, but he never sought employment. A job would have interfered with his mission. Registering with the local authorities would also have exposed him to conscription into the army or the Volkssturm. He never left the house during the day and emerged only for brief walks after dark. Seven other people, besides his hosts, lived in the three-story building, wholly unaware of his presence. In the house next door lived a militant Nazi party member.

When his friends were out, he did nothing that might arouse the people living upstairs. He checked himself if he started to hum or sing. He moved about in stocking feet and dared not turn on a tap or flush a toilet while alone. When his protectors were in, he still spoke barely above a whisper. If visitors rang the doorbell during a meal, Kappius picked up his plate and utensils and disappeared before they entered.

The nation into which Jupp Kappius had parachuted was a supreme police state held for the past eleven years in a grip of steel. The reverses of the war had not weakened that hold, only shifted its leverage. Fear, to a degree, had supplanted chauvinism in sustaining allegiance to the Nazi regime, a fear made all the more palpable after the savage extermination of the plotters of July 20, 1944. The regime's chief instrument of terror was the Geheime Staatspolizei, the Gestapo, the secret state police which Hermann Göring had created in 1933. The sybarite Nazi established the secret police as a branch of the Prussian Ministry of the Interior to impose Hitler's will upon all opponents and rivals within the Nazi party. The Gestapo was thus originally part of the government of Prussia, the state which embraced more than half of Germany and had Berlin as its capital.

Within a year, the SS chief, Heinrich Himmler, intrigued his way into the deputy leadership of the Gestapo and finally absorbed full control. Within two years, Himmler succeeded in making the Gestapo the political police of all Germany and won for it extraordinary powers. The statute of February 10, 1936, eliminated any appeal from the decisions of the Gestapo and forbade the judiciary to review its cases. Acts of the Gestapo could be neither investigated nor challenged. If the courts acquitted a defendant, the Gestapo could arrest him on his way out of the courtroom and dispatch him to a concentration camp, without further resort to law. The Gestapo had become a law unto itself, answerable to no one.

Himmler brought the Gestapo under the SS, the elitist corps of the Nazi party. Thus the secret police became a bureaucratic hybrid, part government and part political. It was as though, in America, the Democrats or Republicans, upon coming to power, would have their own police force with uncontested authority to arrest and imprison.

Understanding the interconnecting parts of the Nazi apparatus, never a simple task, is best begun with the SA. The SA, for Sturmabteilung, the "Assault Detachment," was the Nazi party's military arm and had provided Hitler with muscle in his early struggle for power. Its members were the brown-shirted, Jew-baiting storm troopers, the political bullies behind the "night of crystal" and other infamies presaging the nature of Hitler's rule.

Within the SA there had emerged an elite, personal bodyguard for Hitler, called the SS, the Schutzstaffel, or "Guard Detachment." The black-uniformed SS soon looked with condescension on the coarser ranks of its parent SA. The SA included men who naïvely believed in the socialism of the National Socialist German Workers' Party and who had actual revolutionary impulses. Its leaders wanted to wrench control of the army from its traditional masters, the Prussian aristocracy. It was this threat from the SA which led the German military mandarins to make common cause with the socially ludicrous Hitler.

If Hitler would turn on his more radical supporters and crush the SA, along with its threat to the army, then he could have the Junkers' support. This Hitler did, bloodily, thus winning a new source of powerful backers and erasing rivals within the SA—all in one treacherous stroke. The generals were freed of the SA, and Germany was eventually yoked, instead, to the SS and the Gestapo.

Himmler gradually built the SS into a state within a state. Its several branches comprised elites in whole areas of German society. The "General SS" included major government officials, diplomats, industrialists, lawyers, doctors, and other establishment figures. It was largely an honorary body. The Waffen SS was strictly military; some of its crack units fought ably and honorably. The Totenkopfverbände, or "Death's Head Detachments," were SS units which operated the concentration camps. The most powerful element of the SS was the state security section, or RSHA for "Reichssicherheitshauptamt," originally under Reinhard Heydrich.

The Gestapo, the secret-police component of the RSHA, cast the longest and darkest shadow over everyday German life. It assumed responsibilities for political security, intelligence, counterintelligence, frontier control, the press, Jews, sabotage, foreign exchange, concentration camps, Russian prisoners of war, commandos, and, as OSS agents were aware, enemy parachutists. The Gestapo best exemplified the motto of the SS: "Blest be all that hardens."

The cream of the RSHA, an elite within an elite, was the Sicherheitsdienst, or SD, the largely independent long-range intelligence branch. The SD had three thousand carefully picked members and was conceded, within and without Germany, to be a corps of formidable intelligence professionals. Normally, the much looser Abwehr, the military intelligence organization, took precedence over the SD in the domain of intelligence. The SD and the Abwehr were thus, inevitably, jealous rivals while the Abwehr lasted.

This competition was resolved in February 1944. In response to Himmler's insistent pressure for the unification of German intelligence services, Hitler removed Admiral Canaris as chief of the Abwehr and folded military intelligence into Himmler's SS. However, some Abwehr units managed to hold on to their separate identity, within the SS, for nearly a year more.

The lines of responsibility between the Gestapo and the SD were fuzzed, perhaps deliberately, by the man to whom both were ultimately responsible, the cold-blooded "Reichsführer," Himmler. The SS chief was too brilliant a student of power to let even one of his own deadly instruments attain unchecked independence.

Though Göring had fathered the Gestapo, and Himmler adopted it, a man named Heinrich Müller raised the secret police to its dread maturity. The chain of command thus ran: commander of all SS, Himmler; commander of the RSHA security services, first Reinhard Heydrich, later Ernst Kaltenbrunner (after Heydrich was assassinated); and chief of the Gestapo, Heinrich Müller.

Müller was an unabashed admirer of Russian methods and modeled the Gestapo on the Soviet secret police. He built a pyramidal cell structure reaching down, literally, into every German home. Ordinary citizens became honorary members of the Gestapo as block wardens. The concierge of an apartment house, for example, as block warden, watched over all families living in his building. Block wardens reported political misdemeanors and seditious talk. They brokered minor problems between their charges and the state or party. By the summer of 1943, the Gestapo had enlisted 482,000 block wardens whose principal purpose was to inform on their neighbors.

Spontaneous informing by other citizens was also encouraged as an act of patriotism. Voluntary informers were generally motivated by spite or a desire to ingratiate themselves with authorities, and their information was usually useless. Yet the knowledge that one could be denounced by virtually anybody produced the desired climate of fear. Everyone had committed an indiscretion at some point and feared its exposure. The knowledge that one was constantly being watched managed to hold an entire people in check and sapped the will to resist even among those who most despised the system. Another advantage of this nationwide network of honorary and voluntary squealers was that it cost the government nothing.

Those who ran afoul of the Gestapo experienced remarkably consistent treatment. Whether this uniformity was officially prescribed or natural to the sadist mentality is not clear. But the patterns of torture were so unvarying, at home and in the occupied countries, as to suggest that the Gestapo practiced barbarism from a standard operating manual.

Before an interrogation began, the suspect was routinely roughed up for the shock value. The effect of this arbitrary viciousness was to daze, humiliate, and throw prisoners off balance at the outset in the contest of wills with their inquisitors.

Anyone picked up by the Gestapo was presumed to have some information of subversive activities, no matter how remote. Even suspects with virtually no evidence against them were tortured on the off chance that they might divulge something. A prisoner would be grilled, often on matters about which he was totally ignorant. One line of questioning would eventually be dropped and another taken up at random. Once begun, the process was nearly irreversible. If the prisoner had nothing to say under mild torture, the screws were progressively tightened. He might be dead or dying before his tormentors could bring themselves to accept that he did indeed know nothing.

An honor code of sorts figured in the Gestapo scheme of justice, almost a suggestion of the Anglo-Saxon protection against self-incrimination. A person could be tortured to extract information on other subversive organizations, persons, or activities. But torture was not to be employed simply to force suspects to admit their own guilt.

The only physical punishments officially sanctioned by the Gestapo, according to RSHA regulations, were flogging and "rigorous examination" to consist of not more than twenty-five blows with a stick. The secret police displayed considerably more imagination.

Prisoners were routinely beaten until their kidneys were torn from their protective tissue. They were punched and kicked until the face was a toothless, shapeless mass. The Gestapo tool chest included a small vise for crushing testicles, electrodes which sent a current from the penis to the anus, an iron ring to tighten around the skull, and a soldering iron for searing flesh. Torquemada would have felt at home in a typical Gestapo headquarters.

The Gestapo chief of Milan had a genius for the work. This officer's most effective technique was to suspend the prisoner from a bar by handcuffs, insert a stick, the thickness of a broom handle, into the prisoner's rectum, then beat on the protruding part of the stick. But the Gestapo did draw a line. There is no evidence that the Nazi secret police ever used the rack.

On October 18, 1942, Hitler issued a top-secret order that clarified any existing confusion over the treatment of secret agents captured within the Reich: ". . . all enemies on commando missions, even if they are in uniform, armed or unarmed, in battle or in flight, are to be slaughtered to the last man. . . . If it should be necessary initially to spare one man or two, for interrogation, then they are to be shot immediately after this is completed."

By the time the United States began to plan the large-scale penetration of Germany, the failure of the July 20 plot had cemented the Gestapo's grip of terror more securely than ever over the Reich. After the attempt on Hitler's life, the barbarism of the Nazis reached a shrill crescendo. The Gestapo made over 7000 arrests. According to one estimate, 4980 lives were forfeited for the failed blow. When the killing was over, not only had the leaders of the plot been exterminated but waves of fear swelled outward from the plot's center to wash away virtually any important trace of anti-Nazi resistance in the Reich. The power of the German General Staff was broken. Admiral Canaris, former head of the Abwehr and the Gestapo's chief rival in the intelligence field, was hanged for allegedly aiding the conspirators.

Ignoring the havoc which Hitler's leadership had brought to the fatherland, the majority of Germans still viewed their Führer as a savior and were outraged by the attempt to kill him. In the Germany into which the OSS had begun to infiltrate its agents, active resistance against Hitler was virtually dead, and control over the country incontestably in the hands of the Gestapo.

Lieutenant Anthony Turano submitted cheerfully to the limp jests of his fellow officers at the OSS London Air Dispatch Section. His mission was to escort two women spies from England to France, where they would slip over the Swiss border and ultimately be infiltrated into the Reich.

Turano picked up the women late in September 1944 at Area O, a lovely English country manor used as an OSS staging facility. To Turano, the women were foreign in the most elemental sense. Their plainness had a relentless quality to it. They resembled scrubbed nuns in drab, secular dress. Their severe appearance was relieved only by a shy, unaffected manner. The women spoke a precise, German-accented English, but Turano had not the faintest idea of what to say to them. One of the women was Anne Kappius, wife of Jupp Kappius, the OSS agent in Bochum; the other was Hilde Meisel, a fellow member of the ISK.

Arthur Goldberg had come to know Hilde Meisel during his duty in London and had been moved by her simplistic idealism and the serenity with which she faced her mission. He had talked to the woman just before her departure and felt a strange foreboding as he studied her calm face and accepted that OSS was quite possibly sending Hilde Meisel to her death.

Anne Kappius was to travel from Switzerland to the Ruhr disguised as a Red Cross nurse and serve as a courier for her husband. Hilde was to go to the Vienna area and set up an espionage network among fellow radical Socialists. She was code-named "Crocus."

They flew a C-47 cargo plane from England to the French town of Thonon on the shores of the Lake of Geneva. The small talk en route had been painful and sparse. They were met at Thonon by another OSS officer who took the party to overnight accommodations in the home of a French professor. The Frenchman and his wife beamingly served a great roast and white bread. Turano noted, and their French host politely ignored, the fact that the two women passed up the roast and quietly ate only the bread.

After dinner, the women blushingly revealed to Turano an unexpected prankishness. They handed him a role of film and asked if he would have it developed before their return. Throughout the flight, they had secretly taken pictures of him with a concealed match-box camera.

The following morning, Turano bade them good-bye. Normally, he would have kissed women agents. These political nuns discouraged that kind of intimacy. He shook their hands and the women left for Switzerland.

The arrival of Jupp Kappius had a galvanizing effect on the moribund anti-Nazi movement in the Ruhr. Only a stroke of luck had saved its members from total annihilation after the twentieth of July plot failed. The ISK was deeply involved in the conspiracy through an unlikely alliance with the militarics. Under the arrangement, the Socialists believed that they were to govern in western Germany after the Nazis were brought down. But the ISK courier who had been sent to launch the uprising in the Ruhr sensed that something had gone awry and never gave the signal.

Kappius found the anti-Nazis in September of 1944 badly demoralized. If the generals, with all their power, had failed to dislodge Hitler, what could a beleaguered band of Socialists do? They were also painfully aware that well-armed uprisings in Warsaw that fall and in Czechoslovakia the year before had been brutally crushed by SS troops. They still lived in fear of the Gestapo dragnet which had snared suspected plotters by the thousands. Some Socialists slept with pistols at their bedside, determined to take their own lives before the Gestapo could seize them.

But as the Allied armies approached from the west, the intrepid among them were sufficiently inspired by Kappius's arrival to consider military action to hasten the conquest of the Ruhr.

The agent's immediate circle of lieutenants eventually numbered fifteen, each of whom ran a subgroup of agents. Three-quarters of the members in the total network were factory workers or miners. Others were middle-class managers, some in sensitive positions. Kappius also enlisted the director of the Deutsche Bank in Essen, a director of a mining firm, a publisher, a high official in the Krupp armament works, an executive of the Stinnes Company, and an official of the German railways with intimate knowledge of train movements.

He took allies where he could find them—liberals, Socialists, and individual Communists; but he refused to deal with the underground Communist apparatus. The party was notoriously infiltrated by the Gestapo.

At the end of September, Kappius's wife, Anne, arrived from Switzerland. Though he had been in Germany less than a month, Kappius was ready to report to her the organization of a resistance cadre spread throughout Bochum, Essen, Witten, and other cities in the Ruhr and linked to Cologne, Hanover, Breslau, Hamburg, Göttingen, Frankfurt, and Berlin. Kappius had also found a safe address in nearby Dortmund, where his London partner, Willi Drucker, could stay as soon as he was infiltrated.

Kappius's key message was that he was ready to launch an armed uprising. Through penetration of the security system at the Krupp arms plant, Kappius had two hundred fifty rifles available. The police chief of Witten had also agreed to turn over all his arms. The plan was to exploit the interval of chaos just before the Allied armies struck the Ruhr and after the German armies began to retreat. His partisans would blow up rail lines and seal off the escape routes of Nazi party leaders. They intended to save factories, food, and vital supplies from the scorched-earth policy which the Nazis were threatening.

Kappius had selected a pinpoint. All that was needed was for the Allies to drop another hundred Sten guns, fifty revolvers, fifty grenades, and fifty incendiaries. Jupp Kappius sent his wife back to Switzerland, eager to receive instructions for his next move.

Jupp Kappius spent anxious hours listening to coded gibberish over the BBC: "Is your pen leaking?" "Roses will bloom in the spring." "Mary's tonsils have been removed." The messages were transmitted via ordinary radio and could be heard by anybody in Germany with a short-wave band. Each message would be repeated several times in a maddeningly precise and toneless voice for the benefit of foreign agents. Kappius waited for a message saying *"Grossmutter hat drei Kinder"* (Grandmother has three children), the code signaling his expected air drop.

As days stretched into weeks, as the men in his network grew skeptical, Kappius hoped even for word that "Grandmother" was aborted, to end the frustration of his men. Kappius did not know that the RAF had rejected his pinpoint because a Nazi searchlight team and antiaircraft battery were known to be located nearby. What the RAF did not know was that Kappius had arranged to eliminate them.

While pursuing his mission, Kappius was also recording social conditions in the Reich during this sixth year of the war. What had struck him most forcibly on his arrival in September was the normality of life in the Ruhr. Factories and mines operated. Trains and trolleys ran on time. Mail and newspapers were delivered punctually. Telephones worked. Gas, water, and electricity were supplied without restrictions. Food was rationed and some items were occasionally short; but no one went hungry. Kappius was amazed that he always ate real butter, never margarine. People were well dressed, too. This fact surprised him, until he was reminded that Germany had ransacked the whole of Europe for clothes. Altogether, an aura of muted prosperity pervaded the Ruhr.

Then, on November 4, 1944, Bochum discovered Allied air power. Over thirty-five hundred tons of bombs shook the city for forty minutes. From that point on, life in Bochum began to decline. As the battering from the air continued, conditions on the railroads and trams deteriorated until regular schedules were abandoned. Telephone lines went dead, and mail delivery virtually ceased. Electrical power came and went. Kappius noticed that the hottest items in the barter system, which soon largely replaced cash, were candles. Food supplies became uncertain. Water was often short.

The bombing had the curious effect of improving people's dress. Fearing the loss of their best clothes in air raids, the Germans preferred to wear them. Kappius was astonished that every woman in the Ruhr seemed to own a fur coat.

His neighbors lived with suitcases packed with clothing, personal articles, valuables, and important papers, ready to move at a moment's notice. Beds were usually kept in the cellar. Apartment dwellers hung their clothes in the basement with no thought that someone might take them. To steal a neighbor's clothes in these times was unthinkable. Homes in town were sparsely furnished. Instead, farmhouses throughout the region were stacked to the ceiling with the furniture sent by friends and relatives living in cities under bombing attack.

Of the first great raid Kappius noted, "It was terrific, the crashing and the effect of petrol and phosphorus bombs. I saw it all standing upright, leaning against a telephone pole. The nearest burning house was 200 yards away. God damn it, I thought, the world was going down!"

Kappius could not risk the safety of an air-raid shelter for fear of attracting the attention of the bunker warden. On rare occasions when he did seek protection, he usually found a cellar full of women, shrieking with terror in a building rocked by the blasts. The screaming unnerved him more than being exposed aboveground.

The raids did not anger the Germans; rather, they numbed people into apathy, a sense that they were hapless pawns. They became obsessed with the mechanics of daily existence. Their priorities were elemental—where to spend the night if one were bombed out, how to stretch a ration coupon or get an extra bar of soap. There were Germans, like Kappius, willing to risk their lives because they detested Nazism. But they were notable, above all, for their rarity. Resistance, he concluded, as he observed the passivity of the mass of people, was the work of fools, divinely touched fools.

The Nazis, Kappius was forced to concede, had done their work well. The years of tyranny had robbed people of the will or capacity for independent thought. The Germans, a highly intelligent and educated people, lived under Hitler in an intellectual fog. The propagandists had beaten into their heads one point of view. The suppression of free expression, the crushing of dissent left no place for alternative ideas to circulate. People went about perpetually puzzled, uncertain what to believe, distrusting their own judgment.

Even anti-Nazis fell into an intellectual funk. Many educated Germans had not read a newspaper in years, ever since the Nazis had prostituted the papers into party organs. One could not believe anything the Nazis said, and in the absence of countervailing opinion, a person did not know what to believe. Lacking facts, or any faith in the official line, people tended to substitute clichéd sentiment for thoughtful analysis. Thinking became flabby.

Virtually everyone, including the Nazis, listened to foreign broadcasts, particularly those beamed from England, although the penalty for doing so was punishment by hard labor, and the dissemination of such information was a capital offense. But here, too, psychological conditioning eroded confidence in what one heard. How could they know how much to believe of the English and Americans?

The systematic terror of Nazism had also isolated people, physically and mentally. There was little opportunity to test one's ideas against another's. The spirited give-and-take of political discussion in a *Bierstube* or café had long since vanished. Any unauthorized public congregation was suspect. An entire nation manifested the symptoms of social exile similar to what the deaf and dumb suffer.

It was hardly a climate favorable to recruiting a large following willing to resist the system. There was a conspicuous lack of leadership, as well, since most of those unable to tolerate Nazism were dead, in concentration camps, or in exile.

Jupp Kappius found the prospects for enlisting the working classes in the resistance especially bleak. The Nazis had pursued a parallel policy of fear and full stomachs. Skilled workers were highly paid and enjoyed a comfortable living standard. They received extra rations of schnapps, cigarettes, meat, and chocolate. Well paid and well fed, they had little quarrel with Nazism.

Kappius was also disappointed by the possibility of recruiting conscript workers. The term was misleading. Contrary to his expectation, few foreign workers in the Ruhr had been forcibly conscripted. Most had come seeking work. Many got along well with German workers and expressed a desire to stay on in Germany after the war.

Kappius lived in the midst of a nation where bombs rained and the structures of society were collapsing. But little serious talk was ever devoted to the war. Facetious cynicism seemed the outer limit of political comment. One joke making the rounds told of the latest secret weapon, the V-5, a giant submarine made of India rubber which would circle the English coast until Britain was erased. Another secret-weapon story described the V-6, a hollowed-out oak which was to be filled with high explosives and floated to England. The problem in producing it was a critical shortage of acorns to grow the oaks.

Most Germans, Kappius concluded, accepted that the war was lost, were content to laugh grimly about it, and, as good Germans, keep on doing what they were told.

Back in England the London Labor Division waited impatiently for a second report from Jupp Kappius. The original plan had been to provide him with a radio and operator. But Kappius did not want to risk having a radio as long as his wife could serve as his courier. Not until mid-January 1945 had Anne Kappius, disguised as a nurse, managed to reach Bochum again. This time she brought back to OSS a tightly packed thirteen-page account of budding resistance.

Kappius reported an increase in industrial sabotage. Railroad men from outlawed trade unions were deliberately bottlenecking trainloads of tanks and cannons headed for the front. The pacifist owner of a Bochum steam turbine plant, the Luftkuehler A.G., had managed to drag his feet, exaggerate bomb damage, and invent shortages until the factory was out of operation by 1945. Luftkuehler A.G. had produced cooling systems for steam turbines used in key industries and on German submarines. Another anti-Nazi sympathizer, whose job was to consider leave applications of war workers, issued approvals like handbills, even encouraging workers that they needed a rest.

Kappius reported that I. G. Farben in Frankfurt am Main was running full blast with twenty-five thousand workers. A generating complex near Cologne which supplied two-thirds of the electricity to the Ruhr had, as of December, suffered only five small bomb blasts. Thereafter, Allied aircraft flattened the Farben works and the electrical-power plants.

He reported a startling statistic. With almost invariable consistency, nearly one out of every three five-thousand-pound bombs dropped by Allied planes was a dud. In a clear, daylight raid on the Göttingen railroad station, three hundred bombs had miraculously missed the station and landed in a nearby field. One hundred had failed to explode.

After four and a half months at Burgstrasse 15, Kappius was tipped off of an impending Gestapo raid and had to leave the home of his friend, the kitchen-supply dealer. Thereafter, he moved constantly, rarely staying more than a week in one place. He rotated quarters among five neighboring cities in the Ruhr.

As Kappius moved about, he developed a high respect for the briefing and preparation he had received from Lazare Teper's BACH Section in London. His clothes were inconspicuously appropriate. He found himself well versed on background and events in Bochum and other towns. He could chat volubly and confidently, as though he had never left.

He became an expert practitioner of the ask-them-before-they-ask-you technique for allaying the suspicions of police officials. Several times he had felt that policemen were watching him. He would immediately ask the officer an innocent question. The man was invariably distracted from his original concern and became helpful. Kappius felt that he came in for an unexpected share of suspicion because, on one point, BACH had failed him. Almost no young man in Germany wore a mustache. His soon came off.

Both ISK women, Anne Kappius and Hilde Meisel, completed their missions. Frau Kappius had traveled twice from Switzerland deep into Germany to carry out the intelligence gathered by her husband in Bochum. Before returning to Switzerland, she had also debriefed ISK contacts in six other major German cities.

Hilde Meisel, the plain young woman whom Arthur Goldberg had so much admired, was slipped across the Swiss border into Austria early in 1945. As agent Crocus, she proceeded to Vienna, where she established an intelligence chain among ISK sympathizers. On her return, she had reached the Austrian border with Switzerland where two associates were waiting to escort her back to safety. As she was about to cross over, Hilde Meisel stumbled into an SS patrol. An expert marksman brought her down with a shot that shattered both her legs. Before the Germans could reach her, Hilde had bitten into her "L" pill, a capsule of cyanide, which killed her instantly.

VI

The Birth of Sergeant Steinhauser

✠ ✠ ✠

Communicating with the outside world continued to present a monumental challenge to the OSS staff in Bern. Nothing of a confidential nature could be sent through the mail. No military aircraft were allowed to fly into Switzerland and Swiss international commercial air service had been suspended, except with Germany.

The remaining channels were commercial cable and transatlantic radio telephone. The encoding and decoding of messages over the commercial lines made this method cumbersome and maddeningly slow. Dulles relied heavily on radio telephone calls to Washington, placed four or five evenings a week directly from his home. The conversations were scrambled by an electronic device and thus unintelligible to German monitors, but not, evidently, to the Swiss. One evening Dulles found himself seated at a dinner next to a member of the Swiss Council of Ministers. "I hear," the man began—and then related to Dulles, in dismaying detail, the American's report to Washington of the evening before.

Dulles's staff lived with an awareness that not only transatlantic calls but all their telephone conversations were being tapped by the Swiss. They operated under an iron rule of never discussing confidential matters over the telephone. On the one occasion when this rule had been broken, in an emergency attempt to set up a rendezvous, the Swiss police had arrested the agent within hours.

The Germans also intercepted more messages than the Americans realized. Wilhem Höttl, an SD officer, writing after the war, revealed the extent of German code-cracking and, coincidentally, offered a commentary on the Dulles operation. He noted, "Since the autumn of 1944, we had been listening in fairly regularly to the reports from the American embassy in Bern. Those to which the Ambassador Harrison put his name were of very little interest to us. But there were others so judicious and so unusual in their grasp of the political situation that they soon made a deep impression. We discovered that they came from the head of the American secret service, OSS for central Europe."

To Gary Van Arkel, at thirty-seven, war seemed a game for younger men. Van Arkel had received orders to transfer from London to Bern, his fourth move since the war. In September 1944, he flew out of England to Paris, where he and the air crew spent the night. In the morning, he went out to the airfield of Le Bourget and reboarded the plane. There was room neither to sit nor stand. Van Arkel had to hunch behind the twenty-year-old pilot, the oldest of the crew, all of whom had spent the night in a memorable Paris fling ending only hours before.

Before heading toward their destination, the pilot paid a fond farewell to the city. He flew up the Champs-Elysées at treetop level as Parisians scattered like leaves in every direction. He circled the Arch of Triumph, then bore down on the Eiffel Tower. He announced that they were going to fly under it. He swerved away at the last second and reluctantly turned the plane toward their goal, a French airfield near the Swiss border. They hedge-hopped German-held territory at an altitude between two hundred and three hundred feet with frequent detours, as the pilot joyously fired rockets into ammunition dumps and strafed trains.

With the liberation of France, the border with Switzerland had been reopened, and after landing, Van Arkel was able to cross legally into Switzerland. He had been selected for Bern because Allen Dulles wanted a civilian with valid papers who could work there legitimately. The Swiss official at the frontier post had not seen an American passport for years. He glanced at a signature on Van Arkel's document and noted in his records that, on that date, a Mr. Cordell Hull entered Switzerland.

Van Arkel, a tall, spare man with a quiet, reassuring voice, and one of the earliest OSS officers concerned with the penetration of Germany, was supposed to set up a labor operation in Switzerland as he had done earlier in North Africa and Italy. But in Bern, Van Arkel was swept up in the whoever-is-available administrative style of Allen Dulles and instead found himself mastering something called "Kutter's Formula." He was to report to the Sixth and Twelfth Army groups in France the daily water levels of the Rhine River. The Allies feared that the Germans would blow up dams on the Upper Rhine or its tributaries, to flood out any pontoon bridges or landing craft crossing the Rhine. Changes in the water levels upriver, as reported by Van Arkel, would be the tip-off.

Dulles also found the discreet Van Arkel a good contact man with his stable of foreign agents. Van Arkel could neither phone nor write these contacts. He never revealed his real name, nor knew the names of the agents. All meetings were prearranged for a particular time and place. If the appointment failed, the contact, probably months in the making, was broken and not easily repaired.

In the small Swiss capital, meetings in cafés, restaurants, and hotels were too risky. Van Arkel preferred to meet his people on roads outside of town. He would drive around the city until he was sure he was not being followed, then pick up the agent at the appointed spot and transact their business in the moving car. Van Arkel would then drop the agent off at a different point, always deeply relieved when the passenger left.

Gary Van Arkel found the deception, the anonymity, the reflexive suspicion, the living with one eye constantly looking over his shoulder hardly glamorous. It was to him nerve-racking, emotionally draining, and ultimately dehumanizing work. He was soon to undergo his most exhausting espionage experience with a rather remarkable young Austrian.

Allied agents infiltrated into Austria faced perils no less fearsome than in Germany itself. Since 1938, Austria had been absorbed into Germany as an integral part of the Third Reich. Among prominent Nazis born or raised in Austria were Ernst Kaltenbrunner, Heydrich's successor as the head of the RSHA; Waffen SS General Josef ("Sepp") Dietrich, a personal favorite of Hitler; SS Major Otto Skorzeny, the daring rescuer of Mussolini; SS Colonel Adolf Eichmann, chief of the Gestapo's Jewish Section; and Hitler himself. The National Redoubt, the expected last stronghold of Nazism, was located in an area embracing roughly equal expanses of southern Germany and western Austria.

After the Anschluss, Hitler had crossed the Austrian border on the afternoon of March 12, 1938, near his birthplace of Braunau-am-Inn, and received a frenzied welcome. At Linz, a city of 120,000, a crowd of 100,000 turned out to cheer their new Führer. From an open Mercedes-

Benz, Hitler smiled and saluted a sea of outstretched arms and radiant faces. One account noted, "When Hitler entered Austria it was to the clamorous strains of the Nazi 'Horst Wessel' *Lied* pouring from middle-class throats." Hitler had received the affectionate reception of a local boy who had made good.

But there were Austrians who did not cheer. They were a heterogeneous minority bound by nothing more than a shared loathing of the Nazis. Their ranks contained monarchists and nationalists who cherished Austrian independence. They included believers in democracy and Communists, the congenital foes of National Socialism. Some were pan-Germans, who believed that union with Germany was desirable, but unity under the likes of Hitler and his gang was abhorrent. The dissidents contained many of the finest and bravest leaders in Austrian society. In the first warm flush of Teutonic brotherhood, there was little that they could do. But, in time, anti-Nazis who fled Austria and some of those who stayed began to fight back.

The men of the German 356th Infantry Division had been sent into reserve after weeks of bitter fighting in Italy at Montecassino. On January 22, 1943, their respite was cut short. The division was hurled against an American and British surprise landing at Anzio.

The American troops moved cautiously at first. For ten days they held within a small perimeter on the beach. Then they broke out. Among the troops of the 356th harassing their advance was a young Austrian private named Fritz Molden. Molden fought as savagely as the next man against the invaders. But the enemies before him represented only an immediate, impersonal menace to his life, and he fought in the way one would struggle to escape a burning building. His true enemy was the system that he was now perversely defending. For, at age nineteen, Molden had been an anti-Nazi activist for five years and had already served in prison as a political criminal.

Fritz Molden was born in Vienna into a cultivated and public-spirited family, strongly opposed to Nazism. His father, Ernst Molden, was a prominent journalist with Vienna's *Neue Freie Presse,* and his mother a talented writer. Molden had joined the Wehrmacht because it offered an alternative to serving out the remainder of his prison sentence. He had originally been assigned to a *Strafbataillon.* He was sent first to Russia, where SS units used men from the *Strafbataillon* as scouts. Their mortality was measured in months.

In Russia, Molden experienced that inexplicable kindness of strangers

—which happened repeatedly during the war among Germans and Austrians—who felt a shared but unspoken anti-Nazism. While he was being treated for a strained heart, an army doctor stripped his dossier of derogatory material, which enabled Molden to be reassigned out of the *Strafbataillon* and the Pripet Swamps of Russia and into Paris as an interpreter.

In France, he again linked up with Austrian anti-Nazis. But within a few months the specter of the Russian front loomed again. Once more, an unknown benefactor intervened. Thousands of soft-duty soldiers were being rounded up for transfer to Russia, but Molden received orders to Italy.

After he had fought at Anzio, Fritz Molden made contact with Italian partisans. In the summer of 1944, returning to camp after a short leave in Florence, Molden was tipped off that several of his partisan comrades had been arrested. He decided that it was dangerous to return to his unit and fled to the mountains. On his way, he encountered grisly good fortune. A German convoy had been attacked and several bodies lay scattered among the smoking wreckage. He dragged one corpse into the woods, where he switched uniforms and identification with the dead man. He loaded the body back into the truck and set it on fire.

Molden then left for Milan, where he had other contacts among the Italians, including a brilliant and beautiful young woman named Adriana Del Piano.* She was one of the youngest women in Italy to hold a law degree, a practicing idealist possessed of great personal courage and an extravagant style which captivated Molden. The Italian resistance had already cost the life of her partisan brother, Giancarlo, who was killed in a shoot-out in the Piedmont in the winter of 1943. She and Fritz Molden became linked politically and romantically. In Milan, Molden stayed with Adriana and her mother. There, he adopted the identity of Luigi Brentini, student, and plunged back into the resistance.

In August 1944, Molden left for Switzerland, under instructions from an embryonic Austrian resistance movement to make contact with the British through their consulate in Lugano. On this mission, the young Austrian tripped himself up, but managed to recover through an audacious stratagem. He had paid two smugglers to slip him across the Swiss border and was relaxing with a cigarette at a café when a man asked him for a light. Molden realized his error as soon as he committed it. The matches betrayed his recent arrival from Italy. The man identified himself as a Swiss police officer and arrested the Austrian.

*A pseudonym.

During his interrogation, Molden confidently told the Swiss that he was the representative of a rather well-developed, if largely unknown, Austrian resistance movement. Switzerland at that time perched like an uneasy sparrow between the claws of the Nazi eagle. The Swiss were hungry for information revealing troop movements along the borders they shared with the Germans. This obviously intelligent, brash young fellow could be useful. Instead of being interned, Molden was enlisted in Swiss intelligence.

Molden established his base in Zurich and soon became one of the Austrian anti-Nazis slipping into Kurt Grimm's apartment at the Bellerive au Lac. He and other young Austrian exiles came to look upon Grimm as a youthful father who would take care of them when they were harassed by Swiss authorities, needed cash, a safe house, or a useful contact. Grimm had been particularly impressed by Molden's successful infiltrations into Italy for the Swiss. Here, Grimm thought, was a young man whom Allen Dulles ought to know.

The first meeting was set for September 1944. Molden was to get out of the train two stops before Bern, then take a bus, then a commuter train to Bern, then proceed on foot to an arch in one of the medieval city's arcades. There, he was to meet the German-American businessman and Dulles confidant Gero von Gaevernitz, who had earlier presented Hans Gisevius to Dulles.

Von Gaevernitz took Molden to the Dulles apartment at Herrengasse 23, where the Austrian and the American sparred cautiously during this first encounter. Molden had been forewarned by the Swiss that American intelligence was a sieve. The Swiss were especially disturbed by Dulles's association with Gisevius, the ex-Gestapo official. Molden's mentor, Kurt Grimm, was also uneasy about Dulles's involvement with Gisevius. The German, in Grimm's view, lived in a style obviously beyond the capacity of a mere operative of the Abwehr.

Though Molden tried to maintain his reserve, he was desperately eager to impress Dulles. He realized the enormous potential of an association with the Americans, and he had immediately found Dulles an engaging and magnetic figure.

He told Dulles that he represented an anti-Nazi Austrian national committee. The American was not so easily satisfied. Who, he wanted to know, were the members of this national committee? Molden confidently rattled off an honors list of Austrians, all of whom would have been surprised to learn not only of their membership in this organization but of its existence. The people he named were all anti-Nazis, but in no way as formally united as he maintained. Molden's confident assertions had potentially placed all their necks in a Nazi noose. When he left the Dulles apartment that autumn night, Molden was euphoric. Here is a man, he thought, with authority, responsibility, and faith. Now we will win the war against the Germans.

Molden, like Fritz Kolbe and Hans Gisevius, had also approached the British and, like them, had been turned away. The British warned the Americans against this glib fellow. He was quite likely an *agent provocateur*. Dulles really ought to turn him over to the Swiss police. Dulles decided, instead, to gamble on Molden and handed him to Gary Van Arkel for day-to-day management. Van Arkel was introduced to a tall, pale young man with a lean, sensual face and hooded eyes that seemed continually to be searching his surroundings and measuring his listener.

What struck Van Arkel most was Molden's total self-possession. He asked the Americans for virtually nothing—only that they accept the reality of an Austrian resistance movement and reap the intelligence benefits from it. He asked for no documents, money, or clothing. Almost everything he needed had already been supplied by the Swiss. The Americans were quite willing to buy into this ready-made arrangement.

Early in September, Fritz Molden took a train from Zurich for the Swiss-Italian border near Lake Como. Swiss intelligence had previously supplied him with a German Army uniform, appropriate identification, and orders. The uniform had been sent ahead to Milan by Italian smugglers who combined patriotism and profit. Molden followed their route to Milan to the home of his mistress-collaborator, Adriana Del Piano. Here, he completed a metamorphosis to Hans Steinhauser, Feldwebel in the German Army.

Molden favored military cover as least conspicuous for an able-bodied young male traveling in the Reich in wartime. He assumed the rank of Feldwebel, roughly the level of a U.S. technical sergeant, because this rank occupied a strategic position between enlisted men and officers. No lesser rank dared cross a Feldwebel, and, since these men ran the companies for lieutenants and captains, they were valued and respected by their superiors. Military police units who checked documents were usually headed by Feldwebels, and there was something of a lodge-brother fellowship among men of this rank. Molden was perhaps young for a grizzled noncom. But he exuded tough self-assurance; by age twenty, little of the boy remained in Fritz Molden.

On September 7, 1944, Paula Molden received an anxious telephone call from her niece, asking her to come over quickly. At the young woman's home, Frau Molden learned that her son, reported missing in action in Italy over a year before, was alive and in Vienna.

On his arrival, Fritz Molden had routinely presented his orders to army billeting officials, had been assigned a room in a hotel, and from there called his cousin. He met his mother later that day in the Stadtpark. The next day, he was reunited with his father at a streetcar stop in Vienna's Third District.

With the elder Molden's guidance, he quickly set about creating the national resistance organization which he had told the Americans already existed. He soon learned the pitfalls of the task. For a few wild hours on July 20, 1944, scattered resistance groups had seized key points in Vienna. Then, when the coup against Hitler failed, the Nazis had struck back almost as savagely there as in Berlin. Many of the earlier resistance leaders had been shot or jailed by the time Molden arrived in Vienna.

One of the men he had mentioned to Allen Dulles as a member of the Austrian national committee was a distinguished Viennese professor of international law. Early in his Vienna visit, Molden had waited in the darkened hallway of the man's home for his return.

"My God!" The professor was startled. "I thought you were dead!"

"No, I am with the resistance."

"Are you crazy? You'll have us all hanging from the gallows."

The professor ordered him to leave the house immediately and warned Molden never to come back. "It's too late," Molden said on leaving. "You are already a member of the Austrian national committee."

Molden's political objective was clear. Every Nazi-occupied country had a provisional body, a government-in-exile, which dealt on a respected footing with the Allied governments. If Austria were to avoid treatment in the postwar world as a conquered province of the Third Reich, it too must have a provisional government, recognized by the Allies, and it must carry out a credible resistance.

Molden was mindful of the provision insisted on by the Russians in the Allies' Moscow Declaration of October 1943. In the postwar world, Austria was to be considered as a liberated country rather than a conquered enemy. But in the final settlement, account would be taken of the degree to which she had contributed to her own liberation.

Thus, Molden sought people from those surviving the bloodletting after the twentieth of July who could form a unified Austrian resistance movement. The remnants he had to work with were fragmented, small groups, individuals, bound only by their hatred of Nazism.

There was, however, one promising anti-Nazi nucleus which Molden learned had been created in the spring of 1944 by a scattering of resistance groups with military connections. By the time of Molden's arrival in September, they were affiliated under the symbol O5.* In truth, O5 was more symbol than resistance. But the existence of the organization did give Molden something tangible to report to the Allies in support of his claim that Austrians were willing to fight their way out of Hitler's grip.

Molden's hope was to see the disparate elements of anti-Nazi Austrians stitched together into one organization so that on his return he could present an entity to the Allies with clear outlines and thus win for Austria treatment as an independent, if temporarily subjugated, nation.

Before he left Switzerland, a friend had suggested to Molden that while in Vienna he should contact a woman code-named "Circe." She might prove useful. Molden arranged to meet her at the Hotel Excelsior.

Circe was then in her late thirties, a feline woman, small, quick, with something faintly disconcerting in her attractiveness. She had been a leading photographer in Berlin, with numerous important Germans, along with Mussolini and Count Ciano, among her subjects. The woman was an Isherwood character, a practitioner of the headlong hedonism of Berlin in the 1920s. She had left Berlin after having been bombed out three times and was now settled temporarily in Vienna.

Circe had earlier been enlisted by the Abwehr and was going on an assignment which quickened Fritz Molden's interest. She was to travel in northern Italy taking photos of industrial sites which the Germans intended to confiscate. She would be moving between Turin and Milan. This obviously clever woman could provide Molden with another base in northern Italy.

Circe was eager to help. The fellow was too young to appeal to her amorously, but he intrigued her. Here was someone standing up to and thus far outwitting the Nazis. There was a "craziness" about Molden that fascinated her. Circe agreed. They would meet again in Milan.

While his main objective in Vienna involved Austria's political future, Molden was aware that the Americans valued him solely as a source of intelligence. Thus he worked on two levels. With his father and other leading Austrians, he sought to unify liberals, monarchists, Christian Democrats, Socialists, and the military into the Austrian national committee. At the same time, he was organizing a secret-intelligence network.

Before his arrival in Vienna, Molden had already stopped at Innsbruck,

---

*O5 was a code abbreviation for "Oesterreich," O for the first letter and 5 representing E, the fifth letter of the alphabet.

Salzburg, and Linz and established intelligence cells. On his return to Switzerland he traveled by way of Graz and Klagenfurt for the same purpose. In each city he built the classic espionage pyramid, a group of from three to five agents, of whom only the leader knew Molden. Each of these agents, in turn, set up subnetworks unknown to each other.

In Innsbruck, Molden had an uncle on the university faculty, a professor who had been blinded in World War I and who was regarded as above suspicion. In the professor's offices, Molden set up his Innsbruck headquarters, including his radio. The room was conveniently located next to the university's own communications laboratory.

Twenty days after his departure, Fritz Molden was back in Switzerland and had his first debriefing with Gary Van Arkel.

VII

"I Swear Allegiance to Adolf Hitler"

✠ ✠ ✠

Within OSS, one intelligence adversary commanded genuine esteem—not the Gestapo, which functioned largely through brute force and which was too large for consistent quality, but the Sicherheitsdienst, the SD, the Nazi Security Service, a small, select elite and the rival of any nation's espionage apparatus. To penetrate the SD headquarters in Berlin represented a formidable challenge and a rich prize. In totalitarian societies, the best secrets were obtained from penetration of their intelligence services. Eventually, all secrets passed through or resided there. What was happening militarily, politically, and diplomatically inside Germany was known to the SD. In the fall of 1944, Bert Jolis, with the OSS unit at Saint-Germain-en-Laye, outside Paris, had a long-shot prospect of penetrating the SD.

Nearly two years before, Arthur Goldberg had heeded the advice of Omar Becu, the Belgian secretary of the International Transport Workers Federation, to track down Jolis. Goldberg's staff had proceeded despite the seeming anomaly: a labor leader recommending an international diamond merchant to marshal seamen, truck drivers, and railroad workers to engage in Allied espionage.

The diamond merchant, when located, had since become an American buck private undergoing training as a military policeman in the *terra incognita* of Pine Camp in far-western New York State. "I had visions," Jolis recalled, "of spending the rest of the war guarding a bridge in Maine."

One day, while engaged in close-order drill, Jolis heard his name shouted. He was instructed to report to his commanding officer, who eyed him quizzically and handed Jolis a slip of paper. It read that Jolis was to proceed to New York City, where he would meet a man identified as Morton Kollender at one of the restaurants adjoining the ice-skating rink at Rockefeller Center. "I don't know anything else," the officer said. "Just report back when you are through."

In the winter of 1942, Albert Jolis found himself with Kollender watching the glissando of skaters in mid-town Manhattan. The man revealed nothing of himself, but carefully drew out Jolis's background. Kollender learned that Albert Jolis was thirty years old, born in England, and now an American citizen. His family had been in the diamond business for generations and, like most diamond families, traced its roots to Amsterdam.

Through the family's enterprises, Bert Jolis had extensive contact with non-Communist labor-union leaders, particularly in the transport industry. Thus he had come to know Omar Becu of the ITWF, who had originally suggested his name to OSS. The two fervent anti-Communists, one a capitalist, the other a trade unionist, had worked together in 1940 to stem a disturbing Soviet strategy.

During the time in which the Russians were linked in unholy alliance with the Nazis, they had waged a strenuous propaganda campaign against Great Britain. The Russians preached that the war was an imperialist con game, and that no honest workingman should be sucked up in a struggle to save capitalism. The British, the Russians charged, were cruelly prolonging the war by spurning Hitler's honest overtures for peace.

Foreign Minister Vyacheslav Molotov had opened the seventh session of the USSR's Supreme Council with a ringing call to Communist parties throughout the world to induce workers in capitalist countries to foment strikes and work stoppages in defense plants; to obstruct the loading of ships; and to induce merchant seamen to jump ship on the waterfronts of the United States, the Caribbean, and Latin America. Had this appeal succeeded, Britain would have been strangled.

After his work with Becu to stave off Soviet subversion of merchant seamen, Jolis had settled in the United States, where he had been swallowed up in the draft. At Becu's suggestion, Arthur Goldberg had sent Mort Kollender to look over Jolis. Kollender, like George Pratt and Gary

Van Arkel, had been recruited into OSS from the National Labor Relations Board.

He asked Jolis, "Would you be willing to volunteer for secret, dangerous work?" "Sure," Jolis said, "if it means getting out of the military police." Not until then did Kollender reveal that he was working with General Donovan, whom President Roosevelt had recently named to head the office of the Coordinator of Information, OSS's original designation. Bert Jolis had not the faintest idea of what the man was talking about.

He returned to Pine Camp, fearing, as the weeks passed, that even this strange opportunity to escape the military police had passed him by. Finally, he was called and sent to Washington, where he met Arthur Goldberg and joined the OSS labor organization. He entered the training course, and remembered, most vividly, planting sea mines on the walls of swimming pools at luxurious estates around Washington.

Jolis followed the common path of labor officers, working for a time with Gary Van Arkel in North Africa, then joining George Pratt's Labor Division in London. He was sent to Paris after the liberation, and there he handled his most significant agent, a man who had little connection with honest labor.

One of Jolis's staff had brought him a White Russian émigré named Youri Vinogradov, a tall, blond, good-looking fellow, in his early twenties, with the slick, ingratiating manner of one raised on the impoverished fringe of polite society. His parents were refugees from the Russian Revolution who had settled in Berlin, where Youri was born and had lived most of his life.

After the liberation of Paris, Youri had managed to get through the lines to the French capital and was supporting himself dealing in the black market. It was there that he offered his services to OSS.

To Jolis, it was all too pat. A young Russian flees Germany for the west professing his anti-Nazism and dangling interesting connections with the SD before American intelligence officials. How, Jolis wondered, had this healthy young fellow spent the war years in Germany without being drafted? How had he slipped through the battle lines to reach Paris? How did he happen to have SD contacts?

Youri presented Jolis with a classic intelligence dilemma. "In all these cases," Jolis noted, "the degree of ideological commitment versus the degree of opportunism of someone who offers to become an agent is extremely difficult to assess. One of the first things you want to know is the motivation. Is he a double? You're never absolutely sure. You have to get to know him as an individual. Time is really the element."

Jolis moved Youri into his villa headquarters outside Paris to observe him and decide if Youri were capable of the audacious stroke he proposed. The Russian had confidently told Jolis that he could penetrate SD headquarters in Berlin. Jolis finally put aside his doubts. "We weren't looking for simon-pure motives; we were looking for someone who could do a specific job." Youri's mission was designated RUPPERT.

Youri was undoubtedly an adventurer and an opportunist. He had come to Paris, Jolis figured, when the invasion of France presaged ultimate Allied victory. But he did possess political sophistication and was a talented conniver. He might make good his boast. The vain Russian was put into army fatigues and reduced to the anonymity of an American GI assigned to the villa while he prepared for his mission.

In the fall of 1944, OSS did not yet have the capability of flying an agent all the way to Berlin. Youri was to be slipped through the lines. He was to use his own identity, but he would have to pretend to be an SD agent in order to get through the German lines. Then, once in Berlin, he would try to lure the SD into offering him genuine employment.

He would claim that he had been caught in Paris by the Allied advance, had been unable to find work, and had gotten into trouble with French authorities as well. He also had a sick mother living in Berlin whom he wanted to rejoin, which was true. But, above all, he had returned to Germany because he was appalled at the upsurge of communism in liberated France. As a White Russian, he feared for his fate, in light of the Soviet partnership with the western Allies, and he had returned to Germany as the only country still sharing his abhorrence of Bolshevism.

Just prior to his departure, Youri demonstrated the sort of cheek which annoyed the OSS staff. He refused to carry large sums of reichsmarks through the German lines. He instead persuaded his superiors to give him gold and silver jewelry, valued at approximately $10,000, to be sewn into the linings of his clothing.

By the fall of 1944, the Seventh Army's rapid advance up the Rhone Valley had mired down about thirty-five miles from the German border in the cold, the mud, and unanticipated stubbornness of Nazi defenders in the Vosges Mountains. Infiltrating an agent had become an intricate *pas de deux*, requiring first that the man pass through the Allied lines, then through the German side.

Bert Jolis and Youri had arrived from Paris on October 31. Jolis had made arrangements with the Seventh Army OSS Detachment to prepare the way for the line crossing. The two men, with a driver and Jack Nyle, the Seventh Army OSS officer who had laid out the plan, left Epinal on November 2, late in the afternoon during a heavy rainfall. As they churned their jeep through the mud, up the twisting roads of the Vosges, Jolis was fascinated by the scene unfolding. They wove through sodden files of American troops moving up to the front, the heavy silence disturbed only by the shouts and curses of MPs directing traffic. Coming down the opposite side of the road, crowded against the hedgerows, was a column of Goums, Berber tribesmen recruited by the French in Morocco, wearing turbans, and rain-soaked capes, riding on horseback or leading mules. To Jolis, the rain, the mud-caked silent men, and bony animals formed a haunting tableau out of World War I. Until that moment it had all been theory. Now he found himself flushed with excitement at taking in his first agent. Youri remained maddeningly unimpressed.

In his report, written four days later, Jolis described his last moments with the Russian as he delivered him into no-man's-land:

> The infiltration point was in the zone of operations of the First French Army. At battalion headquarters, we were stopped by a French guard and told that the enemy had just commenced shelling the road ahead and that no vehicles could proceed farther. We consequently left the car and continued the remaining two miles on foot to the outpost. Parts of the road were under enemy observation and it was necessary for the agent to wear a helmet and a GI overcoat over his civilian clothing. Due to the failing visibility, however, and the pouring rain, there is every reason to suppose that we were not seen by the enemy.
>
> The agent was handed over to the farmer who lived in the first of three farmhouses. It was planned that he spend the night at this first house and make his way at daybreak the following morning via the other two houses to Gérardmer. From there he was to make his way to Saint-Dié.

The farmer let them in without a word. Jolis and Nyle stayed long enough only to take Youri's GI helmet and overcoat. Jolis shook the Russian's hand and briefly embraced him. The Americans left.

At eight o'clock the next morning, Youri set out from the farmhouse. He followed a path toward the German lines until he was challenged by a sentry hidden in a blockhouse. Youri drew out his papers and gave the correct SD password. Then he ordered the soldier to direct him to the nearest intelligence officer. The soldier let him pass and sent him to the company command post.

There, Youri fretted, impatient and overbearing, as the officer in charge apologized for having to search his luggage. His men, he said, had found two Frenchmen crossing the lines the night before by the same route Youri had used. The Germans had discovered radio equipment on the two Frenchmen and had shot them.

Youri refused to tell the officer anything about his activities, insisting that he could not speak with anyone at mere company level. He demanded transportation to division headquarters. Youri set out for Gérardmer with a German Army major and a driver in a staff car. En route, an American artillery shell exploded nearby, mortally wounding the major, but leaving Youri unharmed. At Gérardmer, Youri underwent a routine interrogation by army intelligence officers, and sailed through it.

From Gérardmer, he traveled by train and reported to SD headquarters at Strasbourg. There, during questioning by two SD men, he confronted disaster. They wanted to telephone SD headquarters in Berlin to verify his story.

Youri coolly told them to go ahead, but not to expect to find him in the regular SD register. He worked, he said, for a man named Michel Kedia, like himself an anti-Communist Russian who was connected to the eastern espionage service of the SD. Kedia was, in fact, one of the names that Youri had traded on in selling himself to OSS Paris. The device worked sufficiently to get Youri past the Strasbourg SD office. But he was ordered to report directly to Baden-Baden, where Standartenführer Bichler, the SD chief for Western Europe, wanted to meet him personally.

In Baden-Baden, Youri underwent his first professional grilling. His SD interrogators pressed him, in fine detail, on his journey from Paris—dates, times, places, and means of transportation. He was questioned about the location and movements of Allied units in the area where he had crossed. He was ready for them. Seventh Army officers had provided him with stale but accurate intelligence which he was authorized to divulge to the Germans.

Youri was then presented to the chief, Bichler, and found himself something of a celebrity. He was the first presumed SD man to return since the fall of Paris, and his colleagues were hungry for news of the French capital. He found them tough, smart, realistic men, except on one score: they were willing to swallow virtually anything he told them of the flowering of communism in France now that the protecting bulwark of Nazism had been removed.

Youri remained for three days as a guest of the SD at Baden-Baden, where he was privy to internal SD office gossip which could prove invaluable both to OSS counterintelligence and to himself when he attempted to penetrate the main SD headquarters in Berlin.

Some days after Youri's departure, Gary Van Arkel, in Bern, was scanning a copy of a German daily, the *Berliner Morgenpost.* In the classified section he found an ad for a furnished room. The phone number given was 66–87–46. Van Arkel went to his files and compared the number with one he had been given. He went immediately to the communications office and had a message sent to Bert Jolis in Paris. It had worked. Youri was safely in Berlin. The ad had appeared on November 7, five days after Jolis had left the Russian in the farmhouse near Gérardmer.

The Seventh Army OSS Detachment that had arranged to put Youri through the lines was a curious amalgam. Its people epitomized the privileged centers of American life from which OSS drew heavily for its staff—the grandson of a tycoon, the son of a distinguished motion-picture director, the scion of a wine fortune, a daughter of the Philadelphia Main Line. Yet the Seventh Army Detachment operated not out of London town houses but within earshot of roaring artillery and moved with the troops close behind the lines. Its members drank cheap apéritifs in obscure mountain villages in the Vosges, then might take over the wine cellar of a splendid château. The detachment recruited its agents not from anti-Nazi intellectuals and expatriate social theoreticians in Bern or London, but from the ranks of disaffected German soldiers in grim prisoner-of-war cages in places like Sarreguemines and Nancy.

OSS had other units attached to armies in the field. Largely ineffectual detachments served with the Third and Ninth armies. The First Army had thrown out its OSS detachment soon after D day and had later been caught by surprise at the outbreak of the Battle of the Bulge. Only the OSS unit attached to the U.S. Seventh Army enjoyed genuine standing in the field, a reputation won largely through its meticulous inventory of Nazi defenses in advance of the invasion of southern France.

The Seventh Army drive from the Riviera beaches to a junction with the Third Army at Epinal had moved in two stages. The first six weeks witnessed a headlong gallop 270 miles deep into occupied France within six weeks. On September 21, the Moselle was crossed, barely 50 miles from the German border. In the second phase, the backs of the Germans stiffened, the Allied advance stalled, and the opposing lines hardened.

As weeks of stalemate stretched into months, the commander of the Seventh Army, Lieutenant General Alexander Patch, turned to one of the authors of the intelligence triumph that had paved the invasion of southern France, the OSS detachment's SI chief, Henry Hyde. Hyde, then barely thirty, balding, looking older, was an expatriate American who hardly knew the United States until he entered Harvard Law School at the age of twenty. Hyde's grandfather had amassed a fortune as founder of the Equitable Life Assurance Society of the United States. When the U.S. government launched a potentially embarrassing investigation of his business holdings, Hyde's father had elected an elegant exile in France. There, in Paris, Henry Hyde was born. Until Harvard, he had been educated in the public schools of England and grew up a thorough cosmopolitan in outlook and style. His speech was a curious meld of upper-class American with British mannerisms ("Dear boy") and studded with a clearly enunciated profanity.

Hyde was electric, testy, high-strung, exacting, and worshipped by his staff. There was little malice in his flashes of temper, only impatience with minds that did not race along with his own. His fits of pique were mercifully brief and partly calculated, since Henry Hyde was a talented performer.

He was a hotly competitive man as well, and able to infuse his people with a fierce sense of "us" against "them." Hyde was perpetually jousting against pig-headed regular army officers, uncooperative air force people, resentful G-2 intelligence rivals, and know-it-alls from the OSS front office in London.

His searing criticisms were, however, kept within hearing of his own people, uniting them further in their sense of superiority against the fumbling world outside. In his personal dealings with that other world, Hyde was the consummate politician, matching his performance to the target to be wooed, down-to-earth where it helped, sophisticated where it mattered, and capable of devastating charm. When he wanted to persuade, a faint smile played across his lips, making his listener an accomplice in their delicious secret. Working with Henry Hyde, for all his petulance and impatience, was, his staff found, great fun.

General Patch called Hyde to his headquarters in November 1944 and wanted to know why the Seventh Army was no longer getting the kind of intelligence that had eased its march into France. OSS seemed to have dried up. What, Patch wanted to know, had happened?

The honest answer was that Hyde had run out of agents. The Frenchmen who had served so well in infiltrating their homeland were mostly unsuited to penetrate Germany and secure the deep tactical intelligence that Patch and his commanders expected. But, in Patch's complaint,

Hyde saw a faint shaft of hope for a long-contemplated scheme. He seized the moment.

"General, it's getting very difficult. This place is empty. The Alsatians don't have the right accents. We don't have good papers or cover stories for them. And the Nazis have sent all able-bodied men to work in Germany. There's no one left but old men, women, and children." Then Hyde played his hole card. "We could try to use some German POWs." A few weeks before, Hyde had met Allen Dulles in France and the OSS Switzerland chief had made an intriguing point: "You know, there is an awful lot of dissidence among the Germans. You fellows ought to be taking advantage of it."

Using POWs as agents was then expressly forbidden by SHAEF, and the prohibition against recruiting German soldiers had been rigorously respected by the British. Canvassing potential spies among POWs was questionable as well under the Geneva Convention.

Patch was nothing if not practical. He told Hyde to go ahead and use prisoners of war. Hyde reminded him of the SHAEF prohibition. Patch asked who was the key to evading this obstacle. "General Donovan," Hyde informed him.

Hyde flew to London to meet Donovan and to perform the kind of Jesuitry which was second nature to him. Before his departure, Patch had said, restraining a wink, that if Hyde could not follow his orders, then he was finished with the Seventh Army. General Donovan conveniently agreed that Hyde had no choice but to follow his field commander's dictum; therefore, Donovan's hands were clean. The SHAEF prohibition on using POWs was thus quietly sidestepped. On his return, Hyde informed his people that their objective now lay across the Rhine. Recruiting began immediately.

Hyde had on his staff three fluent German-speaking Americans to do the canvassing. Peter Viertel, the son of a Hollywood director, was a brash fellow with an appetite for adventure which had drawn him first into the Marine Corps, then to OSS. Viertel had been raised in the Babylonian Hollywood of the thirties, where his female companions had been leading film stars. By age twenty-four Viertel was wise beyond his years.

A second occasional recruiter was the unit's finance officer, Peter Sichel, from a family of noted German wine merchants. The Sichels had simply walked away from their properties as the fate of the Jews remaining in Germany became obvious. Sichel had been educated in England and spoke a clipped, elegant English, laced with occasional distracting Teutonisms. In 1941, the family had gone to live in the United States.

The third recruiting officer, Carl Muecke, though American-born, had a good command of German learned from parents who had emigrated from the old country.

The three men worked the receiving cages through which freshly captured prisoners were funneled, rather than permanent camps, where the POWs' identities and associations had already become fixed. What first struck the Americans on entering the cages was the physical contrast—the Germans, on the whole, were shorter and much blonder than Americans. Sullenness usually pervaded the camps, reflecting resignation among most of the men and a glowering defiance from a few, particularly SS troops. The prisoners tended to cluster together, army and Luftwaffe men together, preferring their own company, both avoiding the SS.

OSS had army intelligence officers screen potential agent material. The clues often came unexpectedly. A prisoner might drop a hint to the doctor at sick call. Another might whisper to a mess-hall guard that he had something important to reveal. The camp staff had been alerted to recognize these signals.

Hyde's German-speaking officers could sometimes provoke anti-Nazis into revealing themselves. One of them would strike up a casual conversation and profess grudging admiration for Hitler, then wait to see who disagreed. A quick litmus test was to ask which prisoners had served in punishment battalions. They would screen from this group the genuine misfits and concentrate on political offenders. Peter Sichel, gregarious and open-mannered, had a particular advantage. He was a gifted mimic with a good ear and able to imitate regional German dialects and accents. Sichel established easy rapport with the prisoners.

Potential recruits were called out, always in work details, never singly. Then a prospect would be peeled off from the work party and shunted to a cubicle where the Americans worked on him.

The candidates fell roughly into three classes: the young, the old, and opportunists of all ages. Younger recruits were usually Germans of good middle-class families—reluctant, last-minute conscripts into the Wehrmacht who shared their parents' scorn of Hitler. The older prisoners who might turn were frequently Socialists from the industrial areas who had been squeezed out in the last wringing of Germany's manpower reserves.

Even sheer opportunists could be valuable, provided they stayed bought. The recruiters dangled prospects of lucrative business deals before them—a good job after the war or, the most powerful lure, the possibility of emigrating to the United States.

For those more nobly motivated, the problem was to help them overcome the odium of treachery. These Germans had pledged, on entering the armed forces: "I swear before God to give my unconditional obedience to Adolf Hitler, Führer of the Reich and of the German People, Supreme Commander of the *Wehrmacht,* and I pledge my word as a brave soldier to observe this oath always, even at peril of my life." The recruiters had to offer a bridge of honorable rationalization for these men to cross over to the other side.

The Americans began by arguing that their cause was lost. "If you really want to do something for the Fatherland, you will help end this war. The longer it goes on, the more cities will be destroyed, the more lives will be wasted. If you are truly a good German, you will help us to shorten the war."

Henry Hyde could be marvelously persuasive with the more promising candidates brought to him. Before seeing a prisoner, Hyde would absorb the usable elements of the man's background. He would learn about wives, children, politics, and vanities.

He then gazed intently into a man's eyes with that knowing smile playing across his lips. "We have a common enemy. This crazy Hitler, he's going to bring destruction on your homes, your families. He is going to cause more people to be killed. He's a mad dog. We need to get rid of this fellow and get on with the business of rebuilding Germany."

Hyde anticipated their objections. If they feared retribution, he promised that they would operate far from their home cities. Or, he would "disinfect" them after the war by getting them resettled in a new area.

Even through an interpreter, Hyde could mesmerize. "Look, the jig is up. You know it. We know it. But Hitler won't quit. He'll go down in some *Walpurgisnacht.*" It was not treachery. It was sanity and a sensible patriotism that the Americans were preaching.

For all the embellishment, the arguments were elemental: You want to get out of the POW cage? You want to eat better? You want adventure? You want a job after the war? You want to go to America? Here is a way.

Carl Muecke sometimes wondered if the recruiters' most persuasive argument was not simply Teutonic worship of authority. These Americans were the new masters, and a good German was obedient. Muecke had once gone into a cage to collect documents for agent cover. He stood on a jeep before ten thousand prisoners and spoke to them through a loudspeaker. He told the prisoners that he wanted them to turn in their leave and hospital passes, travel permits, and ration coupons. One soldier objected. "Under the Geneva Convention we don't have to give these things to you." A dozen other men jumped to their feet and shouted the man down. "Be quiet. Can't you see, an officer is speaking?"

The Americans had not, in fact, concerned themselves much with the fine points of the Geneva Convention. Seventh Army officers looked the other way and erased any trace of a prisoner having been in their custody by turning over to OSS all agent records if a man was chosen as a possible agent.

Prisoners selected were blindfolded and driven to a safe house. There, they signed a contract and personally saw it locked in a safe. The storing of the contract was as if the man had filed away his true identity. Thereafter, he was known only by his code name.

After the inducements and appeals to conscience, Henry Hyde sealed the bargain with a practical enforcement clause. The Allies were obviously going to win the war. If the German agents doubled, the Americans would get them in the end, or get their wives or children. They believed him. They had no reason to expect that the Americans would behave any differently than their own.

Spies, like baseball players, movie stars, and authors, signed written contracts, at least under OSS procedures. Early in the war, arrangements had been less formal. Those recruited at the beginning of the Italian campaign, for example, had bound themselves to a contract devised by an officer of poetic bent: "This contract will continue in force until the Allies have sighted the top of the Alps."

But as experience with agents raised unanticipated questions of legal responsibility, OSS lawyers sought to bring uniformity and fairness to the terms of employment. A contract could avoid conflicts and misunderstandings. What, for instance, was the obligation to a family in the event of an agent's death? How were claims to be adjudicated? How were primary OSS agents to be treated, as contrasted to subagents whom primary agents enlisted after they landed behind the lines? OSS lawyers eventually worked out standard language:

> Between agent and the Government of the United States which witnesseth: That employer shall pay employee the sum of ＿＿ dollars each month while said contract is in force; that employee shall faithfully perform all duties which may be assigned to him by the employer; that employee further agrees a) to subscribe freely and without reservation to any oath of office prescribed by employer and b) to keep forever secret his employment and all information which he may obtain by reason there-

of, and further, that this contract is a voluntary act of employee undertaken without duress. . . .

The contract was usually made out in the agent's pseudonym. Most recruits preferred not to have their own names recorded. If they were French, for example, the Gaullist faction took the position that anyone who worked for a foreign intelligence service was, automatically, a traitor to France.

German agents were naturally leery of having the fact recorded that they had contrived against their own nation. But if a German agent was killed on a mission, how was the beneficiary to be paid without revealing the agent's association with U.S. intelligence? The solution was to list as the beneficiary some imaginary relative living in the United States who presumably had died and left the money to the family in Germany. The amount of the death benefit had been computed for OSS by the U.S. Employees' Compensation Commission based on comparable benefits for government employees.

In the end, the contract was no more than a gentlemen's agreement. A contract agreed to by a German citizen and the government of the United States in a POW cage in France raised serious questions of jurisdiction. The contracts were probably not enforceable in any court of law.

To those who saw the function of intelligence not only as a wartime exigency but as a permanent game of nations, these files identifying people who had secretly collaborated with the United States could have interesting uses extending well beyond this war.

The man responsible for cover stories and documentation for Seventh Army missions was George Howe, a handsome and urbane architect of middle age, with an almost fanatic commitment to his work. Howe seemed to take childlike delight in this late-blooming career in professional deception. His lively imagination in devising covers was aided by an unusually qualified POW. Under Howe was a Wehrmacht battalion adjutant, a former lawyer from Dresden, who was doing for the Americans the same thing that he had done in the German Army: seeing that a man's papers were in order.

A German soldier, Howe learned, had to have a credible answer to simple but critical questions: "Where are you coming from? Where did you spend last night? Where are you going?" They were obvious; yet lack of an acceptable response could prove disastrous. An agent's papers would be frequently checked, since he was always supposedly in a travel status to give him maximum mobility. A soldier in transit had to have his papers verified every day.

The initial efforts by Hyde's unit to use German POWs as agents were a disaster. These missions had been modest exercises in tactical espionage. Agents in German uniform, carrying phony leave papers, usually for a death in the family or a brief hospital stay for venereal disease, were to slip a few miles behind the lines, then return, reporting the location of artillery, tank parks, and ammunition dumps. To facilitate their movement through the lines, their papers usually identified them as members of units known to be facing the Americans.

The agent confronted German land mines and machine-gun nests on the way out and American defenses on the way back. Of twenty-one line crossings attempted in January and February of 1945, only ten succeeded in getting through. Mines took a particularly heavy toll of the rest.

If anything, the agent's return through the American units was more unnerving than crossing the German lines. German soldiers were willing to wait long enough to distinguish a cow from an enemy. The Americans, with no shortage of ammunition, tended to fire at anything that moved.

OSS officers also faced an exasperating thickheadedness about clandestine operations among the conventional troops. Peter Viertel would bring agents up to the line and ask for the infantry's help in infiltrating them. "You want us to walk a Kraut through a minefield?"

Viertel had tried to put one agent through who was hit before reaching the German lines. The man was suffering excruciating pain from a severed nerve when Viertel brought him back to an aid station. He pleaded with several army doctors not to leave the suffering man in agony at the end of the line. The only sympathetic doctor, a Jew, asked Viertel why the man had gone on the mission. He was anti-Nazi, Viertel said. The doctor gave the wounded agent a shot of morphine.

Viertel eventually designed, with Henry Hyde, a system for cutting in half the danger of line crossings. They called the new scheme "tourist" missions. The agent would parachute fifty to sixty miles behind the lines, then follow an itinerary of points of interest to the army. On completing the tour, usually timed for a week to ten days, the agent would make his way back through the lines. Twenty of the first thirty-one tourist missions were successful.

It was not the stuff of espionage melodrama. They did not plot the assassination of tyrants or filch secrets from a cabinet minister's safe.

What they reported mostly were numbers: map coordinates signifying where bombs and shells should be dropped to destroy concentrations of the enemy's tanks, aircraft, and troops.

An agent code-named "Vacuum" completed a typical tourist mission. Vacuum was dropped in Bavaria and began a nine-day journey which took him to Munich, Ulm, Stuttgart, Pforzheim, then back through the American lines. He filed a report which included this observation:

> On the north side of the RR line MUNICH-STRAUBING agent saw a single continuous underground factory 12 kms long extending from a point at (map coordinate) Y-711581 west to a point at (map coordinate) Y-624588 between the road and the RR tracks. Six individual bunker entrances set at 2 km intervals . . . tracks join the entrances to the main RR line . . . agent was told by a Salzburg Hauptquartier employee that the factory was used for manufacture of poison gas, and V-1 type shells as containers for the gas. Name of the gas is "Influensia Inzitus Eukalyptus." It was said at Hauptquartier that Hitler would use gas at the time of the last great breakthrough.

Vacuum's report was then distributed to ground and air forces for appropriate exploitation.

VIII

A Dentist with a Mission

✠ ✠ ✠

There was on the outskirts of the drab Adriatic port of Bari a villa which in palmier days had some small claim to elegance. Now, in the summer of 1944, Villa Suppa presented a weary, seamed face to the world. This former residence of an Italian general named Suppa had about it the same wan indifference of Italy in this fifth year of the war. The Villa Suppa nevertheless met the needs of the 2677th OSS Regiment—numerous rooms, some land, and a surrounding wall.

Just before the invasion of Italy, General Donovan had suggested to General Mark Clark that some of his OSS people in the Mediterranean be assigned as an integral unit of Clark's Fifth Army. Thus, the 2677th OSS Regiment came into being in July 1944. The unusual designation of "regiment" for an intelligence unit testified to the acceptance this OSS staff had won from Clark's forces. When Allied Forces Headquarters relocated from Algiers to Caserta, the 2677th Regiment moved there as well and established a field office at Bari.

The intransigence which the Germans were demonstrating on the western front hardly surprised the Allied armies in Italy, where the enemy had yielded every inch grudgingly. During the Italian campaign, OSS had infiltrated hundreds of agents into enemy-held territory to nourish Italian partisans. Now, attention shifted farther north to Austria, the southern boundary of the Reich and the expected locus of the National Redoubt. It was from Bari that OSS launched another intelligence invasion of the Third Reich.

The German-Austrian section at Bari was initially headed by Major John B. McCulloch, a wealthy, pleasant man, educated at Oxford, who before the war had edited a learned journal on Latin America for the Foreign Policy Association. McCulloch spoke German, Spanish, and French. He was a likable fellow and an indifferent commander, his junior officers thought.

McCulloch enjoyed recruiting for the opportunity it gave him to exercise his German and his amiability among initially cowed and suspicious prisoners of war. He left chores like shaking down prisoners for personal items and clothing to the lesser ranks in the camps they scoured from Aversa to Leghorn. McCulloch would take a list of likely candidates provided by G-2 and engage them in disarming small talk. In one camp, McCulloch had been tipped off that a certain Wehrmacht officer might be useful for his high-level connections in German society. On interrogation, the man unapologetically affirmed his Nazism. McCulloch played another card. He showed the German a newsclip reporting that the man's uncle, a distinguished figure in Germany, had been arrested in the aftermath of the July twentieth plot against Hitler. The man thought deeply, then announced, "I *was* a Nazi."

McCulloch was aided in the recruiting by two German-American refugees from Nazism, Dyno Lowenstein and Walter Haass. Lowenstein's father had been a school superintendent in Germany and a fervent Social Democrat. The family had made the refugee odyssey—first to Czechoslovakia, then to France, ultimately to the United States via Martinique. The Lowensteins had been admitted to the United States through the intercession of American trade unions. In America, Dyno Lowenstein met Arthur Goldberg before being drafted into the army and believed Goldberg was responsible for his ultimate transfer to OSS.

Walter Haass had fought against the Nazis from his early teens, helping his father spirit refugees out of Germany. He too had become an American citizen through the U.S. Army after the family emigrated to America.

Lowenstein and Haass made an effective pair in the POW cages. Lowenstein's manner was classic European intellectual, down to the cigarette held between thumb and index finger in an upturned hand. He had a lean face and lank black hair, was slender, and spoke with habitual grace. Haass was a short, powerful man with a thick neck, and a broad, flat face capable of a menacing aspect.

They had perfected a classic station-house technique. They entered the cages posing as American counterintelligence officers looking for German spies. Lowenstein played the "police commissioner," cultivated, soft-spoken, understanding, calmly pointing out the rewards of cooperation and the folly of stubbornness. Haass loomed threateningly in the background, the "second-grade detective," moving in with blunt, jarring interrogatories, when the gentle Lowenstein, his patience exhausted, would throw up his hands in despair.

Some prisoners were quick to protest their innocence. They could not possibly be German spies because, they said, they opposed the Nazi regime. The two Americans now had an opening. They would ask a professed anti-Nazi prisoner more about his political beliefs, his family background, and any run-ins he might have had with the Nazis. They would ask if any fellow prisoners shared his sympathies.

An approach which Lowenstein found particularly effective and which he played with total conviction was to ask in a softly chilling voice, "Do you know what you did to my people?" This approach offered an irresistible opening for anti-Nazi confessionals.

OSS Bari found a serviceable, if awkward, label for prospective agents drawn from prisoner cages. They were officially "Deserter-Volunteers," and soon, simply, DVs. In the fall of 1944 in Bari, DVs were assigned to two villas, with twenty usually assigned to the Villa Suppa and others to the neighboring Villa Pasqua. The compounds were guarded by an implausibly hybrid gendarmerie—sometimes Americans, sometimes Italians, and at one point by Chinese seamen who had been stranded at Bari.

Within the post, the agents in training wore GI fatigues and were kept from contact with American personnel other than OSS. The day was long and the training rigorous. Parachute training was a compound of anxiety and exhilaration. Word of jumping accidents inevitably filtered through to the trainees. One which cast particular gloom over the camp involved an agent flown to the north of Italy. The man's lines had become entangled on leaving the plane, and he had been pounded to death on the bottom of the fuselage. The apocryphal story, which inevitably made the rounds, was of the agent so nervous that he had jumped without first hooking up his static line.

For recreation, DVs occasionally were taken into town for dinner or the opera. Women were supposedly out-of-bounds for agents in training, a rule which was occasionally blinked at by tolerant chaperons.

The atmosphere at Bari was a curiously strained informality. The secret nature of the operations, the intimate daily association of a relatively small group made strict military deportment impractical. The deserters were told by their American officers, "Just call me Al" or "John." It was not an easy transition for German Army veterans accustomed to the class striations of European society and the tight caste structure of the Wehrmacht.

The officer cadet was slim and straight, blue-eyed, with thick sandy hair brushed straight back from a studiously earnest face. "Sergeant, I want to scout the American lines." The rumpled noncom eyed this seeming paragon of Hitler Youth with weary tolerance and waved in the direction of nearby foothills.

The cadet had arrived at the front with a draft of replacements on January 7, 1944, at San Vittorio, near Cassino. The new men had been briefed immediately on the position of the opposing armies. German forces, the map showed, occupied the hill country. The Americans held the lower ground to the south.

After a half hour's brisk walk, the cadet cleared the German lines and entered a hilly no-man's-land. He swung his rifle from his shoulder and pitched it into the brush. He kept walking for another hour until he saw below him a cluster of deep-green tents, shadowed by the late-afternoon sun. He could see no one around them. He approached the nearest tent and stood before it, breathing slowly and deeply before pulling the tent flap aside. Inside, four American soldiers dozed. He tugged at a blanket. The man who was curled under it raised his head and stared at him vacantly.

"I am Austrian." His English was excellent, only lightly accented. "I want to help you."

Within two hours of arriving at the front, Ernst Ebbing had accomplished his sole ambition since becoming a soldier of the Third Reich. He had deserted at the first opportunity.

Young Ebbing had been raised in a Viennese Catholic family. His father, a lawyer and a rabid anti-Nazi, had been a member of the Austrian "Fatherland Front," a nationalist coalition. Ebbing senior was also a personal friend of the murdered Austrian chancellor, Engelbert Dolfuss. The father had served ten months in a Nazi prison for political dissidence, which, however, had not saved him from being drafted into the Luftwaffe, where he was commissioned a captain in communications.

In December 1942, Ernst Ebbing was also drafted into the German Army. Ebbing had originally been assigned choice duty in Vienna with the signal corps. He proved a gifted malingerer, feigning illness, getting himself hospitalized, rubbing thermometers to raise the readings to fever level. His evasions eventually earned him a transfer to the infantry. While young Ebbing awaited assignment to a combat zone, his father used his connections to have the son sent to the Italian rather than the Russian front.

OSS quickly plucked Ebbing from the prisoner-of-war cage at Aversa after his desertion and assigned him to Morale and Operations, the propaganda unit. Ebbing's knowledge of English and his flair for writing made him a useful recruit for psychological warfare. He wrote propaganda leaflets and occasionally took on more daring assignments. Dressed again in German uniform, he would slip through the lines to circulate phony proclamations in the name of various German officers ordering all units under their command to surrender.

Ebbing was rescued from the silly-tricks department in May 1944 by Major John McCulloch. McCulloch offered Ebbing the opportunity he had long sought: to strike a serious blow against the Nazis. Ebbing was quite willing, if necessary, to forfeit his life in the process. At Bari, he was to meet an American who was equally willing to give him that chance, John Hedrick Taylor, a navy lieutenant.

Jack Taylor was a thirty-three-year-old orthodontist practicing in California when America entered the war. Taylor's Los Angeles home provided a marvelous vista of the Pacific, and the sea had a far firmer hold on Jack Taylor than the meticulous dentistry which he performed. Jack Taylor's passion was not simply the sea but any natural frontier against which he could pit his strength and will. He had navigated in five Honolulu yacht races and two to Bermuda. He was a licensed pilot. During an expedition to the Yukon, he had been trapped for two days in a gold mine after an earthquake struck. Between adventures, Jack Taylor prescribed retainers and installed braces.

When the war came along, Taylor rejected an assured commission in the medical corps and became a naval officer aboard a sub-chaser. OSS needed men who knew small boats, who could navigate unknown coastlines in the night, and slip ashore into enemy-held lands. The intelligence agency acquired Jack Taylor from the navy and made him an instructor in boat-handling, navigation, seamanship, and underwater demolition at a school operated on the Potomac River, near Washington, D.C.

Taylor was a tall man with short-cropped light-brown hair and impassive good looks. His students remembered him as all business with little use for amenities. Few students or associates knew that this laconic expert on marine warfare had been a dentist briefly before. Indeed, they knew little of Taylor at all, since he took no part in their life after-hours.

From the moment he learned of the DUPONT Mission scheduled for the fall of 1944, Lieutenant Alfred C. Ulmer, Jr., of the Bari Austrian-German section, viewed it with profound skepticism. Four men, one American and three Austrian DVs, were to parachute near the industrial city of Wiener Neustadt, about twenty-five miles south of Vienna. Here was located a major nexus of the German transportation system supplying the Italian front and the Rax Werke, a key German aviation plant. Here, as well, the Germans were said to be constructing a major barrier against an Allied advance from the south, the Southeast Wall.

The Allies might be able to marshal a resistance movement around Wiener Neustadt from among the many anti-Naxi Austrians believed to live in the area. American military forces had not one source of intelligence from this region of the Reich. Successful penetration of Wiener Neustadt and the surrounding country could yield an intelligence harvest. Yet, observing the men and the plan, Lieutenant Ulmer doubted that the DUPONT Mission was the answer.

Ulmer was a twenty-eight-year-old Floridian, a former reporter and advertising executive. He seemed to the European agents a recruiting-poster American with his fresh-faced, boyish manner. He also possessed, they learned quickly, a tough, quick mind and a deadly seriousness about his work.

Since his arrival in Bari, Ulmer had felt uneasy about the leadership of the German-Austrian section in which he initially served as second in command. To Ulmer, the section seemed to be "learning on company time." The planning of the DUPONT Mission confirmed his fears. Preparations for the mission appeared casual at best. DUPONT suffered an even deeper flaw not immediately visible. Ideally, members of a team operating in enemy territory should possess a mutual affinity described as "a good marriage." The Austrian members of DUPONT did not particularly like each other. One of the three was Ernst Ebbing, who had deserted nine months before at San Vittorio. Leading the mission was Lieutenant Jack Taylor, the erstwhile dentist.

On a trip to POW Camp 326 at Aversa, Major John McCulloch selected the two men who would join Ebbing and Lieutenant Taylor on DUPONT. McCulloch had driven over from Bari and had made an encouraging catch. Of over one hundred prospects interviewed, he had chosen seventeen as potential agent material. As they drove the twisting, rutted road from Aversa back to Bari, a thought struck him. The Germans had all been screened; still, only his driver's M-1 stood between the two Americans and seventeen recent members of the Wehrmacht riding in the back of an open truck.

Ernst Ebbing disliked the two Austrians immediately. In his Europe, where such things mattered deeply, they were of another class. One of the new recruits was a genial, twenty-three-year-old, dark-haired, brawny former stonemason named Felix Huppmann, from the tiny village of Saint Margarethen, conveniently situated near their drop point. His family were anti-Nazi Social Democrats, though Huppmann himself lacked political sophistication. He had the equivalent of a grammar-school education, concluded at age fourteen. He also had a strong and undiscriminating sexual appetite. Huppmann had been a parachutist when he deserted in May 1944. He had talked a woman in Perugia into getting him a set of civilian clothes and had eventually worked his way south into American hands.

The other Austrian recruited by McCulloch was Anton Graf, a corporal in the Luftwaffe. During the interrogation, Graf described himself as a former medical student in Prague and a qualified pilot with six hundred hours of flying time. He gave his citizenship as Austrian, though he regarded himself essentially as a Czech. Graf said he had been married in April 1944, one week before departing for the Italian front, where he had deserted on July 1. Major McCulloch had found the voluble Graf, an Aryan prototype with lank blond hair and gray eyes, a marvelously promising prospect.

Though Graf claimed to have been a university man and said his father served as a director for a glassworks in the Sudetenland, Ebbing still lumped him, with Huppmann, among the proletariat. Ebbing may have been unaware of Graf's background. Or, Graf's story may have been imaginative, for Ebbing suspected early that Graf had a problem distinguishing the truth from his own inventions. Graf was also a man of volatile moods, confident and euphoric one moment, morose and whining the next. As for the stonemason, Huppmann, Ebbing found him irresponsible, rash, and maybe a little insane.

Ebbing's trust rested in Jack Taylor. He stood in awe of this quiet, confident American from the far-off golden shores of California. He felt secure in the strength which Taylor radiated. Ebbing had also learned, through the Bari grapevine, that Taylor was one of OSS's most experienced officers in operating behind the lines. The Californian had completed fifteen sorties into Corfu, Yugoslavia, and Albania. He had recently survived, alone, for forty-five days on an enemy island off the Albanian coast.

Ebbing especially enjoyed the knowledge that he outranked the other two Austrians, at least in Taylor's esteem. So it seemed, since Taylor kept Ebbing constantly at his side during the preparations for the DUPONT Mission. His closeness to Taylor may also have been explained by the fact that Ebbing was the only one of the three Austrians who spoke fluent English, while Taylor, who would soon parachute into the Reich, spoke no German at all.

In daily relations, Taylor seemed to treat all three members of his team with as much warmth as his muted character permitted. Ebbing sometimes wondered if this silent American had any real grasp of the oddly mated Middle European personalities he had inherited. But Ebbing kept his questions to himself.

Not everyone at Bari shared Ernst Ebbing's unalloyed worship of Jack Taylor. Captain George Vujnovich, the Bari unit's air operations officer, recalled a perpetually tense man with a remoteness in his eyes, forever flicking his tongue over dry lips. Taylor, to him, was a humorless loner, forever disciplining an inner impulsiveness through stony self-control. The man, he noted, said little, but when he did speak, it was with excessive intensity.

Captain Rob Thompson, who had worked with Taylor on Yugoslavian missions before he was eventually transferred to DIP in London, saw him as a daredevil bent on having his own show, the more hazardous the better, a man impatient with the painstaking preparations a well-executed mission demanded and a hip shooter inclined to action for action's sake. Another OSS officer who had briefly known Taylor was John Hamilton, who ran guns across the Adriatic to Yugoslav partisans. Hamilton, better known in peacetime as the actor Sterling Hayden, had found Jack Taylor "an oddly chilling guy."

Al Ulmer questioned whether this taciturn figure possessed that touch of the con man so valuable in clandestine life. Ulmer confided to Taylor, as candidly as tact permitted, his misgivings about the DUPONT Mission. Taylor countered with a terse recital of his extensive experience behind the lines. Ulmer did not press the point that Taylor's earlier efforts had produced little useful intelligence, and that the last time out he had had to be rescued from the islet off Albania where he had become stranded.

Ulmer also raised the question of the language barrier. His ignorance of German did not trouble Taylor at all. The presence of an American was what mattered. His simply being there would keep the other agents from melting into the environment, using OSS, in effect, for a free ride home. The presence of an American officer was also of vital importance to impress anti-Nazis and to encourage the formation of resistance groups. But Taylor's strongest argument for pressing on with DUPONT was simply, "I was promised this mission and I want it."

Ernst Ebbing was an implacable anti-Nazi and independent enough to act on his convictions. He was also young, just twenty, and the product of an authoritarian society. Otherwise, he might have voiced his own reservations about DUPONT with more force. It was heady experience for a common soldier, a recent prisoner of war, to sit with American officers and plot a bold gambit against the Nazis, especially exhilarating when the two other DUPONT Austrians were excluded from these strategy sessions. When asked his views, Ebbing would quietly state the advantages of a drop into partisan-held territory, rather than deep into Austria. Such a drop, say, on the northern Yugoslavian border, would still allow them to slip into Austria. Yugoslavia would also provide a base of partisan support and a sanctuary to which they could withdraw. But Ebbing did not express his views with great force.

Instead, they were to drop into a desolate marshland on the eastern edge of the Neusiedlersee, a vast lake about thirty-five miles southeast of Vienna. They would land blind, counting only on Huppmann's unsuspecting family and a few other untested contacts to give them refuge.

The DUPONT plan's chief advocate was a middle-aged OSS civilian who had served in Austria with the Hoover Commission after World War I. On the basis of this experience, over twenty years before, the man had arrogated to himself all expertise on Austria. Ebbing endured the man's inanities quietly. No one else seriously questioned him, certainly not Jack Taylor, who displayed only a testy impatience to get on with the mission.

Yet for reasons incomprehensible to his Austrian team, Taylor reacted angrily when the mission was finally scheduled. He argued with unaccustomed passion for a new date. But the next moon period was too far off. Reluctantly, Taylor accepted that the DUPONT Mission would depart for the Reich on Friday, October 13, 1944.

The order was clear. No OSS officers, except for crewmen, were to accompany agents on flights to their destination. The rule was designed expressly to prevent men with the kind of knowledge which John McCulloch possessed from falling into enemy hands. But, at least, McCulloch intended to accompany the DUPONT team on the drive from Bari to the airfield at Brindisi. He owed Jack Taylor that much. McCulloch had become fond of this quiet man, and now Taylor was about to parachute deep into enemy territory with three strangers. In Bari, betting odds that the DUPONT team would survive were one in ten.

Just before their departure, the three Austrians signed the last piece of paperwork. The form read: "In the event of my death, I hereby appoint as beneficiary of any payments due me by the Office of Strategic Services the following person _____." They were then issued money for the mission. Taylor received 200 gold napoleons, $200 in American money, 100 Swiss francs, and 10,000 reichsmarks. The three Austrians each received 5 gold napoleons and 1000 reichsmarks. The reichsmark, valued at 40 cents well into the war, had declined with Germany's military fortunes, and was now rated by the OSS at 10 to the dollar.

They rode in heavy silence through the Italian countryside in the back of a battered army six-wheeler, the three Austrians staring blankly ahead. At Brindisi, they pulled up to a shack near the airstrip where they ate a hasty meal in continuing silence. The air-crew dispatcher then hauled out their parachutes and jump suits.

Jack Taylor was wearing a rarely used brown navy officer's uniform designed for ground combat. With it he wore a black tie and a small silver insignia pinned through one collar tab. To Europeans, his garb might pass for rather odd-looking work clothes. Technically, his clothing met the uniform requirements of the Geneva Convention classifying him as a combatant rather than a spy.

The Austrians took off their GI fatigues and put on Wehrmacht uniforms under their jump suits. The dispatcher then helped them strap on their parachutes. They made their way to an RAF aircraft, where Taylor was relieved to find that the Polish pilot spoke reasonably good English. But Taylor was alarmed by the Pole's total ignorance of the unusual demands of the DUPONT Mission. He eyed Taylor with amused disbelief as the American explained that no signal lights on the ground would lead the plane to the drop point. Jump procedure was also to be reversed. Usually, agents dropped first. Then, as the plane circled above, the men on the ground would prepare to receive the parachutes with their equipment containers on a subsequent run. But, on this mission, Taylor explained, there would be only one run. The agents would jump from the doorway, while three chutes bearing the equipment would be dropped, simultaneously, from the bomb bay. Two of the containers had duplicate radio equipment. The third held the rest of their supplies. Above all,

Taylor insisted, the aircraft was not to circle. One run. One drop. No more. The entire approach was to be compressed into the briefest possible time to minimize opportunities for the enemy to spot them.

They boarded the plane and slowly lowered themselves with backs braced against the fuselage. Taylor looked up to see John McCulloch pulling himself through the doorway. Though it was against regulations, McCulloch had asked the British flight dispatcher if he might go along as an observer. "By all means, go, old man," the Britisher had agreed. He sat down next to Taylor and the two men smiled at each other. The pilot came back from the cockpit and warned McCulloch that he had no extra parachute for him. That did not matter, McCulloch assured him. If anything happened to the aircraft, he did not intend to be taken alive. At 7:15 P.M. the plane was airborne.

Almost as soon as they were aloft, Ernst Ebbing discovered that he had left his gold pieces in his GI uniform back at Brindisi. Major McCulloch waved the problem aside with fatherly forbearance. He would pick up Ebbing's napoleons on the return trip.

The low moan of engines was the only sound in the back of the plane, broken occasionally by the crackle of Polish over the intercom. Graf and Huppmann remained locked in silence. Taylor lost himself in studying their maps.

At 10:15 P.M. a red light flashed overhead and the dispatcher yanked a plywood cover off the jump hole. McCulloch quickly shook each man's hand and backed out of the way. The agents pulled themselves to their feet. Taylor settled himself on the rim of the hole. Below, he saw patches of fog floating across the glistening black surface of the Neusiedlersee. At 10:30 P.M., just as the plane crossed over the shoreline, action stations sounded. The plane descended to the barest minimum jumping altitude, four hundred feet, the height approximately of a thirty-story building. A green light flashed, and Taylor pushed himself out. The three others jumped close behind him. The signal to jump had stirred Ebbing from a daze. He didn't know whether the plane had been aloft for minutes or hours. As his turn came to perch over the jump hole he thought, This is the Goddamned end.

Amid tall reeds spiking the eastern shore of the Neusiedlersee, the untimely call of marsh birds sounded in the night. The members of the DUPONT team were sounding their prearranged rendezvous signal. As they found each other, the men smiled broadly, not so much as friends reunited but as individuals affirming their survival. They stripped off their jump suits and buried them with the parachutes. Taylor ordered the men to start searching for the chutes bearing their equipment. They looked up toward the drone of an approaching aircraft. The plane circled overhead, straightened out along the original drop path, and flew directly above them. Taylor stifled a cry of helpless rage. The men looked from the plane to their leader. He ordered them to keep searching for the equipment.

Huppmann shouted. He had found one container. As Taylor was opening it, the plane returned and again traced the same flight path above their heads. Searchlights stabbed the darkness and red-orange bursts of antiaircraft fire illuminated the sky. The pilot threw the plane into a tight, evasive maneuver and disappeared to the south.

Just before he jumped, Ebbing said, he had noticed a crewman kicking at two containers, which seemed to be jammed in the bomb bay. Maybe, he suggested, the pilot had made the other runs to drop the supplies. Taylor shook his head ruefully. DUPONT's arrival on enemy soil had been announced with fireworks and flashing lights.

As the men finished burying the last of their gear, the parachutes bearing their radios were floating down onto the calm surface of the Neusiedlersee.

The Buchleitners had not seen Anton Graf since he had spent his leave with them the previous Christmas. Now, he was back in their little village of Stixneusiedl, descending on them in the middle of the night, accompanied by a stranger, telling them that he was a spy for the Americans and that he had an American officer and still another Austrian hidden away near the Neusiedlersee. He wanted the Buchleitners to hide the four of them.

Herr Buchleitner knew that Graf could be careless with the truth. But, basically, he liked and trusted this young fellow who had worked for him for a time as a butcher's helper before the war. There was also the matter of his daughter, Margrit. She had some sort of understanding with Graf, though not an engagement precisely. The Buchleitners could not know that Graf had married a girl from Brunn-am-Walde six months earlier, before leaving for the Italian front.

Herr Buchleitner was sympathetic. His own son had also granted himself an early discharge from the Wehrmacht. He gave his rather guarded permission, and Graf and Huppmann returned to the hideout among the reeds to bring back the rest of the team.

While walking back to Stixneusiedl, Ernst Ebbing's heart began to pound irregularly. He was out of breath and struggled to keep up with the others. Taylor told him to stay behind until he felt better. He could catch up later.

Anton Graf bore Ebbing no ill will. But events had obviously worked to raise his own worth in Taylor's eyes and to dim Ebbing's. It was he, Graf, who had immediately found a safe house. This other smart fellow had fared badly from the start. Ebbing had cut his hand deeply on the reeds while trying to brake his roll after the jump. Now, he had had to stay behind while Graf was returning to his friends, the Buchleitners, with the American intelligence officer in tow.

On their way back to Stixneusiedl, the group passed near gangs of laborers working on a stretch of the Southeast Wall between the Neu-siedlersee and the Leithagebirge, a range of hills to the west. At night, they gave wide berth to a huge camp for Russian prisoners of war at Kaisersteinbruch. They passed near enough to make out high barbed-wire fences punctuated by guard towers. The brilliantly lit camp glowed against the sky for miles.

They slipped back into the Buchleitner home in the dead of night. The family had waited up for them. Jack Taylor exhausted the few words of German he had picked up during training as he sought to express his gratitude to his anxious hosts for the risks they were taking. But he was already preoccupied. Taylor had begun to grasp the intelligence potential in this area. The work on the Southeast Wall and the Russian POW camp were early indications. But, with no radio, his information was useless.

Their first night in Stixneusiedl did little to relieve Taylor's frustration. They had barely fallen asleep in a spare bedroom which Buchleitner had provided when the man was pounding on their door. German troops were arriving in the village. They would have to leave immediately. Taylor firmly refused. The frightened butcher then agreed to let them move to a more secure refuge in his hayloft.

As Taylor lay shivering in the straw, he decided that he had no choice but to violate security. He would have to try to contact another OSS team operating in the area, a mission which, if Bari security had functioned effectively, he should have known nothing about.

In the next few days, Taylor decided to gamble on Margrit, the Buch-leitners' daughter. The girl attended apprentice classes at the Augarten Porzellan Manufaktur in Vienna. Another student there traveled home frequently across the border into Czechoslovakia. Jack Taylor knew that Holt Green, another naval lieutenant, was supposed to have led a mission code-named DAWES into Czechoslovakia. Margrit was to ask the girl if she would take a message to Green through Czech partisans. Taylor hoped to have Green then get word to Bari to drop another radio for his DU-PONT Mission at a specified pinpoint. Margrit Buchleitner took the message and set out for her friend's room in Vienna.

A connection with Holt Green had become increasingly important, since they could not remain much longer at the Buchleitners'. Constant fear had quickly eroded the novelty of playing host to enemy spies. Taylor occasionally pressed a gold piece or a fistful of reichsmarks on the butcher, but the good effect was short-lived.

When Margrit Buchleitner arrived in Vienna she found the city smoking from the last American air raid. The Fifteenth Air Force was now leveling military and civilian areas of the city indiscriminately. Margrit found what remained of the house where her friend had lived. The girl who was to contact the DAWES Mission for Jack Taylor was dead.

At nightfall on October 19, 1944, Jack Taylor and his men departed Stixneusiedl for Hornstein, a larger town eighteen miles away. Felix Huppmann had a café-owner friend there who might shelter them. They would ordinarily have traveled by field and forest. But the night was black, they had much ground to cover, and they chanced the roads. The aged villagers who manned the control points were satisfied with a muttered *"Heil Hitler"* or *"Soldaten. "* At dawn, the team halted in a woods bordering Hornstein. Huppmann and Graf went into town to see the café owner. He could not take them. He was sorry, but he had just completed a prison term himself for a political crime, and the Gestapo had placed a permanent guest in his home. Nor could he suggest anyone else helpful in Hornstein. People were frightened, he warned.

The man had gauged the temper of his neighbors accurately. At the end of a day of discreet inquiries, the two agents finally found an anti-Nazi who could put them up, but only for one night. They went back to the woods to get Taylor.

At their host's house they met his son, a wounded veteran, who now worked as a guard at the huge Blumau ammunition works nearby. What the guard told them baffled Taylor. Blumau was operating near full capacity with about ten thousand workers. Just before leaving Bari, Fifteenth Air Force officers had briefed Taylor and showed him photographic proof that the Blumau plant had been completely destroyed. Taylor mentally filed this information with his growing store of undelivered intelligence.

The nightly moves from one tenuous refuge to another began to exact an emotional toll from the DUPONT team. Taylor knew that he had to anchor his men somewhere. He resorted to a long-deferred possibility. Their next hideout was to be at the home of Huppmann's family in Saint Margarethen. Huppmann had discouraged Taylor from seeking refuge at his home earlier because he could not predict his father's behavior. Under pressure, he knew that his father would likely turn to drink.

They arrived at the Huppmann house, located across the street from a barnlike structure that had been converted to military use. The building was under heavy guard. They met the utterly dazed parents of Huppmann briefly, and the father then secreted them in his hayloft.

Jack Taylor awoke on the morning of October 22, 1944, to the sound of sharp, shouted commands rising above a muffled din. He crept to the front of the loft and peered out cautiously. Hundreds of slave laborers were pouring from the building across the road and were being herded into formation by Organization Todt officers and SS men. Taylor had worked with cadavers as a medical student and thought himself hardened to the human body debased. But he was not prepared for these stooped, skeletal figures apathetically enduring a rain of abuse and blows. Taylor went back to his pack for his camera. He tried to get shots of the SS officers, showing the bold, black swastikas on their brassards. These were the first Nazis he had seen at work. Most of the laborers, Taylor later learned, were Ukrainians, with a scattering of Poles, Czechs, and French. They, too, were working on the Southeast Wall.

While the DUPONT team hid at Saint Margarethen, Ebbing rejoined them. After his inexplicable heart condition had passed, he had made his way to Stixneusiedl, only to find the others already gone. But they had gotten word to him. He arrived at Saint Margarethen just as this refuge was becoming untenable.

The terror they had witnessed in the Buchleitners' faces was now visible among the Huppmanns. The father was drinking continuously. He complained that the SS posted across the road would surely spot the four men. His son could remain; but the rest would have to leave.

Anton Graf's mercurial moods while they had been in Bari seemed to stabilize at a level of wholly unwarranted optimism now that they were in Austria. He cheerfully told Huppmann that they would simply have to continue to search for a new safe house.

At Schützen, a small rail junction a few miles to the west, they found a farmer's wife who accepted the story that they were soldiers who had missed a train. She agreed to put them up for one night. Early the next morning, she was pressuring them to be on their way. Taylor balked. He had to stabilize his operation somewhere if he wanted to salvage this mission. He told Ebbing to have the woman bring her husband around. The man turned out to be an anti-Nazi, but hardly of the heroic stripe. Taylor pressed Herr Kaufman to keep them, and he offered the man several gold pieces. Kaufman pocketed the money uneasily. They could stay, he said, maybe for a few weeks. Kaufman put them up in their now customary quarters, a hayloft, this one over his winery. DUPONT now had a home. And Jack Taylor had a plan.

Taylor had failed in his attempt to contact Holt Green's DAWES Mission through Margrit Buchleitner, but he had another possibility. Second Lieutenant Miles Pavlovich, another fellow officer at OSS Bari, was supposed to take a team designated DILLON into Carinthia, a hundred and fifty miles to the southwest. One member of Pavlovich's team was Karl Lippe, an Austrian whose family lived not too far from the winter-resort town of Spittal. Ernst Ebbing had earlier managed to slip a message to his mother in Vienna, and she had volunteered to help them contact Pavlovich by trying to arrange a brief vacation to Spittal. While there, she would attempt to reach Pavlovich through Lippe's family. She would convey the same message that Taylor had tried unsuccessfully to get to Holt Green: Bari must drop him another radio.

Ebbing felt particularly good about the possibility of their reaching Pavlovich. He liked Pavlovich and had been flattered that this officer had also wanted him for the DILLON Mission.

The Kaufman farmhouse was a sprawling, U-shaped structure with a courtyard in the U's enclosure. Taylor and Ebbing stayed in the hayloft over the winery in the wing opposite the Kaufmans' living quarters. Graf and Huppmann reported frequently, though the stonemason lived at his home in Saint Margarethen, while Graf stayed with Huppmann's aunt in the same town. While they waited for Frau Ebbing to make arrangements for the Spittal trip, life at Schützen took on an unaccustomed regularity for the DUPONT team.

Taylor and Ebbing passed the days working out endless variations on a solution to their plight. Every night, at seven, they climbed down from the loft to find the simple supper which Frau Kaufman had left for them in a small room off the winery. After dark, they went to the courtyard and exercised muscles grown stiff from inaction. Sometimes, late at night, they would go into the Kaufmans' home and listen to the BBC over a short-wave radio.

Herr Kaufman often had visitors, sympathetic anti-Nazis who dropped by to discuss the war. To those he trusted, Kaufman revealed the secret of the hayloft. Then Ebbing would come down and chat with the visitors. If they seemed promising, Ebbing would bring Taylor down, who would make notes of any useful intelligence which the guests disclosed.

One of Taylor's favorite visitors was Josef Preiler, community secretary of Schützen, a man of surprisingly broad-ranging interests for the insular town he served. They had conversations lasting deep into the night, with Ebbing translating. As their friendship ripened, Taylor learned that the war had already cost the life of one of Preiler's sons, and that the man risked these visits while being carried on the Nazi security lists as a political unreliable.

Graf and Huppmann came by to report their lack of success in finding future hideouts and their considerable success in unearthing new intelligence. By now, the harvest had become exasperatingly abundant. Taylor had pieced together a complete picture of the Southeast Wall, including the location of fortifications, minefields, tank traps, pillboxes, and artillery emplacements. When the Allied armies finally broke out of the top of the Italian boot, it was this rampart which they would confront in eastern Austria. Taylor also knew the locations of fifty thousand foreign workers and Hitler Youth who were racing to complete the wall by January 1, 1945. He knew the sites of the Rax Werke aviation plant, hidden airfields, a gunpowder factory employing two thousand workers, and the major depots in Vienna storing foodstuffs, petroleum, and coal supplies. In spite of relentless bombing, he knew that the locomotive works in Wiener Neustadt was still producing one new engine a day.

But the knowledge which Taylor wanted most impatiently to transmit was the political intelligence he had gathered in the region. If he could get this information to Bari, the Allies might use it to sap any remaining will to resist among the Austrians. His informants had convinced him that, in the countryside, less than five percent of the people were confirmed Nazis. The remainder ranged from rabidly anti-Nazi to the politically inert. He was told that in Vienna under twenty percent seriously espoused the Nazi cause. But American bombings of purely civilian targets, residential neighborhoods, the beloved Vienna opera house, and fine-arts museum were welding the Austrians to Germany. American bombs were doing more to discourage anti-Nazism than six years of Gestapo terror.

From Kaufman's visitors, Taylor also heard disquieting reports that Graf and Huppmann were endangering the mission by their open and extravagant pursuit of local women. When Taylor confronted the men with this information, they responded only with knowing grins. Taylor failed to press the matter. They were producing invaluable information. If only he could get it out.

On October 28, Taylor's latest scheme collapsed. Ebbing's mother came from Vienna to see them. All able-bodied women, she said, had been ordered to make themselves immediately available for war work. She would not be able to make the vacation trip to Spittal, and Taylor would not be able to contact Pavlovich's DILLON Mission.

Days lengthened into weeks at the Kaufman farmhouse. From a crack in the hayloft, Jack Taylor spent hours watching officers from the Wehrmacht and the Organization Todt sponge off the Kaufman family. They drank Kaufman's wine all day and often had to be carried out at night. In between, they let slip useful nuggets of intelligence that Kaufman reported to Taylor, who added them to his store. Once Taylor had been able to talk briefly from the hayloft with some startled English POWs who were digging an antitank trap nearby.

Late in November, Graf brought promising news to Schützen. Through an acquaintance, Gustav Bauditsch, a train dispatcher in Wiener Neustadt, Graf was sure that he could get Taylor and Ebbing onto a freight train to Klagenfurt. From there, they could slip into Yugoslavia and eventually make their way back to Italy. Graf said that Bauditsch could also be depended upon to hide the two men until they could catch the train. Since both Graf and Huppmann were in uniform, they could try to make their way via troop trains to Udine, then slip south to Bari. Taylor liked the idea. Dividing the team doubled the chances that one pair would get through.

On November 17, Graf returned from Wiener Neustadt claiming that he had made all necessary arrangements. Herr Bauditsch had been out, he said, but Frau Bauditsch and her daughter, Erika, had agreed to hide the team while they waited for transportation. Graf gave Taylor the Bauditsches' address and a rather vague description of the house.

Shortly after this plan was broached, Taylor met Ernst Ebbing's father, the former lawyer, now a captain in the Luftwaffe. The elder Ebbing had been transferred from Upper Silesia to Vienna, awaiting reassignment. While at home he learned from his wife that his son had returned to Austria. He immediately made his way to Schützen and put himself at the team's disposal. Captain Ebbing proved a mine of intelligence. Allied bombers, he said, had thus far spared prime targets in Upper Silesia, a heavily industrial area and a hotbed of Nazi fanaticism. He mentioned

Gleiwitz, Oppeln, Breslau, and other industrial centers virtually untouched by bombs. He also provided Taylor with information on recent developments in German jet aircraft.

While ignoring so much industrial muscle, American bombers were punishing innocent civilians. Austrian Communists were having a propaganda field day at the Allies' expense. The Russians, the Viennese believed, were fighting a clean war on the battlefield, while the Allies were waging war against old people, women, and children. And why, in August, when Warsaw partisans had tried to rise up against their Nazi masters, had the Allies failed to offer help? Taylor leaped at the opportunity to correct the record. During the uprising, he explained, the Allies had dispatched ten to fifteen supply planes a night, diverted from Italy and England, while nearby Russian forces failed to lift a finger.

A mutual respect quickly grew between the two men. Taylor outlined his latest plan to return to Italy to the elder Ebbing and enlisted his help. By now Jack Taylor had reluctantly accepted the younger Ebbing's contention that Graf's word could not be automatically accepted. The man apparently had an emotional compulsion to please Taylor, even if it meant lying. Taylor asked Captain Ebbing if he would double-check any arrangements which Graf was supposed to have made with Bauditsch, the train dispatcher in Wiener Neustadt. Ebbing agreed to help. He shook hands with Taylor, embraced his son, and was gone.

The man who knocked at the door at Fischelgasse 25 in Wiener Neustadt introduced himself as a Luftwaffe officer, although he wore civilian clothes. He was not, he assured Frau Bauditsch, with the Gestapo. She asked him to step inside quickly. Her daughter, Erika, an attractive young woman, was standing near the doorway. The man spoke carefully, determined to gather more information than he gave. Yes, Frau Bauditsch knew Anton Graf. But she and the girl both said they had not seen him since he had passed through Wiener Neustadt on his way to the front months before.

Ebbing took a desperate gamble. He explained that Graf had since parachuted to the area as an American agent, that his team had lost its radio equipment and was eager to get back to Italy. He reminded her of arrangements which Graf was supposed to have made with her husband. She knew nothing of them. But she said she could put up the men, and her husband would help them get on a train. Ebbing thanked her warmly and left. Frau Bauditsch immediately went to the railway station, where she described Captain Ebbing's strange visit to her husband. Herr Bauditsch told her to go to the Gestapo immediately and tell them the full story.

A few days later, Jack Taylor received a note from Captain Ebbing describing his visit to Wiener Neustadt. Graf had not been to see the Bauditsches, as he had claimed. His description of their home, the team's promised hideout, was wholly fabricated. When Taylor confronted Graf with Captain Ebbing's information, the man responded only with a hurt silence.

But, at least, the resourceful Captain Ebbing had made good the scheme that Graf had invented. They had an escape plan, and would act on it.

The day before they were to leave Schützen, Taylor sent Graf and Huppmann to make one last canvass of the Hornstein area for possible hideouts on their return from Bari. They had long since exhausted their welcome at the Kaufman farm. The two men were to return the following night to Schützen; then all four men would walk through the night, arriving at the Bauditsch home in Wiener Neustadt just before dawn. Taylor and Ebbing, with Bauditsch's aid, would hop the first freight train to Klagenfurt. Graf and Huppmann would then take a passenger train to Udine.

The temperature in the hayloft was now often below freezing. Taylor bundled himself in an old coat, an extra pair of trousers, wrapped himself in his thin blanket, and burrowed into the hay for what he hoped would be his last night in Schützen.

Early the next morning, Graf and Huppmann left the hayloft. By ten-thirty, they were in Wiener Neustadt, not in Hornstein, as Taylor had ordered. They headed for the Central Post Office, near the Bahnhofplatz, where Graf hoped to see Erika Bauditsch. She was not there. They then went to her home at Fischelgasse 25. Graf told Huppmann that he would enter the house first. If he did not come out in ten minutes, Huppmann was to look for him. Graf went up the stairs and knocked on the door of the Bauditsches' second-floor apartment. Frau Bauditsch greeted him with stiff courtesy and asked him in. She led him to Erika's bedroom and excused herself. As Erika and Graf chatted uneasily, two armed Gestapo agents burst through the door and wrestled Graf to the floor.

The door of the apartment house opened and a young woman waved to Huppmann. Was he Anton's friend? Then please come in. He followed her upstairs and into her room, where two gun barrels greeted him. On the floor Huppmann saw Anton Graf bound hand and foot. "Where is the American?" they demanded.

Jack Taylor felt under the eaves of the hayloft and pulled out the hidden money belt, camera, cipher pads, signal plan, and radio crystals. He knew, if he were ever captured, that this equipment would constitute devastating evidence. But he still harbored hopes that if they did not get back to Italy, Bari might yet drop another radio to them. At seven o'clock he and Ebbing made their descent from the hayloft to eat their supper in the small room next to the winery. The watchdog barked. Someone was approaching the house. It was not unusual; a stream of callers visited Kaufman. Taylor turned off the light and they remained quiet. Now someone was coming to their door, probably a member of the family sounding the usual "all clear." The door opened slowly. Eight plain-clothesmen rushed in. The two agents fought savagely. Taylor finally sagged under the repeated hammering of a blackjack. He and Ebbing were dragged out into the night where other Gestapo officers trained subma-chine guns on them.

After Major John McCulloch had returned from dropping the DU-PONT team, he had immediately fallen into a deep slumber at his quarters in Bari. That evening he met his superior, Robert Joyce, at the officers' club bar. "I understand you took an unauthorized trip last night."
McCulloch said nothing.
"I should reprimand you." Joyce broke into a broad grin. "But I'd have done the same damn thing. Suppose, instead, I buy you a drink."
Then a month had passed with no word from the DUPONT Mission. Standard procedure was to stop monitoring the radio frequencies of a team which had not been heard from for thirty days. But because DU-PONT had involved unusual risks, the radio watch was extended for two more weeks; then, at McCulloch's insistence, extended again. Finally, on January 22, 1945, 101 days after he had jumped into Austria, OSS Italy officially listed Lieutenant Jack Taylor as missing in action. For security reasons, no notification was made to his next of kin.

The DUPONT team had fallen into the hands of Johann Sanitzer, a Gestapo expert in tracking down enemy agents and persuading them to play back their radios under his control. He had been designated chief of all *Funkspiele*, phony playbacks, in Austria. Sanitzer had known for months that a team had landed in the Wiener Neustadt area, ever since he had received reports in October of parachutes seen floating on the Neusiedlersee. He had expected that his quarry was a French team and was amazed to find an American in his net. He immediately informed the RSHA in Berlin. Sanitzer left Ebbing, Huppmann, and Graf to his subordinates and took Taylor, personally, in his own car to Vienna the evening of the arrest.

The DUPONT team was confined to Gestapo headquarters in the Metropol Hotel, where Sanitzer quickly introduced his professional style to Taylor and Ebbing. He pointed to the insignia on Taylor's collar and asked what it was. Taylor answered *"Hauptmann,"* captain, which was the army equivalent of his navy rank. Sanitzer delivered Taylor a stinging slap across the face. "False!" He repeated the procedure, alternating slaps and kicks, never raising his voice. He then beat Ernst Ebbing until the Austrian abandoned his code identity of "Underwood" and admitted to his real name.

To Sanitzer the interrogation was a charade, a psychological conditioner, a test of the men's strength. He already knew the answers to the questions he had asked, since Graf and Huppmann, in Sanitzer's phrase, had "talked like a book." He respected Taylor and Ebbing, who, thus far, had revealed nothing to him.

Sanitzer advised the two men to spare themselves any further grief and told them that he had already picked up Graf and Huppmann earlier in Wiener Neustadt. Taylor smiled bitterly. He had sent Graf and Huppmann to Hornstein to find a safe house. They had been captured, instead, in Wiener Neustadt at the Bauditsch home. When Taylor remembered that Bauditsch had an attractive daughter, what had happened became painfully clear. When asked who else was operating in the area, Graf and Huppmann unhesitatingly told what they knew of Miles Pavlovich's DILLON Mission. They said that the team was supposed to have dropped in Carinthia, north of Spittal near the Katschberg Pass, and that one of the agents, named Karl Lippe, came from that area. They told Sanitzer where Lippe's family might be found. Sanitzer's imagination fairly danced. He might be able to carry off a double *Funkspiel* as soon as his men nabbed the DILLON team.

With the necessity for deception out of the way, Sanitzer and his cohorts adopted a less brutal manner. The talk shifted between interrogation and conversation. Taylor admitted to having been a dentist and an amateur radio operator and learned that he had communicated via ham radio before the war with one of his inquisitors, Flieger-Hauptmann Hannesbauer.

The Germans were deeply curious about America. Through a woman interpreter, they posed astonishing questions to Taylor. Why were the Americans bombing Germany? they asked, sounding almost hurt. Germany was not bombing America. Yes, Taylor agreed, but only because the United States was beyond the range of German bombers. But why was America waging war against Germany at all? Taylor tactfully pointed out that it was Germany which had declared war on the United States after Pearl Harbor. Sanitzer asked him how much longer he thought the war would last. Six months, Taylor estimated. The Germans agreed. Though, to Taylor's amazement, they believed that the Allies would quit by then. Was Taylor unaware of the miracle V-weapons, and that the Americans were retreating from Aachen, and that the Wehrmacht would soon retake France?

His captors demonstrated a detailed knowledge of OSS operations. They showed Taylor charts, complete with names and titles, indicating the relationships between field organizations and the Washington headquarters. Their knowledge of OSS operations among the partisans in northern Italy far exceeded anything Taylor knew, much of it gained from torturing members of Holt Green's captured DAWES Mission, on which Taylor had vainly staked his hopes.

Sanitzer told Taylor that intercepted messages between OSS headquarters and partisans' outposts were routinely circulated among RSHA officers in Berlin. He knew that some agents who dropped into Germany came out of OSS London, that southern Germany and Austria were covered by missions originating in Bari and flown out of Brindisi under overall control of an officer named Chapin stationed at Caserta.

Sanitzer had a fairly complete knowledge of how certain OSS codes worked. He took obvious delight in giving Taylor a demonstration of his mastery of the one-time pad, a highly secure system in which messages were encoded using pages of constantly changing random letters. Stamped across the face of the pad on which Sanitzer demonstrated his expertise was the word HOUSEBOAT, the name of another team captured along with the DAWES Mission.

Taylor proposed a deal. The Germans seemed obsessed by Allied bombings. Taylor believed he could persuade the Fifteenth Air Force that the indiscriminate bombing of civilians was counterproductive. Taylor said that if his captors would spare the lives of all members of the DUPONT team, he would make contact with the Fifteenth Air Force and guarantee that its bombers would confine themselves, henceforth, to military targets.

Sanitzer agreed to present this proposal to RSHA headquarters in Berlin. A few days later, Kaltenbrunner's staff answered. Not only was Taylor's proposal absurd but Sanitzer was reminded of Hitler's edict that all captured officers attached to foreign missions were to be executed, precisely the sentence meted out to the spies connected with the DAWES and HOUSEBOAT missions.

The day after the arrest of the DUPONT team, two Gestapo officers came to the home of Josef Preiler, the community secretary of Schützen who had frequently come to the Kaufman farm to give information to Taylor. They brushed past Preiler's daughter, Angela, and went into the man's bedroom, where they found Preiler on the edge of the bed putting on his shoes. One of the agents had a pistol. A shot was fired and Preiler fell back. When Angela Preiler came into the room, she was informed that her father had committed suicide. The Gestapo officer pointed to the pistol on her father's night table. It had not been there, she was sure, when she had been in the room earlier that morning.

After he extracted from Graf and Huppmann that another American team was supposedly operating in Carinthia, Johann Sanitzer sent one of his men to the Katschberg Pass to search for the family of the DILLON team member named Karl Lippe. Sanitzer's man came unknowingly close, but failed to locate the family. Lippe's mother lived approximately three miles south of the Katschberg Pass, and her son had indeed parachuted with the DILLON Mission in nearby mountains. DILLON could have done Jack Taylor no good, in any case. The DUPONT team had been captured before the DILLON Mission left Italy.

DILLON, under Second Lieutenant Miles Pavlovich, was the largest mission sent into the Reich. Like DUPONT, the operation was too far along to be aborted, though Lieutenant Al Ulmer also had deep reservations about DILLON, most of which began with Miles Pavlovich.

Pavlovich, in his late twenties, of Yugoslav descent, was a languid, slender, blond-haired man with a romantic vision of his role in OSS. To Ulmer, he was an adolescent poseur, lacking the requisite mental and physical energy for a serious mission. Still, Pavlovich did possess undeniable courage and was a likable enough fellow.

The man Ulmer counted on to back up Pavlovich in the DILLON Mission was a tough, taciturn Yugoslav merchant marine radio operator named Julio Prester, a man in his late thirties, with the weathered look of a life spent at sea. Prester expressed himself poorly in English, but in his seamed face there was an integrity and an untutored intelligence. Prester's ship had been impounded in New York Harbor by American authorities earlier in the war. There, he had been interviewed by OSS officers gathering intelligence on European ports. Finding Prester a devout anti-Nazi, OSS subsequently recruited him for operations into Yugoslavia. He had later been switched to the Austrian mission, which was to take him and Pavlovich, along with three deserters from the German Army, to the vicinity of Spittal, about thirty miles north of the Yugoslav border. It was to this area that Ernst Ebbing's mother had tried to come on vacation in order to put the DUPONT Mission in touch with Pavlovich's DILLON team.

Two of the deserter-volunteers troubled Ulmer almost as much as Lieutenant Pavlovich. Karl Lippe had the surface polish of a peasant who had picked up minor graces while working in the manor house. He was small, garrulous, and unctuous toward those whom he considered his superiors. The second man, Viktor Ruthi, seemed merely dim, with no discernible qualification or motivation for the sensitive mission on which he was embarking. The third man, Ernst Fiechter, was intelligent and appeared reliable. All three came from the area into which they were to be parachuted and believed they could establish friendly contacts there.

The DILLON team flew out of Brindisi aboard a Halifax bomber two days after Christmas of 1944. The three Austrians were in Wehrmacht uniforms. Pavlovich and Prester wore minimal U.S. military dress. The drop, in snow-capped mountains, at an elevation of 6037 feet, went well enough for the men, but their radio equipment was damaged on landing and none of their other containers could be found.

After two fruitless days of searching, Lieutenant Pavlovich sent Karl Lippe to a nearby village for food. The man returned two days later, empty-handed, which seemed odd to Julio Prester; but Lieutenant Pavlovich appeared unconcerned.

After looking for three more days, the group hiked for eight hours through deep snows to a house where Karl Lippe said they would be safe. During the march, Ernst Fiechter's foot became badly frozen. When the exhausted men arrived at the house, Karl went inside and returned later with the news that they would have to spend the night in the stable and leave the next morning. The family could not be trusted, Karl said. He failed to mention that the house belonged to his brother.

They pushed on the next day to a tiny village called Treffenboden, passing en route near Karl's hometown of Eisentratten. In Treffenboden, they found a politically sympathetic mother and daughter. One of the women had just finished a three-month jail sentence for an offense against the regime. For the first time since their arrival, one week before, the men ate well. The women washed their clothes and arranged through other anti-Nazis for a secure nearby ski hut, which could serve as their hideaway. The women also found a doctor to care for Ernst Fiechter's foot.

For the next four weeks, the team made two- and three-day forays into the drop zone, searching for their lost equipment. They tramped a huge "V" into the snow and marked it with shreds of a German flag which Julio Prester had discovered. The "V" was a prearranged signal to Allied reconnaissance planes coming out of Italy that they needed additional radio equipment.

The "V" was spotted on January 14 by an Allied photo-reconnaissance aircraft. At Bari, OSS Operations Officer Hart Perry tested an idea for a more precise drop of the second radio. Instead of using a high-flying bomber, he arranged to have the drop made close to earth by a P-38 fighter.

On a cold January 30, the DILLON team was again scouring the drop zone for its lost equipment. At high noon, through howling winds, they detected the purr of an approaching aircraft. Out of the bright sunlight, a plane with the body of a dragonfly streaked low against the mountainside and disgorged its cargo. The DILLON team watched the parachutes settle to earth and sprang after them. In the containers were food, equipment, and a new radio. They had not watched the P-38 alone, however. High on a mountain peak, near Kremsbrücke, an air-warning post flashed a message to the police in Gmünd and Eisentratten that an enemy aircraft had just made a parachute drop.

The DILLON team took its supplies back to Treffenboden, to the home of the two women who had originally given them sanctuary. There, they found a visitor named Martha Frais, who evidently knew Karl Lippe. Karl's frequent unexplained absences suddenly became clear. He showed a preening proprietary interest in this provocative woman. She seemed to tolerate Karl, but with no reciprocal enthusiasm. Lieutenant Pavlovich did not take his eyes from her.

Martha Frais said that she might be able to arrange for more food for the team to be sent up to Treffenboden from her village of Gmünd, one mile south. The DILLON team then retreated to its ski-hut hideout on a mountain outside Treffenboden to await the delivery. The next day, Karl Lippe was sent back to Treffenboden to pick up the food which Martha Frais was to have sent. He did not return for two days. When he did come back, he told Pavlovich that the food had cost him seven hundred reichs-marks.

Julio Prester said nothing to the others, but traveled to Gmünd and confronted Martha Frais. The confused and hurt young woman denied asking any money for the food. It had been given freely by her and other friends, she convinced him.

On his return to the ski hut, Prester laid before Miles Pavlovich his case against Karl Lippe. That he had stolen from other members of the team, they already knew. He had disappeared on frequent unauthorized absences. Now, he had sought to profit from the kindness and courage of local people without whose support their mission was doomed. This man, Prester argued, was a menace and could cost them their lives. He brought in the other two Austrian agents. They, too, had no faith in Karl and no desire to work further with him. Prester reminded Pavlovich that as leader of the team, his word was law. Prester recommended that he and Miles hold a court-martial on Karl Lippe. Miles Pavlovich went along with Prester's plea.

Prester ordered Karl to come before them and sent Ruthi and Fiechter to wait outside the hut. Miles explained to Karl, uneasily, that he was on trial. Prester, with his slow, serious speech, enumerated the charges against him. Karl answered each accusation with nervous amusement, shrugging his shoulders and smiling foolishly in Pavlovich's direction.

They sent Karl out of the hut while they deliberated. Julio called him back shortly. He informed Karl Lippe that the court had found him guilty and had sentenced him to death. Karl turned, trembling, uncomprehend-ing, to Miles Pavlovich, who wordlessly rose and left the hut. Tears streamed down Karl's face. He seized Prester's hand between his hands imploring the taciturn Yugoslav to show him mercy. For the next three hours he pleaded for his life. In the end, Prester relented. But Karl, he warned, was now on probation.

Later that day, Prester took the seemingly chastened Austrian to Tref-fenboden, where they borrowed a horse and wagon from a farmer to haul food supplies and the new radio from the village back to the ski hut. At one o'clock in the morning, after they had unloaded, Prester sent Karl back to Treffenboden to return the horse and wagon. He ordered Karl to return immediately afterward.

Karl, instead, took the horse to Gmünd, where he spent two days with Martha Frais. The farmer, in the meantime, informed the police that strangers hiding in the mountains had stolen his horse.

When Karl Lippe finally returned, only Prester and Ernst Fiechter, still nursing his frozen foot, were at the hut. Pavlovich and the other Austrian, Viktor Ruthi, had gone to Treffenboden. Prester noticed immediately that Karl was wearing a different Wehrmacht uniform, for which he had no explanation. Prester ordered Karl outside and informed him that he had violated his probation. When the other two agents returned to the lodge, two hours later, Prester told Miles Pavlovich, "I've carried out the sentence of the court-martial on Karl."

They buried the body that night and set out for Gmünd, where they thought they would be safe for a few days while they looked for a new mountain retreat. They feared that the farmer whose horse Karl had taken might lead the police to the old hideout. In the village, they met another peasant, named Josef Wegscheider, who was willing to accommodate them on his remote farm near Malta, a village four miles northwest of Gmünd.

Early in February, the DILLON team set out after dark for Wegscheider's farm. As they walked along a country road in the pitch-dark night, Julio Prester realized that Miles Pavlovich was no longer with them. It was too late to turn back to look for him, so they continued on to the farm. On their arrival, they were led by Wegscheider to another mountain ski hut, three miles away, which seemed secure.

Five days passed before Prester learned from a visitor what had happened to Miles Pavlovich. The team's leader claimed that he had become separated in the dark and had decided to turn back to Gmünd. He had since been staying at the home of Martha Frais.

On February 17, Prester went to the woman's home and confronted Pavlovich. What exactly was their leader's plan, he wanted to know? Pavlovich told Prester that he had arranged a better mountain retreat for them. Prester explained that they were already in a safe hideaway. Pavlovich insisted; they were to get their gear packed. He would then have someone transport them and the equipment to the new refuge where he would join them later. In the meantime, he would continue to stay with Martha Frais. Ernst Fiechter could remain with him, since his foot was still in bad condition.

Julio Prester left perplexed. None of the airy plans which Pavlovich had tossed off matched the realities of their situation. Nevertheless, he and the other Austrian, Viktor Ruthi, headed back to the hideout and on the way stopped to inform the peasant Wegscheider that they were moving. The man seemed upset, but said nothing. As soon as they were gone, Wegscheider went to his brother, a village official in Malta, and reported them.

Julio Prester and Viktor Ruthi waited most of the next day for someone to take their equipment to the hideout which Miles Pavlovich had chosen. At three o'clock in the afternoon, they heard voices outside the hut. Three policemen, bearing submachine guns, suddenly broke through the doorway. Behind them a squad of Volkssturm waited. The two agents were marched, their hands bound behind them, down the mountain roads past taunting villagers to the police station in Gmünd.

During the march, Julio Prester could read the terror in Viktor Ruthi's face. "It's all fate," Prester consoled him. "In war, some men get killed at the front, and some like this. If they shoot us, it won't matter. Just keep your mouth shut and don't say anything." Ruthi promised he would not talk. But he was bound to view his situation differently from Prester's. Prester was a legitimate foe, a secret agent. Ruthi was a traitor.

On their arrival at the Gmünd station, the prisoners were ordered to empty their pockets on a table. As soon as he laid down his paybook, Ruthi volunteered that it was a fake and did not bear his true name. Prester heard him in helpless rage. The police chief put through a call to Gestapo headquarters at Spittal and advised the secret police of his catch.

At midnight, the Gestapo chief arrived from Spittal and took Ruthi away. Prester was left with a policeman who untied his hands and offered him a cigarette. He sat for hours in the station and finally dozed off. At about 3:00 A.M. he was awakened by gunfire.

After the Gestapo officer had separated Julio Prester and the deserter, Viktor Ruthi, the latter immediately told his captors that there were other members of the DILLON team in Gmünd, the American leader and another Austrian.

A thirty-foot rope was tied to Ruthi and he was ordered to walk ahead and lead the Gestapo chief and a body of local police to the house of Martha Frais. Ruthi approached the door, accompanied by a policeman named Josef Hartlieb. He gave the DILLON team's secret knock. Miles Pavlovich, in bed with Martha Frais, woke her and told her to answer the door. As she opened it, Hartlieb was standing in the doorway with his pistol drawn. "Put your hands up." Pavlovich reached for his own gun and Hartlieb shot the American through the stomach. Pavlovich fired back erratically and the policeman quickly retreated.

Two hand grenades were tossed through a window and exploded inside the house. Martha Frais became hysterical, screaming that the Gestapo was going to kill her. Pavlovich shot her through the heart, then put a bullet through his own head. Ernst Fiechter watched helplessly. He sat alone for hours in the darkened silence of the room, with the two bodies, waiting for the police to storm the house. At dawn, SS troops edged slowly toward the doorway and arrested the last member of the DILLON team.

The mayor of Gmünd, Josef Oberlechner, ordered that Lieutenant Pavlovich and Martha Frais be buried without coffins or ceremony. They were dumped into two shallow holes, not large enough to accommodate the full length of their bodies. Mayor Oberlechner kicked at the crumpled figures to force them into their cramped graves.

Though both were American missions, DUPONT and DILLON had been flown out of Italy in RAF aircraft manned by Polish fliers, because American fliers were not yet prepared to handle them. The 334th Wing RAF, created especially for secret operations, flew both British and American agents in Halifaxes or Bristols out of Brindisi. Walter Haass, who went frequently as dispatcher, recalled the plywood Bristols as bitterly cold with barely enough room for a man to stand. The discomfort was softened only by the invariable serving in midflight of tea and crumpets.

Lieutenant General Ira C. Eaker had taken command of Mediterranean Allied Air Forces in January 1944. Eaker, possibly with one eye on the postwar world, wanted Americans "to get some credit in delivering knives, guns, and explosives to the Balkan patriots with which to kill Germans." Out of Eaker's objective was born the American 885th Heavy Bomber Squadron, a special unit of the Fifteenth Air Force commanded by Colonel Monro MacCloskey, which arrived on October 2, 1944, to share the airfield with the RAF at Brindisi. The 885th comprised eight black aircraft and was soon engaged in dropping agents and supplies into the Balkans and northern Italy, but not into the Reich.

To officers of the German-Austrian section at Bari, the situation at the Brindisi field was symptomatic of a deeper malaise in their operation. The planes of their own nation's air force, with all the communications and logistics advantages they offered, were denied them for the infiltration of the Reich. Instead, they were compelled to rely on the RAF, where, in the order of priority, the American missions were assigned, as one member observed, "hind titty."

The OSS people had no quarrel with the British aircraft or crews. They found the Polish RAF pilots, in particular, "crazy" but consummately skilled, willing to fly anywhere, in any weather. The difficulty was getting their agents aboard the British aircraft. Primed American teams were left waiting, often for weeks, which eroded their state of readiness.

The officers of the German-Austrian section resented this second-class treatment at the hands of the RAF. They were appalled by the inept planning of DUPONT and DILLON. The problem, they believed, lay in the well-intentioned yet ineffectual leadership of their unit.

Hart Perry, the operations officer of the section, and Dyno Lowenstein gathered their courage for a visit to Lieutenant Colonel Howard Chapin, the SI chief at Caserta. Their argument was direct. The German-Austrian section was a poor piece of work. If the thing were worth doing at all, it must have firmer direction. They wanted a new boss at Bari for the German operations. They wanted Lieutenant Al Ulmer. They then went to the Fifteenth Air Force to see if they could not be cut in on the service of Colonel MacCloskey's 885th Bomber Squadron.

IX

A Spy's Fate

✠ ✠ ✠

The infiltration of Willi Drucker was set for New Year's Eve of December 1944 at the small border town of Stein-am-Rhein. The Swiss frontier guards had been bribed. On the German side, patrols might be dulled from toasting in the new year and fighting off the biting cold with schnapps. Drucker stood serene and erect on the edge of the woods as the others in the party stamped their feet and batted their hands together. If they succeeded in slipping him across the border, Drucker was eventually to proceed north to the Ruhr and join Jupp Kappius.

Drucker's twinkling blue eyes contrasted with an otherwise impassive appearance. With his copper-colored skin, planed cheekbones, and great hawk nose, Drucker resembled nothing so much as an American Indian, except for the eyes.

Eleven years had passed since Willi Drucker had left his native Germany. In 1933, he had been sacked as a policeman in Dortmund for refusing to join the Nazi party. Later, he served a jail sentence when the Gestapo caught him helping anti-Nazi fugitives. He had fled to Saarbrücken, where he lived until 1935, and then moved to France when Hitler marched into the Rhineland.

Drucker prided himself that he was one of probably less than a thousand German police officers who had refused to go along with the Nazis.

And he was one of a handful to become involved in active resistance.

In 1942, after a stint with the French foreign legion, Drucker found himself in North Africa in a French work battalion. As one of the earliest agents recruited by Gary Van Arkel, he had been waiting for two years for the day when he would penetrate Germany. His movements since then had paralleled Van Arkel's—Bari for a time, then England. Now he was in Switzerland to perform at last the mission for which Van Arkel had originally selected him.

While in England, Drucker had passed tedious months with the BACH staff, reading newspapers smuggled from the Ruhr, studying city directories, going over briefing notes, and learning the latest conditions in Dortmund, where Kappius had arranged a safe house for him. He also underwent a simulated Gestapo interrogation. Drucker was told to imagine that he had been caught in Germany carrying a sketch of a tank factory. He was given fifteen minutes to devise his defense, then marched into a darkened room. A spotlight impaled him, and from behind the light, unseen inquisitors began a harsh interrogation. Drucker, who had undergone actual Gestapo questioning, found the simulation harrowingly accurate.

After-hours, Drucker and other Socialists gathered to talk long into the night on the kind of Germany they wanted to build after the war. They were as one in their desire not simply to restore their homeland but to erect a wholly new German society. Drucker's ambition was to lead the organization of a democratic German police system.

Willi Drucker, at thirty-seven, was still driven by unalloyed, almost childlike enthusiasm. His OSS instructor had written of him: "He is of average intelligence, slow in grasping new ideas, but once he has understood them can be depended upon to apply them in practice. He has no great imagination or inventive powers but he is careful, shrewd, and determined. He appears reliable and loyal and has self-confidence. A straightforward and likable personality. He was keen and worked hard, a good average student."

The solid, steady Drucker had soon won the confidence of the more cerebral Jupp Kappius. The latter looked forward to having this dependable rock of a man join him.

Drucker left England five weeks after the departure of Kappius. He was flown to Thonon and was then smuggled into Switzerland. There, ISK contacts looked after Drucker while he waited to slip into Germany. Gary Van Arkel used Drucker's police background to build a cover for him as a Gestapo agent. Van Arkel had located a buyable Gestapo chief named

Kriner who was assigned to Feldkirch, just across the Swiss border in Germany. Kriner had already provided Van Arkel with enough intelligence to appear reliable. Drucker was to report to Kriner, who would arrange authentic Gestapo orders enabling him to proceed to the Ruhr. His mission was designated RAGWEED.

Anne Kappius had returned from Germany with her first report from her husband, Jupp, and the safe address in Dortmund for Drucker in October. But soon after, the Germans sealed the Swiss border and Drucker was stalled in Switzerland for weeks. Then, on New Year's Eve, the gamble was made to infiltrate him across the border.

As the party waited in the raw night, one of the men realized that Drucker was about to cross the snow-covered terrain into Germany wearing a dark overcoat. He hurriedly switched with Drucker, giving the agent his light-colored coat. Willi Drucker then walked off alone into a copse of evergreens. Two hundred yards later he emerged, inside Germany. The ground was starched white, and the night air clean with the cold. From overhead, a full moon gave the snow a marvelous luminescence. Drucker felt absolutely calm, almost euphoric. He fully expected, after twelve years under the Nazi heel, that the German people would welcome him.

Gary Van Arkel was becoming concerned. He had received a brief message on January 2, two days after the border crossing, that Willi Drucker had arrived safely at Feldkirch and had contacted Kriner, the Gestapo chief who was to put Drucker's papers in order for the trip to the Ruhr. Then, for weeks, nothing more.

In mid-January 1944, Anne Kappius made her second courier run to her husband in Bochum and on her return on February 8 reported to Van Arkel that Willi Drucker had never reached his destination in Dortmund. Van Arkel assumed Drucker was captured or dead.

All might have gone well in Germany for Willi Drucker, but for the Battle of the Bulge. After crossing the border on New Year's Eve, Drucker had hitched a ride with an SS officer from the city of Singen to Constance. The man was the first German with whom Drucker had prolonged contact after slipping across the frontier. He was discouraged by the officer's stubborn faith in eventual German victory. The man spoke ecstatically of the stunning German offensive in the Ardennes, proof of the Führer's continuing military genius. Drucker gladly left him at Constance, where he ferried across the Bodensee to Friedrichshafen and took a train to Feldkirch. He was safe at last. Drucker presented himself to Herr Kriner, the Feldkirch Gestapo chief, and then passed the message through a trusted border guard to Van Arkel that all had gone well.

During their first meeting, Kriner had said that he could not help Drucker right away with the papers for travel to the Ruhr. He was to come back the next day and join Kriner for lunch. The delay had puzzled Drucker, but he tried to dismiss his anxiety.

The lunch the next day was a round of cautious probing. When Kriner finally looked Drucker in the eye, it was to say, "You know, the war is not yet lost." Kriner referred to von Rundstedt's counterthrust. "What will happen to us now?" "Nothing," Drucker answered. "Nothing will happen to those who work with us." Kriner wanted to know where Drucker had crossed the border; who were his other contacts in Feldkirch; where was he going next—questions never raised between trustworthy agents. Drucker lied and told Kriner he was going to Friedrichshafen, then to Nuremberg. At the end of the lunch, Kriner again said that he could not yet get Drucker's Gestapo papers renewed. He would need a few more days.

Drucker went immediately from Kriner's office to the railroad station. Kriner, he assumed, had reassessed his bets in light of the sudden shift of German fortunes on the western front. In the station, Drucker picked up an attractive woman and invited her to have a drink with him. It was not difficult. He had money, ration coupons, and cigarettes. A woman companion would be pleasant and safer for the journey he still intended to Dortmund.

They took a train to Friedrichshafen and were in the station, waiting to board a train to the Ruhr, when three men seized Drucker's arms and handcuffed him. "We've been waiting for you," one of them said. The woman fainted.

Five months after the plot on Hitler's life, Hans Bernd Gisevius was still in Berlin, living like a hunted animal. Allen Dulles felt a deep obligation to save this courageous German from the unrelenting Gestapo manhunt. After his September visit to General Donovan in France, Dulles had gone on to England for further talks with David Bruce. While there, he had urged Bruce to have his people give high priority to a scheme for spiriting Gisevius out of Germany.

The best and boldest plan was to deliver to Gisevius in Berlin the documents of a Gestapo official, including orders for him to proceed to Switzerland. This cover would be challengeable only by other Gestapo officials, and Gisevius, as a former Gestapo officer, could play the role convincingly.

(Above) William J. Casey, OSS Chief of Secret Intelligence for Europe, the man responsible for organizing operations in England which put 102 missions into the Third Reich. *Courtesy William J. Casey.*

(Left) Lieutenant Commander Stephen H. Simpson, Jr., developer of the Joan-Eleanor communications system, with WAC major Joan Marshall, for whom half of the system was named. *Courtesy Stephen H. Simpson, Jr.*

(Above) The British De Havilland Mosquito, a fighter-bomber, perhaps the most versatile plane of the war and the aircraft used for Joan-Eleanor missions. *Courtesy U.S. Air Force.*

(Left) The hand-held Joan-Eleanor transmitter-receiver used by American agents inside Germany, approximately 2½" × 6¼" × 1¼". Antenna, left, unfolds to one foot. *Courtesy Stephen H. Simpson, Jr.*

(Opposite, above) The Douglas A-26, a small, fast bomber adapted by OSS for missions deep into Germany, such as HAMMER, which penetrated Berlin. *Courtesy U.S. Air Force.*

(Opposite, below) OSS printshop in London, where documents were counterfeited. *Courtesy Carl Strahle.*

DEUTSCHES REICH

VORLÄUFIGER
FREMDENPASS

Name des Paßinhabers

Sedillot   Pierre

Der Paßinhaber
besitzt nicht die deutsche Reichsangehörigkeit

Nr. 245/42

Dieser Paß enthält 16 Seiten

A 54a (8. 42)

A provisional passport for alien residents in Germany, forged by OSS London Documents Section, used by an agent posing as a French conscript worker. *Courtesy Orpha Van Dyck.*

(Right) A "Work Permit" counterfeited by OSS London Documents Section for Emil Van Dyck, who penetrated an SS facility in Munich on the PAINTER Mission. *Courtesy Orpha Van Dyck.*

Arbeitskarte

für belgische Arbeitskräfte

aus Belgien

und Bescheinigung über eingezahlte Lohnansprüche*)

*) Nichtzutreffendenfalls streichen

linker Zeigefinger

Raum für Fingerabdruck

rechter Zeigefinger

(Below) Adjustable rubber stamp which enabled OSS London counterfeiters to duplicate the stamp of virtually every German military unit. *Courtesy Carl Strahle.*

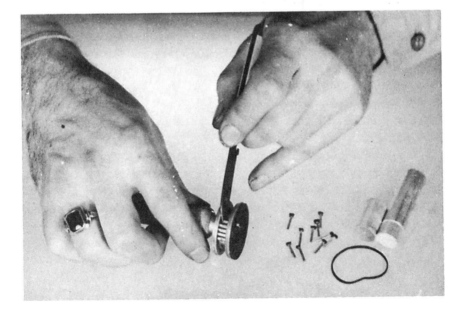

(Above) The Gestapo Silver Warrant Identity Disk of the type counterfeited for Hans Gisevius in his escape from Germany. *(Below)* The reverse side of serially numbered Gestapo Silver Warrant Identity Disk. *Courtesy Gerhard Van Arkel.*

Practice forgeries by staff of OSS London Documents Section. *Courtesy Carl Strahle.*

(Above) An OSS tailor alters clothing at London shop for an agent about to enter Germany as a conscript worker. *Courtesy Carl Strahle.*

(Below) An agent being fitted out for a mission into Germany at the Clothing Depot on Brook Street in London. *Courtesy Carl Strahle.*

(Above) OSS London staff plot missions into Germany from war room. Note status board of missions on right. Left to right: H. H. Proctor, Hans Tofte, Lieutenant Normand (standing), Robert Thompson, William Grell, Fred Gerke, Lazare Teper, by then a lieutenant. *Courtesy George O. Pratt.*

(Right) Lieutenant Junior Grade Mike Burke, OSS London, who helped unsnarl the logistics of penetrating the Reich. After the war, he became president of the New York Yankees and president of Madison Square Garden. *Courtesy George O. Pratt.*

(Above) Château Gleisol, near Lyons, an early base of the Seventh Army OSS Detachment from which agents were dispatched into Germany. *Courtesy Ann Willets Boyd.*

(Below) Third from right, Henry B. Hyde, who led Seventh Army OSS penetration of Germany, with his staff. On far left is George Howe, who manufactured documents and identities for the agents. Seated, Ann Willets Boyd, Hyde's aide. *Courtesy Ann Willets Boyd.*

(Right) Mary Bancroft, a
colleague of Allen Dulles in
Bern, worked with Hans
Gisevius, twentieth of July
plotter. *Courtesy Mary
Bancroft.*

(Right) Kurt Grimm, exiled
Austrian financier, whose
apartment in the Hotel
Bellerive au Lac in Zurich was
an unofficial headquarters for
Austrian agents penetrating the
Reich. *Courtesy Verlag
Molden, Vienna.*

(Above) Paybook of "Feldwebel Steinhauser," the identity assumed by Fritz Molden on missions into Austria. Note attention to differing handwriting and inks on three forged promotion entries. *Courtesy Verlag Molden, Vienna.*

(Left) Ernst Lemberger, prominent Austrian Socialist, later ambassador to the United States. Posing as a German Army private, he completed a vital mission to Vienna with Fritz Molden. *Courtesy Verlag Molden, Vienna.*

(Right) Lothar Koenigsreuter, Austrian Socialist, killed on an OSS mission near Innsbruck in a shootout with SS troops. *Courtesy Verlag Molden, Vienna.*

(Below) Wehrmacht "Deserter Volunteers" (and one woman) recruited for missions into the Reich, seen at Bari, Italy. Fifth from left is Dyno Lowenstein, seventh from left is Walter Haass, two German-Americans whose families had fled the Nazis. *Courtesy Dyno Lowenstein.*

(Above) The Sulztaler Ferner, the 10,000-foot Alpine glacier where the three-man GREENUP Mission parachuted in midwinter, 1945. *Courtesy Fred Mayer.*

(Left) The GREENUP team, which penetrated Innsbruck, seen shortly after the liberation. Left to right, Franz Weber, Hans Wynberg, and Frederick Mayer, who led the team. *Courtesy Franz Weber.*

(Above, left) Fred Mayer, leader of the GREENUP Mission, in the German uniform he wore in Innsbruck, posing as a lieutenant in the 106th High Alpine Troops. *Courtesy Fred Mayer.*

(Above, right) Lieutenant John H. Taylor, leader of the DUPONT Mission, who was captured and sentenced to death at Mauthausen concentration camp. Seen here on an earlier mission to Albania. *Courtesy Dr. Harry Cimring.*

(Right) Martha Frais, killed by Miles Pavlovich of the DILLON Mission; he also killed himself to prevent their capture by the Gestapo. *Courtesy Josefine Neunegger.*

(Above, left) Lieutenant Alfred C. Ulmer, Jr., who developed missions from Italy into the Reich, seen here in Vienna after the war. Sign offers employment in upcoming winter, but warns no ex-Nazis need apply. *Courtesy Alfred C. Ulmer, Jr.*

(Above, right) American personnel who trained and led the IRON CROSS Mission. Left rear is Aaron Bank, the U.S. Army captain who headed the mission. Others identified are Sergeant Baumgold (left, kneeling) and Sergeant Goldbeck (right, kneeling). *Courtesy Aaron Bank.*

Members of the IRON CROSS Mission, the phony company of German infantry, which was to penetrate the National Redoubt to try to capture Hitler and other Nazi chiefs. Front row, left, is Aaron Bank, the mission leader. *Courtesy Aaron Bank.*

The 186 "Death Steps" in the stone quarry at Mauthausen, the concentration camp where several OSS secret agents were executed. *Courtesy Netherlands State Institute for War Documentation.*

(Above) American troops liberate Mauthausen. *Courtesy Archives, Mauthausen Museum.*

(Left) General William ("Wild Bill") J. Donovan, father of the OSS. *Courtesy William F. Grell.*

The first obstacle was to locate a photograph of Gisevius. No individual picture could be found, only a group shot. A Swiss photographer enlarged the picture so that a passport-size photo could be cut from it. This shot and some stolen Gestapo stationery were rushed from Switzerland to London. The BACH operation and the counterfeiters worked together on a German passport and a set of orders from Gestapo headquarters informing government officials and party members to provide all necessary assistance to "Dr. Hoffmann," in whose name the documents were made out. Dr. Hoffmann was ostensibly en route from Berlin on a secret mission to Switzerland. Bob Work, one of Bill Reddick's best men, forged the orders and a phony letter signed "Heinrich Himmler," which was included among Dr. Hoffmann's effects.

Forgery had by now descended from an art to a routine in the London office. Lazare Teper had recently experienced a minor crisis in getting a document out to an agent awaiting departure from Area O. The man had signed his pseudonym to a pass for the Hermann Göring Werke in Linz, Austria. The pass was later to be laminated and sent out to him. In the sealing process, the card had been burned. Teper fretted over the time that would be lost in bringing the agent back to London to sign a new pass. One of the forgers said, "That's not necessary." He glanced at the signature and reproduced it on a new blank. The man, Teper noticed, had not bothered to take a practice stroke.

A difficult but vital item in Hans Gisevius's cover was the Silver Warrant Identity Disk, a gray medallion of an unknown alloy, serially numbered, which provided a Gestapo officer with unlimited right of access and power to arrest. The authentic medals were believed to contain a slight, deliberate flaw to help expose counterfeits.

The medallion was beyond the depth of OSS London. Bill Reddick sought help from the British. They agreed to produce it, but had little faith in the operation. They were working against the calendar, since the Germans usually changed the format of their documents annually, and it was now December 1944.

Reddick's trusted associate, Bill Turnbull, personally delivered the documents and medallion into the hands of a Dulles agent near the French-Swiss border. Gary Van Arkel examined the forgeries first with admiration, then with horror. The passport lacked a vital stamp. Precious days would be lost returning the passport to London. Van Arkel entrusted the document to Daniel Margulies, an OSS officer then returning to London from Switzerland. Margulies was to take the passport to London and have the missing stamp added.

In Paris, while Margulies was switching planes, a military policeman asked to check his papers. Margulies foolishly displayed the German passport. The MP immediately seized it and said that a document of that nature could only go by top-secret army pouch. OSS had long ago learned that any document entrusted to the army was inevitably consigned to oblivion. Four more days were lost extricating the passport from army security officials.

January 20, 1945, the six-month anniversary of the failed plot against Hitler, found Hans Gisevius holed up in a girl friend's apartment in Berlin. The bell rang. Gisevius approached the door with reflexive caution. He heard the hum of a motor driving off, then opened the door. The package he found on the doorstep had traveled from London to Gary Van Arkel in Switzerland, then to a German publisher named Goverts, who delivered it to Berlin. The Gestapo medallion, orders, and passport made out to "Dr. Hoffmann" had arrived virtually at the eleventh hour. After January 21, the following day, no more civilian passenger trains would run and even official travelers would first have to obtain special travel permits from the police. Gisevius had to get on a train that day.

He took a subway to the railway station. There, his documents underwent their first official scrutiny. The ticket agent seemed to linger overly long before he gave Gisevius a ticket to Stuttgart, where he planned to change trains for the Swiss border.

The platform from which he was to depart was bedlam. Ranks of unexpected SS guards and officers shoved civilians and lesser military passengers aside. Gisevius asked a few questions and learned that he had stepped into the hive of a Nazi queen bee. Ernst Kaltenbrunner, chief of all security forces, including the Gestapo, and thus "Dr. Hoffmann's" superior, was soon expected to board the Vienna Express to his Austrian homeland.

The train for Stuttgart was impossibly crowded. Gisevius headed toward the front of the train to try to bribe the conductor to get him aboard. At the baggage car, he encountered a furious commotion. On the platform, the conductor and baggage master were shouting at a crowd pressing around the baggage-car doorway. People cursed and shrieked back at the train officials.

Gisevius drew from deep within himself an authority which he hardly felt. He rudely shouldered his towering bulk through the crowd to the beleaguered trainmen. He flashed the Gestapo medallion and demanded to know what was wrong. It was the first time he had spoken openly in public in six months.

The conductor told him that he and the baggage master could not even board their own train because of the crowd. The conductor gratefully accepted Gisevius's offer to clear the baggage car. He began shouting "Gestapo! Gestapo!" and bulled his way through the doorway as people fell back on either side. As soon as he reached the conductor's bench inside the car, his officious manner evaporated. He sat down, took two children on his knees, and let the mob pour in behind him. From the platform, he could still hear the two railroad men shouting to him for help.

When the conductor finally regained control of the baggage car, he thanked Gisevius for trying to assist him and informed him that there was a special compartment up ahead reserved for high officials. No, Gisevius said, he preferred to stay where he was. After a seeming eternity, the train, with people clinging desperately to every opening, finally pulled out of the station.

Two days later, at Kreuzlingen, a tiny border crossing, Hans Gisevius faced the last two Germans standing between him and Switzerland. One was a simple enough hurdle, a customs official. The other was Gestapo.

Gisevius's position was absurd. He had arrived on foot at six o'clock in the morning at a flyspeck station where no official of consequence ever came, bearing papers signed by Heinrich Himmler. It was midwinter, and he still had on the same summer suit he had worn since the twentieth of July. Over it he wore a torn, filthy spring coat. He had stolen a hat from someone on the train, and it fit him poorly. For months he had cut his own hair with nail scissors, and it hardly followed the neat, close-cropped style favored by the Gestapo, including the agent now checking his papers. He felt faint from hunger and the exertions of deceit. He sank into utter despair as the Gestapo official continued to shift his glance from the papers to the huge, strange figure before him. Then, the gate was swung open. Gisevius limply returned their Nazi salute and walked into freedom.

X

The Courtship of Joan-Eleanor

✠ ✠ ✠

On New Year's Day, 1945, the Battle of the Bulge still raged; the Germans had launched a second offensive to the south in Alsace. These desperate Nazi lunges had to be beaten back; then Germany had to be invaded, and OSS had only three active agents to provide intelligence from inside the Reich: Jupp Kappius in the Ruhr, Youri Vinogradov in Berlin, and Fritz Molden in Austria. The others were either lying low, captured, or dead.

The pressure on Bill Casey, and through him on George Pratt's Division of Intelligence Procurement, to get more agents into Germany now became intense.

Throughout the fall, DIP had organized swiftly and effectively for the task. But one obstacle persisted. The staff could recruit agents, equip and document them, even extricate them from Germany independently. But, alone, it could not parachute people into the Reich. For this step, OSS was at the mercy of the U.S. Army Air Force.

During the French operations, two squadrons of bombers had been made available to OSS for agent drops. The squadrons designated for this work were drawn from the 492d Bombardment Group, Eighth Air Force, stationed at Harrington Air Field, outside London. The missions were designated the "Carpetbagger Project."

Carpetbagger crews flew weathered B-24 Liberators, most of them punctured by rusting, unrepaired shell holes from enemy fire. The planes were painted a glossy black to deflect light, thus rendering them virtually invisible, even when passing through the beams of enemy searchlights. The ball turret in each bomber's belly had been removed and a round plywood door placed over the hole. It was through this space that the agents parachuted. Flame-dampeners were attached to reduce the fiery glow of the plane's exhaust. The nose compartment was curtained from the rest of the plane, leaving the bombardier in total darkness. From this black aerie, he could better spot visual-reference points for the navigator —a shoreline, a bend in a river, lakes, and mountains. Prisoner-of-war camps, with their bright lights to prevent escapes, were particularly useful beacons.

The twin curses of the aviators were foul weather and "flak," from the German *Flugzeugabwehrkanone*, or antiaircraft gun. Of the two, airmen seemed to prefer man-made perils. Evading enemy fighters and antiaircraft fire was all-consuming work which crowded out fear. But flying on instruments over the fog-shrouded English Channel—in total silence, in a small capsule high above the earth—produced a silent, helpless terror.

During the campaign in France, the 492d had gained extensive experience in the peculiar demands of carpetbagging and had dispatched over one thousand agents from its B-24s. The techniques differed sharply from conventional bombing missions. On bombing runs, each plane flew as a ship in a vast armada twenty thousand feet above the earth, guarded by fighter planes. Carpetbaggers flew alone at altitudes as low as five hundred feet, as slowly as 120 miles an hour over the drop zone. Navigation was less critical on bombing missions, since planes in formation usually played follow-the-leader. For the solitary aircraft on a dropping mission, navigation was the difference between depositing an agent accurately and safely or leaving him hopelessly lost.

Each mode of flying had its perils. The massed bombers flew with relentless fatalism into an aerial valley of death formed of waiting antiaircraft below and enemy fighters above. The lone plane on a dropping mission risked the treacherous hazards of low-level navigation, particularly as it wove through mountain passes. A heavy bomber, flaps down, flying barely above stalling speed at low altitudes, running in to drop an agent was a pigeon for enemy fighter aircraft.

After the breakout from Saint-Lô in the summer of 1944, the 492d was shifted from dropping agents to hauling gasoline to the mechanized forces racing through France and Belgium. The 492d flew what it was told was its last Carpetbagger mission on September 16, 1944. Soon after, OSS advised the group commander that there was probably no further need for Carpetbagger flights, since the war would probably soon end. The 492d was then assigned to conventional bombing, leaving a few aircraft behind for unanticipated OSS needs.

For men of the 492d, the change was a welcome return to the mainstream of Eighth Air Force flying. The crews were freed of the odd demands, stifling secrecy, and occasional smugness of OSS officers. They could again swap tales of their last mission with other bomber crews at the officers' club. Then, on the last day of 1944, as the penetration of Germany assumed priority, OSS was back again, knocking at the hangars of the 492d Bombardment Group.

The resumption of relations between OSS London and the 492d Bombardment Group began badly, and went downhill. The air unit no longer had the planes and experienced crews which it had placed at OSS's disposal earlier. One of the 492d's squadrons had been transferred to Italy in December. Other crews were engaged in night raids on marshaling yards and supply depots inside Germany. The remaining crews showed little enthusiasm or understanding of OSS missions. The attitude began at the top. In December 1944, the 492d had been assigned a new commanding officer, Colonel Hudson H. Upham, described, tactfully, by Lieutenant Colonel Charles C. Bowman of OSS, Bill Casey's executive officer, as "a very fine officer, recently arrived from the United States with no experience of our type of activity and unwilling to make definite decisions."

Colonel Upham did make one decision. He sharply limited the scope of OSS's ambitions for Germany. He forbade his aircraft to fly missions outside a southwestern corner of Germany bounded roughly by Stuttgart, Ingolstadt, and Munich. Colonel Upham feared that lone aircraft operating beyond these limits were too vulnerable to German night fighters and heavy flak, and would find too few navigation aids. The 492d did agree to fly to Holland, but not across the German-Dutch border. In a period of nine weeks the group flew only one OSS mission.

As agents began completing training for the German missions, OSS requested more support from the 492d. The OSS air-liaison officer to the bomber group, an amiable, unaggressive man, found himself suddenly saddled with an uncomfortable and unaccustomed burden of responsibility. He was sent from London with one of Colonel Upham's officers to establish a base at Lyons from which missions could be flown into Germany. Lyons could also provide air transportation for Henry Hyde's Seventh Army missions.

Just as the pressure intensified to get more planes into the air, the weather worsened. The winter of 1944–45 was the coldest in forty years. Freezing temperatures and unaccustomed snowfalls settled in December and covered the ground until the end of January. For the first three weeks of February, the skies were obscured with fog, rain, and low-stratus clouds. Only five missions were dispatched from the new Lyons base during the January–February moon period. Another six missions got off during the February–March moon, a time also plagued by storms. As agents continued to pour from the training program, the facility at Lyons and the OSS air-liaison officer sagged under the responsibility, and thirty more missions were backed up awaiting the next period.

Bernard Shaw had anticipated Stephen H. Simpson, Jr., when he observed: "The reasonable man adapts himself to the world; the unreasonable one persists in trying to adapt the world to himself. Therefore all progress depends on the unreasonable man." Those who failed to grasp Stephen Simpson's vision found him clearly unreasonable. Those who shared it also found Simpson unreasonable, but worth the pain.

One evening in the fall of 1944, Lieutenant Commander Simpson was dining with Bill Casey and other OSS London officers. They were discussing the problems of communicating with agents inside Germany. What had worked well in France posed grave danger within the Reich. In occupied territories, agents had communicated via wireless radio from safe houses. They were able, to a degree, to thwart German radio direction-finding equipment by changing houses frequently. The standard radio was called the suitcase model, since that was how it was usually carried. It was not the kind of luggage which one would gladly carry into Germany.

There, where safe houses would be few or nonexistent, wireless transmission, with its widely dispersed signal, would expose agents to detection by radio direction finders. These "gonio" vans, for radiogoniometry, could pick up a radio signal twenty miles from its source and home in on it until, at one hundred yards, monitors could hear the clacking of the radio keys.

Steve Simpson confidently told his dinner companions that given the right people and the right planes he could come up, within months, with a clandestine communications system safe for use inside Germany. A claim by Steve Simpson was not to be dismissed lightly.

He was a man seemingly composed of equal parts of ability and irascibility, a thirty-seven-year-old Texas mustang with a twanging accent and a healthy ego. When men carried out their duties with unusual courage and intelligence, Simpson was quick to praise, writing letters to their superiors, recommending appropriate decorations. When men were lost, he wrote touching letters to their families. When someone failed to meet his exacting standards, he was scathing.

His colleagues found him, variously, "cheerful, always smiling," "fiercely independent," "a very collected human being," "a belligerent man masquerading as a naval officer."

Before the war, Simpson had been an RCA scientist with a long interest in radio-transmission technology dating back to 1928. As a young man, Simpson had worked on a pioneer RCA project to rebroadcast the Christmas tolling of Big Ben via shortwave from London to New York over radio station WJZ. Sixteen years later, Simpson found himself a navy lieutenant commander attached to OSS London, still probing the potential of radiowave propagation.

Simpson's solution to the German communications problem had been simmering in his imagination since he had first gone to work for COI to establish a worldwide communications network in 1942. He envisioned a system in which an agent on the ground could speak directly to an operator in a plane circling overhead via a radio beam so narrow that it would be virtually undetectable by enemy direction finders. Within twenty-four hours after he had told Casey that he could perfect such a system, he received official approval to proceed.

Simpson turned immediately to DeWitt R. Goddard, a research engineer and RCA colleague then working at the company's Riverhead, Long Island, laboratories. Goddard was given a commission by the navy and flown to England so precipitously that his first stop was at Selfridges to buy a uniform. He brought with him to England experimental equipment which he, Simpson, and other colleagues had worked out in the course of frenetic transatlantic trips and telephone calls before his arrival in England.

The Simpson-Goddard team produced a system designed to fill Simpson's specifications, a transmitter-receiver small enough to be easily concealed by an agent on the ground, and another larger set to be installed aboard a plane. The equipment on the plane was to be connected to a novel device, a machine which could record conversations on a spool of wire. The radio carried by the agent was six and a half inches long, two and a quarter inches wide, one and a half inches thick, and weighed three-quarters of a pound. It was powered by long-life batteries. The equipment aboard the plane weighed under forty pounds.

The British had earlier developed a prototype called the S-Phone. But it had serious drawbacks for use inside Germany. The S-Phone equipment carried by the man on the ground was so large that it had to be strapped to his back, and its signal to the plane was good only up to ten thousand feet, well within lethal antiaircraft range.

Simpson named his system "Joan-Eleanor": Joan, for a major in the WACs whom he much admired; and Eleanor, for DeWitt Goddard's wife. The Joan component was carried by the agent on the ground, and Eleanor was the equipment aboard the plane.

While Simpson and Goddard had been perfecting their device, the Germans had made a technological leap of their own. The Eighth Air Force informed Simpson that the Germans had developed an antiaircraft gun directed by radar which ruled out the original plan to use B-17s for Joan-Eleanor missions. To fly a lumbering B-17 in circles within the range of a weapon of such lethal accuracy would be suicidal. Simpson argued that the potential gains justified the risks. The air force was adamant. It would provide no clay pigeons for OSS spy games.

Simpson determined to adapt his gear for another aircraft. He had been reading about the British De Havilland Mosquito and was much impressed by its virtuosity, particularly the model used in photo reconnaissance. The small, swift and spirited Mosquito, the "jeep of airplanes," with some daring modifications, could be adapted to carry Joan-Eleanor equipment. Simpson and his team were assigned to an airfield at Watton in East Anglia, where the American air force maintained its only squadron of British Mosquitoes, procured under a form of reverse lend-lease. Initially, Simpson managed to pry one Mosquito, #676, from the air force for Joan-Eleanor testing.

Simpson first shed the Mosquito of every pound of dispensable weight to compensate for the addition of the Joan-Eleanor operator and equipment. All guns were torn out, the Mosquito would fly unarmed. Simpson covetously eyed another few pounds in the "IFF" system, Identification, Friend or Foe. He was warned that if the IFF were removed, he risked having the plane shot down by friendly planes and antiaircraft. The IFF system came out.

Flying the Mosquito proved vexing to American pilots. The propellers of the British plane, unlike American aircraft, spun in the same direction, causing the Mosquito, in the hands of inexperienced pilots, to drift on landing. OSS had to find American pilots who had flown British Mosquitoes with the RAF before Pearl Harbor for the Joan-Eleanor project.

Simpson thought he detected another distinction between British and American aviators. Plagued by chronic aircraft shortages, the British attitude, it seemed to him, put irreplaceable planes before dispensable pilots. RAF fliers were to take extreme risks to save the plane. To part with any aircraft was painful enough to the British. Consequently, the additional Mosquitoes finally given to the Americans by the RAF were, not surprisingly, basket cases.

Whipping these planes into flying condition and adapting them for Joan-Eleanor would have taxed the talents of master mechanics. Simpson, instead, found himself supervising inexperienced workmen who demonstrated little comprehension of the project's significance and who wielded their tools with a heavy hand. For Stephen Simpson, to whom a workbench was an altar and the purring of engines a hymn, the experience was excruciating. He drove this indifferent crew and himself ruthlessly to get results. One of his colleagues described him during this period as "obsessed, superefficient," and added, "he was unflappable, except if things didn't go right."

The purpose of the BOBBIE Mission was to establish an underground route along which OSS agents could be infiltrated from Holland into Germany. BOBBIE, actually Anton Schrader, was a twenty-seven-year-old engineer from Soerabaja, Dutch East Indies. After attending the University of Utrecht, he had been trapped in Holland by the German occupation. Schrader escaped to England, worked with Dutch intelligence first, then signed a contract with OSS to undertake the mission to establish the secret path into Germany. On November 10, 1944, BOBBIE parachuted, for the first time in his life, near Ulrum in Nazi-occupied Holland. There had been no time for jump training. Stephen Simpson had demanded to be notified immediately if BOBBIE had dropped successfully. The agent was the first to penetrate enemy territory equipped with Simpson's Joan-Eleanor radio.

Eleven days after BOBBIE had departed, Stephen Simpson crawled into the tapered tail of Mosquito #707, the second aircraft which the British had supplied the Americans for Joan-Eleanor missions. Two earlier attempts to contact BOBBIE through Simpson's system had failed. During the first effort, with the ailing Mosquito #676, the elevator controls had jammed, wrenching control of the plane from the pilot. On the second try, BOBBIE could not be contacted and #676 had been badly damaged on landing.

Mosquito #707 had been hurriedly pressed into service for the third attempt, with Captain Doroski as pilot and Lieutenant Mishko as navigator. Simpson braced himself for the takeoff on a bench behind the bomb bay, where his equipment had been installed. As they passed over the Dutch coast, Captain Doroski descended to twenty thousand feet to try to catch BOBBIE's signal. Simpson impatiently tore open a hatch and stared below. Beneath him there unfolded a gorgeous fireworks. The plane shuddered with each burst. He knew he would have to straighten out the pilot. Simpson seized the intercom. "We're in a storm, Captain. You'd better get us out of here." "Commander, that's no storm." Doroski was patient. "You're being shot at." Simpson slammed the hatch shut and resumed his position behind his radio gear.

The aircraft gained altitude and now cruised seven miles above the earth. Air scoops sucked a strong draft into the plane's tail, whipping Simpson's oxygen mask with a cold, hard stream. He manipulated his dials through thick gloves, which, like his flight suit and boots, were electrically heated to ward off temperatures that plunged to twenty degrees below zero at this altitude.

The pilot cruised along a prearranged bearing while Simpson played his directional antenna back and forth across the flight path. The receiver began to hum and crackle. Simpson locked the antenna onto the bearing that had yielded the response. The pilot brought the plane around to the same heading. Simpson turned on the wire recorder. "The time is now twenty-three–fifty-eight." His voice was taut and his speech exaggeratedly precise. "Steve calling BOBBIE, Steve calling BOBBIE. The time is now twenty-four hundred. This is Steve calling BOBBIE. Steve to BOBBIE." Static danced along the circuit.

"Thank God! Thank God!" Simpson's voice choked. The other voice was faint, ethereal. ". . . am quite all right." Simpson's ear picked out words through the noises. BOBBIE became louder as the plane pursued the radio beam, then swung into a tight circle thirty thousand feet above the agent on the ground. "I landed in a big ditch and lost part of my luggage. I have a car now." Simpson grinned. "I need new maps, new batteries, five flashlights, two sets of five automobile tires, one set sixteen by five twenty-five and one seventeen by five fifty." Simpson eyed the spinning spool of recording wire contentedly.

BOBBIE reported a Panzer regiment headed toward Arnhem and pinpointed a railroad bridge over the Ems Canal at Leeuwarden. If Allied bombers destroyed the bridge, he said, they would paralyze traffic from this key junction into Germany. BOBBIE then asked permission to break off the conversation. "I am standing here near German posts. It is very dangerous." Simpson said good-bye, raised the pilot on the intercom, and told him to head home. Joan-Eleanor worked.

The OSS now had a system for communicating with agents in Germany which was virtually foolproof against direction-finding equipment. Since the chance of interception was unlikely, the plane and the agent could converse in plain language. Freed from the necessity of enciphering messages, tediously tapped out in Morse code, Joan-Eleanor could convey more information in twenty minutes than could be sent by wireless radio in three days. Garbles and misunderstandings could be clarified on the spot.

The hand-me-down Mosquitoes, when finally patched together, were well mated to Joan-Eleanor missions. The plane could fly at thirty thousand feet and higher. It was highly maneuverable and able to elude enemy radar. With the successful test of BOBBIE in Holland now behind him, Stephen Simpson did some heady calculations. Stripped of a bit more weight, a Mosquito could fly a Joan-Eleanor Mission directly to Berlin.

Lieutenant Commander Stephen Simpson had flown over a dozen test missions to BOBBIE in Holland as his own Joan-Eleanor operator. It was an ideal arrangement. No one understood the radio system better than Simpson, its creator, and BOBBIE spoke fluent English. But as Joan-Eleanor equipment was entrusted to agents bound for Germany who spoke little or no English, foreign-speaking operators had to be recruited to work aboard the aircraft. The first Joan-Eleanor linguist reported to Watton, on February 21, 1945. His name was Calhoun Ancrum.

Lieutenant Ancrum had blond good looks and a square, solid frame. He had displayed unquestioning fatalism at jumping out of aircraft or flying Joan-Eleanor missions. Yet he seemed an incongruous figure to crawl into the tail of a small, unarmed plane and fly into Nazi Germany. There was something of the aesthete in Calhoun Ancrum—in his movements and the measured precision of his speech.

As a civilian, Ancrum had done some itinerant writing and editing. He was recruited by OSS for his knowledge of Scandinavian languages and German. He had been trained, originally, for a drop behind the lines.

After the liberation of France, Ancrum was at loose ends, haunting OSS corridors on Grosvenor Street. Here, he first stumbled onto the budding Joan-Eleanor project. It appealed to him immediately. Particularly, it offered Ancrum a fresh start after having been unhorsed in several jousts with military authority. Lieutenant Ancrum, a warm, generous friend to his peers, compassionate and understanding toward the lesser ranks, had a poorly concealed impatience with military superiors whose intellectual candlepower he suspected. Idiots, Ancrum believed, ought to be made aware of their condition, whatever their exalted rank.

After being assigned to the Joan-Eleanor project, he quickly became snagged on Stephen Simpson's barbed character. The Texan drilled Ancrum in the rudiments of Joan-Eleanor with a classroom manner combining impatience, sarcasm, and wonder at the density of the human mind. They came away from the experience with widely differing views of each other. Ancrum accepted that he had fallen into the snare of a tyrant. He particularly disliked the raw, Texas political conservatism of the engineer. Simpson concluded that in Ancrum he had acquired a bright man and a gifted linguist. He admired the young officer's abilities and drove him fiercely, along with everybody else, to help perfect his dream.

Most German Communists in exile were associated with an organization appealingly called the "Free Germany Committee." After the Nazi defeat at Stalingrad, the Russians had persuaded captured German commanders, including Field Marshal Friedrich Paulus and General Walter von Seydlitz, to work for the defeat of the Nazi regime. One offshoot of this effort had been the formation of the Free Germany Committee, in actuality a political wedge designed to initiate Communist domination of Germany after the war. Subsequently, branches of the Free Germany Committee emerged in France, Switzerland, Sweden, England—virtually anyplace where refugee German Communists had fled.

Noel Field, an American Communist in Switzerland and Allen Dulles's link to the far left, suggested that OSS ought to set up a relationship with the western elements of the Free Germany Committee in France. This move could, he believed, open a rich vein of highly motivated anti-Nazi Germans to serve as espionage agents.

Dulles sent Field to Paris to pursue the idea. But there, Field was stopped cold, in no small measure by the efforts of Bert Jolis, the erstwhile diamond merchant who had become a key OSS link to the non-Communist trade unions and who had infiltrated Youri Vinogradov, the White Russian, into Berlin. Jolis was aghast at the shortsightedness of OSS in considering the use of German Communists. Looking to the postwar world, he found the prospect of arming Reds and positioning them where they could grasp power in Germany to be naïve in the extreme.

But General Donovan, a Catholic, a Wall Street Republican, and a thoroughgoing establishment figure, was not overly concerned with the side effects of any nostrum which might promote victory. He had once said, "I'd put Stalin on the OSS payroll if I thought it would help defeat Hitler."

David Bruce, Donovan's man in London, agreed. "Why not use everybody?" As Allen Dulles in Bern saw the issue: "An intelligence officer should be free to talk to the devil himself if he could gain any useful knowledge for the conduct or termination of the war." The matter was formally resolved in a directive issued by Bill Casey to his SI staff on February 22, 1945. This document listed among potential agent recruits, "the Free Germany Committee or other Communist groups, anybody who fought in the Spanish civil war."

German labor exiles in England were split roughly between adherents of the German Socialist Party and the German Communist Party. George Pratt's Labor Division had extensively used laborites, but had done nothing to exploit the Communists. When OSS London decided to explore the untapped Communist reserve, the recruitment task fell to Joseph Gould, a round-faced, bespectacled young army lieutenant assigned to the Labor Division.

Gould's only exposure to trade unionism had occurred at a fairly rarefied level, as a member of the Screen Publicists Guild. He came into Arthur Goldberg's orbit late in 1943, which led eventually to his assignment to the Labor Division. The former motion-picture publicist and the first German V-1 both arrived in London on the same day in June 1944.

Knowing nothing of Communist organization in England, Gould set about his assignment with elemental directness. As a New Yorker, he assumed that every large city must have its political bookshop. Inquiries led him to a bookstore operated by a British couple, where he ingratiated himself and, after a decent interval, asked who was important in the Free Germany Committee in Great Britain.

Thus, Gould learned of Dr. Jürgen Kusczynski, a distinguished German-refugee economist. Gould's approach to Kusczynski was as unadorned as his strategy in the bookstore. He called upon Kusczynski in his London flat on an August afternoon. He met a lean man in early middle age, deeply enmeshed in his writing, but open and friendly.

Gould, though dressed in civilian clothes, introduced himself as a lieutenant in the U.S. Army, involved in intelligence. He explained that he was looking for agents capable of undertaking delicate and highly hazardous missions inside Germany. Kusczynski was equally direct. Gould, he said, was the first intelligence officer of any Allied nation to approach him, and, however belated, he regarded it as a mutually fortunate meeting. He understood precisely what Gould needed and told him where they would meet again in one week.

Gould next saw Kusczynski in a London restaurant. With the economist was a small group of men looking uncomfortable in inexpensive suits and neckties. Kusczynski introduced them as German labor exiles and explained that they were eager to cooperate with the Americans.

Over the following weeks, Gould continued to meet with Kusczynski's people. He inquired about their backgrounds, what cities they knew, where they might have contacts, who might shelter them. He hammered at his key concern: physically and emotionally, were they prepared to parachute into Germany?

Kusczynski had chosen wisely. Every man wanted the job. Beyond a minimal assurance of security for their families, they had only the most passing interest in what they would be paid. They had suffered at the hands of the Nazis and were eager to have an opportunity to strike back. They stressed their desire to demonstrate to the world a finer dimension of the German national character than Nazism. Gould found them impressive, politically sophisticated, and accustomed to organizing effectively for the achievement of their objectives.

From them he chose seven men with the physical stamina to carry off a mission and the intelligence and resourcefulness likely to produce information once inside Germany. They ranged in age from thirty to forty-one. All of Gould's recruits were authentic workers—a bricklayer, a plumber, an iron molder, a turner, a miner, a welder, a maker of artificial limbs. All were employed at their trades when Gould enlisted them—which may have explained their relatively comfortable lives, compared to the near-destitute Socialist German refugees whom George Pratt was aiding.

Gould's actions had to be approved by Pratt, who was his chief. His recruits also needed clearance by British counterintelligence. Presumably, the enrollment of these men had at least the tacit approval of the labor chief of all OSS, Arthur Goldberg, though in later years Goldberg would deny that Communists were ever knowingly used in his labor operations.

Late in the fall of 1944, Gould entered his recruits into eight weeks of training. Except for parachute school, the student spies led a life indistinguishable from that of hundreds of thousands of Londoners. They took the tubes and buses to downtown offices for OSS training. Most were married and lived at home. They were, in effect, commuters.

Gould's students were a pleasure to their instructors—serious, hardworking, quick, ready with original ideas. Their politics, however, were not revealed to other agents attached to the Labor Division. The Socialists and democratic laborites thought they had allied themselves with OSS to fight both Nazism and communism. The employment of Gould's recruits would have perplexed them.

Joe Gould was now carried on the OSS roster as a training officer, which enabled him to be with his agents at all times. Between classes, he took them to Lazare Teper's BACH operation to work out their cover stories and their documentation. He had them outfitted at the clothing depot on Brook Street, and had them photographed. Bob Work, the star forger in the Bill Reddick operation, also served as photographer and took the pictures of agents for the false identification they would carry. Work found himself studying their faces, searching vainly for some clue that marked them as unusual. He was continually surprised by their ordinariness.

The home of one agent, Paul Land, became unofficial headquarters for the Communists. Gould spent a memorable Christmas in December 1944 at Land's modest, comfortable flat. He, the agents, their wives and children, ate, drank, laughed, and sang "O Tannenbaum" and other Christmas songs in German.

It was a happy crew. The aura of good feeling prevailed on and off the job. Still, the Germans were insistent as to what role they expected the Free Germany Committee to play in the postwar political life of their nation. It was a ticklish point for the Americans, which they handled, largely, by ignoring it. No promises, no commitments were made. Gould and other OSS people dealing with Communist agents drew a careful distinction. They were dealing with individuals, not with the Free Germany Committee.

The clothing depot on Brook Street, where Joe Gould had taken his agents to be outfitted, was located in a brownstone, recently a private residence. It now resembled the sort of thrift shop where well-to-do women sell last season's fashions to raise money for charity. The jarring note, amid the racks and piles of suits, dresses, hats, and shoes, was the German uniforms here in a house in Mayfair.

The clothing depot served both OSS and British intelligence operations. Some of its stock had been acquired from refugees, like those who had sailed to New York aboard the Portuguese liner *Serpa Pinto* three years before. The clothing came from exiles in Britain, North Africa— wherever people had fled Nazi rule. The common denominator was that all the goods—the suits, shirts, ties, hats, belt buckles, cufflinks, billfolds, suspenders, tiepins, shoelaces—had been manufactured in Germany or in countries under the German heel.

Another source of clothing for the depot was prisoner-of-war camps in the English countryside. There, Lazare Teper would employ ersatz chumminess on his scavenging missions. "Hi. Where are you from? What do you hear from home?" Elite SS troops greeted these overtures with sullen defiance. But Teper found the dregs of the Wehrmacht, the frightened old men and homesick boys, pliant and grateful for a friendly word. Conversation drifted easily to an offer to trade a cigarette for a prisoner's comb or pocket mirror—maybe a whole pack for a fountain pen. Teper also absorbed the bits of information which his conversations produced on conditions inside German cities, grist for the BACH operations coverstory mill.

Other supply procurers were more direct. At a racetrack outside of London, converted into a POW cage, the guards blew their whistles whenever intelligence officers arrived, signaling the prisoners to muster. The intelligence people then took whatever they needed, observing the letter, if not the spirit, of the Geneva Convention. If an army cap was taken, another was supplied. If the substitute cap engulfed the prisoner's head, the Geneva Convention was not specific on sizes. A noncom carried a bag which filled quickly with clothes, cameras, and other personal articles.

Sweden also supplied the clothing depot. German-made luggage, razors, perfume, and eyeglasses were purchased there and shipped from Stockholm through the State Department's diplomatic pouch.

The depot maintained its own tailor shop, which made alterations or fabricated wholly new items when necessary. New clothing would be deliberately dirtied and laundered again and again, until it lost its stiff newness.

The clothing depot's most prolific supplier was Captain Edward C. Miller. Miller, an OSS supply officer, abhorred forms and formal channels. He always had someone, a friend of a friend, always in another outfit, who could get it, fix it, find it, or borrow it. One of Miller's tactics was to have an enlisted man place a call to a supply depot for "General Miller." Miller would then gleefully seize the phone, rattle off a list of items which his men urgently needed, and announce that he was sending a truck to pick up the material right away.

Miller was slightly paunched, with a retreating hairline, a genial man, clearly relishing life. He maintained an inexplicably lavish apartment in London. Invitations to an Eddy Miller party meant good food, liquor, poker, craps, good-looking women, and an attentive and gracious host.

As preparations for the missions to Germany began to deplete stocks at the clothing depot, Captain Miller was directed to apply his talents to the problem. Miller flew to the front and arrived in time to enter Cologne just behind the infantry.

He remained on the Continent for two weeks working areas liberated by the First Army. Some supplies he purchased from terrified German civilians and shopkeepers. Most of it he "liberated." The official OSS inventory from his scavenging mission showed 106 men's suits; 102 women's dresses; 400 neckties; 156 hats; 150 pairs of shoes, rubbers, and boots; 52 sets of ladies' underwear; 98 cigarette lighters; and 500 miscellaneous items ranging from toothpaste to flashlights, flown back to London in three crammed C-47s.

The pieces were fitting nicely for Lieutenant Commander Stephen Simpson. Joan-Eleanor had been successfully tested with the British Mosquitoes. The OSS had found, in the new batch of agents recruited by Joe Gould, two natives of Berlin. Everything was almost in order for Simpson's vision, the mission designated as HAMMER. HAMMER would drive deeper into the Reich than any mission before, all the way to Berlin. The mission would stretch the capacity of men, aircraft, and the Joan-Eleanor system to their outer limits, and it would prove Simpson's theories of clandestine communication.

Through Simpson's efforts, a wholly new plane had been procured which could fly the distance from England to Berlin, drop the agents, and return. Securing aircraft was not Simpson's province, and OSS had been reasonably satisfied thus far with the performance of B-24s for agent drops. But Simpson had overheard pilots describing the graces of the A-26, a new, lightweight attack bomber with a maximum speed of 373 miles an hour. The A-26 had been designed to make swift descents to treetop level, drop its bombs, and arch steeply out of antiaircraft range. Simpson wondered: If the A-26 could drop bombs this way, why not agents? He began to read hungrily about the plane's characteristics. It had maneuverability and speed far surpassing the B-24 and was, in fact, one of the fastest bombers in the world. The A-26 had a maximum range of 1400 miles, well above the 1160 miles required for the round trip to Berlin.

Lieutenant Colonel John Bross, of London OSS, worked with Simpson to persuade a reluctant Eighth Air Force to assign A-26s for missions deep into Germany. Simpson told Bross that they ought to go to air force brass and demand that "OSS damn well be given A-26s." Bross convinced Simpson that they might improve their prospects with a persuasive written case. They then drafted a memorandum to present to an air force intelligence general.

On the appointed morning, Bross and a restless Simpson waited for the general to arrive. The air force officer came in at ten-thirty, bearing the marks of a low-level mission over Piccadilly the night before. One arm was cradled in a sling. He gazed blearily at the memorandum for an uncomfortable interval. Bross then described what was in it. "How many do you need?" "Two," Bross answered. As the general began to sign his approval to the memorandum, Simpson began to argue for three A-26s. Bross quickly maneuvered Simpson out of the office. "Why did you do that? You almost killed it." Simpson laughed. "It was getting too damned easy."

One obstacle still stood in Simpson's path. The minimum safe flying speed for the A-26 was 155 miles per hour, too fast for a guaranteed safe opening of parachutes. The B-24 Liberator usually slowed to 120 to 130 miles per hour for jumps.

Early in February 1945, modifications were hurriedly begun to see if the A-26 might be adapted for agent drops. By February 24, the aircraft was ready for tests at the hitherto unsafe speeds. Simpson boarded the modified aircraft at Beaulieu, the British airborne experimental station, along with his favorite pilot, Captain Robert P. Walker, and two test parachutists.

The A-26 leveled off for the first run. Chutes of two test dummies were pushed through the jump hole. They struck the bulbous turret of the belly gun. A live chutist would have been bashed to death. They took the plane down and attached longer static lines to the parachutes. On the next run, both dummies cleared. Gunnery Sergeant Lawrence N. Elder of the U.S. Marine Corps and Sergeant George Usher of the RAF, the test jumpers, said they were ready. As they jumped, their bodies were snatched from the bomb bay by a swift airstream. But the chutes blossomed clear of the aircraft.

The components were now there for Simpson's long-schemed mission to Berlin. It would be tight. The A-26 had the range to drop the agents and return. But the Mosquito, which would follow and make the Joan-Eleanor contact with the agents on the ground, had a proven range of only eleven hundred miles. The round trip to Berlin was a shade longer.

The HAMMER Mission to Berlin was planned with scrupulous precision. Lieutenant Commander Simpson enlisted the group's outstanding navigator, Major John W. Walch, to design the flight. Walch was more than a navigator. He was a serious student of aeronautics, able to integrate aircraft characteristics, meteorology, navigation, and pilot capabilities into a successful whole.

Major Walch spent two weeks plotting a detailed flight plan. His calculations had to take into account several weather zones which the aircraft would transit. He designed a sinuous course permitting the plane to fly blind, by instruments, around German gun batteries and mountains, sometimes at altitudes as low as two hundred feet. He shaped the course along large bodies of water, the only reference points which would be visible on the night selected for the HAMMER Mission.

The two native Berliners chosen for the HAMMER Mission were Paul Land and Toni Ruh, both Communists living in English exile and chosen by Joe Gould. The two men had also worked together for ten years in the anti-Nazi movement.

Paul Land was thirty-four years old, a small, coiled spring of a man, intense and propelled by inexhaustible energy. Gould's dossier on Land read, "Face: Squarish, small. Complexion: Usually pale. Subject notes that the fitter he feels, the more often he is asked if he is ill . . . will wrinkle brow when hunting for word, may toss head occasionally, but usually keeps head absolutely fixed during talking. No use of hands." Under "Distinguishing marks," Gould reported, "Red mark to right of nose bridge and under left eye, received from knuckle ring at hands of Nazis. . . . Also bayonet scar, upper-right-hand buttock from SA handling in 1933, a distinct scar in the shape of a bayonet blade."

Land had begun to resist the Nazis years before as a member of the Labor League of Youth. In 1935, with the Gestapo after him, he fled to Czechoslovakia, where he worked with an underground movement spiriting fugitives out of Germany. When Czechoslovakian independence was bartered to Germany by Allied appeasers in 1938, Paul Land left for England, where he was interned as a "dangerous alien." He was deported to Canada until March 1942, and then allowed to return to England. When Joe Gould met him, Paul Land was working as a toolmaker in a British factory. Gould found Land to be that rarity: a true proletarian intellectual accepted by middle- and upper-class leftists.

His partner for the Berlin mission was a year younger and almost a head taller than Land. Toni Ruh also carried impeccable anti-Nazi credentials. Ruh had gone underground on the night of the Reichstag fire, was subsequently arrested, and spent seven months in prison for anti-State activities. He was unexpectedly released, so that the Gestapo might follow him to other members of his ring. Instead, he fled in May 1934 to Czecho-slovakia, where he and Land worked together. Ruh also went to England, only to be deported to Australia as a danger to the Crown. He was allowed to return in the spring of 1941 and found work as a welder. Both men were married and each had one child.

Ruh was a large man with graying hair and a quiet, reassuring solidity. He provided the requisite counterpoise to the volatile Paul Land. Joe Gould felt more comfortable with the engaging Land than with Ruh. But he wrote in his evaluation: "This was a balanced team in which the individual characteristics of the two men combined effectively."

The Germans possessed other qualities which would serve them well on the mission. Both were in prime physical condition. Land was accus-tomed to riding a bicycle up to fifty miles a day. Ruh was a devotee of hiking, boating, and bicycling. Both were avid skiers. They were going to need strength and stamina for this mission. They would be the first to parachute from the swift A-26 on an actual operation.

HAMMER became a pampered mission. The complex flight plan was rehearsed on four practice runs to Berlin, during which the navigator recorded each checkpoint with a stopwatch and compass. On March 1, the night set for the agents' departure, a special precaution had been taken. They would not leave until a weather plane returned and declared conditions for the drop favorable over Berlin.

Paul Land and Toni Ruh arrived at 9:30 P.M. at Watton Air Field accompanied by their mother hen over the past five months, Lieutenant Joe Gould. Also awaiting them was the architect of the HAMMER Mission, Lieutenant Commander Stephen Simpson, and the gruff DIP operations officer, Captain Rob Thompson.

The sensation that he was living a movie scenario bothered Gould, the former Hollywood publicist. He had committed the professional sin of growing too close to these men, and the drama of the moment seemed to be at their expense. On the drive out to the airport, Gould had passed around a flask of brandy. He sipped lightly himself, but noticed that Land and Ruh had taken deep, pulling drafts.

The audacity of the HAMMER Mission had inspired the documents and cover staffs to extraordinary efforts. The agents carried the finest papers which Carl Strahle's printshop could falsify. Each carried a *Kenn-karte* and a work order from the Berlin Labor Office. Paul Land, acting as the senior partner, also carried a *Wehrpassbuch*, exempting him from military service as a skilled defense worker, and a Nazi party membership card.

Lazare Teper's BACH Section had fashioned new lives for them as a German toolmaker and a Czech welder. Paul Land had committed to memory his life as "Ewald Engelke":

I was born on 10 May 1909 in Frankfurt a/Oder a son of Paul Engelke, cabinetmaker, and of Hermine (maiden name) Baum, housewife. My father was born on 9 May 1886 in Frankfurt a/Oder; my mother on 27 June 1886 also in Frankfurt a/Oder. We lived at Goerlitzerstrasse 32, Frankfurt a/Oder, where my father was running a little cabinetmaker's shop. I am single and evangelisch-lutherisch.

From 1915 to 1920 I went to elementary school *(Volksschule)* in Frankfurt a/Oder, and from 1920 to 1923 I went to the Staatliches Friedrichsgymnasium und Realgymnasium in Frankfurt a/Oder. I had to quit the Realgymnasium in 1923 because my father's cabinetmaker's shop went into bankruptcy at that time.

I started as a toolmaker apprentice in 1923 at SCHMIEDT & DIETRICH, Geepelstrasse 59, Frankfurt a/Oder, which lasted until 1927. During these four years apprenticeship I went to the Städtische Gewerbliche Berufsfachschule in Frankfurt a/Oder. As soon as my apprenticeship was ended, I was fired. I moved to Königsberg, Konitzerstrasse 3, where my family had moved in 1925, to live with them again.

In Königsberg I got a job at the ODINWERKE MASCHINENFABRIK u. GIESSEREI BARTLICK & ROGLER, Ayeider Allee 59/65. There were about 300 workers employed then on the production of car components and machinery. I was working in the lathe and toolmaking department, making precision parts, gearshifts, universal joints, axle and axle housings, etc. In 1940 I was made a foreman of the toolmaking department of that firm.

On 21 Nov. 1938 I was issued the *Arbeiterbuch* by the Arbeitsamt in Königsberg.

On 8 February 1939 I was issued the *Kennkarte* from the Polizeipräsidium in Königsberg.

In February 1940 I was called up and declared unfit for military service because of kidney trouble.

My *Wehrpass* was issued by the Wehrbezirkskommando I in Königsberg, 4 March 1940, I also received an *Ausmusterungsschein* for this reason.

The ODINWERKE were destroyed during a Russian air attack and when I reported to the Labor Office, I was ordered to evacuate to Berlin and report there to the Labor Office.

I carry a letter from Arbeitsamt Königsberg to Arbeitsamt Berlin, written in February 1945.

My mother has been sick and in bed for the last two months with rheumatism and my father stayed with her since she was unable to evacuate. Since then I don't know what became of them.

The red mark (scar) to right nose bridge was caused when as a child I fell on a rock. The scar on the upper-right-hand buttock was caused on my job at the ODINWERKE when handling sheet metal in 1932.

Toni Ruh was given a new identity as Antonin Vesely.

I was born on 20 February 1907, at Mährisch-Ostrau Protectorate, the son of Jan Vesely, a railroad worker, and of Maria (maiden name) Jirka, housewife. I am a Roman Catholic and single. My father was born on 15 March 1877 and died of angina pectoris on 22 April 1938. He was buried at the city cemetery in Mährisch-Ostrau. My mother, Maria Vesely, maiden name Jirka, was born on 7 August 1883 in Mährisch-Ostrau as the only daughter of the cobbler Franto Jirka, Mährisch-Ostrau; she died on 10 January 1944 of heart failure and is buried with my father there in the family grave.

I went to elementary school *(Volksschule)* in Mährisch-Ostrau from 1913 to 1921 and graduated there. From October 1921 to October 1924 I was apprentice at the machine and repair shop Jaroslav Janiszeck in Mährisch-Ostrau, where I learned welding and lathe-band operating. I continued to work with this firm with minor interruptions until summer 1940, when by recommendation of my uncle who was foreman at the RINGHOFFERTATRAWERKE A.G. (ZAVODY RINGHOFFER TATRA A.S.—Czech name for firm) in PRAHA-SMECHOV, Martouzska 200, I quit my job in Mährisch-Ostrau to work with this firm in the welding department. There were about 4000 to 5000 workers employed in 1940 on the production of cars and trucks. In Prague I lived at: PRAHA-SARCHOV, Zborouska 27.

Kennkarte was issued by the Polizeidirektion in Prague on 4 February 1941.

In May 1944 I was transferred by the Labor Office in Prague to the JUNKERSWERKE, STRIEGAUERSTR. (near Gaudon airport) to work again as a welder in the welding department on repair of fuselages, steering mechanism and wings. There were about 1800 workers of which 75% were foreigners. The plant consisted of 6 large buildings. I lived in Breslau at Tauentzienstrasse 175.

The plant was nearly completely destroyed by Russian air attacks and most of the machinery was damaged or destroyed. I was told to report to the Labor Office in Breslau where I was given an order to evacuate to Berlin and report there at the Arbeitsamt.

Letter from Arbeitsamt in Breslau, dated. . . . 1945 to the Arbeitsamt in Berlin. The scar on center of upper lip, under nostrils was caused when as a child I fell on a pointed rock, which pierced the lip. Burns on the right elbow were caused through an accident in 1938 on my job in Mährisch-Ostrau.

Should they succeed in establishing themselves in Berlin, the HAM-MER team had three objectives: to make contact with the Free Germany Committee (particularly members living in areas of immediate military significance), to procure and transmit intelligence from these sources, and to prepare for the reception of additional agents (specifically Adolf Buchholz, another Communist recruit from the Gould group).

Land and Ruh finished supper at Watton Air Field and were taken to the operations hut, where Gunnery Sergeant Lawrence Elder waited to help them don their parachute gear. The marine was introduced as one of the men who had safely test-jumped from the A-26. The men shook his hand, but said nothing.

Before putting on jump suits, their documents, .32-caliber pistols, and money were checked again. They carried reichsmarks equivalent to $700 apiece and each had a diamond valued at $200. Joe Gould went over their communications plan one last time. The team was to identify itself in Joan-Eleanor contacts as "Heinz." If another name were used, this would alert London base that they were in trouble. The radio operator in the plane would use the name "Vic." They went over the exit plan with Sergeant Derr, the dispatcher, who warned them that from the moment he tapped their helmets, they and their containers had eight seconds to clear the plane if they were to land close to the pinpoint. The rest of the crew was a star aggregation hand-picked by Lieutenant Commander Simpson. Robert Walker, Simpson's favorite, would pilot the plane. The squadron's best navigator, John Walch, who had designed the course, would guide them to Berlin aided by another able navigator, Lieutenant Mishko, who had flown in early Joan-Eleanor tests.

Ten minutes before midnight the weather aircraft returned. A light rain was falling at Watton, but over Berlin the weathermen reported the night clear and moonlit with a thirty percent cloud cover. The pinpoint had been sighted visually and confirmed by navigational aids. Commander Simpson gave the order for the team to depart. A-26 #524 pulled up to within fifty feet of the operations hut. The rain gave its black body a glistening sheen. The roar of the engines overpowered their voices. The party bent against the blast of the propeller and edged toward the glow of light from the open bomb bay. Gould and Derr helped boost the two Germans through the opening. Gould shook their hands quickly, ducked under the fuselage, and headed back to the operations hut.

He, Simpson, and Thompson stood huddled against the rain and deafening engine noise. A fuel truck pulled up to the aircraft. The engine warm-up had consumed seventy-five to one hundred gallons of fuel, and the tanks were being filled again just before takeoff. The trip to Berlin and back was expected virtually to dry the tanks. Demolition charges had been attached to the Joan-Eleanor equipment in case the plane fell into enemy hands.

The A-26 began to move, slowly at first, then faster, then streaked down the runway. As the wheels cleared the ground, Commander Simpson checked his watch. It was one minute past midnight.

Gould and Simpson were awakened four hours later. They had dozed off in the warmth of the Watton operations hut and began to shiver on re-entering the raw night. Their vigil was short. The aircraft soon appeared, dipping one wing tip. Simpson knew what Captain Walker's signal meant. Minutes later, the A-26 rolled to a halt before the hangar. The huge frame of Derr, the dispatcher, reared from the plastic blister at the top of the plane. He shot his arms into the air, thumbs up. The mission to Berlin was in. Inside the cockpit, Captain Walker noted that his fuel gauge showed one hundred gallons.

The HAMMER team walked the streets of Berlin in a silence born of awe and disbelief. The capital of Nazi despotism, which they had fled ten years before, now cowered under the lash of Allied bombers. Berlin had become a curious mosaic of stateliness and ruin, part-functioning, part-shattered, like a handsome woman with gaping wounds.

The pair had dropped thirty miles to the west, near Alt-Friesack. They had walked all the way and on their arrival in Berlin, on the evening of March 2, headed for the home of Paul Land's parents. They were greeted first by shock, then tears of joy. Later, when his parents had time to regain their composure, Paul Land noted proudly that the fire of defiance still burned in them. Both were fifty-seven years old and still militant foes of the regime. The father said to Paul, "We knew you would come back someday to fight the Nazis."

The agents were hidden in an empty bungalow left in the care of Paul's father by fleeing neighbors. They spent their first week becoming Berliners again, learning the catechism of wartime behavior in the city, and relearning the layout of this sprawling capital. They were by turns impressed and annoyed by the uneven information provided on Berlin by the BACH staff. In their pose as workingmen, they found that they had been provided with unnecessarily shabby clothes. Even foreign workers presented a better appearance, sometimes superior to working-class Berliners, since the foreigners seemed to possess better contacts with the black market.

The faked ration stamps issued in London, however, held up admirably in both the open and black markets. The coffee and fourteen hundred American cigarettes they carried proved to be the strongest currency in the barter economy of Berlin. On one occasion they traded a half pound of coffee for seven loaves of bread and a half pound of meat. On another occasion twenty cigarettes netted thirty pounds of potatoes. Their prize transaction had taken place in the country, where they acquired a large sheep for sixty cigarettes and a half pound of coffee.

The information that they brought from London on the air-raid warning system was amazingly accurate. They found Berlin in the early spring of 1945 a city ruled by Allied raids. Work, travel, shopping, eating, sleeping were all dictated by the wail of sirens.

In the eleven weeks preceding their arrival, Berlin had been struck over eighty times. Every third home was destroyed or uninhabitable. Streets were often no more than paths between the rubble. On their sixteenth day there, the city was staggered by the awful devastation of thirteen hundred U.S. bombers.

Yet the effects of the raids were curiously sporadic, both on stone and flesh. Gutted shells with empty eyesockets for windows stood next to virtually unscathed buildings, like the seemingly charmed Gestapo headquarters on the Prinz Albrechtstrasse. The raids had killed an estimated fifty thousand Berliners. But life went on with a dogged regularity, like a madman wordlessly ramming his bloodied head against a wall. Milkmen and mailmen delivered. Garbage men collected. Phones rang, subways and elevated railways ran, fitfully, it was true, since this was the nerve most damaged in the city. People traveled from battered homes to shattered offices and factories. Bake shops opened, grocers and beauty salons operated. Newspapers were published daily, still promising miracle weapons to win the war and reporting fresh rifts among the Allies. A few theaters, symphonies, and movie houses continued to function. Restaurants were crowded, even if menus were tedious. People seemed chronically tired and irritable. But no one spoke of the war, just as the blind do not complain perpetually of their cross. Particularly astonishing to the HAMMER Mission, two-thirds of Berlin's industry continued to function.

The psychic effects of the raids, which people seemed largely to suppress aboveground, were frequently exposed in the confinement and enforced idleness of the shelters. Hysterics, shouted abuse, and fights—

among the young, old men, women, the infirm and the able—were common. On one occasion Paul Land found himself taking charge of a small shelter when the warden lost all control.

On March 12, 1945, Calhoun Ancrum, huddled in the tail of a British Mosquito bomber, realized Stephen Simpson's highest hopes for Joan-Eleanor. Eleven days after the HAMMER team had parachuted near Berlin, Ancrum talked to Paul Land, who stood in a field six miles below on the outskirts of the German capital. Admittedly, this first contact had been more a technical than an espionage triumph, a frustrating exchange of code names: "Is that you, Heinz?" "Is that you, Vic?" "Can you hear me, Heinz?" "I can't hear you, Vic." Nevertheless, through Joan-Eleanor, OSS had communicated with an agent directly from the German capital. Simpson knew that subsequent contacts would be more productive. But his triumph was short-lived. The next day, the bottom fell out.

The small fleet of Mosquitoes and A-26s assigned to OSS was ordered from Watton Air Field and transferred to the 492d Bombardment Group at Harrington. Simpson received no explanation for the move. He could tie it only to a change of leadership in the photo-reconnaissance squadron that had flown the Joan-Eleanor missions. Command had passed from an officer who had supported Simpson's project to Colonel Elliot Roosevelt, the president's son, whom Simpson, for no provable reason, believed to be unsympathetic to his work.

From a field accustomed to handling the special demands of air-reconnaissance and Joan-Eleanor missions, the Simpson crew was destined for a facility engaged almost wholly in mass-bombing missions. From an officer who had appreciated and abetted Simpson's efforts, they passed into the unsympathetic hands of Colonel Hudson H. Upham, commander of the 492d, who already resented having to assign any of his B-24s to OSS missions.

The Mosquitoes and A-26s flew from Watton to Harrington in a storm of confusion. No preparations had been made for their arrival. Officers and men were left to search on their own for billets where they might spend the night. The mechanics who tended OSS aircraft reeled under conflicting orders from three different engineering staffs at Harrington.

In subsequent days, Simpson was horrified to find green pilots taxiing his painfully rehabilitated Mosquitoes up and down Harrington runways for practice. He inevitably collided with Colonel Upham, who questioned the authority of this domineering, apparently dry-docked naval officer.

They battled bitterly over who had operational control over agent flights, the air force, or OSS.

The first Joan-Eleanor Mission flown out of the new base was a chilling portent. On March 17, Lieutenant Ancrum and the crew of Mosquito #725 set out for another rendezvous with HAMMER. The navigator scheduled for this run, Lieutenant John Jackson, had to beg for weather information. Air corps intelligence failed to provide the customary briefing on German air defenses which the plane might encounter. The VHF radio circuit did not work. The plane's mechanics had to scramble over the Harrington field at the last minute begging for oxygen and fuel.

Other Joan-Eleanor crews were left waiting for ground transportation which never arrived. On one occasion, the fliers had to commandeer a jeep to get from the mess hall to their plane.

These high-altitude aviators were supposed to eat a special diet of non–gas-forming food prior to missions—broiled steaks, toast, grapefruit, sliced tomatoes. A gaseous diet could cause excruciating cramps at high levels. Harrington cooks concluded that these fliers could damn well eat what every other crew ate. Ancrum remembered the almost diabolical menu before one Joan-Eleanor mission: hot dogs and sauerkraut. On March 21, the ultimate indignity occurred. Stephen Simpson's log noted, "All sheets removed from our quarters. No coal. Told to fend for ourselves."

The Joan-Eleanor teams met indifference from the control tower as well. Kingdon Knapp, the most seasoned Joan-Eleanor pilot, returned on April 2 from his thirtieth mission. After failing repeatedly to raise the tower for landing instructions, he finally had to put the plane down at the old field at Watton. The next morning he again attempted to return to Harrington. As he circled, a warning light indicated that his landing gear had failed to lower. He called the tower for visual confirmation, but got no answer. Knapp had faced a near identical problem on his previous mission, when only one wheel had dropped. At that time he had heard from the tower belatedly that, indeed, he was on one wheel. Knapp had solved the problem by smacking the runway with such force that the other wheel popped out.

After that experience, Knapp had told Lieutenant Anthony Turano, the deputy OSS air operations officer, "I'd like a little more attention from the tower." Turano had relayed the complaint to Colonel Upham. "Our boys deserve just as much attention as yours," Turano tactfully suggested.

Now Knapp faced another tense moment, with the control tower again ignoring him. He wheeled the plane around, bore down on the tower, and skimmed closely over it. He dove toward the tents where the mechanics worked, coming so close that his backwash tore the shelters out of the ground. All over the field, figures darted and dove for cover. Fire engines and ambulances rolled onto the tarmac. Knapp ordered Lieutenant Jackson to maintain pressure on the landing gear with a hand pump; Knapp was going to try to crash-land. He brought the aircraft to a smooth stop. The landing gear had not jammed. The warning lights had malfunctioned.

Air force officials rejected Knapp's argument that he had buzzed the field only to draw the tower's attention to his plight. He was threatened with a court-martial. Lieutenant Turano tried unsuccessfully to dissuade the air corps officers. Turano then informed Lieutenant Colonel Charles Bowman, the SI executive officer and a skilled peacemaker, of Knapp's situation. Bowman invited Colonel Upham to London for lunch. No one knew exactly what took place. But Simpson heard later that Bowman, with disarming innocence, had raised the subject of countercharges for gross mismanagement and negligence by the air corps at Harrington. The charges against Kingdon Knapp were dropped. But the acrimony on the ground was destined, inevitably, to be reflected in the sky.

The perversity of it all enraged Stephen Simpson. Most of his problems at Harrington Air Field had been in trying to get the 492d Bombardment Group to fly agent missions. Now, Colonel Upham was demanding action when inaction was the course of wisdom.

The CHISEL Mission was scheduled to drop Karl Macht near his birthplace at Hamm, Germany, on March 19. Macht was another of the seven Communist agents recruited by Lieutenant Joe Gould from the Free Germany Committee. The sky was an unnatural habitat for Karl Macht. He was a creature of the earth who had worked as a coal miner in Germany and, after he was run out, returned to the mines in Scotland. He was thirty-three years old and another proletarian intellectual who wrote articles for the trade-union press on the German labor movement. Macht was a practicing internationalist and well enough thought of, though a German, to have been elected an officer of the National Union of Scottish Mine Workers. He had been primed for this operation by a rough practice stint in a prisoner-of-war cage as a phony POW. He faced his mission with a quiet, earnest fatalism.

The A-26 scheduled to fly the mission was #524, the same aircraft that had deposited the HAMMER team in Berlin. Its navigation gear badly needed calibrating. The engines were overdue for their hundred-hour check. The weather on the day of the mission began ugly and overcast. The flight was scrubbed, then rescheduled, then scrubbed again. The plane was finally grounded for repair.

At four o'clock that afternoon, Lieutenant Commander Simpson was stunned to learn that CHISEL had been rescheduled. He rushed to Colonel Upham's office and demanded an explanation. Upham parroted the order of an unnamed general who, he said, demanded that the mission be flown. Simpson explained that both engines had been torn down and that the radio was malfunctioning. The crew assigned to the CHISEL mission had never flown together. The pilot, Lieutenant Oliver Emmel, had not yet completed training for an A-26. The weather report showed a heavy front moving across Harrington and foul conditions on the Continent as well. Flak was said to be heavy along their route.

The navigator on the flight was to be Major John Walch, the finest in the group, the man who had brought the HAMMER team to a perfect drop near Berlin. Simpson hated to see Walch board that aircraft. Upham was adamant. The plane was to be patched together as soon as possible and go.

At ten-thirty that evening the agent, Karl Macht, arrived at Harrington. Just prior to takeoff, the pilot, navigator, and bombardier all told Colonel Upham that they believed the mission was impractical. Upham replied with the ultimate taunt to proud aviators. If they were afraid, he would fly the plane himself. Lieutenant Emmel, the pilot, said this would not be necessary. The crew boarded A-26 #524 and took off in harsh, stiff winds that drove sheets of rain across her black fuselage. Simpson watched the plane disappear into the blackness. The aircraft never returned.

XI

Belgian Roulette

✠ ✠ ✠

OSS had initially recruited Ray Brittenham for his ties to Belgium. Brittenham had grown up there while his father served as an overseas executive of International Harvester. He had returned to America to attend law school and had barely begun to practice in Chicago when he was called on by a university professor who asked if he wanted to do something interesting for his country. The man refused to be more specific. Brittenham was leery. He described the spare, strange conversation to his father, who said simply, "If your Uncle Sam wants you to do something, why don't you do it?"

His initiation into OSS in 1942 had struck Brittenham as sophomoric. He was given a train ticket to Washington and an envelope with orders not to open it until after his arrival. He obediently waited until the train was in Union Station. In the envelope were instructions for him to stand on a particular Washington corner on a certain date at 9:00 A.M. Brittenham complied, and precisely at the designated hour a car pulled up and the driver waved him in.

Matters thereafter took a more serious turn. Brittenham underwent OSS training at several posh estates around Washington. There, he mixed with anonymous men whose identities were concealed under army fatigues and false names. Some of their talents he discovered in the weapons-training session. The Sten gun behaved in Brittenham's hands like an untamed bronco. The man after him fired the weapon in short bursts, clean through the center of the target. Later, Brittenham learned that the man was a veteran of the Abraham Lincoln Brigade in the Spanish civil war.

Brittenham was eventually assigned to the Washington OSS office handling the reports of Hans Gisevius, Fritz Kolbe, and other Allen Dulles sources in Switzerland. It was a pleasant enough war, but one which Brittenham found intolerable. He managed a transfer to London, where he helped to mount operations supporting the Belgian underground.

In the spring of 1944, as the invasion of Europe approached, Brittenham began thinking about the geographic advantages of Belgium as a base for the infiltration of Germany. But British intelligence then had a virtual lock on Belgian secret operations. In a May 23, 1944, memo to Whitney Shepardson, then chief of SI in London, Brittenham wrote:

> At the present time, the Belgian Sûreté is bound by certain very firm agreements with the British to which they are holding which prevent them from having relations with other intelligence services. One of these is that they will tell the British of every agent who goes in and comes out of Belgium. The British apparently have complete control over all communications between the Sûreté here and the underground now in Belgium. The underground networks are directed from London, much of the direction and control being done by the British.

But after D day, with General Patton's Third Army reaching Luxembourg, and as it became obvious that American armies would soon enter their homeland, the Belgians became eager to free themselves from British domination. Thus was born ESPINETTE, a joint group representing OSS and the Belgian Sûreté. Captain Brittenham went to France on September 5 as head of ESPINETTE, along with several Belgian colleagues. Their objective was to establish contact with Belgian underground agents as they were overrun by Allied armies and to recruit them for subsequent operations into Germany.

On September 15, ESPINETTE set up headquarters in Brussels. In its recruiting, the group had to tiptoe around a 1942 OSS restriction imposed by the British stating that "no efforts were to be made to send OSS agents for intelligence purposes into Belgium, nor to recruit Belgians in the U.K. for intelligence work."

The first Belgian team recruited was sent to England for training in

October. Brittenham's primary criteria were that prospective agents spoke German, had a knowledge of the country, had espionage experience, and were highly motivated. The latter standard was not easily met, since the most reliable motive, the desire to liberate one's nation from the Nazis, had largely been achieved in Belgium.

OSS recruiters had undergone a similar and even more dispiriting experience with the French. After the liberation, OSS officers canvassed scores of former French operatives and Maquis veterans. One discouraged recruiter reported after returning empty-handed from a foray to Nancy and Marseilles, "The trouble was simply that no one wanted to go on missions into Germany." OSS wound up signing on a half-dozen French freebooters, none of whose operations succeeded.

Brittenham, too, was forced to deal with adventurers. By the time ESPINETTE had been organized in Brussels, Belgian espionage had virtually shut down. Most agents had returned to conventional lives. Brittenham was left with those who had tasted life behind the lines and who had acquired a craving for danger. The possibility of continuing with the Americans in the unfinished war had a powerful appeal to the soldier-of-fortune mentality.

Brittenham still resisted enlisting sheer thrill-seekers. Besides the formal security clearance by X-2 and Belgian authorities, he sent members of the ESPINETTE staff to check out a prospective agent—in his home-town, among friends, relatives, the local priest—to find out what really propelled him.

Even to the well motivated, the prospect of parachuting into Germany had to be broached carefully. Brittenham found himself manipulating the recruits indirectly toward that objective. He first revealed only that they would be involved with the Americans in extremely dangerous work. Most assumed he meant that they would serve as liaison officers and interpreters at the front and make a brief tactical incursion behind the lines now and then. By the time Brittenham revealed the true scope of the missions, most felt their honor too firmly committed to back down.

When the Germans broke through the Ardennes in December, Brittenham was diverted temporarily from long-term espionage planning to finding agents who could slip through the lines on quick reconnaissance missions to detect a troublesome gun, troop movements, or the number and firepower of enemy tanks. He found these darting intrusions a not always reliable test of a man's fitness for long-term missions into Germany. The short mission was the challenge of the sprinter, a heady burst of excitement followed by immediate accolades for success. The long missions demanded endurance, solitude, and offered only long-deferred rewards.

Brittenham had become particularly fond of a red-haired agent named Louis, who had successfully completed four short infiltrations during the Battle of the Bulge. Between missions, Louis returned to his home in a nearby Belgian village. When the man asked for a fifth mission, Brittenham turned him down. The agent was sorely testing the odds, Brittenham warned. Louis pleaded. When he slipped through the lines, he explained, he did his job, then sought refuge in a barn or hilltop where he knew perfect serenity. But when he came back to his village and his wife, he also returned to his mother-in-law, who made life hell. He preferred to face the Germans.

By the end of January 1945, Brittenham had sent five teams to London for training. In February, Bill Casey created a Belgian desk as another unit of the Division of Intelligence Procurement to handle Brittenham's recruits. Casey named Major William F. Grell, one of a handful of U.S. Marines in Europe, to head the Belgian desk.

Grell had been born Willy François Angélique Grell in Antwerp and had become an American citizen during the 1930s. He was working as assistant general manager of the St. Regis Hotel in New York City when the war began. Grell, then in his early forties, tried to enlist in the army and navy, but was turned down as too old. Much to his astonishment, he was accepted by the Marine Corps. But his excitement ebbed when the recent hotelier learned that he had been commissioned expressly to manage a marine officers' mess. Grell rebelled and pulled enough strings to have OSS enlist him—on the condition that he would undertake missions behind the lines. He had accepted without hesitation.

On reporting to Washington, Grell, too, was subjected to the spy-thriller conceits of rear-echelon security officers. He arrived in Washington in his Marine Corps uniform and was told to buy himself a civilian suit, to cut all the labels out of it and any other identifying marks from any other clothing, then to wait in his room at the Statler Hotel for a phone call. A few days later, he received a message to stand on the corner of 17th and K streets until a gray panel truck came by. Grell, who had spent two years in the trenches of World War I before he was eighteen, tolerated it all with an amused shrug.

He eventually went to Europe and completed a highly successful mission to Limoges in southwest France, an operation that resulted in the surrender of a large German force.

At the peak, Grell had eleven Belgian teams in training which Brittenham had recruited on the Continent. Their principal objective was to penetrate the National Redoubt. Brittenham's highest hopes rested with three teams code-named DOCTOR, CHAUFFEUR, and PAINTER.

Jean Smets, the younger of the two DOCTOR agents, was the twenty-four-year-old son of a well-to-do Belgian government official. Young Smets had never done a day's conventional work in his life. He was six feet tall, with dark hair, heavy brows, gray-green eyes and a devilish smile—a handsome fellow exuding facile charm. He had studied catalytic chemistry at the universities of Louvain and Brussels, though student cafés seem to have been the primary focus of his academic career.

Of Smets his OSS evaluator wrote: "He can easily understand . . . but is lazy and rather frequently tries to screen his ignorance of a point he should have studied. He has done little personal study. He is interested in women and nightlife. In order to go to town on two occasions, he trespassed strong contrary advice given by the C.O. of the area. He dodged morning physical exercises on two occasions, is not particularly punctual."

The only trade Smets had ever plied was sabotage as an underground agent of the British SOE in his occupied homeland. This background had brought him to Ray Brittenham's attention.

Smets was to serve as the DOCTOR team's observer. The radioman chosen was a friend of Smets's, also from the Belgian resistance, a man of far different and, fortunately, complementary character. Lucien Blonttrock was a physically and emotionally solid man of thirty-three who, before the war, had held white-collar jobs while studying law at night. He was evaluated during training in England as: "seriously interested by his work . . . although he is not a 'brilliant' type. He is security-conscious and punctual." In one respect Blonttrock and Smets were alike: both were wholly apolitical, with Smets's penchant for high living matched by Blonttrock's single-minded obsession with athletics.

The BACH Section asked air force photo-reconnaissance to come up with a bombed-out factory in Munich which could be used in a cover story as the former place of employment of the two agents. The air force produced the name of the Optische Werke A.G., Rodenstock, a key optics plant which had been struck on February 25. The DOCTOR cover story was that the men had left the plant after it had been bombed to go on a brief vacation in Kufstein, Austria, before seeking work again. The counterfeiters provided an *Urlaubsschein*, a leave permit from work, along with other standard documentation. Since they were officially carried as Belgian officers on the OSS roster, they were to be paid the Belgian Sûreté rate of £8 per week, about $40, and were informed that a life-insurance policy of $2500 had been settled on them, should they be killed.

If the outlines of the Redoubt had a geographical center, it was the drop zone selected for the DOCTOR team. The prospective pinpoint was a plateau lying between the ice-blue crags of the Kitzbüheler Alps, at an elevation of approximately 6300 feet.

The team's objective was to report on rail traffic out of the Reich supplying the Italian front, military installations in the Tirol, and to unveil any plans of the Nazis to form their own alpine Maquis, once they were defeated in the field.

As the date approached for the DOCTOR team to depart, Jean Smets made a request of the Belgian desk officer, Captain Grell, which amazed his shyer teammate. It would bolster their morale, Smets said, if they had an opportunity to meet some of the top OSS people who were determining their destiny. The request was unusual, Grell thought, but not unreasonable.

George Pratt, as chief of the DIP, took the two men to dinner in London. He strengthened their confidence in OSS by his honesty as to the odds they faced and by his obvious commitment to the work, all conveyed with Pratt's habitual understated humor. Smets was perfectly at ease and lighthearted; Blonttrock serious and impressed. It had been a successful evening, George Pratt thought afterward, except that neither the host nor the guests ever knew each other's names.

The DOCTOR and PAINTER teams were scheduled to fly out of England together at the beginning of the February–March moon period. On the night of their departure, they were accompanied to the airport by Pratt's superior, Bill Casey. Casey found Smets's resolute nonchalance rather hollow that night, confirming a pattern he had sensed in departing agents—either labored gaiety or a tight-lipped grimness.

The two teams landed at the airfield at Lyons and stepped immediately into the three-cornered cross fire between the 492d Bombardment Group, OSS London, and the Seventh Army OSS Detachment.

The two teams were, on their arrival at Lyons, boarded at a rundown, insecure hotel in the center of town and fed in a sleazy black-market restaurant. Everyone in Lyons seemed to know who they were. Jean Smets recalled strangers approaching them on the street wanting to know how soon they would be leaving and wishing them *bon voyage*. Eventually, they had to be temporarily returned to London, since the 492d Bombardment Group was unable to arrange their flight.

Among the Belgians recruited and dispatched to London, André Renaix typified Ray Brittenham's nagging concern. His unease was summed up succinctly at the end of Renaix's evaluation report. "Has no political interests." If a thirty-five-year-old man was not politically motivated, then why would he agree to undertake a highly hazardous secret mission? If solely for money or adventure, how reliable would his performance be? What kind of man, Brittenham had to ask himself, would graduate from the University of Brussels, hold down a responsible executive position, then chuck it all to join the French foreign legion? Part of the answer, he recognized, was, the same kind of man who would jump out of an airplane into Nazi Germany.

André Renaix, blond, blue-eyed, with a well-formed physique and ruddy complexion, described as "typically Ardennais," had returned to the business world after serving five years with the foreign legion. He then worked for two years as a sales director for a French firm in Casablanca. He left that job, went to England in 1943, and trained as an agent for the British SOE. Renaix had parachuted into Belgium three months before D day. After his homeland was liberated, Renaix worked the front lines for the Canadian Army.

Brittenham had found Renaix while looking for a radio operator to team up with another agent already sent to England. Direction Action, the intelligence branch of the Belgian Army, offered him André Renaix. The offer puzzled Brittenham. Direction Action was desperately short of radio operators, he knew. Yet, they were willing to part with this man.

Renaix had performed his work with undeniable intelligence and dedication. He also had the background to move easily in most social circles. But he lacked self-discipline when the pressures of a mission were removed. Belgium intelligence people had diagnosed Renaix as a "legionnaire" personality, the dependable barracks soldier who inevitably goes on a spree when he hits town. Renaix had gone AWOL twice while working with the Canadians, and his behavior was viewed as demoralizing to the other men. Brittenham, for lack of better, took his chances with the Belgian.

In England, Renaix was paired with a man twelve years his junior who would, nevertheless, head their mission. Michel Dehandtshutter's adult life had been passed almost wholly as an agent. He had begun with the

Belgian underground at the age of eighteen. Dehandtshutter had only a grammar-school education, but earned impressive credentials in the resistance. He had been planted by Belgian intelligence as an employee of the Gestapo in Brussels during the occupation. In the year spent there, he had managed to steal important documents, including lists of Belgian collaborators with the Nazis. Eventually, sixteen subagents reported to Dehandtshutter.

He gained a first-hand knowledge of German security methods, both as Gestapo employee and victim. One of Dehandtshutter's co-workers had denounced him for a minor infraction unrelated to his undercover work. He was arrested and tortured, but never talked. He was completing a jail sentence for this offense when Brussels was liberated.

Dehandtshutter dismissed OSS's initial concern that his Gestapo record would unduly endanger him inside Germany. They had his picture, he pointed out, but they had failed to fingerprint him. He suggested his own cover solution, which the BACH Section regarded as unconventional but promising. He adopted the name of an actual friend, a Belgian then working in Berlin. He had a picture of his friend, and there was a reasonable resemblance. Should the police check his papers against their own records, they would find that such a man did exist.

The CHAUFFEUR agents carried an unusually large amount of cash —50,000 reichsmarks, then worth about $5000, another $350 in American money—and a supply of cigarettes.

The Belgians were documented with the common cover of conscript worker. They were supposedly fleeing from Nuremberg and looking for work in Regensburg. They carried forged factory passes from the Siemens-Schuckert Werke.

If they had to leave Germany, they were authorized to slip into Switzerland and contact the American consul in any major Swiss city. The password given them for this contingency might make for a curious introduction: *"Je suis l'idiot du village."*

The CHAUFFEUR Mission was to be dropped outside of Regensburg, near the site of a vast plant assembling the Messerschmitt ME-109 fighter plane. CHAUFFEUR was to report on industrial and political conditions and troop and train movements. The B-24 crew assigned to fly them in took on the job with little enthusiasm. Among German cities, Regensburg was respected for its deadly air defenses; a fiery ring of fighters and antiaircraft stood guard there. The first major American strike on the city, the year before, had cost 24 of 146 Flying Fortresses, one of the heaviest prices ever paid by American fliers.

Most spies going into Germany were compensated according to a fairly uniform salary scale, $231 per month prior to parachute training and $331 per month afterward. A $2500 death benefit was standard.

Agents also had to have money to bribe officials, buy equipment, and pay any subagents they might recruit. Obtaining large quantities of German reichsmarks for these purposes could be difficult. Some German funds were bought from neutral diplomats moving in and out of Germany for whom OSS made it profitable to take out large sums. Reichsmarks were also obtained from French, Belgian, and other laborers returning from Germany.

Crisp new bills needed to be aged. They could not simply be buried, because the soil left a telltale residue. The Office of Special Funds in London hit upon a simple and effective technique: the staff locked the office door and scattered hundreds of thousands of reichsmarks on the floor, then went about its work; a few days of trampling underfoot produced a well-worn appearance in the money.

Obviously, large sums of cash would arouse suspicion if found on an agent posing as a conscript worker, a common soldier, or a minor official. To compress the most purchasing power into the smallest form, agents were often supplied with jewelry. The Americans were agreeably surprised to learn that solid-gold watches, rings, cigarette cases, and lighters were fairly common personal possessions among Europeans. Agents were often supplied with these valuables in lieu of large amounts of cash. If the possession of too many gold items conflicted with an agent's humble cover status, the valuables would be nickel-plated. The baser metal could be removed when the agent wanted to sell the ring or cigarette lighter.

The most convenient, universally accepted currency was diamonds, which were sewn into the linings of an agent's clothing. Along with his responsibility for the counterfeiting and clothing operations, Willis Reddick was responsible for the procurement of diamonds. He would buy as many as two hundred at a time among London jewelers. The one-carat size was most handy and Reddick paid in cash, about $200 per diamond. He was always surprised when, after missions, agents returned their unused diamonds.

XII

Armistice with the Air Force

✠ ✠ ✠

The 492d Bombardment Group had done a wretched job of preparing to fly agents out of Lyons into Germany, though long warned of the coming build-up. But the Lyons operation was a casualty, as well, of the rivalry between OSS London and Henry Hyde's Seventh Army OSS staff. Hyde balked at the presumption of authority coming out of London. Nominally, his operation was subordinate, having been transferred in November 1944 from the Mediterranean Theater of Operations, headquartered in Italy, to the European Theater of Operations, run out of London. But Hyde had not grown up under that roof. His group had come out of North Africa, then went into southern France with the Seventh Army invaders as part of the Mediterranean OSS command.

His SI unit, with over one hundred people, was larger than Bill Casey's parent London SI operation and had already successfully attacked problems of agent recruitment, documentation, cover, air support, and communications on its own during the invasion of southern France. For Hyde, London was like a stepfather one acquires as an adult. The new parent deserved respect, but should expect to exercise little control. To Hyde, working feverishly to dispatch his own missions, the arrivals from London to Lyons were an unwanted intrusion, guests on a Monday morning. Nevertheless, the Lyons operation fell within his geographic jurisdiction and he was expected to accommodate London's agents.

Back in London, the crumbling relationship between OSS and the 492d Bombardment Group troubled Lieutenant Anthony Turano, the conscientious OSS deputy air operations officer. Turano, a well-regarded officer, was often handed odd assignments for his reliability. It was he who had escorted the ISK women, Anne Kappius and Hilde Meisel, to Switzerland prior to the latter's fatal mission into Austria.

The war had plucked Tony Turano from Brooklyn, put him down in the Pacific as an infantryman, returned him to military intelligence in the United States, then shuttled him to a replacement depot in England during the preparations for D day. Turano was destined to miss the invasion.

Before the war, he had studied art and had worked as a photographer. This background attracted OSS and spared him the beaches of Normandy. Lieutenant Turano was pulled out of the replacement depot and assigned to the OSS London Air Dispatch Section. He was made responsible, primarily, for selecting the pinpoints in Germany where agents would be dropped.

The assignment proved arduous, requiring long hours bent over maps and aerial photographs, which had to be scrutinized in microscopic detail. The selection of a poor pinpoint undid months of costly effort and was likely to doom agents to capture, torture, possibly death. The twenty-seven-year-old Turano, a slight, handsome, intent man, had a quick, uncluttered aptitude for the technical demands of the task and a conscience for the human consequences of his decisions. He often found himself agonizing for hours after choosing the longitudes and latitudes by which other men might live or die.

The first requirement in choosing a pinpoint was to overcome the apprehensions of the air force by finding reasonably flak-free corridors. One wall of Turano's office at 72 Grosvenor Street carried a huge map of western Europe. On it he plotted data fed in by the British Air Ministry, the U.S. Army Air Corps, and field units on the Continent. Clustered pins formed forbidding rings around major industrial cities, rail junctions, and military installations in the Reich, signaling expected flak zones.

Turano chose the pinpoints working with the country desk handling the agent, the operations staff, and, occasionally, the agents themselves. Once a drop zone had been tentatively agreed upon, the ideal next step was to obtain fresh reconnaissance photos. Turano's reconnaissance requests were not always granted. A plane poking about an area might tip off the enemy that something was afoot. Turano, therefore, often had to work with dated photographs or maps. In one instance, a photo was so obsolete that what had appeared on it as an open space had since become overgrown with trees, a discovery made by a parachutist rather late to select a new site. An inviting field shown on an old map might now be sown with barracks, gun emplacements, and pillboxes.

The model pinpoint was a flat field distant from antiaircraft, nightfighter bases, and inhabited areas. It should be near a woods which could provide shelter, with a road close by for easy egress, and a readily-identifiable natural feature—a lake or distinct point on a river—marking it. When the importance of a mission warranted it, OSS specialists constructed a plaster mock-up of the pinpoint for agents to study before their mission.

Turano's duties required a close working relationship with the air force, and he became one OSS officer who won the fliers' trust. Turano continued to select pinpoints, but was increasingly employed as a respected broker between the air force and his own comrades in OSS. When important joint meetings were scheduled, Turano found that his superiors always sent him along with his less forceful chief. When the 492d Bombardment Group had a gripe with OSS, its officers usually communicated it through Turano.

Turano and Rob Thompson, the DIP operations officer, detected a maddening nonchalance among air force crews toward their OSS cargo. Nearly half of all agents were dropped far enough from their pinpoints for the mission to be classified as "error in drop." An accurate drop was considered anything within a half-mile square around the pinpoint. Even accounting for the difficulty of blind drops at night, errors of twenty miles or more from the pinpoint seemed excessive.

Tony Turano sensed immediately when a drop had gone badly. The crew would return muttering about heavy clouds over the drop zone or the fierceness of the flak. His queries brought vague, impatient reassurances. "Sure. Went fine. Don't worry." The fliers were exhausted emotionally and physically from the mission and still faced their own intelligence officers for debriefing before receiving their "two-ounce medicinal ration of whisky," a hot breakfast, and a long-postponed night's sleep. Turano was dismayed that his superior in the Air Dispatch Section seemed a reflexive apologist for air force miscues.

One extravagant inaccuracy had occurred in dropping the mission designated as PITT, which had gone into Germany under Waffen SS cover. The two agents were to have been dropped on January 2, 1945, near an SS division posted in the Black Forest near Karlsruhe. They had landed on a night when the German troops were outside watching a movie. Their parachutes settled to earth in full view of the stunned and amused audience. One chutist landed on a barracks roof.

The Germans were usually of two minds in treating spies caught so red-handed. One school favored summary execution. A second approach, particularly if the agents carried a radio, was to play them back. These two men agreed to transmit under control, but managed to tip off OSS through their danger signal. The radioman had always spelled his name in the anglicized fashion, "Carl." OSS received its first warning signal from "Karl."

OSS fed the two PITT agents truthful but harmless intelligence, known as "chicken feed," which kept them alive until they were later overrun by Allied troops.

Rob Thompson was incensed at the wasted weeks of planning and the disregard for human lives caused by inaccurate drops. He was convinced that many failures were the fruit of pilot-error, of excessive skittishness when the flak began or when clouds thickened. He blistered one crew after a particularly slipshod drop, "This isn't a damned bombing run. That's a human being you just dumped to save your own asses." He demanded that the negligent crew be relieved from further OSS missions.

To Thompson, Turano, and others engaged in flight coordination, it seemed that OSS missions were treated by the air corps as diversions from serious work and, therefore, merited air crews of commensurate quality. Thompson found himself practicing a rough Darwinism. The most promising agents were assigned to the better air crews. The least reliable fliers carried the most expendable agents.

After seven teams had been stranded on the ground at Lyons, between January and February, Bill Casey called his top staff to a meeting. The poisoned relationship with the air corps had to end. Casey was under intense pressure, as the Allied armies crossed the Rhine, and the demand for intelligence from within Germany had reached a clamor. Teams scheduled for May and June missions were moved up to the March–April moon period. The OSS sections preparing agents, operations, clothing, documents, training, and BACH, were all maintaining a killing pace only, it seemed, to have their efforts frustrated by the air corps.

Air crews frequently lacked commitment to OSS missions simply because they had no true understanding of their purpose. Upper-echelon air force officials had failed to communicate to their subordinates an appreciation of the importance of intelligence operations. To harried air base commanders, the peculiar demands of OSS were so much more lumber added to the cross they already bore. OSS had also deliberately fostered an ignorance of its purposes in its desire for secrecy.

The crews knew when, how, and where missions were flown, but rarely why. A hard choice had been made between motivating crews with knowledge of the mission's importance and risking disclosure of that knowledge, should a crew fall into enemy hands. Among ground crews and support staff, there was wild speculation over the actual purposes of these blackened aircraft. Some thought that the planes were landing in Germany to exchange high-ranking prisoners. Others believed they had a secret device for jamming enemy radar.

Healthier rapport had to be established with the air corps, and authority for air operations had to be centralized in London to resolve the family bickering between London SI and the Seventh Army group. Most important, a respected hand had to replace the present OSS liaison officer with the fliers. Bill Casey announced in the latter part of March 1945 that he was putting Lieutenant Colonel Charles Bowman, his executive officer, in charge of air operations. Bowman was a skilled diplomat of deceptive toughness. He also knew the real and imagined obstacles facing the aviators. Bowman was a flier and had been shot down himself.

Even with the organizational snags unsnarled, OSS still could not provide the strategic intelligence which Army G-2 wanted from the Redoubt, Berlin, and other deep enemy areas so long as the 492d refused to fly outside the southwest quadrant of Germany.

Soon after Bowman took over his new responsibilities, the Eighth Air Force came around. Colonel Upham was removed as commander of the 492d Bombardment Group and his more understanding deputy, Colonel Jack M. Dickerson, took over. The U.S. Strategic and Tactical Air Force ordered the 492d to fly its B-24s beyond southwest Germany.

The ill-starred Lyons operation was ended. The air corps shifted OSS operations to fields at Dijon and Namur, Belgium. The new locations afforded deeper penetration into Germany and gave the strained relationship with OSS a fresh start.

The exuberant Danish-American Major Hans Tofte was dispatched to manage operations from the new Dijon field. Casey's right hand, and an able negotiator, Lieutenant Commander Milton Katz, took up the corresponding post at Namur.

To Katz, a legal scholar, a contemplative man who had thus far spent the war desk-bound at strategic-planning altitudes, this first exposure to field operations was a revelation. He sat, in the middle of the night, in the communications hut at Namur watching as mere youths, surrounded by dials, gauges, knobs, switches, and squawk boxes, translated the grand schemes hatched by OSS London into stumbling reality.

From somewhere out in a black infinity the voice of a pilot flying an agent mission blared over the radio. "I think I've got a bogey on my tail; I'm not sure." A controller consecutively flipped switches linked to a chain of radar stations spaced fifty miles apart. He gave each station a bearing, "You got one plane or two?" Each in turn answered, "One." The controller shouted over to his radioman, "Tell him he ain't got nobody on his tail." In their execution, London's sophisticated schemes seemed hardly different from dispatching taxicabs.

At Dijon, air operations rapidly improved and relations between OSS and the air force became harmonious under the new commander of the 492d. As the backlog of waiting missions grew, OSS sold the air force on a bold gamble. Accurate drops required precise navigation, and navigation was presumably abetted by moonlight, when the outlines of a road, a railroad track, a lakeshore, or a mountaintop could be seen. But waiting for moon periods, with over fifty teams now backed up and the armies hungry for information, became a luxury. It was found, over an experimental period, that thirty-eight percent of drops made during moonlight hit the pinpoint, and almost the same percentage by the dark of the moon. Thereafter, agents were dropped every night, moonlit or not, whenever the weather permitted.

The moonless experiment had, however, produced a record error. Two agents forming the PLANTER'S PUNCH team were deposited on the wrong side of the Elbe River, forty-eight miles from their pinpoint.

When DOCTOR and PAINTER next flew to France to attempt again their flight into Germany, it was to the new field at Dijon. The Belgians were met by Hans Tofte and taken to the handsome Château Brochon, situated six miles south of Dijon in the village of Gevrey-Chambertin. They arrived on a Sunday evening and were served a dinner befitting their new surroundings.

Château Brochon had been commandeered from an elderly, world-weary nobleman who accepted his guests uncomplainingly, if not warmly. "I have been occupied by many people," he observed to Hans Tofte. "One group is as bad as another."

The château was richly furnished with Oriental rugs, porcelains, paintings, and furniture accumulated over three centuries. Tofte watched uneasily as anywhere from thirty to sixty agents and staff camped amid its treasures. Tofte suggested to their host that he move into one wing and take his most valued possessions with him. OSS would then take over the rest of the château. The only part of his property that the owner could not secure under the bargain was his wine cellar, which Tofte noted was a reliable morale builder. Château Brochon was located at the gateway to the vineyards of Burgundy. A tour of neighboring villages suggested a fine wine list: Chambertin-Clos de Bèze, Les Musigny, Clos de Vougeot.

At any given moment, there were at the dinner table of the château Frenchmen, Belgians, Dutch, and Germans. They sat together, but did not mix together. They could not discuss their missions or reveal their actual identities. Their cultural differences also formed an effective barrier. The atmosphere of Château Brochon fell somewhere between a grand hotel and a minimum-security prison.

Some of the men wore bandages and walked, when outside, on crutches. Parked on the château grounds were vehicles with Red Cross markings, in clear violation of the Geneva Convention. The château pretended to be a rest area for wounded officers.

It was just as well that the 492d Bombardment Group personnel knew nothing of châteaux and fine wines. The new site at Dijon had been chosen in large part to get the tottering OSS-air corps relationship off to a better start after the disaster at Lyons. But to air corps ground crews, the world looked much the same at Dijon. They lived in cold wind-buffeted tents, with no floors or running water, not far from the Château Brochon.

After dinner at the château, agents scheduled to depart that night would go to the stables, where parachutes and gear for the jump were stowed. American enlisted men helped them to dress and, usually by 9:00 P.M., they piled into ambulances for the ride to the airstrip.

Hans Tofte was masterful at departures. He wore his parachutist wings to let the agents know that they were not in the hands of some Mayfair commando. In talking to anxious Belgian, German, and Dutch agents, he quickly shed his eager new Americanism and again became a European. Tofte radiated a contagious optimism which he did not particularly feel. The chances of serious injury on the drop were high. One agent had recently been killed when a gust of wind took his chute and slammed his head against a tree. If the jump went well, there was still the strong possibility of capture.

Tofte talked one March night to two German agents under the wing of a black Liberator. "Oh, I've done it many times myself. You won't have any trouble. You have good paper. You are going back to your own country. Germany is a mess. There are fellows like yourselves running around loose all over the place, cut off from their units. It's really a cinch." Tofte's farewell before an agent boarded the aircraft was a warm smile, a firm handshake, and a determinedly casual "See you soon."

On Monday, March 19, the DOCTOR and PAINTER teams were taken to the airstrip. The dressing and final checkout ran late because the men had gone heavily into the Burgundy during what was mordantly called the Last Supper. Five hours later they were back at the château exhausted and angered. The pilot had encountered heavy flak near their drop zone. He had been driven off course, was briefly lost, then brought them back to Dijon.

They tried again the next night. This time the PAINTER team was dropped, but bad weather forced DOCTOR back to the château. On Wednesday they were to try again. Jean Smets would not go. Each abortive flight had meant hours of exhausting tension and each had taken its toll.

Tofte knew the symptoms. In the lull between flights, the château staff tried to occupy the agents with movies, chess, bridge, Ping-Pong, and phonograph records. There was always additional training to be done on radio operations and coding, and late-arriving information from London to be absorbed. But a man could not remain psychologically primed indefinitely.

Tofte spent the day after Smets balked talking to the man, more often simply listening. He took Smets for a ride among the vineyards. The important point was not to leave the agent to ruminate alone. By nightfall, Tofte had the young Belgian prepared to reboard the B-24. Again the mission aborted.

The delay of the DOCTOR team offered an opportunity to test a new psychological approach which had been discussed between OSS and air force people to improve rapport between the crews and agents. A training officer had hatched the idea that it might prove helpful to have the pilot explain the aeronautical demands of the drop to the men making it. Jean Smets and Lucien Blonttrock met with their pilot, Lieutenant Bledsoe, who described how he would have to fly over a mountain, quickly spot a terrace on the other side of it, and get them onto it virtually within seconds. The terrace was about a mile and a half long and thirteen hundred feet wide. If they overshot it, the agents would drop into an inhabited valley. It was difficult to know how much this information reassured the agents.

DOCTOR was given an extra day to rest. On March 23, on the sixth attempt—counting two earlier failures out of London—the team parachuted into the Reich.

Jean Smets and Lucien Blonttrock, the DOCTOR team, looked out over the Kitzbüheler Alps in utter despair. Smets, so assured in demanding to meet George Pratt and Bill Casey during his training in London, was now visibly shaken. His fear had infected Blonttrock, the older, quiet partner who had always been reassured by Smets's breezy confidence.

They had overcome the early mishaps of their drop through brute will. But now the DOCTOR team appeared undone. Winding up the stiff snows, obviously on their trail, they could see three distant figures. Military police? An alpine patrol? Gestapo?

Smets and Blonttrock had been dropped shortly after midnight on March 24 on a mountainside about eight miles southeast of Kufstein. They had been told to expect about a foot of snow on the ground, but sank into five feet of it and assumed that the pilot had missed the pinpoint.

They trudged about for three hours, by the light of the moon, searching for their containers. On finding them, they buried their chutes, jump suits, and equipment that they planned to reclaim later. During the search they learned how cruelly nature had toyed with them. Two containers with white parachutes had fallen into the snow. And the equipment dropped with a brown parachute had fallen into the woods and spread itself over a dark tree.

The DOCTOR cover story proved one of the less insightful of the BACH preparations. The agents were in deep alpine snow, wearing cheap dark suits and ordinary street shoes. Private Lazare Teper had persuaded them that mountain shoes had gone out with the war, and that they would be conspicuous wearing them. Smets quickly cut two large white swatches from their parachutes to put over their clothing as camouflage. After the exhausting search and burial of the equipment, they dragged themselves into a woods and prepared to crawl into sleeping bags, another item taken over Teper's objections.

Jean Smets took out a flask of cognac. He drank deeply from it and passed it to Lucien Blonttrock. Smets then finished off the cognac and fell asleep. Blonttrock remained on watch. Hours later, in the silver dawn,

Lucien had spotted, several miles off, the three dots moving against the white horizon. He then woke up Smets. As they watched, Jean shoved handfuls of snow into his mouth to quench a fierce thirst created by the cognac he had consumed.

Miles away, the three men climbing the mountainside felt marvelously aglow. They were German Army deserters who had been hiding in the Alps for months, feeling a helpless impotence, wanting to strike at the Nazis, yet lacking any means. Their leader was Rudolf Steiner; his subordinates were Matteus Hornmacher and a man named Hachselberger. Steiner was a one-time Hitler Youth leader who had become disenchanted with Nazism in 1942, and whose defection had been a hard blow to his loyal Hitlerite family.

This sunny morning was Steiner's hour of triumph. American bombers, flying overhead daily had given him an idea. The day before they had spread a huge red-and-white Austrian flag on a mountaintop as a signal. Then, they waited in a nearby hut. It seemed incredible. That very night they heard the engines of a B-24 which seemed to graze the mountain peaks and hang briefly suspended above them. At first light they headed for the spot over which the plane had hovered. They quickly tracked down the place where the DOCTOR team had buried its three containers. They then began to trace the parachutists' footprints into the woods.

Smets and Blonttrock watched them approach for almost two hours. As they came within firing range, Smets hid under a sheet of white parachute silk and trained his pistol on the lead figure. Two of the men stopped and Rudolf Steiner continued on, obviously unarmed, with his shirt opened against the cold, almost as proof of his peaceful intentions. Smets sent Blonttrock ahead to meet him.

As they approached each other in the deep snow, miles from the nearest evidence of civilization, Blonttrock said, "We are Belgian workers on leave from our jobs." Steiner smiled tolerantly. He knew, he said, that they were parachutists who had been dropped in response to his flag signal, and that they had nothing to fear. They were in the company of fellow anti-Nazis. Blonttrock called for Smets to come down and meet their new friends.

Steiner told the story of spreading out the flag and their amazed reaction to the Americans' instant response. The two Belgians did not disabuse him of his interpretation of their arrival.

They spent the day in the woods, learning from the Austrians the extent of anti-Nazi sentiment in the area and gathering whatever military intelligence the men possessed. Under cover of night, they hiked for four hours to the village of Scheffau, where the agents found a sympathetic farmer to shelter them.

That night, Blonttrock radioed the first message to London announcing the team's safe arrival and asking that a test message be sent over the BBC, saying: "The Reich is the arsenal of the enemy through cruelty."

From Rudolf Steiner they learned that they had indeed been dropped several miles from their pinpoint, a fortuitous error. Lieutenant Turano had been unable to obtain photo-reconnaissance in advance, and the drop site he had selected was now a training area for German mountain troops.

They also learned from Steiner that the cover story which BACH had devised, that they were foreign workers on vacation in Kufstein, was a potential disaster. Producing their leave papers would have meant almost certain arrest. At that point, it was virtually impossible for a foreign worker to get a vacation.

Four days after they landed, the DOCTOR Mission transmitted a message to London asking for a drop to arm and equip twenty men as the cadre of a resistance army that would ultimately liberate the Kufstein area. They wanted rifles, grenades, German mountain infantry uniforms, explosives, maps, medicine, typewriters, cigarettes, sugar, and chocolate. They stressed, "Our prestige and full accomplishment of aims of mission depend on aid sent."

They next radioed an additional plan. The Itter Castle at Brixlegg had been converted by the Nazis into a VIP bastille, and among its prisoners, DOCTOR reported, were Edouard Daladier, the former French premier who had signed the Munich Pact; Maurice Gamelin, generalissimo of the French armed forces at the outbreak of the war; Paul Reynaud, the French premier just prior to the 1940 defeat; Stalin's son; and at least fifty other prominent prisoners. "It is possible that we can free them," DOCTOR said, "if we receive arms and you authorize this action."

These requests alarmed OSS London. "You are authorized to equip twenty men for your protection," the home base responded. "But you must avoid all sabotage for the moment. Use these men for military intelligence on roads and railroads." The restraints were hard to explain to Austrians who had long chafed at Nazi domination and now wanted the satisfaction of kicking the staggering giant as he fell.

The DOCTOR team abandoned its hope to lead a guerrilla army and thereafter became the most garrulous informant in the Reich. In forty-five days in enemy territory, the men radioed fifty-two messages to London, mostly from a hut which they had built in a mountain forest near Scheffau, and the rest from the homes of sympathetic farmers in neighboring villages.

Some women felt defensive about joining the Women's Army Corps, instantly and ungallantly acronymed the WACs. The concept made sense and was used by virtually every nation at war—have women take over noncombatant jobs and thus free more men to carry guns. Still, it took a reservoir of self-esteem for a girl to face the heavy-handed gibes and snide asides about women who enlisted, especially when the girl's own family, including a soldier brother, was uneasy with the decision.

Orpha Gresham had been working at the Bendix Corporation in South Bend, Indiana, as a secretary when the war started. She was vaguely bothered by an awareness that the world was undergoing epic convulsions and that her life went on untouched. She joined the army and was sent first to Fort Oglethorpe, Georgia. There OSS recruited her for a secretarial job in London. She arrived four days before Thanksgiving in 1942 and was assigned to the Schools and Training Branch. She lived in a billet on Upper Brook Street with eighty other WACs.

Area F was a walled estate outside of London where OSS agents trained. One night early in January 1945 Orpha Gresham found herself at Area F with her boss, Captain Ezra Shine. She had now served in London for nearly two and a half years and had that privileged view of an organization available to an alert secretary. She had stayed late at Area F to watch a movie being shown for the agents and OSS staff, *None but the Lonely Heart.*

Well into the movie, she became aware of a pair of eyes fixed on her. The man was disheveled, unshaven, and slightly drunk. He had stumbled conspicuously into the room with two other men in similar condition. They had settled themselves unaccountably with their backs to the screen and were looking out over the audience. Sergeant Gresham's admirer was one of Ray Brittenham's Belgian agents, a man of twenty-five named Emil Van Dyck. He looked to Orpha Gresham that night like a tramp.

Emil Van Dyck was born in the city of Malines, the youngest of six children of a Belgian civil servant. He had been studying to become a teacher of retarded children when he was called up, just before Hitler's armies blitzkrieged Belgium. He had been taken prisoner but later escaped and thereafter worked with the Belgian underground until his country was liberated.

Ray Brittenham had used Van Dyck for missions behind the lines during the Battle of the Bulge. His life for the previous five years had been lived in military posts, prisons, internment camps, barns, cellars, attics, and roadside ditches. When one adventure passed, Van Dyck hungered for the next. He had been sent to England by Brittenham with a Belgian of like mind and experience, a radioman named François Flour who, before the war, had been a foreign student at Johns Hopkins University in Baltimore.

In training, the two men were quick and serious. But when the day was over, they found the constraints OSS tried to place on their freedom laughable. Men who had known the mercies of the Gestapo and who were about to risk themselves against the Germans again were not inclined to pass their free hours playing Ping-Pong or watching movies in a country house, not with a city like London nearby. If liberty was not authorized, they simply went over the wall.

It was after returning from an unapproved trip to London that Emil Van Dyck had spotted Orpha Gresham as she watched the movie. When he next saw Ray Brittenham, Van Dyck said that he wanted to meet the girl. To comply would be a gross breach of security. But Brittenham weighed what he was asking this man to do and what this man was asking him to do, and said he would try. If it was just a question of a woman, that could be arranged. No, Van Dyck said, he wanted to meet this girl.

Orpha Gresham was scandalized. She lived by the rigid regulations of OSS security, and she remembered only too uncomfortably the bleary gaze of the Belgian. Brittenham spent over an hour describing the brave acts Van Dyck had performed in the Belgian resistance, his good character and trustworthiness. He capped his argument by telling Orpha that he would provide his jeep, and his driver as chaperon, but she must go out with Emil Van Dyck.

Orpha Gresham then went to her superior, Captain Shine, and explained to the incredulous training officer what she had agreed to do. She assured him that it would only happen this time.

Emil was a romantic figure to the girl from South Bend. He laughed easily, was thoughtful, considerate, and knew his way around London. Despite the restraints on agents, he had quickly managed to join something called the Gargoyle Club, popular with the military, and took a much impressed Orpha Gresham there as his guest. They saw each other whenever possible and within weeks regarded themselves as engaged.

On March 1, 1945, Orpha Gresham had a date to meet Emil Van Dyck at 8:00 P.M. At 2:00 P.M. she received a call at the Schools and Training Branch to have agents Van Dyck and Flour pulled out of their communications class to report to Area O, the staging facility. They were to fly to France on the first leg of their mission as the PAINTER team. They would then be flown to Germany and parachuted outside Munich. PAINTER was to make its way to that city and carry out espionage against the SS.

They spent galling days in Lyons with DOCTOR and other teams marooned in that chaotic outpost. On March 19, they and the DOCTOR team had been the first agents to attempt to fly from the new facility at Dijon. After the first abortive flight, the PAINTER agents were dropped near Munich the next night.

Orpha Gresham was in a position to follow the progress of the teams in Germany. DOCTOR, she discovered, was the joy of OSS London, reporting almost daily and providing a river of intelligence. But when nearly six weeks had passed with no word from PAINTER, she learned that OSS had declared her Emil and his partner, François Flour, as missing in action.

An OSS London operations directive neatly described four priorities for German missions. Of first priority were missions to report on military movements. Here, an agent's age, sex, and nationality were unimportant. Only the physical strength and cunning to survive and gather intelligence mattered. Second priority were missions requiring persons with special-ized backgrounds to infiltrate the German industrial machine, to deter-mine production, plant locations, and technology. Third priority were political missions to evaluate the potential of anti-Nazi resistance, particu-larly among presumed Nazi antagonists, labor people, religious associa-tions, career civil servants, and ethnic groups. Fourth priority were mis-sions involving people who might be useful as "Post-Collapse Personnel" —agents who could pass as Germans and thus infiltrate and expose Nazi elements planning to burrow underground after the conflict ended.

In actual practice, missions were born of shotgun matings between a sudden need for intelligence and the agents available. SHAEF would want a report on jet planes being launched from a stretch of the autobahn. The request would be sent to Bill Casey. Down the line, the operations staff of DIP would approach the nationality desks. "What do you have that we can put into Munich?" "We've got a good Belgian, tough man, with one mission under his belt." Then, to the prospective agent: "Are you ready to go? Are you willing?" "Fine. Pick a radioman—somebody you like and trust for your partner."

The operations officer then coordinated each phase: training, documents, clothing, cover story, communications, the flight plan.

When they were ready, the luckier agents out of OSS London waited to depart from the splendid isolation of Area O, the lovely manor house outside London. The house, in a lush, green park, was operated by British enlisted personnel and girls from the countryside who worked in the kitchen and dining room. The staff had been screened by MI-5, British domestic intelligence. Overflow agents were billeted in safe houses located around London.

As the number of missions mounted, elements of mass production entered into the processing of agents in England. It was an unwanted and unhealthy atmosphere for men embarking on a highly individualistic enterprise. A conducting officer, often a lieutenant, was therefore assigned to each team to cater to the agents' final needs and whims. The conducting officer looked after last-minute financial arrangements, insurance, the writing of wills, the companionship of a woman.

Bill Casey described his attitude: "They got any damn thing they wanted. These guys were the kings. We were all working for them, to get them off in the right frame of mind, to get them functioning in the right place, the right way."

Bill Grell's brother, Leon, though still a Belgian citizen, was commissioned in the U.S. Marine Corps and assigned full time as a conducting officer. An air corps historian recorded Grell's role:

At 4:45 P.M., Captain Leon Grell rang the bell at an anonymous side-street address in London. The house was largely empty. Knots of men and women sat around a bare, utilitarian table talking quietly. A thumbtack held a message written in red crayon over the fireplace: "Restaurant Colesta on Queen Street is out-of-bounds for students."

After a two-hour drive to the airfield at Harrington, Grell took the agents to a hangar, where they underwent a last security check. Pockets were turned inside out to find train stubs or other evidence revealing their recent life in London. The men were also checked to insure that a double agent was not spiriting anything valuable out of the country. Then a second security officer completely repeated the process.

Leon Grell put the agents' personal items into envelopes—letters, English money, billfolds. He sealed them and wrote each agent's code name across the front. "You can pick it up when you get back to London," he advised.

Grell went over their papers, ID card, ration card, census card, work card, birth certificate. He opened the suitcase he had brought from London and began distributing items. "Wear this money belt around your waist. Keep your big money in it. Remember, you're a conscript laborer. Live like one. Only put short-term money in your wallet. Stuff these radio crystals in the front of your jump suit. There's room there for a baby grand."

Grell gave each man a set of pills. The blue pill was benzedrine sulfate to overcome fatigue. The white pills were knockout drops which would put someone out for six hours. The third was the cyanide-laden "L" pill. The capsule was encased in rubber. To kill himself, the agent would have to bite into it. The rubber casing would otherwise allow the pill to be swallowed harmlessly.

Grell had the agents sign for the pills. He loaded .32-caliber pistols and Smith & Wesson .45s and gave the men one of each. OSS found that pistols were a psychological obsession among agents. They were supposed to be used only in the event that a team landed to a hostile reception. Otherwise, guns were to be buried along with chutes and jump suits, a rule usually violated.

The agents removed their shoes. The dispatcher bandaged their ankles and placed rubber cushions under their heels. The jump suit, with extra-wide arms and legs, fit easily over civilian clothing. It was zippered completely down the front so that an agent could step out of it instantly. The jump suit was made of heavy canvas camouflaged in green and mustard brown. It contained several generous pockets to hold items which would be needed immediately on landing, the pistols, a flashlight, a knife to cut a parachute free from a tree, and a short spade with a removable handle to bury equipment.

The agents put on helmets with sponge-rubber cushioning, then goggles and leather gantlets. The dispatcher helped them on with the parachute. He checked each strap and tested the release mechanism several times. It seemed to Leon Grell like dressing a bride for a wedding. Then, the quick handshakes. They boarded the plane and were quickly airborne.

Tony Turano, who picked pinpoints, smoothed over quarrels with the air force, and escorted agents to the field, had a new assignment. He was to work with the Direction Générale des Etudes et Recherches (DGER), a French intelligence operation, which was planning its first mission into Germany since the liberation of France. The DGER was delighted with the agent it had found and wanted him trained through OSS facilities in London. Turano was to serve as liaison.

The American instantly distrusted the DGER's recruit. The agent was no more than eighteen, a POW who had formerly been a model member of the Hitler Youth. Turano suspected that this much too clever fellow was simply looking for a way home. Turano balked at exposing OSS secrets to so unconvincing a convert.

He expressed his concern to Colonel Bowman, the SI London executive officer who was also then handling air operations. Bowman cut through to the nub of Turano's problem. "Knock him off," Bowman advised. On the flight out, Turano, or else the dispatcher, could shoot the agent as he left the plane. No one would be the wiser.

Turano was uncomfortable with the colonel's solution. He was willing to do whatever was necessary to protect the security of American intelligence; but he was not that positive of the German youth's duplicity. Bowman shrugged and left the matter up to Turano. Nevertheless, Bowman told him, this first mission was important to French pride and, one way or another, had to be carried out.

In the end, Turano could not overcome his doubts and contented himself with revealing as little of OSS operations as possible to his young German charge. When it was time to take the agent to the airfield for his flight, Turano had him blindfolded, and the blindfold was not removed until they had driven a deliberately long, circuitous route to the field and the German was aboard the plane.

Some time after the agent had been dropped into Germany, Turano asked his French colleagues how the mission was going. "Strange, monsieur. He seems to ask so many more questions than he answers."

From a speck orbiting in the night, high above the earth, Cal Ancrum's words danced along an unseen beam to a man crouched in a field outside Berlin. The voice coming back in response quickened Ancrum's pulse. It warmed him against the subzero cold seeping through the metal hull of the Mosquito aircraft. His fierce concentration on the static-riddled phrases distracted him from the stiffness, the aching in his back and legs as he sat wedged behind the Joan-Eleanor gear in the small oval of the plane's tail.

Lieutenant Commander Stephen Simpson had been right. Though the first Joan-Eleanor contact with the HAMMER team in Berlin had gone poorly, subsequent transmissions opened a rich vein of intelligence directly from the German capital.

On this day, March 29, Lieutenant Calhoun Ancrum talked at length to the men on the ground. The HAMMER agents, Paul Land and Toni Ruh, reported the Klingenberg power plant, on the Rommelsbergsee, fully operational and providing power to defense industries. A successful strike on the still functioning railroad system could, they said, induce total paralysis. One marshaling yard bulged with twenty-six freight and eighteen passenger trains.

In later contact, Ancrum asked if they could provide information on tank factories still operating. HAMMER gathered the intelligence within a week. From their Volkssturm contacts they were also able to give an up-to-the-minute status of Berlin's defenses and the deployment of troops.

In one conversation, the agents made a puzzling request for "medicine that soldiers can take in order to become ill." This message was later interpreted to mean that OSS should provide some substance that would allow war-weary soldiers to feign sickness.

Then someone entered their circle who sent a chill through the HAMMER team. Paul Land's twenty-one-year-old sister, like her parents, had aided the agents' efforts from the moment of their arrival. But they had not reckoned on her husband. Otto Malzer arrived unexpectedly from the Russian front in the last week in March. He was twenty-four years old, had been raised in the Hitler Youth Movement, and knew no religion but Nazism. Otto had been granted special leave after winning the Iron Cross, First Class, for knocking out three Russian tanks single-handed with a Panzerfaust, a bazooka-type weapon. The hero arrived home to find his wife's family harboring enemy spies.

The HAMMER agents had either to abandon their painstakingly constructed network of informants and flee, or accept the belief of Paul's sister that her soldier husband could be persuaded to their cause. They took the risk, building on the slim reed that Otto genuinely liked his in-laws. The two men led the soldier through long explanations of what had shaped their lives, painting en route a picture of Nazism that had never occurred to him. They discovered that the young man was more good soldier than good Nazi. What Otto had seen happen to his comrades during the invasion and retreat from Russia confirmed what these two older men were telling him of the nature of the Hitler regime.

They also had a remarkable knowledge of how the paper of bureaucracy was generated and assured Otto that he would not have to desert the army to join them. They would simply get his leave extended and thus avoid his imminent return to the front.

Paul Land wrote out on the back of Otto's leave papers a request that his stay be extended for twenty days so that he might search for his bombed-out wife. The request was forged with the name of Otto's commanding officer. Using the damp surface of a freshly hard-boiled egg, Paul transferred an impression of the validating stamp from the front to the back of the leave papers.

The three men then proceeded to a small village just outside Berlin where Otto presented his leave request to the adjutant of a field regiment. He wore his Iron Cross. Under guard in the adjutant's room were several deserters. The officer in charge barely glanced at the papers but studied Otto's medal reverently. He berated the deserters, pointing to Otto Malzer as an exemplar of the true German soldier. Otto's leave request was quickly approved. He was also given a special food-ration card for men on leave, and the officer asked him to take along a list of deserters the regiment was hunting.

The HAMMER Mission was by now badly in need of resupply. A drop had been arranged at a point thirty miles outside of Berlin. The two agents made the journey on April 1, Easter Sunday. No trains were running and they traveled the entire distance on foot. Wehrmacht troops, encamped across their path, forced them into a lengthy detour. They were uncertain whether the drop was set for this night or the next, and so, when no plane appeared, they went to sleep in an open field.

They awoke the next morning to the muffled rumble of voices. They saw army tents and heard the movement and clatter of soldiers beginning a new day. They had unwittingly passed the night in the midst of a bivouac. They would have to forgo the air drop, slip through a nearby woods, then break out to a road leading back to town.

Concealed in a satchel was their Joan-Eleanor set and a batch of intelligence papers, covered by dirty laundry. They carried the laundry at all times to support their story that they were displaced workers newly arrived in Berlin. They made their way to the road and were headed toward the city when a young lieutenant in the Hermann Göring SS Division roared up on a motorcycle. He demanded to see their papers. Both men reached into their pockets and, in a single practiced motion, slipped the safety catch off their .32s, without taking them out. They gave the lieutenant the documents.

The two men then assumed well-rehearsed roles: Paul the bright German, and Toni his obtuse Czech sidekick. Paul produced his Nazi party membership card. The lieutenant nodded approvingly, but still insisted on searching their luggage. Paul explained impatiently to the slack-jawed Toni, in Czech, what the officer wanted. Toni began, clumsily, piece by piece, to draw soiled shirts and underwear from the sack. Paul's overbearing manner toward this thick-skulled Czech produced the desired bond of superiority between him and the young German officer. Still, Paul was growing uneasy. He returned the papers to his pocket and let his hand rest on the pistol handle. The SS man, finally bored with the game, told Paul they could pass. As he sped off, Paul was almost disappointed. "I would have gladly shot him," he muttered.

Daily life at Grosvenor Street in the winter of 1945 was a mixture of the incongruous. It meant safety from the battlefronts and exposure to German rockets; grueling, twenty-four–hour days spent getting agents into the air and all-night parties catered with black-market luxuries; lunch at Claridge's and cold rations in a shed at Harrington Air Field.

The V-1 and V-2 attacks, which had begun the summer before, were initially explained by British authorities as gas-main explosions to conceal the truth that the enemy possessed a new weapon of horrifying aspect. Londoners were soon referring to the Nazi missiles as "flying gas mains."

There were OSS agents who left London to jump from airplanes into a brutal tyranny. And there were OSS officers whose work was "oh-so-secret" that no one ever knew exactly what they did, if anything. Mike Burke had run across one of these hush-hush figures, "a man who had never shouldered anything heavier than a major's oak leaf," who appeared one day with two heavily bandaged arms. "My God, have you actually seen action?" "No," the man answered cheerily. "I was crossing Brook Street with a champagne bottle under each arm and, well, fell off the curb."

It was a nomadic existence. Round-the-clock duty schedules, continual transfers from London to France, to Switzerland, to Italy and back made daily life in London a game of musical beds, with ever-shifting roommates and changes of address.

The eclectic character of OSS threw unlikely comrades together. The patrician OSS European chief, Colonel David Bruce, was sent two unwanted assistants by General Donovan. The men were, Donovan boasted, the best safecrackers in America. They had been paroled and given navy enlisted rank through the machinations of OSS Washington. Bruce protested that he could not use their talents in an Allied country. Donovan insisted. "These are rare specimens, and I'm sending them to you."

The two men duly arrived but soon grew weary doing nothing. Bruce suggested that they enjoy the British capital. "It's better than being in Sing Sing." They were concerned that their talent was rusting. They asked Bruce if he would allow them to practice on his office safe, which held top-secret documents. "Go ahead, so long as you don't use dynamite."

Bruce went about a series of meetings that day. If his visitors wondered what the two men sandpapering their fingertips were up to, they said nothing.

The men had been working for over three hours when one turned to Bruce. "Colonel, would you like to take a look?" Bruce watched, aghast, as the door swung open. "I think you fellows had better go back to your quarters."

His interest in safecrackers and militarized con men was part of General Donovan's ravenous curiosity. He possessed a tolerant view of human failings as well. One of the WACs assigned to David Bruce's staff had become pregnant and had to be sent home. Donovan directed his top assistant in New York, Otto Doering, to meet the young woman on arrival. "Ollie, I want you to welcome that woman, and I want you to make her feel that she is a casualty of the war."

Some of it was ridiculous and futile, some of it was helping to end the war. Jay Gold, a member of the OSS London Research and Analysis staff, spent his days reading cables and determining what should be sent to whom. Gold had a phrase for the information winging from one in-box to another. They were "buying each other's wastebaskets." He recalled spending an entire night with Labor Division people, huddled over a garbled message from an agent in Germany. The man had been injured in parachuting and they debated for hours whether he was asking for a truss or a crutch.

The payoff for their efforts, when it did come, was usually oblique. George Pratt would pass Colonel Bruce or Bill Casey in a hallway. "George, the air corps said some nice things about the HAMMER reports. Keep it up." Nothing more.

XIII

The Jew Who Dared Return

✠ ✠ ✠

The *Offizierskasino* in Innsbruck was a nostalgic reminder of the good army life before the Reich began to crumble. Distant from the front, unscarred by a single bomb, set in the startling beauty of the Tirol, the club put the war, however briefly, out of mind. Here, officers passed treasured days between assignments. Convalescents from the local military hospital waited, with admirable patience, for wounds to heal before returning to the front. Orderlies were still assigned to each officer to polish boots, to see that uniforms were pressed and clean, and to run errands. Food was in fair if monotonous supply, and drinks still cheap.

On the night of April 3, 1945, a party sat around a table listening distractedly to a tedious drunk from the army engineers. The man had returned twelve days before from Berlin, where he had worked, he said, on the construction of an underground bunker for the Führer and his staff. The quiet officer at the table, with swarthy features and Swabian accent, wearing the field gray of a first lieutenant in the alpine troops, was Frederick Mayer. The name was his own, but nothing else that his companions believed about him was true. For Mayer was actually a Jew, from Brooklyn, New York, and, even as he sat among them, a sergeant in the U.S. Army.

When the group broke up, Mayer went to his room and wrote:

Führer Hauptquartier located one and one half km southeast of station Zossen Lager near Berlin. Pay attention to group of houses five each on parallel facing each other. One is lengthwise in center of east end. Roofs very steep and camouflaged black, white, and green. Houses built of reinforced concrete. All walls one meter thick. Ten rooms per floor. Lowest 13 meters underground under four ceilings one meter each. Air-warning tower in center of house group. Last attack hit officers' club only. First house in southwest end is Adolf. Two courier trains under steam at Rehbrücke, 24 cars each. One with SS guards at Barth. Adolf at present in Reichskanzlerei where each night 2200 hours generals of staff come to visit. Adolf tired of living. Watched last attack from balcony. Alternative headquarters at Ohrdruf, Thuringia. Not Obersalzberg. Source is Austrian staff officer who left HQ March 21.

He made arrangements to have the message delivered through a courier to his radio man, secreted in a tiny village outside of Innsbruck called Oberperfuss.

The path which led Fred Mayer to the officers' club in Innsbruck had begun years before to the north, in the German city of Freiburg, from which his family had fled in 1938. The departure had been a devastating experience for Mayer's father, who had served the fatherland honorably as an officer during World War I.

The Mayers settled in Brooklyn, where Fred took a job in a Ford plant. When the war came, he volunteered for the draft and was on maneuvers with the U.S. Rangers when OSS recruited him for his German background and linguistic skills. Mayer spoke French, Spanish, and English, along with his native tongue. He was eventually sent to Bari, Italy.

Frederick Mayer looked most like a Middle Easterner, with black wavy hair, olive skin, and gleaming teeth often revealed in an easy smile. He was not tall, but had a powerful frame and possessed animal vitality. He seemed totally oblivious of physical danger. One friend observed, "Fred's fear nerve is dead." He was ready to undertake any assignment against the Nazis, yet felt no consuming hatred for them. He was a man of curious innocence with a tolerant view of mankind.

Mayer also had a quick, plausible imagination. One friend at Bari believed that Fred had been a Luftwaffe pilot. Fred had told the fellow a chilling account of how he once had a Gestapo agent aboard his plane and had pushed him out "without benefit of parachute." Another friend believed that Fred had served in the U.S. Marines. Dissembling was not a wasted talent for someone to whom deception was about to become a way of life.

In Italy, Fred Mayer was teamed with four other soldiers with parallel backgrounds—Jewish refugees who had lived in America until the war brought them back to Europe in American uniform. The five men had been assembled into a reconnaissance battalion to work behind enemy lines. After a year of training they had still seen no action.

In the fall of 1944, Lieutenant Colonel Howard Chapin, the SI chief in Italy, learned of their dissatisfaction and saw a place for them. OSS Bari had recently established a revitalized German-Austrian section now effectively under navy lieutenant Al Ulmer's control.

The ill-conceived and ill-fated DUPONT Mission, under Jack Taylor, and the DILLON Mission, under Miles Pavlovich, were then still training at Bari, but too far down the track for Ulmer to derail them. With this new group of prospects, Ulmer was determined to develop sound missions from the ground up.

He and his superior, Lieutenant Colonel Chapin, interviewed the five men. They found Fred Mayer impetuous and unsophisticated, perhaps, but the man clearly possessed spirit and cunning. They paired him with a Dutch Jew named Hans Wynberg. The two made an unlikely and thus well-balanced pair.

Wynberg was tall, shy, and scholarly, with a child's innocent face. When asked if they could kill, Fred Mayer had unhesitatingly answered, "Yes." Hans Wynberg had said, "No." Wynberg's quiet passion was chemistry, and his aim in life to become a college professor.

Al Ulmer discussed the nature of the missions into Germany, "Do you appreciate what can happen to you?" Fred Mayer spoke for them: "It's more our war than yours."

In the course of their training, the two men were encouraged to develop their own ideas for missions on the assumption that, as natives of Europe, they might have the best grasp of what they could achieve inside the Reich.

Dyno Lowenstein, then serving as one of Ulmer's deputies, recalled Fred Mayer's original suggestion. Mayer had proposed that a heavily armed team be dropped into the concentration camp at Dachau to lead an uprising. Lieutenant Lowenstein listened patiently. When Mayer finished, he asked, "Why don't you jump out of the window now? It would be cheaper and more practical."

Mayer and Wynberg soon met the sturdy, taciturn Walter Haass, who with Dyno Lowenstein had grilled prisoners on recruiting missions to POW cages. Haass also helped train agents and, as their dispatcher, would be the last person to see them as they parachuted into the Reich. Haass, too, was a refugee who had migrated to the United States only three years before. His face was broad and flat. His chest, legs, arms, and hands all thick and powerful. Haass would have made a model Wehrmacht Feldwebel. One could imagine him bullying recruits into cringing submission. But the image of brutal power was moderated by his voice. Haass spoke softly in quiet, measured tones.

He struck it off immediately with the brash Mayer and the quiet Wynberg, but had one deep reservation. They seemed to him, in their eagerness, to be "medal hunters." Haass saw no reason for Mayer's theatrics.

With their training complete, the Fifteenth Air Force suggested a target for the Mayer-Wynberg team. American bombers needed intelligence on traffic moving through the Brenner Pass, the supply aorta for Field Marshal Albert Kesselring's forces in Italy. Innsbruck, at the head of the rail line and less than twenty miles from the pass, offered an attractive watch on the Brenner. Mayer and Wynberg were to be dropped near Innsbruck and report on movements through the pass. The mission was designated GREENUP.

Fred Mayer was to lead GREENUP with Hans Wynberg serving as radioman. They needed one more member, an Austrian who knew the Innsbruck area and who could possibly provide safe houses. The third man was found in December 1944 in a POW cage outside Naples. He was Franz Weber, a lieutenant in the Wehrmacht's Forty-fifth Infantry Division.

Weber lived by a stiff, old-style moralism. When asked a question he invariably paused before speaking, then expressed himself with laconic precision. When the Americans wanted to know if he was willing to undertake a mission against the Reich, Weber had answered, "If the action you propose is in compliance with my conscience."

Weber came from a Tirolean culture honoring the soldierly tradition. But, even before he had entered the army, Weber knew where his true allegiance lay. He was a practicing Catholic and expected, if Hitler won the war, that he would destroy the Church. Weber thought that a Nazi victory would be a disaster and that if he, personally, did nothing to prevent it, then he would have been morally remiss. He did not want to hear himself saying years later, "Of course, I was always against them, but . . ." He had deserted immediately upon reaching the Italian front and was not prepared to rest with this act of negative resistance.

Fred Mayer and Hans Wynberg liked this serious, thoughtful fellow with the look about him of his mountain homeland—steep, sharp planes in his face, a jutting chin, and a fine alp of a nose. Most promising, Weber was an experienced mountaineer from a small town just six miles from Innsbruck, called Oberperfuss, where his fiancée's mother ran an inn in which he believed the team could hide. Weber was honored to be accepted by these fine American fellows and puzzled and flattered that they had trusted him so readily.

Their days were occupied with planning the mission. The three team members, Mayer, Wynberg, and Weber, with Lieutenant Ulmer and his staff, plotted drop points, procured equipment, set up their communications plan, and mulled over intelligence targets. The team lived at the Villa Suppa, on the outskirts of Bari, where the DUPONT teams had lived before departing in October. Part of the villa had been set aside as a primitive laboratory for Hans Wynberg, where he pursued his chemistry studies in spare moments.

During their preparations, Fred Mayer carried on a form of on-the-job training. He persuaded the OSS document counterfeiter to draw up orders for an imaginary company supposedly recently arrived in the area. Mayer had himself designated as supply sergeant of the ghost company and made weekly runs to the supply depot for rations. He also acquired a refrigerator, which was installed in Lieutenant Ulmer's office, and which, thereafter, was rarely unburdened of steaks, turkeys, and hams.

Fred Mayer and Walter Haass were amused by a rigid new operations officer who arrived at Bari bearing the fate of the war on his young shoulders. They took the lieutenant aside for a briefing. They told him, even though he spoke no German, that he was to be parachuted alone into Berlin on an extraordinarily critical mission. Dyno Lowenstein presented him with a convincing set of orders and told him that he would immediately begin parachute training under their guidance. They maintained the charade for days, while the young officer, who had expected a prestigious staff job, faced his martyrdom with baffled stoicism.

The GREENUP team was carefully isolated from all other military personnel at Bari and under firm orders to discuss nothing of the mission with other agents in training. They had little freedom to explore the drab port city, still half-crippled from the devastating German raid of December 2, 1943. Wynberg and Mayer once attended the Bari opera house, where they sat with combat boots propped comfortably on the next row. The next day's newspaper carried a picture of them with a caption deploring the behavior of American primitives in the presence of Barese culture.

The thorniest problem GREENUP faced was to find a suitable pin-point. All the flat areas near Innsbruck were inhabited. The surrounding Alps were towering and treacherous, even in fairest weather, and they were to jump in midwinter.

Fred Mayer suggested a desperate scheme to turn winter to advantage. On the map, he spied two small lakes wedged between the mountain crags. They would be frozen and provide flat surfaces for a parachute landing. The point was thirty miles southwest of Innsbruck. They could ski down to the lowlands and ultimately make their way to the expected safe house at the inn in Oberperfuss.

The German-Austrian section was directed first to the RAF 334th Wing to arrange the drop. On January 11, they received a forthright reply. Squadron Leader H. F. Brown declared the pinpoint "not acceptable." At that time of year, he feared, it would be extremely difficult to locate the area and make a reasonably precise drop. To reach it, the aircraft would also have to fly at sixteen thousand feet without ground navigational aids, which, Brown said, was unsafe.

Hart Perry, Ulmer's operations officer, then went to the American air force. Colonel Monro MacCloskey's 885th Heavy Bomber Squadron had just the man, Captain Billings, a red-haired pilot who would "rather fly than eat." Perry was told, "If you're crazy enough to jump there, we're crazy enough to fly you."

By February 1945, the GREENUP team was at its peak of preparation and eager to move. The three men were told candidly the fate of agents who had preceded them. The first OSS team to penetrate Austria out of Italy, ORCHID, had crossed over from Yugoslavia in August 1944. Two of the men were presumed dead. The third member had been evacuated. On January 24, 1945, German Transocean Radio reported that eighteen members of an Anglo-American group of agents had been captured in Slovakia and executed. OSS Bari suspected that the victims included members of the DAWES and HOUSEBOAT missions, who had been dispatched to penetrate Austria from Czechoslovakia. The assumption was correct. Lieutenant Holt Green, heading DAWES, and nine other OSS men were among the captives taken to Mauthausen concentration camp and shot. OSS Bari did not know that the DUPONT team, which had tried unsuccessfully to contact Holt Green, was also in the hands of the Gestapo.

The GREENUP team was still impatient to get on with the mission. But bad weather repeatedly foiled photo-reconnaissance of the proposed drop zone. Mayer was willing to go without photos and ready to rely on maps alone.

Just before departing Bari, the team was given a new priority. Along with intelligence on the Brenner Pass, they were to unearth whatever they could on Nazi plans for burrowing underground after the war. Information on the National Redoubt was to be radioed at considerable risk.

They finished packing at the Villa Suppa, where Hans Wynberg used part of the priceless space in his bag to pack a chemistry book. As the team's radio operator, he explained to a puzzled Al Ulmer, he would have long, idle periods between transmissions. He could use the time to study.

In February 1945, they were driven to an airport at Brindisi, and with their dispatcher, Walter Haass, crawled into the belly of Captain Billings' B-24. The four-hour flight was uneventful until they reached the drop area. There they found the mountain peaks obscured by clouds. Billings would have to search out a break in the thick fleece beneath him, locate the narrow valley where the pinpoint lay, drop the agents, and fly a tight U-turn out of the steep mountainsides.

Billings saw his break. He slipped through a hole in the cloud cover and turned on the position lights to see if his wing tips were clearing the mountains.

Walter Haass removed the hatch from the jump hole. Jagged peaks rose up to meet the plane. As they descended into the valley, Fred Mayer looked straight down one thousand feet into a cold, forbidding void. The two small lakes were not visible amid the gray-white crags. Mayer lowered himself into the hole, a heavy container strapped to his left leg. Lined up behind him were Weber and Wynberg. He pushed himself free and sailed out of sight. "Jump! Jump!" Hans Wynberg screamed at Weber, who stood stock-still, as critical hundreds of feet raced beneath the aircraft. Walter Haass shot forward and pushed Weber out of the plane. Hans Wynberg did not bother to sit. He simply stepped out of the hole from a standing position.

Billings wheeled his aircraft from a fast-approaching mountainside. As he cleared the top, the plane's propellers blew snow off the peak.

As the GREENUP team was beginning its Austrian mission, the captain of the first aerial team to precede them out of Bari languished in a Gestapo prison in Vienna. Jack Taylor, who led the DUPONT mission, had been assigned a cell on the top floor of the converted Hotel Metropol, the Gestapo headquarters. After his capture in the hayloft in Schützen and his interrogation by Johann Sanitzer, the radio *Funkspiel* expert, he had been left in solitary confinement.

His loyal subordinate, Ernst Ebbing, was also in the prison, along with Ebbing's mother and father, the Luftwaffe captain who had tried to aid DUPONT. Taylor knew nothing of the whereabouts of Felix Huppmann and Anton Graf, whose womanizing had compromised his team.

Taylor, expecting to be executed any day, slept poorly and ate little. He began to count on Allied bombing raids to break his isolation and save him from the corrosive depression into which he was slipping. When the alert sounded, he was removed from his cell and taken to the Metropol's basement air-raid shelter. There, he met his fellow prisoners from the fifth floor. In these sporadic moments, while trying to learn German from them, he discovered that most of the fifth-floor prisoners were Viennese Communists who had been spies for the Russians. They had saved their lives by agreeing to deceive Soviet intelligence. Every day they were taken to the radio room, where they dutifully transmitted to Moscow bogus messages prepared for them by their captors. The favorite German ruse was to try to convince the Russians to send in new agents. To Sanitzer, this wholesale deception of the Russians was his masterwork.

Among his air-raid shelter acquaintances, Jack Taylor met a Viennese woman, Tanya Souchek, who deeply impressed him. When he became ill with dysentery and pneumonia, a guard allowed Tanya to visit Taylor. She soothed him, placed cold towels on his burning forehead, and told him of her life. She had been a Communist for fourteen years. Her husband was last known to be fighting with Russian partisans. She told Taylor that the Soviets were probably aware that most of the transmissions from the fifth-floor prisoners were controlled and that they played along only to keep their agents alive and to mislead the Germans. Taylor asked for her Vienna address. Should they survive the war, he wanted to renew their friendship. Tanya Souchek agreed, but added, unemotionally, that she and the other Communists would surely be executed at the last moment, just before the Russians arrived. When Taylor suggested that her prospects might not be quite so bleak, the woman laughed. "I have no fear. I am a Communist."

One day Taylor was assigned a new roommate who possessed an unexpected luxury, a radio. Someone had tampered with it, and the shortwave band did not work. Taylor fashioned an antenna from a small piece of magnetic wire and turned the shortwave tuner. A hauntingly familiar voice pierced through the sputtering and crackling. ". . . Almighty God has blessed our land in many ways. He has given our people stout hearts and strong arms with which to strike mighty blows for freedom and truth. . . ."

Franklin Roosevelt, in a Spartan wartime inauguration in front of the White House, had just taken his fourth oath of office. For the first time since his captivity, Jack Taylor cried.

Early in March, American bombers did Taylor another service. A heavy bomb destroyed a large part of the Metropol and Taylor had to be transferred to a handsome villa in the Turkstein Park area of Vienna. Here he began to regain his strength. He was put to work pruning trees and splitting wood under the first sun he had seen in five months.

His good fortune in staying at the villa was at the expense of the Austrian industrialist from whom the Nazis had confiscated it, Dr. Franz Josef Messner, general director of the Semperit Rubber Company, and the man who had passed intelligence on Peenemünde to Allen Dulles. Elsewhere in the prison were the other members of the ring, the priest Heinrich Maier and the pianist Barbara Issikides. They all faced death sentences. For a few days, Dr. Messner had been a cellmate, in the Metropol, of Anton Graf, one of the members of Taylor's team. Messner told Graf that he had been arrested after becoming involved with inept OSS agents in Istanbul, precisely what Dulles had warned him against.

Jack Taylor's comparative idyll at the Messner villa was brief. A Berlin court rejected his defense that he was not a spy but a legitimate combatant. He was found guilty of espionage and ordered to the concentration camp at Mauthausen to be executed. Anton Graf, Felix Huppmann, Ernst Ebbing, and Ebbing's father were also found guilty and sentenced to be beheaded.

The family of Gustav Bauditsch, the train dispatcher in Wiener Neustadt, who supposedly was to help Taylor's team escape from Austria, provided the key evidence in all their convictions. The witnesses had included Bauditsch's daughter, Erika, who had caused Anton Graf to compromise the mission by his rash pursuit of the girl.

Whenever Gary Van Arkel was notified in Bern that Fritz Molden had returned from another mission into Austria, he braced himself for at least thirty-six hours of nonstop debriefing. Sometimes they met in Zurich at a safe house on a little street leading to a lake. Once they met in Van Arkel's apartment on the Schlosshaldenstrasse in Bern. Molden favored another safe house made available by a trusted woman in Zurich. The woman was attractive, and Molden discovered rewards in arriving an hour or so before the appointment with Van Arkel.

The young agent's work astonished Van Arkel. Without a note, he would begin with Austria, run through the military situation, the economic picture, and political and social developments. He would repeat the process for Hungary, Czechoslovakia, and Rumania with rapid-fire precision, all the while sketching on Van Arkel's maps the dispositions of armies and armaments, industries, railroads, and supply centers. Then Molden would meet Gero von Gaevernitz and brief him on political developments inside Germany, leaving Van Arkel to spend wearying hours transmitting stacks of messages to London, Washington, and the Allied military commands.

Molden now had two sanctuaries for his stopovers in Milan—with his sometime mistress Adriana Del Piano, or with Circe, the woman whom he had met on his first trip to Vienna before she went to work as an Abwehr photographer in Italy. Through Molden, Adriana and her mother had become fast friends with Circe, who was then living at the Albergo Grande Milano on Via Manzoni. It was an unlikely and thus unsuspected refuge for an Allied agent, since the Grande Milano was the hotel favored by German intelligence personnel.

Circe remembered Molden arriving from his long, secret journeys from Switzerland, or returning from Austria, "smelling badly," exhausted, sewing insignias on his uniform, eating ravenously, and collapsing on her huge bed.

The intimacy never went beyond the shared bedstead. To Molden, Circe fell outside the ground rule he had set. He might be able to work with a woman after he had known her romantically; but to get involved with a woman after enlisting her as an agent could threaten the professional relationship. For her part, Circe had no dearth of admirers. It became a family affair. She was the beautiful, youthful aunt and he the favorite nephew.

He watched her with awe. She could be maddening, impossible. But her shrieking hysteria, he soon learned, was a shrewdly used weapon. Circe never shrieked the wrong thing, and, he noticed, German intelligence officers at the Albergo Grande Milano ate from her hand.

Molden found that his association with OSS exacted a price. He was accustomed to operating independently, but the Americans expected to possess him. They did not grasp that he was working with them, not for them. On one occasion they persuaded him to take an agent into Italy through his underground route. The experience had been unnerving. The agent was a reasonably attractive woman, which did not disturb Molden, but that she was one-legged and spoke no Italian did annoy him. In the future, he insisted to the Americans, agents with whom he worked must speak the local language and have two legs.

At this point, Molden was involved not only with his native Austrian movement and the Americans but with Swiss and French intelligence as well. Word had traveled the espionage grapevine that he was someone who could get people into the Reich. The French had approached Molden with two agents who violated one of his recent requirements; they could not speak German. French intelligence wanted to establish the men, with a radio, near Salzburg or Innsbruck, to maintain contact with French prisoners in Austria. Molden was eager for new allies to support the political ambitions of the Austrian resistance movement, and agreed to take the two Frenchmen into Austria.

They had to communicate in French, which struck Molden as ironic, since he was again posing as a German Feldwebel, and the two Frenchmen were supposedly German soldiers in his charge. He covered the problem by having papers forged declaring that they were Frenchmen who had volunteered for the Wehrmacht.

The Frenchmen were bringing with them an enormous, old-fashioned radio, the only set they knew how to operate. Molden studied the massive set with resignation. He had it crated and had papers drawn up declaring that the radio was captured Allied equipment which the three men were delivering to German intelligence.

The credits he earned with the French would prove useful as Molden prepared for his grand maneuver. The time had come, he believed, for the Allies to recognize formally the Provisorische Oesterreichische National-komite (POEN), the Provisional Austrian National Committee, the formal title adopted by the group that Molden had helped to establish during his mission to Vienna four months before.

The POEN had to receive this recognition if his country were to be treated as an independent state and spared occupation as a conquered enemy after the war. Molden wanted to see himself and other Austrians who were fighting the Germans recognized officially as liaison officers to Allied military forces, just as French, Belgian, Dutch, Norwegian, and other resistance leaders had been. Until the Austrians achieved this status, they would remain little more than technicians, radiomen, couriers, espionage functionaries with scant influence over their nation's destiny. The level of Allied recognition which he sought could not be achieved in Switzerland. Molden would have to go to Paris to confer with representatives of the Big Three.

He went to Allen Dulles and asked that the American legation sponsor his visit. What Dulles and his colleagues thought of these heady demands from someone not yet twenty-one is unknown, but Dulles initially discouraged him.

"Then I don't need you to go to Paris," Molden informed the Americans. "I can get there myself." He then cashed in his credits with the French. He arranged to be invited to Paris by the intelligence group, Direction Générale des Etudes et Recherches (DGER). Dulles, thereafter, gave his trip a belated blessing and provided some logistic support.

Molden went to Paris as a salesman for the POEN. He visited representatives of the three major Allied powers, but got a serious reception only from the French. American State Department officials were not interested in seeing him. The only Americans who would receive Molden in Paris were OSS and other military intelligence officers. He had not yet broken out of the confines of espionage.

He recognized his cordial interplay with the French for what it was, and was happy to be a profit-sharing partner in it. The French were concerned about being slighted by the Big Three and were making friends wherever they could. So were the Austrians.

As for formal recognition of the POEN, no one moved. More proof was wanting that it was as strong, representative, and organized as Molden claimed. Molden returned to Switzerland with something less than half a loaf. But before he left Paris, he had been told by the OSS labor representative there that a man would soon be sent to Switzerland who would slip into Austria with him to verify the strength of the resistance movement. The man was Ernst Lemberger, a highly regarded Austrian Socialist—then in exile in Paris.

Fritz Molden met Ernst Lemberger at the Hotel National in Basel at the end of January 1945. The two men stood in sharp contrast; Molden, young, tall, confident almost to the point of arrogance, articulate almost to glibness; Lemberger eighteen years older, a small, unassuming man of studious mien who wore glasses and spoke in a quiet voice.

As a Jew and a prominent Socialist, Lemberger had been forced to leave Austria after the Anschluss and had settled in France. There, he joined the French Army and, when France fell, continued to fight with the Maquis. Later, as "Commander Jean Lambert," he became the highest-ranking Austrian in the French Army. With the liberation of France, Lemberger's war was still not over. He turned his energies to his homeland.

He became active in the Austrian refugee community and served as the secretary of the Austrian Socialist Party for France, where he attracted the interest of OSS. He was recruited by the Paris labor desk and worked with Bert Jolis in preparation for a mission into Germany under cover as a German soldier.

Lemberger had then been away from Austria for seven years and had no knowledge of German military life. He was slipped into one of the cages near Compiègne with appropriate uniform and papers and spent three weeks absorbing the idiom and flavor of contemporary Germany. He confided to Bert Jolis afterward that the experience had been terrifying.

The camp Lemberger had entered was divided between unregenerate Nazis, heartened by the Battle of the Bulge then in progress, and those tired of war who were ready to collaborate. The diehards had introduced a reign of terror into the camp against the defeatists. Beatings, kangaroo justice, and occasional killings by the Nazis perpetuated a state of ugly defiance. It was, Jolis thought, a perfect education for Ernst Lemberger.

Jolis was among the Americans whom Fritz Molden had met during his trip to Paris, and it had been Jolis's idea to send Lemberger with Molden into Austria to verify Molden's picture of the Austrian resistance.

OSS Bern bribed a Swiss frontier official at the crossing near Annemasse, enabling Lemberger to get to Basel to join Fritz Molden. They spent three days together designing their mission. Molden was agreeably surprised by the older man. Lemberger lacked the doctrinal inflexibility of many European leftists. He was pragmatic and quite willing to collaborate with Molden, a man not of his party.

The quiet, understated Lemberger and the strongly assertive Molden reached the same conclusion: they needed each other. If a serious Austrian provisional government was, in fact, in the making, Lemberger wanted in for his Socialists. If the POEN were to be effective and to impress the Allies, Molden knew it would have to embrace all political factions, until the Nazis were defeated, when the parties could resume their habitual rivalries.

Molden developed a quick appreciation for the qualities of this unprepossessing fellow Austrian. It was no small heroism for a rather well-known Jewish political activist to return to Nazi Germany during the war as an Allied spy.

On February 16, 1945, the two men left Switzerland for Milan, where their German uniforms were stowed. Molden again assumed the identity of Feldwebel Steinhauser and Lemberger became Private Nowatny. According to the orders they carried, they were on a secret mission for the Abwehr. They arrived in Vienna on February 25, after stops in Innsbruck, Salzburg, and Linz, where Molden tapped his intelligence network and

Lemberger enlisted local Socialist support for the POEN.

In Vienna, the POEN flaunted its existence for the benefit of the new arrivals. Molden and Lemberger found Vienna plastered with posters and walls painted with *"O5 Frieden,"* the slogan of the Austrian resistance. Molden took Lemberger on a round of meetings with resistance leaders. He was particularly eager, through Lemberger's influence, to enlist in the POEN Dr. Adolf Scharf, a leading Socialist who would later become president of Austria. As they moved from offices to homes, Lemberger was able to confirm the claims that Molden had made to the Allies. A movement which originally had been largely created with mirrors began to assume tangible substance.

During their stay, Molden had also taken care of the more immediate interests of their American sponsors. He and Lemberger memorized long reports gathered from Molden's agent network, including recent data on the vital Ploesti oil fields in Rumania and fifteen military targets as yet untouched by Allied bombers.

The two men attended a key meeting of the POEN in the handsome Viennese suburb of Grinzing. In a further show of strength, resistance leaders had secured the area with a detachment of armed O5 guards.

The major positions of the POEN, which Molden and Lemberger were to convey to the Allies, were enunciated at the meeting: Austria should be considered an occupied country and therefore bore no guilt for the war; the POEN would see that Austrian war criminals were punished; postwar Austria was to return to its 1938 borders. More immediately, the POEN protested indiscriminate Allied bombing of Austria: "If our work is to be carried on and if the confidence of the Austrian population in the Allies is to be retained, these bombardments of nonmilitary targets must cease."

For Lemberger, the Viennese mission had been a triumphal return. His mother, Luisa, along with Dr. Scharf, were appointed Socialist members of the POEN. Lemberger and Molden were designated POEN's official representatives to the Allies. The organization now embraced Austrian politics from left to right in one unified, anti-Nazi coalition.

Just before the POEN meeting broke up, SS troops learned of it and moved in on the neighborhood. Fighting broke out with the O5 guards, and an SS man was killed. Molden and Lemberger had to leave Vienna at once.

The weary military policeman inched his way through the troop train checking every man's papers. He read the orders of the Feldwebel and the private with a sly smile. He took some notes and disappeared. Fritz

Molden leaned casually, but spoke anxiously to Ernst Lemberger: "We had better get off at the next station." The military policeman returned before the train stopped, and he ordered them to follow him to the train commander. The shootout the night before between the SS and O5 in Vienna must have exposed them, Molden feared.

The train slowed as they passed through the Vienna Woods. Molden spoke softly to Lemberger: "Get ready to jump." But before they could reach the door of the coach, the train entered a tunnel. Molden unsnapped his pistol holster and told Lemberger to do the same. They would at least take some Germans with them.

They were led to the last car and there met the train commander, an overage and much-harassed captain. The captain apologized, but he was terribly shorthanded and knew from their papers that they were Abwehr. They would have to help check documents on the first half of the train.

The assignment provided an intelligence coup. As Molden and Lemberger moved down the aisle reading orders, a rather complete picture of German troop movements began to emerge. The two men mentally recorded the locations and shifts of various infantry, tank, and artillery units. Molden also took note of the morale of Germany's defenders at this stage of the war. It was, he concluded, not as bad as it should have been.

By March 4, Molden and Lemberger were back in Switzerland reporting to Allen Dulles, and, a few days later, both went on to Paris. There, Molden received a far more respectful hearing than on his earlier visit, even from the U.S. State Department, which had previously ignored him.

On March 10, the two Austrians presented their credentials to General Ivan Susloparov at the Soviet embassy in Paris, where they received a hero's welcome. The Russians looked forward, they said, to seeing the Socialist Lemberger named as Austrian ambassador to the Soviet Union as soon as the war was over. The two men told the Russian general that they had prepared a message to Marshal Stalin reporting the situation inside Austria. He invited them to fly to Moscow to deliver the report personally.

A few days later, a plane bearing a delegation of Poles disappeared en route to Moscow. The Russians maintained that the plane had been shot down by the Germans. But rumors circulated that the Soviets had found a convenient method to rid themselves of a planeload of potentially troublesome Polish non-Communists. The German press seized upon the incident as evidence of a growing split between the western Allies and Russia. In the wake of the incident, Austrian exile leaders forbade any visit by POEN representatives to Moscow.

While Molden and Lemberger were enjoying their Paris triumph, certain elements of OSS poked skeptically at their claims. Bill Casey's London deputy, Milton Katz, raised doubts about the Vienna mission. "It would be perfectly easy," he observed, "for any organization to plaster a city with posters . . . there was no proof that the organization [POEN] was, in fact, on our side." '

The final ignominy occurred when X-2, the OSS counterintelligence branch, insisted that Bern stop using Molden as an agent. The counterspies, ever under the sway of their MI-6 mentors, bought the British line that Molden was probably a German plant. A meeting was called in Paris to debate Molden's fate. OSS officers gathered from London, Paris, Bern, and Caserta. Colonel J. Russell Forgan, who had replaced David Bruce as OSS chief for Europe, attended. John Oakes, of the *New York Times,* another OSS officer, represented X-2.

Allen Dulles regarded the suspicions against Molden as so much rubbish. He dispatched Gary Van Arkel to represent his emphatic viewpoint. During a hot, two-hour debate Van Arkel set aside his recent roles as spy manager and recorder of Rhine water levels and resumed his peacetime profession as a talented lawyer.

He built a tightly woven case, recounting what the young Austrian had contributed in priceless, verified, usable intelligence covering an extraordinary area of the Third Reich. He displayed a coolly controlled fury at the idiocy of casting aside this resource because of baseless rumors. After Van Arkel's presentation, Forgan rendered the verdict: "Keep using him."

The GREENUP team out of Bari—Fred Mayer, Hans Wynberg, and Franz Weber—had not landed as planned on a frozen lake near Innsbruck. At the last minute, clouds had concealed the intended site from the pilot. They had dropped instead on a glacial ridge, the Sulztaler Ferner, at a height of 10,200 feet.

The three men found each other easily; but they tramped for four hours in the mountain passes—in snows at times reaching their armpits—searching for their equipment. They found all of the containers except one that contained a critical pair of skis.

They fashioned a sled out of one pair of skis to carry equipment and gave Franz Weber the other pair. They began to work their way down the slope with Fred and Hans at times on their hands and knees clawing their way through the resisting snows. In ten hours they covered a mile and a half.

They staggered along, soaked through with sweat in the frozen alpine winterscape. Above them, the rock mountainsides trapped the snow in broad white stripes. Even in their exhaustion, the men found these peaks awesome.

At 10:00 P.M., when it seemed they could not raise another limb, they came upon a ski lodge shown on their maps as the Amberger Hütte, a substantial building constructed by the "Friends of the Alps" to accommodate skiers. It was not used at this time of year. The valley lay too deep in snow for even the hardiest sportsman.

They entered the lodge through a window and started a fire before collapsing into a sleep that lasted for most of the next two days. They roused themselves only to eat something from their dwindling rations. Hans tried to radio Bari of their safe arrival, but could not make contact. Then, they started down the mountain valleys.

GREENUP first faced the enemy populace in a tiny snowflake of a village called Greis. The Austrian, Franz Weber, wore the uniform of a German alpine lieutenant. The Americans wore nondescript outfits of mountain winter garb under white capes. Mayer had also wanted to wear a German uniform, but Al Ulmer had thought it would be a too flagrant violation of the Geneva Convention if the team were caught.

Franz ordered tea for them. He told the proprietress that they were ski troops separated from their unit. She directed them to the Bürgermeister, who listened sympathetically to their request for transportation to rejoin their unit. He was eager to help any fighting men, he said, but all he could offer was a sled.

They took the sled and embarked on a trip down the mountain which made the parachute jump seem like a mother's embrace. The sled reached speeds of sixty miles an hour in a sinuous three-and-a-half-hour cascade down the valley. Franz Weber, fully at home in this world, steered, while Fred Mayer tried to brake the sled with a ski pole. Mayer felt fear for the first time on this mission as he watched the steel tip of the ski pole glow red from the friction. After reaching the bottom of the mountains, they made their way to the village of Oberperfuss.

For the first two weeks, Fred Mayer and Franz Weber stayed in the attic of the inn run by the mother of Weber's fiancée. Mayer found Frau Liederkirche, the owner, a frail-looking widow of unexpected strength, a formidable ally. Besides the inn, she ran a farm and bakery and was a power in the village.

Her daughter, Annie, was initially horrified that Franz Weber had returned. She knew that her fiancé had been sentenced to death as a convicted deserter. Now he had rashly returned home with the sentence over his head.

Hans Wynberg was put up near Oberperfuss in the house of a farmer named Schatz, where he rigged a clothesline antenna in the attic for his radio.

In Oberperfuss, Fred Mayer met a foreman who worked in a plane factory in nearby Kematen. The man liked to drink and, more important, to talk. From him the GREENUP Mission collected its first intelligence. Hans Wynberg was able to raise Bari and excitedly tapped out in code: "Messerchmitt Kematen production zero due to lack of resupply for past three months. Formerly made parts for assembly plant in Jenbach. Source, trustworthy worker."

Fred Mayer grew impatient in the village and told Franz Weber that it was time to go into Innsbruck, where Weber's three sisters lived. During the trip, Franz wore his uniform and concealed much of his face behind bandages. His sister Aloisia had obtained papers for him through her hospital job stating that he was on convalescent leave. Mayer wore civilian clothes.

Weber's other two sisters lived together in the city. The elder, Margarete, a widow of thirty, was employed in an office at the University of Innsbruck. Genoveva, twenty-one, worked in a government office. Through the sisters, Mayer met two useful men. One was a truck driver and an admitted member of the Nazi party. He wanted to help, he said, because he was an Austrian patriot first and a Nazi second. The other contact, a black marketeer named Leo, also offered to cooperate, but his patriotism was practiced on a commercial basis.

Mayer made another discovery during the Innsbruck trip. Franz Weber, who had parachuted into the Alps without a single practice jump, who was intrepid at the helm of a careening alpine sled, became unnerved on Innsbruck's streets. Weber had sat near an old acquaintance in the streetcar and was sure that the man failed to recognize him only because of the bandages.

When they returned to Oberperfuss, Fred gently told Franz that he would not have to go into town again. Weber's role in the GREENUP Mission had effectively ended. The man had served well, Mayer reasoned. He had led them to their target and delivered safe houses. Mayer would make his next journey to Innsbruck alone.

Through Franz Weber's sister Aloisia, who worked in the hospital, Mayer managed to acquire the uniform of a lieutenant in the 106th High

Alpine Troops. But he lacked corresponding documents. If he were questioned, Mayer intended to say that Italian partisans had robbed him of his money and his papers while he was en route to the hospital in Innsbruck to have an injured shoulder treated. He supported the story by writing out a statement, "I have lost my paybook." He signed it, "Friedrich Mayer." The name was serviceably German, and Mayer recognized that the best cover was that closest to the truth. Through Aloisia, he also obtained a hospitalization order fixed with the appropriate stamps. Mayer filled out the form himself and, in his new uniform, checked into the *Offizierskasino.*

Through the Austrian truck driver, Mayer met Alois Kuen, an Innsbruck police officer. Kuen was technically part of the SS, since his division, KRIPO, the criminal police, was under Himmler's empire. But he was anti-Nazi. He and a small group within the Innsbruck KRIPO mimeographed and distributed antiparty leaflets and destroyed files of persons threatened with political apprehension. In his boldest act, Kuen, when ordered to arrest ten suspects, had briefly locked up, with calculated incompetence, ten Nazis instead.

Through Kuen, Mayer got in touch with roving bands of deserters hiding in the mountains around Innsbruck and old-line Social Democrats in the Austrian railway. He sent his intelligence reports back for Hans Wynberg to radio to Bari through a system of cut-outs, which broke any direct connection between himself and Wynberg. A steady flow of hard information soon directed Fifteenth Air Force bombers out of Italy:

> Average of fourteen trains are assembled nightly between ten-thirty and twelve in new yards right outside of Hall. Loaded mainly troops from Sprechbacher Kaserne Hall. All trains routed by Vorarlberg Tunnel. Source, railroad employee. Fifty fighter planes expected at new Innsbruck airport. This shipment by rail. . . . Bragging Air Force Major, source.

Mayer also reported that Mussolini was being kept at the Zürshof Hotel in Zürs. Another Mayer transmission provided further evidence that Nazi leaders were withdrawing to the alpine redoubt:

> Night of 17th [April] Himmler arrived with staff at Igls near Innsbruck in Hotel Gruenwalderhof. Three SS divisions are expected but so far only one regiment of Leibstandarte is present.

While reporting bombing targets, troop movements, and resistance activities, Mayer also complained about his corporal's rank. Ulmer radioed from Bari, "Glavin and Chapin have cabled Washington for promotions. Hold your horses." One week later, Ulmer sent another message: "Congratulations to Tech. Sgt. Mayer and Staff Sgt. Wynberg. Families and girls notified."

While Fred Mayer worked out of Innsbruck, Hans Wynberg filled the long hours between transmissions waging his own small clandestine battle from the Schatz farm. He began putting out a typed newspaper, "Freies Oesterreich," in which he reprinted stories he picked up over the BBC, including editorials on leading figures such as Hitler, Roosevelt, and Churchill, and a feature on American life called "Do You Know?" Schatz distributed carbon copies to his anti-Nazi neighbors.

Fred Mayer's interest quickly extended beyond the acquisition of intelligence. He radioed Bari: "If desired can take Innsbruck and area ahead of airborne landings. Political prisoners would need 500 weapons."

AFHQ replied that no airborne landings were feasible at that time.

Mayer then reported: "One thousand partisans of all parties under my command. A full planeload of explosives for bridge sabotage and a quantity of propaganda material should be sent to me at once. . . ."

The air force sent a heavily loaded plane. But along with the arms, explosives, coffee, and PX luxuries, AFHQ packed instructions for Mayer. The Allies had armies and air armadas to prosecute the war. All they needed from the GREENUP team was intelligence. Mayer was to refrain from paramilitary operations that might endanger his valuable flow of information. He was to keep sending useful intelligence such as the message which reported: "Assembled at Hall and Innsbruck main and west stations, 26 trains, 30 to 40 cars each, loaded with ammo, tractors, ack-ack guns, gasoline, light equipment. Leaving for Italy via Brenner April third after 2100 GMT. Trains Guarded. Source, Trainmaster of Hall."

This message resulted in a massive strike by the Fifteenth Air Force in which virtually the entire rail convoy was destroyed while coming out of the Brenner Pass.

Mayer's intelligence had attained not only admirable quality but considerable bulk, including lengthy lists of all Gestapo officials in the Tirol-Vorarlberg, provided to him by Alois Kuen, the police officer. This information could be invaluable in cleaning out Nazi influences when the area was eventually conquered.

Through Franz Weber's sister Margarete, Fred Mayer met a librarian at the University of Innsbruck with ties to the POEN. At the librarian's house Fred encountered a young man described to him as a POEN courier from Switzerland. Mayer had, unknowingly, met Fritz Molden, who was checking with his Innsbruck base located in the offices of his professor uncle. Mayer saw the possibility of delivering his Gestapo membership file through this new associate. He discussed it with Molden, who agreed. The timing, however, could not be worked out and he had to arrange for another courier to carry the pouch. He instructed Hans Wynberg to radio Bari: "On Saturday April 21 you should have person in Vaduz, Liechtenstein, in order to get some important papers. Wire method of recognition and address. Let me know how package is to be marked."

It was the last message OSS Bari ever received from Fred Mayer. OSS Bern sent a man to Vaduz. But the next day, Al Ulmer in Bari received a message from Bern: "Our man kept rendezvous today. No one showed up."

XIV

"Take It Avay, New York!"

✠ ✠ ✠

Though OSS London operated French, Belgian, Polish, Scandinavian, and other nationality desks, the establishment of a German desk was long delayed. The principal explanation was that the British had initially barred the Americans from recruiting German prisoners of war as potential agents, and desirable nonmilitary Germans, such as Socialist and trade-union exiles, had all been monopolized by the OSS London Labor Division.

There had been established in Washington, as early as 1942, a German desk, which was supposed to contemplate the eventual penetration of the Reich, but this listless operation never advanced beyond the contemplative stage. In charge of the German desk was an aging former foreign-service officer, a stationary bureaucrat who did nothing wrong by doing virtually nothing. The man also had an obsession with security. When he wanted to tell an associate something, they would have to go outside to a park bench to carry on the discussion.

To this dry well, an energetic naval lieutenant named Richard Helms reported in 1944. Helms had come to OSS by way of journalism and possessed an impressive credential: as a reporter with the United Press's Berlin bureau, Helms had interviewed and lunched with Hitler at a castle outside Nuremberg in 1936. This experience had left Helms with a view far different from the popular perception of Hitler as a frothing maniac. The hypnotic stare appeared, up close, to be nothing more than protuberant eyeballs. The mesmerizing orator spoke, in normal conversation, plainly, calmly, even diffidently. Helms wrote in his dispatch: "The striking things were the ready intelligence, the understanding of German psychology, the complete assuredness behind every expression of opinion, regardless of what it concerned."

Helms's principal occupation while serving on the Washington German desk was to plot his escape from it, which he managed through a transfer to OSS London.

By the fall of 1944, a German desk was finally operating as one of the London nationality operations of OSS. Major Aubrey Harwood had been dispatched by the new unit's chief to France to look for anti-Nazi Germans who might be brought back and trained as agents.

It was Harwood's effort that sent Ferdinand Appenzell and Leon Lindau to OSS London late in February 1944. They became the charges of Captain Fred Gercke, then serving on the German desk.

Gercke was well aware that the agents given to him were the dregs, troublesome recruits whom no one else wanted. The Labor Division, he knew, had taken the cream of German nationals.

Of one of his new prospects, Ferdinand Appenzell, an OSS psychologist had written: "a rather shrewd and cagey fellow and doubtless something of a grafter. His capacity for accurate objective reporting is not all one could wish . . . [his] activities have been somewhat *persona non grata* not only with the Germans but with the French."

Appenzell was a thirty-year-old German who had worked in the early years of the war as a civilian employee of the Luftwaffe. He was a thickset, swarthy man, ebullient and fast-talking. Appenzell's job was to keep financial accounts and do some buying for the Luftwaffe officers' mess. He followed his unit to Greece and France, and was subsequently sentenced to prison in France for malfeasance. Appenzell maintained that he was jailed for exposing graft among members of the SS intelligence wing, the SD. Given Appenzell's past, one might just as easily believe the reverse.

He escaped from a prison in Paris and wound up, he claimed, fighting with the French resistance, which led eventually to his recruitment by Major Harwood. Appenzell's principal incentive to serve OSS was his understanding that he would be given American citizenship after the war.

When Harwood first met Ferdi Appenzell, the German was broke, recovering from syphilis, and eager to team up with anybody who could help him stay out of either a French or a German jail. Yet, outwardly, he maintained the bumptious confidence of a carnival pitchman.

The man selected as Appenzell's partner was Leon Lindau, whose motivation was rather more pure than Ferdi's. Leon Lindau, born in Munich, age thirty-seven, had enlisted in the French foreign legion when he was twenty. He was discharged in January 1941, after France's defeat. He took a job repairing bicycles in Lyons and subsequently became involved in the French resistance. He regarded himself as a Frenchman first and, while with the resistance, had machine-gunned his former countrymen without a qualm.

Though both men were considered unsavory by other elements of OSS London, Captain Gercke believed in his own tests of character. He got Appenzell and Lindau drunk on several occasions in the belief that he could best judge them with their inhibitions dissolved by alcohol. The Germans apparently satisfied Gercke's standards.

Ferdi Appenzell, by far the quicker mind, was to head the team. Leon Lindau seemed quite content to follow the younger man. Their mission was code-named LUXE. After training in Joan-Eleanor techniques, they were parachuted on April fifth in the vicinity of Weilheim, about thirty miles southwest of Munich.

Ferdi and Leon landed on a farm near the village of Reisting in the vicinity of Weilheim. Soon after their arrival, they met an old peasant woman who owned the property where they had parachuted.

Ferdi Appenzell went immediately for the Germanic jugular. Not for him arguments of freedom lost or justice trampled under Nazi rule. Appenzell knew what moved his countrymen. He told the woman that he was a German parachutist captured in Crete and had been given an opportunity by the Americans to help end the war. He confidentially informed the woman that Himmler had given orders for all cattle in the vicinity to be taken from the farmers and sent to the mountains as a food reserve for the Nazis. The outraged woman immediately offered to aid the American cause and provided the agents temporary refuge in her barn.

After a few days spent consolidating their gear and resting, Ferdi went to the peasant woman's home in the village of Reisting and asked her to put him in touch with someone there who could serve as Bürgermeister after the war. She introduced a man named Dominikus Huttner, who had never associated with the Nazis. Ferdi was much impressed by Huttner, a powerful figure, who told Ferdi that he was fond of Americans and had competed against them as a world-class weight lifter.

Ferdi told Huttner that he needed subagents to collect intelligence and he wanted him to help build the network. If the German cooperated,

Reisting was secure. Ferdi said he was in radio contact with the Allies, and if anything untoward happened to him or his partner, he would have the village blown off the earth. Huttner hastily agreed to help.

Through Huttner, Ferdi and Leon found a suitable hideout. Near Reisting was a cluster of farmhouses, a village called Unterstillern. Two of the houses were inhabited by families that had lived in the United States in the 1920s. Ferdi, Leon, their radio, and other equipment were transported there in a wagon under a load of hay. They were given a hideout under the mosque-style dome of the Unterstillern church. Their presence was known only by two farmers, their wives, and the church sexton. The children of the families and thirty refugees boarding in the other houses were unaware of the agents' presence.

In Unterstillern, the LUXE team met another fugitive, a German Army sergeant named Sommer, who had deserted a few weeks before. Sommer's home was eight miles away in Weilheim. Ferdi immediately snared the deserter. If Sommer helped them, Ferdi said, he would see that he did not become a prisoner after the war ended. If not, Sommer's life would be made unpleasant. He was not about to leave Unterstillern, except with Ferdi's permission, not even to see his wife in Weilheim.

Sommer agreed, and immediately proved his worth. He gave them the locations in Weilheim of the Dornier aircraft factory and the Zarkes plant, where 750 Frenchmen were manufacturing spare parts for Messerschmitts. Ferdi Appenzell was now ready to talk to London.

On April 17, 1945, at fifteen minutes before midnight, First Lieutenant Kingdon Knapp took off from Harrington Air Field for the fifty-second Joan-Eleanor mission. Lieutenant Calhoun Ancrum worked the antenna as though in a trance. He was tired beyond caring. The three-man crew of the Mosquito had been flying the long, tension-racked missions deep into Germany virtually every other day. In one recent week they had flown nine times into the Reich.

They cruised at thirty-five thousand feet. The cold in the unpressurized aircraft increased Ancrum's drowsiness. About forty miles from Weilheim, Ancrum flipped on his transmitter. His voice was toneless. "Hello Ferdi, Vic calling. Do you hear me, Ferdi, Vic calling."

The ever-cocky voice of Appenzell responded. Ancrum gave the pilot the bearing to fly and switched on his wire recorder. As the signal strength increased, he told the pilot to begin orbiting.

The Joan-Eleanor transmitter sent out a cone of sound with a radius of approximately forty miles by the time it reached the ground. The signal was equally strong anywhere within that perimeter. The plane deliberately did not circle directly over the agents, rather, off center, in order not to give their location away. The speaker on the ground and the man in the plane were approximately ten miles apart.

From the onion dome of the church in Unterstillern, Ferdi Appenzell's voice was carried aloft on a beam so narrow at the base that one could hear it by ear alone, before it could be picked up by direction-finding equipment. During one transmission, Ferdi saw a direction-finding truck pass near the church. The truck may have picked up the more diffuse signal from the airplane, but evidently had heard nothing on the ground.

Appenzell reported to Ancrum the promising contacts which he and Leon had made: "The people trust us, but they want us to prove to them who we are and what we can do, and, therefore, I have told them that I shall furnish as proof the bombing of Weilheim . . . the Weilheim railway junction has from forty to fifty trains passing through all night. In Weilheim proper, there are two airplane factories. Number one is the Dornier works and the second is a factory making spare parts for planes. . . . You must absolutely knock out the railway line Weilheim–Peissenberg-Augsburg as soon as possible. This line must be knocked out." Out of concern for Frau Sommer, wife of their informant, and the foreign workers in the Weilheim aircraft plants, Ferdi urged that a warning leaflet be dropped over the city before a raid.

The conversation went on uninterrupted for forty minutes. Ferdi closed with a plea: "You must not bomb Reisting under any circumstances. The people are ninety percent on our side and so is the entire Volkssturm. Reisting! Reisting! Do not bomb it." The entire conversation was carried out in German, except for an English sign-off that Ferdi favored: "Take it *avay*, New York!"

In the early dawn, almost seven hours later, Lieutenant Knapp pulled Mosquito #740 to a stop before a hangar at Harrington Air Field. Calhoun Ancrum slid from the belly of the plane and went into the hangar, where he typed out a quick covering report, which he gave, with the spool of recording wire, to a motorcycle courier. The courier sped the recording to OSS offices in London, where a private named Gerard Hahn, who was fluent in German, translated it and distributed the transcription within the Division of Intelligence Procurement. The information on Weilheim was then relayed to air force intelligence in London, which, in turn, notified the air command responsible for that sector, the Fifteenth Air Force in Italy. On April 19, at 1:49 P.M., approximately thirty-six hours after Ancrum and Appenzell's conversation, seventy-eight P-38 dive bombers appeared over Weilheim. OSS and the air corps had untangled their problems.

On the morning of April 19, Ferdi Appenzell had set out from Reisting for Munich in a truck with two businessmen who had joined his network. Their purpose was to pick up possible air-target intelligence in the Munich area. The two Germans had been reluctant to make the trip, fearing they might be bombed or strafed. Appenzell confidently told them that nothing could happen, since he had alerted the American air forces that he would be on the road that day.

The truck had neared the rail yards in Pasing outside Munich at 11:00 A.M., when a policeman stopped the party and warned that an air-raid alarm had sounded. The two Germans begged Appenzell to let them go into a shelter. He again reminded them that they were safe, but told the driver to pull off the road. They sat and watched the bombardment from a half mile away. The Germans eyed Appenzell uneasily. He sat calmly throughout the raid.

When they dropped Ferdi off late at night in Unterstillern, he found Leon with the deserter, Sergeant Sommer, both much agitated. After Ferdi had left that morning for Munich, Leon had gone into Weilheim to gather more information on the city's airplane factories. Early in the afternoon a preliminary warning had sounded and a low-flying aircraft circled overhead. Leon doubted that this plane presaged a raid, since no warning leaflet had been dropped. Soon after, a wave of American dive bombers flew in at low level and released their charges. Forty minutes later, a second wave swept through and struck the rail yards.

When Leon returned in the evening to their hideaway in the church, he found Sergeant Sommer waiting for him, wild-eyed. They had given him no warning of the raid, Sommer shrieked. No leaflets had been dropped, and now Sommer had been told that his house in Weilheim was destroyed and his wife was missing. He threatened to kill Leon. Not knowing how else to placate Sommer, he told him to go into Weilheim to look for the woman.

Sommer had just returned, even more distraught, when Ferdi arrived. The German deserter had failed to find his wife. He shouted that they had betrayed him and would pay for their treachery. Appenzell's habitual heartiness vanished. He shoved Sommer into a chair and warned him to shut up.

Weilheim had been bombed largely through his own doing, Ferdi reminded him, and if Sommer said another word, he would see that his neighbors learned the source of their grief. Ferdi said he would send somebody into town in the morning to continue the search for the man's wife. But now Sommer was to go back to his hideout and remain there. The deserter slinked out wordlessly. Ferdi told Leon not to go to sleep, but to stand guard over the house where Sommer was staying.

The view of the raid on Weilheim differed depending on whether one saw it from the air or the ground. The Fifteenth Air Force reported that the P-38 Lightning dive bombers had: "Inflicted damage to tracks, rolling stock, in railroad facilities on the Munich–Garmisch-Partenkirchen line. All main lines and siding tracks were completely obstructed by craters and apparently sixty units of rolling stock were destroyed or severely damaged."

Leon Lindau noted that the first wave of bombers hit an unimportant cement-pipe plant, a post office, and a residential area, destroying Sommer's house, among others. Of the four main buildings of the Zarkes airplane factory, only one was damaged.

The second wave of American bombers did strike the railroad junction. The worst damage was inflicted on a clearly marked hospital train. The train had been shuttling between German cities for three weeks seeking a safe haven and finally had settled in Weilheim. It was crowded with wounded Hungarian soldiers, of whom 350 were killed or further injured.

It was Fagin's classroom. The schoolhouse was at Area F, outside London; the curriculum included burglary, bribery, and blackmail. The course was designed to last two months. Students learned to use weapons, operate radios, communicate in code, read maps. They were trained to observe. Where were the enemy arsenals, plane and tank facilities? Where were troops deployed? Artillery? What size, how much, where was it emplaced? Railways? What lines were active, what were they carrying, what was in yards and sidings?

Photographs of four men were flashed on a screen for twenty seconds each, providing the subject's name, age, occupation, and address. The four photos were then scrambled and shown again for thirty seconds without identification. The agent was to write down all the details he could remember about each individual. Instructors found this exercise an excellent test of an agent's powers of observation.

Students learned the mechanics of daily life in Germany: how to mail a letter, buy a railroad ticket, obtain ration stamps, greet a German officer. They learned the vocabulary of the spy's craft: "the safe house," where people would risk harboring an agent; the "cut-out," an intermediary who would handle all of the principal's dealings with subagents so that knowledge of the principal agent would be tightly circumscribed.

They learned the art of silent killing, perfected by W. E. Fairbairn, the legendary British major, sometimes known as "Delicate Dan." Knife strokes, Fairbairn taught, should be upward, from the testicles to the chin. The hand in a "tiger claw" position was most effective for gouging out eyes. A single sheet of newspaper, they learned, could become a crude dagger. Fold the paper to approximately six inches by two inches. Then fold it diagonally to form a sharp point at one end. Drive the pointed end hard into the stomach or under the jaw, just behind the chin.

A graduate spoke of the self-assurance his silent-killing instructor had provided. "He gave us more and more self-confidence, which gradually grew into a sense of physical power and superiority that few men ever acquire. By the time we finished our training, I would have willingly enough tackled any man, whatever his strength, size or ability. . . . One fear that has since, however, haunted me is that of getting entangled in a sudden row and of seriously injuring, or even killing another man before realizing what is happening."

Agents trained in London took a cram course in parachuting lasting three days, compared to the six weeks required of American paratroopers before they made their first jump. Those who mastered the chute had achieved a triumph of will over one of man's most instinctive fears.

They learned the rules of solitude and survival in enemy territory. Walk an extra mile to avoid a village. Take the woods and fields instead of roads. Avoid children, they always talk. Pay for what you take from farmers. Avoid politics and strong drink. When night falls, accept discomfort if necessary. Better to sleep safely in a ditch than to be wakened in bed by the Gestapo. If in the presence of the police and you believe you are being watched, go up and ask a question. "Where is the labor exchange?" A policeman is feared in Germany. Only those with a clear conscience would dare approach him openly.

Agents were schooled in the rudiments of psychology. The OSS training manual advised: "Give the other man a sense of importance. Be a good listener. Encourage others to talk about themselves. Give a man a good reputation to live up to. Practice the 'yes' technique. If you can get a man to say 'yes' twice," the manual advised cryptically, "he will usually say it a third time, as this entails a physical and mental reaction."

Overt bribery was considered dangerous to both parties and was to be avoided. Learn instead the covert forms, the training manual suggested. "Put a man in a position to take your money. 'Forget' your wallet in his office. Sell goods to him below their real value. Buy goods from him above their value. Lose to him at cards. Lose bets to him. . . . [However], in communities where bribery is common or in dealing with a blatant scoundrel, direct methods can be adopted."

The agent who was captured and pressed to talk could take some comfort in knowing that his lips need not be sealed to the death. The British SOE standard was that the captured agent should try to hold out for forty-eight hours. During that time, persons who had been in contact with him would have had enough time to cover their tracks. Thereafter, if the pressures were no longer bearable, the agent was free, honorably, to talk.

The OSS training manual was explicit: "If you are really up against it and realize that the enemy proposes to go on grilling you until they extract all possible information from you, there are only two courses of action open to you, in justice to the other members of your organization—an attempt to escape, or suicide by "L" tablet or other means."

If their captors tried to "turn" them, to persuade them to cooperate by communicating with their base under control, they should go along, and insert the prearranged "captured" signal in their radio messages.

The training manual eschewed sentiment. "The rules of this game are different. The ends justify *any* means. Survival and success go to the quickest, cleverest, most ruthless and the most patiently persistent." Above all, the manual urged, have a good story. "Stick by it. Avoid being conspicuous. Try to be simple, not clever."

Throughout the training, the agent was monitored for clues to his character. How did he act toward other agents socially? At mealtimes? After the training day? Did he display initiative or hang back? Did he master his emotions? Could he endure social isolation? What did he reveal of himself in offhand remarks? How did he play cards? How did he swing himself from the truck on arrival at Area F? Was he agile? Did he lead or lag? His OSS mentors seized any clue that revealed the agent, his motivation, initiative, resourcefulness, discretion, leadership, his being.

Those who did not complete training as agents—because of inability or undesirability—may have learned too much merely to be returned to the prisoner cages or released to their previous life. OSS London had picked a point of no return in the training schedule beyond which the unsuccessful agent had to be stowed in "cold storage." Whether soldier or civilian, the washed-out agent was usually packed off to a camp in the bleak north of Scotland to sit out the war.

The London training staff had never anticipated any problem from the two men sent from Holland. They had been recruited by Jan Laverge, who was to the Dutch what Ray Brittenham was to Belgian operations. While Brittenham had gone to Brussels to recruit agents for Germany, Laverge had gone to Eindhoven to work with Dutch intelligence for the same end. Captain Laverge was admirably suited for the task. He had been born and raised in Doorn, Holland, and had settled in the United States in 1934. As a youth he had gone to parties and played tennis at Doorn with the children of the exiled German Kaiser.

In America, Laverge settled in the South and carried on the same tobacco business which he had pursued in Holland. His speech was undulating Southern, with bewildering Dutch traces. He called his recruitment operation in Eindhoven MELANIE, for the character from *Gone With the Wind*.

Laverge was a meticulous man who took his responsibilities seriously. In November 1944 he sent two Dutchmen, his prize recruits, to England. One was named Hoofdorp and carried excellent credentials. Hoofdorp was well educated and, before the war, had been groomed to work on his father's newspaper. He had worked successfully in the Dutch underground and came to Captain Laverge highly recommended by the Dutch secret service. The other agent, named Wickluis, was equally qualified, a construction engineer by profession, with a good resistance record. There the plaudits ended.

One month after their arrival in London, the Schools and Training Branch reported that the Dutch team "has not shown qualities desirable in good agent material. It has proved itself detrimental to the morale of other students."

Private Lazare Teper of the BACH Section found them overbearing prima donnas. Taken to the clothing depot, they rejected the German suits suggested because they were slightly worn. They insisted instead on stylish, new fashions, which the clothing depot did not stock. As alternatives they wanted well-tailored British suits, which would have been instant giveaways.

Hans Tofte suspected that there might be more than exaggerated ego behind the behavior of the two men. He had seen a report prepared by Polish intelligence indicating that Nazi sympathizers had been insinuated into OSS London among Dutch recruits. He passed his suspicions on to his superiors.

In the meantime, the Dutchmen were schooled in the use of OSS codes. They were trained by Lieutenant Commander Stephen Simpson in Joan-Eleanor techniques. They had been inside OSS headquarters on Grosvenor Street.

The decision to dismiss them was repeatedly deferred until, finally, their potential for harm could no longer be ignored. One of the training officers reported, "If they are left at Area F much longer, the school cannot accept the responsibility of preserving the fine spirit of the other teams." On December 24, Major Hans Tofte informed Commander Simpson that the two Dutchmen were no longer to be let near the Joan-Eleanor operation.

Hoofdorp and Wickluis were subsequently removed from the program. A final report described the two as "unreliable, dishonest, secretive, arrogant, and definitely unwilling to cooperate. They evinced a predilection for deceiving their instructors and for getting away with as much as they could."

What to do with them now? OSS had no facilities for quarantining them. The Dutch would not take them back, and the British refused to allow them into their camps. X-2 believed that they had to be removed from Europe if the German operations were to remain secure.

Captain Laverge manfully accepted his error of judgment. He addressed a memo to SI London: "My opinion is that as agents they are washed out forever, and the sooner we are rid of them the better." But he hardly expected the solution adopted. "When I first heard that they were being sent to Catalina, I was fairly shocked. . . ."

Laverge took some small solace in the dumping of this troublesome pair on unsuspecting colleagues in the home office. "Don't let Washington go wild at the sight of two real agents in the flesh instead of out of a book. I don't feel we have any great obligation to them," Laverge concluded. But if it was thought that some gesture of good will was required to soften their wartime exile on a southern California island, he recommended that the two men be paid $500 each.

EAGLE was an ill-starred exercise in proletarian espionage. Among the two hundred thousand Poles in England were members of a refugee army stationed in Scotland under control of the Polish government-in-exile. The London Labor Division suggested that working-class Poles should be able to pass easily in Germany as conscript workers.

Under Project EAGLE, the Polish government-in-exile provided OSS with forty enlisted men as prospective agents. From them, sixteen teams were formed. The Poles were described in an OSS report as "of the middle and lower type." The prospective agents were placed under the direction of the Polish desk, headed by an exuberant Polish-American, Lieutenant Colonel Joseph Dasher, née Daschiewicz.

However lacking in sophistication, the Poles were high-spirited and strongly motivated. Henry Sutton, preparing their cover stories, was deeply impressed by their simple patriotism. Those who had seen their villages annihilated by the Nazis were fearless and impatient to strike back.

In February 1945, an event occurred which took the heart out of them. At the Yalta Conference, the western Allies ceded a huge portion of prewar Poland to the Soviet Union, and began to shove aside the Polish government-in-exile in favor of the Communist-supported provisional government at Lublin.

"You could just see the deflation of morale in those fellows," Bill Casey observed. "We sensed it when we sent them out. Some were just going through the motions. They had become different people from the time they first went into training." The chief of the Polish desk, the irrepressible Lieutenant Colonel Dasher, tried to fan their flagging spirits. Before Polish agents flew out of Harrington Air Field, Dasher would lead them in rousing choruses of Polish patriotic songs.

A half-dozen Poles were flown to Belgium, then loaded aboard a truck and driven through Brussels en route to Maastricht, Holland. From there, they were to be infiltrated through the lines into Germany. As the vehicle crawled through the city, the months of monasticism that the agents had endured began to tell. Whenever the truck passed a reasonably attractive woman, another Pole quietly dropped from the back. The OSS conducting officer, up front with the driver, turned to find the truck empty. Within several days, the Poles were rounded up and eventually slipped into Germany.

Of the sixteen Polish teams, none ever made radio contact with the London base. Poor initial selection, assembly-line training, political disillusionment after Yalta, all worked against their success. Whatever the roots, the Poles' failure was ironic. Professional Polish intelligence officers were universally rated among the finest. One of the strengths of British intelligence was—after the fall of Poland—that Britain inherited much of the surviving Polish apparatus. In Switzerland, the Olympus of international deception, the word was, "If you have a Pole working for you, you really don't need anyone else."

Adrian was one of the men provided to OSS by the Polish government-in-exile. He was parachuted near Augsburg on March 18, 1945, carrying one of the few faulty sets of papers prepared by the London documents staff. Adrian was forty-one years old and had been a railroad electrician in civilian life. He went into Germany in this role, with the added fiction that he had just left Poznan before the Russian advance and had been ordered to take a job on the railroad in Augsburg. In traveling from the drop point to the city, Adrian passed a large airfield and had drawn a sketch of it.

While having his papers routinely checked in Augsburg, Adrian's cover story collapsed. He supposedly had been ordered to Augsburg, but had no travel papers directing him there. His *Wehrpass* was blank where his physical description was to have been entered. The police had a master list of Poznan railroad workers checked. Adrian's name did not appear in it. He was placed under arrest by the Gestapo and taken by train to Halle. During the ride he managed to swallow, bit by bit, the sketch he had made of the airfield.

At the Halle Gestapo headquarters, Adrian was stripped and his shoes were cut up, layer by layer. The police ripped his clothes apart, but found nothing. They forced him to drink an emetic solution. He refused and was struck in the jaw with a rifle butt which knocked out five of his teeth. He then drank the solution and vomited. The police were still unsatisfied at finding nothing in the discharge. They placed him between two rubber cylinders and rolled his body between them them until everything came up. The contents from his stomach were examined through a large magnifying glass, and parts of the map were discovered.

Adrian was formally accused of spying and ordered to cooperate or lose his life. For the next five days, he was beaten for eight hours a day with rubber clubs, but divulged nothing. On the sixth day, American Flying Fortresses struck Halle. One bomb blew out the doors of the prison block where Adrian was held, and he and several other prisoners escaped.

The document failure which had brought on Adrian's downfall was rare. The London staff had, in fact, shortly after Adrian's departure, scored one of their proudest triumphs in preparing a document for agents such as Adrian.

Lazare Teper had learned from German newspapers that workers fleeing the Russians were now required to carry an evacuation permit. Future OSS agents being sent into Germany under cover as conscript workers running from the Soviet advance would need this paper. The problem, as the more prosaic staff members complained, was how to forge a document which they had never seen.

Teper and Henry Sutton thought about it. The evacuation permit, at this state of administrative disorganization in Germany, would no doubt be issued locally. In small towns, it would probably be typewritten and authenticated by the ubiquitous rubber stamp. OSS London had German paper and typewriters and could reproduce the stamp of any local German government.

Teper worked with the documents people to create what they imagined the evacuation permit ought to look like. They did not believe that anything would be gained by informing agents that the document they carried was not based on any known original. OSS had to wait until agents were recovered at the end of the war to find that their gamble had largely succeeded.

Adrian, half-starved and exhausted after his escape, was found by Russian and Polish conscript workers while sleeping in a forest. They took him in and looked after him. On April 15, when American forces liberated the workers, an army Counter Intelligence Corps unit put Adrian to work tracking down fugitive Nazis in recently conquered areas.

Among a group of suspects hauled into CIC headquarters, Adrian spotted two of his Gestapo tormentors. He pulled a pistol out of an MP's holster and fired two shots, point-blank, into each of the prisoners. No disciplinary action was taken against Adrian. He continued to work with the CIC until the end of the war.

XV

Donovan's Red Army

✠ ✠ ✠

The company of German mountain infantry carried out close-order drill with the bored competence that combat veterans reserve for parade-ground soldiering. *"Habt Acht! Vorwärts, marsch! Kolonne rechts! Halt!"*

The commanding officer put the company at ease, and moved aside. A man stepped out of the ranks and began to speak to the men in serviceable, if hardly perfect, German. His name was Aaron Bank and he was a captain in the U.S. Army. Of all OSS operations planned for Germany, Bank's was the largest and perhaps boldest. He was training a company of ersatz German infantry with the primary objective of capturing Adolf Hitler. The mission was called IRON CROSS.

Bank belonged to SO, the OSS element involved in sabotage, guerrilla warfare, and other paramilitary operations. SO had lived its heyday in the French campaign, training, arming, and fighting with the resistance. During that period, the SI and SO branches of OSS London might as well have been on separate planets for all the contact they had.

Now, with German operations commanding priority, SO stood in the shadows. Germany was largely an SI show, a job for the intelligence side. Emphasis on espionage had been dictated by changed circumstances. In the occupied countries, a handful of SO operatives could catalyze whole populations to resist, particularly when that handful could command air drops of high explosives, machine guns, rifles, ammunition, and satchels of money. But agents infiltrating Germany could count on no conquered people chafing under a foreign master to rally to them.

Saboteurs inside the Reich, unsupported by a native resistance movement, would be as so many fleas blindly assailing the hide of an elephant. So unpromising were guerrilla operations against Germany that Gerald Miller, the new chief of SO London, named late in 1944, was mainly responsible for dismantling the large SO organization which had been built up for the campaign in France.

Miller was an affable man in his early forties who looked every portly inch the Midwestern banker that he was. He had come to OSS from a bank in Detroit, after a tour with the War Production Board. He was one of the old men of OSS and felt more comfortable retaining the rank of civilian. Miller had been recruited by Rob Thompson, the officer who was then working with Hans Tofte and Mike Burke on the operational problems of putting SI agents into Germany.

As Bill Casey's SI operations continued to build up, Jerry Miller's SO organization wound down. But bureaucratic rivalries died hard, even in so young an organization as OSS. There were SO officials in Washington who wondered if their branch could not get just a piece of the German campaign.

Jerry Miller was pressured to get SO into the game on a limited scale. He was given scant encouragement by SO's mentor, Britain's SOE. His British counterparts told Miller to forget about Germany. "You can't get in there; and if you could, you couldn't do anything anyway," a British colleague warned him. Miller was able to mount only a few modest missions and one ambitious effort, IRON CROSS. Aaron Bank became its leader.

Bank was a forty-one-year-old career army officer, a darkly handsome, intensely physical man with a lifelong addiction to adventure. From the age of sixteen and for most of the next fourteen years, Bank was a golden boy, pursuing the beaches of Miami, Long Beach, the Bahamas, and, finally, Biarritz. There, on the Bay of Biscay, he served as chief of life guards for five years at the Hôtel Miramar, a resort then popular with the Prince of Wales and his set.

In 1932 Bank left the "Chambre d'Amour," as the pool and pavilion at the Miramar were called, for a drier career. He went briefly into real-estate investment. But with the Depression deepening and sales declining, Bank joined the army. There he stayed. He spoke fair French and

German, learned from his mother. As a soldier, linguist, and adventurer, Bank was fated for OSS.

The plan was to train an entire company as German infantry to be parachuted into the Inn Valley, roughly midway between Kufstein and Innsbruck. IRON CROSS would conduct sabotage and guerrilla warfare in the Redoubt, induce defections from the German Army, and try to capture high-ranking Nazis trying to take sanctuary in the alpine fastness.

Bank struck a rich vein of anti-Nazi recruits among German civilians interned by the French. Some had been held as political prisoners, others were fugitives from the Gestapo. Some had fought with the French resistance. Bank also canvassed POW cages around Toulouse and Perpignan. His screening was elemental. "Do you oppose the Nazi regime? Will you fight against it?"

By the end of 1944, Bank had gathered an original complement of 175 men. The youngest recruit was twenty, the oldest forty-five. Most ranged between thirty and thirty-five. Nearly all were Communists or Communist sympathizers. Many had fought with the Loyalists in Spain's civil war. At that stage, General Donovan's "but-will-they-kill-Germans?" standard of eligibility still prevailed over admonitions raised against using Communists by people like Bert Jolis.

Besides Bank, the other Americans assigned to IRON CROSS were a lieutenant and three enlisted men, one of whom was to serve as radioman once they arrived in the Reich. For the German underbosses of the company, Bank chose a complementary pair: Klaus, a square-jawed, coarsely attractive man of great physical prowess, rumored to have been a circus strongman, and Horst, suave and ingratiating, with the manner of a maître d'. Both were veterans of the Spanish civil war and undiluted Communists.

As his headquarters, Bank was assigned a French manor house in the Saint-Germain area outside Paris. He and the other Americans moved into the house, while the Germans were quartered in tents outside. There, the company studied a curriculum of ambush, sabotage, traffic disruption, troop defection, insurrection, and the demolition of bridges, culverts, railroads, and power-line pylons.

They were trained in the use of Mauser rifles, Panzerfaust antitank rockets, Luger pistols, and Schmiessen submachine guns for close-up work. They worked with both American plastic and German explosives. The men preferred the latter, but procurement presented problems.

They underwent an abruptly truncated course in parachuting. They jumped from the doorway of a mock-up training plane on the ground and were told only how to roll over on hitting the earth. When the day's classes were over, they practiced close-order drill, so that one day they could march convincingly down the Inn River Valley.

Bank was as exacting as a Prussian. He weeded out the physically unfit, the morally uncommitted, the psychologically undependable, until his original 175 recruits were compressed to 100. Their morale was high—as it is when troops are fairly and firmly disciplined, kept occupied, and have a sense of mission. No guards were necessary around the manor where they trained and no escapes attempted. When absences were reported at bed check, Bank knew in which bordellos the absentees could be found. Bank's infantrymen were paid the equivalent of sixty cents an hour in French francs.

The BACH Section accepted a stiff challenge to its ingenuity in preparing a cover for Captain Aaron Bank. How to explain a German soldier who spoke only fair German, somewhat better French—but with an excruciating accent—as a member of a German mountain infantry company?

Were it not for the terrible accent, Lazare Teper thought that Bank could be passed off as a French Nazi sympathizer. Teper found a solution. He searched the map and located a French-speaking island in the Caribbean. Aaron Bank would be from Martinique. How many Germans could say what the accent of a Frenchman from Martinique should sound like? On this foundation, Teper constructed Bank's cover.

COVER STORY   MARCHAND, HENRI (Captain Bank)

23.11.1902:   born in ST. PIERRE, Martinique.

Religion, Status: Catholic, single.

15.3.1880:   *Father:* died in 1920 of myocarditis. He was an accountant in the Rum Factory St. James Society Anme Coloniale, rue Ernest Deproge, 26, Fort de France.

12.2.1882:   *Mother:* Marie, née Boneau, born in MARSEILLE. She is still living in MARTINIQUE. I have not seen her since 1941.

1907:   When I was 5 years old, we moved from ST. PIERRE to FORT DE FRANCE.
Home Address: rue Victor Hugo, 62.

Population:	Fort de France	46,000
"	St. Pierre	4,300

Education:

1908–18:   Lycée Schoelcher until 1918.

1918–19:   Ecole Commerciale.

Originally it was my parents' and my own wish to become an accountant like my father but, during my study at the Ecole Commerciale I developed an aversion against this profession. On the other hand, during all my youth I was interested in sports and medicine. Because of my father's early death it was financially impossible for me to study medicine, so I decided to try to make a living as a Masseur and Gymnastic Teacher in its rather fashionable Spas around Fort de France. (Les eaux d'Absalon, de Didier, et de Moutte). After a while I succeeded in having many fashionable people as my clients, besides I was employed on a part-time basis at the Clinique Pasteur as a Therapeutical Masseur.

After the German occupation of France, economic conditions on the island deteriorated, I lost quite a few of my well-to-do clients; therefore, I could not earn enough money, especially as I had to support my mother too. On the other hand, I knew that for a trained masseur like myself, there would be plenty of work in France, where the Germans maintained many hospitals. So I sailed on the steamer *Mont Viso* (4500 GT)—(Soc. Gén. de transports Maritimes à vapeur, S.A.) from Fort de France to Marseille via Casablanca.

Left Fort de France 11.11.41,
arrived Casablanca 7.12.41,
left Casablanca 1.1. 42,
arrived Marseille 13.1. 42.

After my arrival I inquired at the German Labor Office and was told to come back in 2 days. I did so and got a slip and was told to report to the Res. Lazarett at Biarritz, where I worked for about two years.

The population considered me a collaborator
and my feelings and my experiences actually were
and made me pro-German. When my superiors
told me that they would see to it that I get a good
job and will improve my position if I would join
the German Army, I decided to do so.

Although jobs in the same capacity did not
materialize, I never regret this step.

I possess the following papers:-
    1) French Identity Card
    2) Soldbuch

In mid-April, Aaron Bank was visited by the chief of Paris SO. The
officer had dined the night before with General Donovan, and the general
had been enthusiastic over the progress of the IRON CROSS Mission.
The thought of an entire company of German infantry marching to the
secret cadence of OSS excited Donovan. But he wanted the emphasis of
the mission changed. If the expected flight to the Redoubt materialized,
IRON CROSS was the right instrument for seizing Goebbels, Göring,
even Hitler. "Tell Bank to get Hitler," Donovan ordered. He tossed off
the idea with a hundred others from his corn-popper imagination and it
was passed down from him with magnified urgency to each succeeding
level.

Aaron Bank now saw IRON CROSS as an operation on the scale of
Skorzeny's dazzling snatch of Mussolini from Allied jailers on September
12, 1943. Bank immediately shifted his training emphasis. Guerrilla warfare and insurrection were subordinated to raiding techniques—how to
storm a building, neutralize its defenders, and make off with a human
prize; how to pluck a man, live, from a motorcade bristling with armaments. The IRON CROSS company was not told who was their prey,
only that they were to take him alive.

The men liked the idea that they would not be used against regular
Wehrmacht units, ordinary fellows like themselves sucked up in the
vortex of Hitler's war. Instead, they would operate only against elite Nazi
SS units. As their departure date neared, Bank sensed a healthy exhilaration in his men. They were as primed as the best troops he had ever seen
on the eve of combat.

Toward the end of April, Bank went to Dijon to lead the advance party.
He, his American radio operator, a sergeant named Goldbeck, and the two
German leaders, Klaus and Horst, were to parachute a few days ahead of
the main body. Bank and the sergeant would wear American uniforms

initially. Their German uniforms would be packed in the equipment containers. If they were caught on landing, proper uniforms might save them from summary execution.

The two Germans were to parachute in civilian clothes. They would carry papers identifying them as construction workers with the Organization Todt. The Germans were to establish themselves as the advance intelligence unit and set up a network to track the movements of key Nazis retreating into the Redoubt.

After the advance team was established, Bank would radio back to have the full company dropped from C-47s in a remote area, a platoon at a time. The drop zone was selected, a point at an elevation of five thousand feet on the west side of the Inn River Valley near a town called Schwaz. The point was sixty miles from Hitler's mountain retreat near Berchtesgaden and in the expected path of any withdrawal into the Redoubt.

The advance party arrived at Dijon, and then waited. During six days at the airport, the air liaison officer canceled their departure six times. Bad weather was the reason he gave.

Soon after the party had reached Dijon, Colonel J. Russell Forgan, David Bruce's successor as OSS commander in the ETO, had called the London chief of SO, Jerry Miller. "I know your IRON CROSS people have worked hard, and they are primed to go," Forgan began. "But, I can tell you, we think this whole German situation is about to fold. It's not wise to risk these fellows' lives. I think we'd better scrub it."

Germany's imminent defeat did not obviate the value of the mission. Rather, it increased the wisdom of having a unit positioned to snare Hitler and his Nazi overlords should they seek to carry on the war from the Alps. But Miller recognized what had happened. Returning a hundred Communists to Germany, on the eve of victory, could create rough political repercussions at home. OSS had gotten cold feet. Miller reluctantly told one of his deputies to call Aaron Bank.

For Bank the hardest part was telling the men. He mustered the IRON CROSS company for the last time. After the commitment they had made, there was little to say, and less that he could promise them. His orders were simply to pay off the men and send them back to POW cages. Their sole reward was to be among the first prisoners released when the fighting ended.

The Seventh Army OSS Detachment, deployed along the western front, had a reputation for style. The detachment's early headquarters in France had been the Château Gleisol, outside Lyons, graceful and turreted, where oil paintings hung from the walls of an ornate salon. The château had earlier served as Marshal Pétain's headquarters. It was also unheated and furnished largely with parachutes, packing crates, and gear strewn over its handsome polished floors. Later, the detachment took over other châteaux, hunting lodges, and villas in the mountains around Lunéville and Saverne, even a convent near Strasbourg.

Still, much of the time, it was a rugged existence interrupted by flashes of amusement, camaraderie, and promiscuity, since male and female agents and the American staff were often housed together. At a Vosges hunting lodge, a Polish prince played songs composed for his children on a piano—which was virtually the only furnishing in the lodge. An American officer, a dancer before the war, performed in a barren room in front of a fireplace for a chilled, huddled audience of aspiring spies. A German agent who boasted of having once been a lion tamer did frantic, wild dances, drank heavily, behaved coarsely, and offended the well-bred young ladies who worked as secretaries for Henry Hyde.

Hyde, their chief, had a generous tolerance of weaknesses of the flesh and lapses of military decorum. But he set an exacting standard of performance. He made one perfunctory gesture toward conventional military comportment—not because it mattered to him but because it had seemed politic. He was at the mercy of the army and the air corps in carrying out his missions. He needed their cooperation, their planes, and equipment, and to obtain these he needed their respect. His solution was to add to his staff a West Point major to impose a semblance of military order on his operation.

On arriving at Hyde's headquarters the West Pointer summoned the officers to a meeting. He coldly surveyed the casual crew which Hyde had assembled and announced that he was going to transform them into a military organization. He then went down the roster and catalogued each man's deficiencies with withering scorn.

The sergeant who managed the motor pool rashly chose that moment to enter the room. He wore a scarf of German parachute silk and sauntered past the officer with a "Hi, Major." He badly needed a shave.

The major seized this target of opportunity. "Attention!" The startled soldier stiffened at the half-forgotten command. He riveted his arms to his pants seams, his chin and chest jutted forward. The major then launched into a protracted lecture on military conduct, offering the sergeant as an object lesson. He concluded, asking, "What do you have to say for yourself now?" "Major, this position sure makes my tits tired."

The major proved, in the end, to be a decent sort. After two months with the Hyde operation he had acquired a scarf of German parachute silk and often needed a shave.

The Seventh Army OSS Detachment continued to confront obtuseness from the army and air corps. Carl Muecke took three agents to the mess hall at the Dijon airfield prior to their takeoff. While they ate, he introduced himself to the officer in charge and explained their purpose.

"Prisoners of war?" The officer studied Muecke incredulously. "Do you have a guard on them?"

"A guard? Of course not."

"Well, they're going to escape."

Muecke shook his head. "Where to?"

The German recruits, though housed and trained with agents of other nationalities, were generally left to themselves. Even the officers who had persuaded them to shift their allegiance never seemed entirely convinced of the conversion. This unspoken suspicion gave rise to rumors passed along to each new generation of German agents. One story had it that when the Americans finally dropped them, it would be with paper parachutes. The counterrumor told of a German who had balked at jumping and who pulled his American dispatcher out with him as he was being pushed from the plane.

Women offered certain clear advantages as secret agents. A woman did not have to explain why she was not in military service. She did not need the sheaf of passes that a working male or soldier had to carry. That a woman might be involved in secret military intelligence simply seemed less likely on the face of it. There were always risks, but the odds of exposure were sharply reduced.

Peter Viertel, of the Seventh Army OSS Detachment, had recruited Ada, Emily, and Maria in the Strasbourg area. His chief, Henry Hyde, was delighted with Viertel's plan. Hyde knew when to dare.

Of the three, Ada possessed the purest motivation. She was an Italian circus acrobat, stranded by the war in Strasbourg. She had once been assaulted and repeatedly raped by German soldiers. Her quest for revenge had a deadly coldness which appealed to intelligence professionals.

Emily, a small, pert brunette, had been recommended to OSS by French intelligence, the Deuxième Bureau. Little more was known of her background beyond her connections with the French.

The third woman, Maria, was young, no more than twenty, and toughened by her early life in a mining town south of Strasbourg. She was an

Alsatian prototype, a straw blonde, sturdy, ruddy-cheeked, a seeming milkmaid come to the city.

Peter Viertel had recruited Maria from a detention camp where she was being held as a Nazi collaborator. Maria was variously reported as having worked in a German hospital and in a German mess hall. The French described her as *"cul et chemise,"* ass and shirttail, with the Germans. She had also been the mistress of a Gestapo officer.

Maria offered a credible if hardly inspiring answer to the forever nagging question of motivation. Life for a Frenchwoman who had bedded down with the Germans was destined to be hard in liberated France. This unsentimental child of poverty and war was determined to land back on her feet even if she had to start from an American airplane. Maria wanted to get the collaborationist burden off her back and wanted something entered into the records proving that she had aided the Americans.

Viertel found Maria resilient, confident, and possessed of a native shrewdness. She was signed on and placed in training, where she received elemental instruction in parachuting and communications, and learned how to identify military units, tanks, aircraft, and guns. As an Alsatian, she spoke German as easily as French and could pass east of the Rhine. She was placed in a mountain retreat maintained outside of Strasbourg for boarding and training agents.

She learned quickly, had no fear of parachuting, and struck her OSS mentors as a promising prospect. This hard-bitten proletarian also succeeded in scandalizing the American women attached to Henry Hyde's staff. Maria was appealing in a base, available way and not particularly critical in satisfying her physical hungers. Between the Americans and other agents, she was rarely lonely.

On February 3, Maria was transferred to the Château Gleisol at Lyons to be parachuted near Stuttgart. She was to travel under cover as an army nurse.

Just before takeoff, Maria presented Peter Viertel with a novel problem. She informed the stunned marine that she was pregnant. Why now? Why had she waited until the last possible minute to tell him? Maria made clear that she had no intention of frustrating the mission. But she wanted to strike a bargain. She expected to be gone less than two weeks. With luck, she would have worked her way back to the American lines by then. After she had thus performed her part of the agreement, she wanted the Americans to arrange an abortion.

To Viertel, it was preposterous. To drop the woman from a plane might solve the problem of the unwanted pregnancy, but this hardly seemed an auspicious beginning for a serious intelligence mission.

Whose baby was it? he wanted to know. Maria said that her Gestapo lover was the father. Viertel found the ironies more annoying than amusing and recommended that the mission be scrubbed.

A great investment had gone into this operation—in planning it, financing it, gaining the cooperation of Seventh Army and, most difficult, getting the 492d Bombardment Group to set up the flight. The girl was not that far along. She was willing to go. The decision was made to proceed. Maria was bundled aboard a B-24, practically lost in the billows of her jump suit. Late on the night of February 3, she dropped into Germany.

She had done a splendid job. All had gone according to the text. After Maria had jumped and disposed of her gear, she successfully carried off her disguise as an army nurse, managed to cover the points on her itinerary and traveled west, back to the front. She was overrun by American troops who accepted her password and turned her over to OSS. Maria was soon being debriefed by the man who had dispatched her, Peter Viertel. She proved sharp-eyed and retentive and reported valuable information on the headquarters of German commands, tank parks, and troop deployments. She had more than fulfilled the expectations of her mentors. Now she wanted her terms met.

Arranging an abortion seemed to fit best under the grab bag of duties assigned to the Seventh Army OSS finance officer, the spirited Peter Sichel. The assignment appealed to Sichel's sense of the absurd, and offered considerable latitude to exercise his talent for invention.

Sichel took the girl, whom he referred to as "the plucky Maria," to a hospital in Strasbourg and explained to the physician in charge a most delicate matter. This young woman, possessed of a passionate hatred for the *Boche,* had carried out the most extraordinary act of heroism behind the lines in Germany, a *Jeanne d'Arc de la résistance.* Her mission inside the Reich had demanded the highest sacrifices of her and, unfortunately, she had become pregnant in the process. The physician indicated complete understanding and told Sichel to leave the girl with him.

Sichel returned several days later to pick up Maria and to square the account with the hospital. The doctor protested vigorously. They did not want a *sou.* After all, what the girl had done was *"pour la belle France."*

Peter Viertel's success with Maria was not duplicated with the two other women he had recruited. Ada, the circus acrobat who had been violated by the Germans, made five flights, none of which, for various reasons, was successful in getting her into Germany.

Emily, the petite little thing recommended by the Deuxième Bureau, carried off a rather ingenious infidelity. She had undergone her training with admirable perseverance. She had mastered the parachute and the radio. After she had landed in Germany, Emily merely substituted the radio crystals provided to her by the Deuxième Bureau for those given her by OSS and broadcast exclusively for the benefit of the French.

On his arrival in Berlin in early November, Youri Vinogradov, the White Russian who had been slipped through the lines at Gérardmer, France, by Bert Jolis, rented a room at Eisenacherstrasse 10. He was picked up for questioning by the Gestapo the day after his arrival, when an acquaintance informed the police that the Russian was just back from Paris.

Youri refused to cooperate until he had an opportunity to talk first with Michel Kedia of the SD. Kedia was president of the National Georgian Government in Germany, officially recognized by the Nazis as something of a "government-in-exile" for the Soviet Republic of Georgia. Kedia was treated by the Germans as the representative of an independent but Soviet-dominated nation. While not precisely a member of the SD, Michel Kedia had worked closely with the Nazi intelligence organization, supplying agents for espionage missions into Russia and plotting anti-Soviet stratagems.

He was one of several Russian ethnic minority leaders whom the Nazis had adroitly manipulated. After Germany invaded Russia, Ukrainians, Tartars, Uzbeks, Kirghiz, Armenians, Georgians like Kedia, and other minorities aligned themselves with the Nazis in the vain hope that they might thus eventually achieve independence for their homelands.

They were not particularly pro-Nazi; indeed, some possessed only the flimsiest comprehension of the issues at stake in the war. Culturally and linguistically they were a disparate group. The Kirghiz, for instance, were Turkic-speaking Muslims. The ethnic leaders were welded together only in their desire to throw off Soviet domination. The Germans had encouraged their aspirations, forming "national" organs within Germany, such as Kedia's Georgian government.

Though they were indulged in the German capital for their propaganda value and capacity to sow disunity in the Soviet Union, the expatriates gradually came to understand the hopelessness of their condition. The Germans had never intended independence for their homelands. The Soviets, their arch nemesis, were now bearing down from the east. These men were viewed in the west as Nazi puppets. The only remaining political capital with which they might possibly bargain among the western democracies was their anticommunism. Thus, they viewed Youri, with his western connections, as a slender thread of hope.

At the Gestapo's request, Michel Kedia came to the headquarters and vouched for Youri, whom he did indeed know well. He knew a good deal more than he revealed to the Germans, including the fact that Youri had left Berlin for Paris months before, expressly to join the Allies.

During questioning by the Gestapo, and later by SD officials, Youri repeated his exaggerated account of rampant communism in France, and again it was lapped up. With his good standing seemingly restored, Youri made known to the SD his interest in working on intelligence matters. He was not without certain assets. Youri had natural links with Russian émigré communities. He spoke French, indeed had been educated for a time in France, and knew western Europe well.

The SD enrolled him as an agent for its Soviet espionage section. Youri was eventually to return to Paris, undercover, to spy among Russian émigrés in the west. He was issued an SD identity card and permits to carry arms and wear the SD uniform. He spent the next several weeks training for his return to Paris, quietly absorbing, at the same time, every facet of the SD, its internal operation, organization, and leading personalities.

The SD paid Youri a bonus of reichsmarks—equivalent to $500—for the information he had given on political conditions in France and a pittance salary of $50 per month. But Youri had $10,000 worth of jewelry, supplied by OSS, which enabled him to launch himself immediately among the magnates of the black market, a sideline which his SD superiors did not find at all reprehensible.

The months dragged on into March 1945, and still Youri had not obtained his orders to return to Paris. In the interim he had successfully survived repeated denunciations by people aware of pro-Allied statements he had made before his last trip to France. In every case, Kedia had managed to protect him. Youri had also cultivated profitable sources, including a woman named Maria Frankenstein, who was a close friend of the wife of Hermann Göring and who associated as well with highly placed figures at Heinrich Himmler's Berlin SS headquarters.

But after his second departure date had been inexplicably canceled by the Gestapo, Youri's habitual aplomb began to fade. Kedia, his protector, was now coming to him with problems, which the Georgian expected Youri to solve.

The Soviets were moving remorselessly on Berlin. When they laid their hands on people like Michel Kedia, Russians who had collaborated openly, publicly, and officially with the Nazis, there could be little question of their fate. Kedia wanted to get out of Germany and make high-level contact with the British and Americans to convince them that the exiled ethnic Russians, while fierce anti-Communists, had little sympathy for the Nazis and were ready to support the Allies. For this move, he needed Youri.

Since Kedia was regarded by the Germans as the representative of a foreign government, he and the other minority leaders were free to travel abroad. Kedia wanted Youri to set up a top-level Allied contact somewhere in Switzerland. Youri agreed and got a message through to Bert Jolis asking that he arrange such a reception upon the arrival of the Russian leaders in Geneva.

He then took his fate into his own hands. If he could not get SD orders to the west, he would work through Kedia's other contacts in the Abwehr. On April 8, without notifying the SD, Youri left Berlin carrying orders and military ID that the Abwehr had provided. He headed in the general direction of Erfurt, where he expected to cross over to the American lines. The ethnic leaders left soon after for Switzerland.

OSS had set up a small subpost in France at Annemasse near the Swiss-French border, about five miles from Geneva. There, Paul Mellon, a fellow OSS officer, told Bert Jolis that he would have to make the trip to Geneva in the trunk of the car. It would not be more than a few minutes before they would be there. Mellon had diplomatic status, but Jolis, as an American combatant, could not enter Switzerland legally.

Jolis had a rendezvous in Geneva with the leaders of the Russian ethnic minorities, as arranged by Youri. He was enthusiastic. Jolis regarded the Russians, with their intimate knowledge of the Nazi apparatus and their influence among restive minorities in the Soviet Union, as both an immediate and a postwar intelligence find. He climbed into the trunk of Mellon's car, an American make with diplomatic plates.

Fifteen minutes later, Mellon let Jolis out on a deserted side street in Geneva. "You're only about twenty minutes away," Mellon advised him, and drove off. Jolis was to meet the Russians in an old Victorian hotel, the d'Angleterre, on the Geneva lakefront. He felt naked. He stood alone, in unfamiliar civilian clothes, in a strange city, carrying no papers. As he began to walk, Jolis heard the chilling tramp of boot heels thudding against the pavement. Around the corner, a platoon of soldiers in ominous field gray and Nazi-style helmets swung toward him. Jolis froze in terror. There had been a terrible mistake. But as the men marched past, he noted their insignia. They were Swiss infantry.

Jolis made his way to the d'Angleterre and entered an imposing lobby under an ornate ceiling hung with rococo chandeliers and with a broad staircase leading down into the huge, gilded reception room. Jolis knew only the name of Michel Kedia and rang the Georgian's room on the house phone. An effusive, richly accented voice informed him, "We'll be right down."

"No, no!" Jolis was horrified. "Let me come up." Kedia was insistent.

Jolis waited at the foot of the grand staircase, unnerved at the prospect of conducting an intelligence operation in a grand-hotel lobby in neutral Switzerland. The elevators opened. Jolis stood in disbelief. Of the seven men, only two wore Western clothes. The rest were attired in fezzes, flowing robes, pantaloons, and kaftans. They marched down the grand staircase looking past Jolis and searching, apparently, for an equally resplendent welcoming committee.

Jolis approached the lead figure hesitantly. He mumbled a pseudonym and extended his hand. The man's disappointment was painfully transparent, but he made a swift recovery. Michel Kedia broke into a broad grin, took Jolis's hand, and bowed deeply. The rest followed suit and crowded around him, smiling and gesticulating excitedly. Some spoke German. Some hazarded French. Others spoke languages that Jolis had never heard. The concierge, the waiters, the bellmen, the guests, everyone in the lobby had stopped to watch.

Jolis whispered to Kedia, "Can't we go upstairs? We can't talk here." He persuaded them to retreat to Kedia's room.

There, Jolis, though a politically sophisticated man, understood fully for the first time how deep was the distortion of reality which Nazism had achieved within the Reich. The ethnic Russians assumed that Jolis was some sort of functionary whose purpose was to escort them to General Eisenhower. To Jolis, this was only a momentary and correctable delusion. What seriously troubled him, however, was their utter confidence that as soon as the Germans were defeated, the western Allies would automatically go to war against the Soviets. As congenital enemies of the Communists, they now regarded themselves as natural allies of the western powers. Would not General Eisenhower welcome them and help restore independence, at long last, to their homelands?

Jolis promptly dismissed the idea of war against Russia. The truth left them crestfallen. What, then, were the Allied plans for their homelands?

What was going to happen to their movement?

Jolis tactfully laid out the realistic alternatives. They could stay in Switzerland and eventually be interned. Or, if they could just remain inconspicuous for a few days, he would arrange to have them slipped into Allied territory, where their knowledge could be useful in the final prosecution of the war and in the removal of lingering Nazi elements afterward.

The fall had been hard. In the scope of an hour, they had plunged from ambassadors of potentially independent nations down to informants for a foreign spy service. They asked Jolis if he could not at least deliver a letter on their behalf to General Eisenhower. Of course he would, he said. The atmosphere was again quickly charged with exuberance. All their energies were concentrated on getting their special interest into the letter to the supreme Allied commander.

Kedia struggled manfully to mediate the babel of tongues and colliding objectives. Their earlier disappointment now seemed forgotten and their self-esteem flowed back as the seven leaders heatedly debated the phrasing of every line. When the document was at last finished, each grandly affixed his signature to it, and Jolis promised to see that the letter reached General Eisenhower. In a few days, he said, they would be contacted by his colleagues in Bern.

As promised, they were approached soon afterward. Arrangements were made to send them to a Red Cross camp in the captured enemy city of Hoechst, where OSS officers questioned them. But the experience again proved bitter. Their interrogators were far more interested in their knowledge of the location and content of SD files than in the hopeless nationalistic delusions of these bizarre figures.

XVI

An American in the Holocaust

✠ ✠ ✠

Fritz Molden arrived in Caserta as something of a mythic figure. A small group of OSS officers in Italy knew of the young Austrian's exploits for Allen Dulles and were aware that he was being received in Italy at the highest levels. His purposes, however, remained mysterious to them.

Molden met with the Allied commander in Italy, General Mark Clark, and with officials of the Fifteenth Air Force. His main objective was to argue the folly of bombing the civilian populace in Austria. This sermonizing, earnest young man evidently put off the air corps brass. Molden later reported their attitude as "arrogant." They at first denied that American aircraft indiscriminately bombed civilians. If they did, these people were all Nazis anyway. And who was Fritz Molden to tell the U.S. Army Air Force what to do?

Molden had better luck with a lesser objective. He and Al Ulmer, who now ran the German-Austrian operations in Italy, had quickly become fast friends. Molden asked Ulmer if among their prospects they might have a good radioman. Bert Jolis was holding Joseph Franckenstein, an Austrian-born American lieutenant, for a mission into the Austrian Tirol until they could find a radio operator. Ulmer took Molden to look over two POWs recently recruited by Dyno Lowenstein.

On one of his canvassings of the cages, Lowenstein had been urged to talk to a Wehrmacht private, an older man named Lothar Koenigsreuter. The camp commandant told Lowenstein that Koenigsreuter was a militant Social Democrat, eager to work against the Nazis. Koenigsreuter had belonged to a *Schutzband*, a guard group, organized to protect labor unions. He had fought with the Socialists in the two brief bloody civil wars that had racked Austria before the Anschluss.

Lowenstein met a tall, stern-looking man of perhaps forty, with steel-straight hair and a fierce mustache. The man had also been involved with the Kinderfreund, the children's organization which Lowenstein's Social Democrat father had headed in Germany. After a long talk, Lowenstein concluded that Koenigsreuter was sincere. He had been deeply impressed by the man's frank admission that he had once briefly flirted with Nazism.

Lowenstein brought Koenigsreuter back to the OSS compound with another recruit named Hermann Pfluger, a sleazy little man with the manner of a ferret. Why, Lieutenant Ulmer wondered, had Dyno brought back this unlikely prospect? "The other fellow is too straight," Lowenstein answered. "The small one can do the black-marketing." Fritz Molden looked over the two, took Koenigsreuter, and quickly rejected Pfluger.

Lieutenant Hart Perry escorted Koenigsreuter to Annemasse, where he was slipped into Switzerland. There, Koenigsreuter teamed with Lieutenant Franckenstein as the HOMESPUN Mission and the two men were infiltrated, with Fritz Molden as their escort, into the Redoubt. Franckenstein and Koenigsreuter set up a training camp for partisans in the mountains near Innsbruck.

They were tracked down by the Nazis, and Al Ulmer's postwar report described the last moments of the HOMESPUN Mission.

> During the night of 27–28 April, Baylor [Lothar Koenigsreuter's code name] arrived at the Kemater Alm, where Horneck [Joseph Franckenstein's code name] had arrived the previous night with an O5 member. The men occupied separate rooms.
>
> On the morning of 28 April, at about 0500, six SD men entered the building and proceeded to Horneck's room. Horneck and his Austrian companion were ordered out of their beds and the room was carefully searched. Then the two men were ordered to dress and to remain under the guard of two SS men while the rest of the raiding group searched the house. After a time Horneck and the Austrian were led down the valley, and in the meantime the house search continued. According to an eyewitness, a girl cook working in the house, Baylor's presence was not discovered by the police. About an hour and a half later Baylor awoke and went down to the kitchen for a bucket of water with which to wash. The cook, hearing Baylor

whistling as he came down the stairs, rushed to warn him of the proximity of the police.

Baylor went back to his room, packed his OSS radio equipment and threw it into the outhouse. Then he packed his rucksack and left the house by the rear exit. During this period, one Gestapo agent was searching the basement and another was on guard on an outside balcony. Shortly after Baylor left the house, the cook heard a challenge and, a moment later, a round of shots.

Baylor's body was not found until some time later after the liberation of the city and the accompanying release of Horneck from enemy imprisonment. On 11 May a searching party sent out by Horneck found the body some distance from the house. It appeared that Baylor must have walked several hundred yards after one shot went through his back and came out of his chest. Another shot, through his head, had been fired from short range.

While handling Fritz Molden and measuring the water levels of the Rhine, Gary Van Arkel was given another lead which could not be ignored. A journalist who had proven reliable in the past handed him an address—no name, just a street and number in Zurich—and suggested that he pay a call.

Late in 1944, Van Arkel traveled the seventy-five miles from Bern to Zurich and traced the address to a neighborhood of drab tenements. He climbed seven flights of stairs and rapped tentatively. The door opened onto two dreary rooms. A threadbare couple eyed him wordlessly. Van Arkel played out a minimum of information in identifying himself. The man asked him in.

In this dank shaft the American found gold. The fellow, he learned, was an Austrian exile, a revolutionary Socialist. He may have fled his homeland out of necessity. He may have settled in Switzerland at the orders of his party. He was scarcely more forthcoming than Van Arkel. He did speak of his contact with another revolutionary Socialist, still in Austria, whose position made Van Arkel's imagination race.

The colleague in Austria had been under party orders to infiltrate a dummy Nazi labor movement. He had succeeded spectacularly and had become the secretary-treasurer of the Nazi-run railroad workers' union. His day-to-day job was that of track inspector for rail lines in western Austria. Once every two weeks he was required to inspect all the major lines under his jurisdiction.

Before he left Zurich, Van Arkel asked the man in the small apartment if there was anything he needed. Only some cigarettes and coffee. Maybe a little cash.

In subsequent meetings in obscure *Bierstuben* around Zurich, Van Arkel and the revolutionary Socialist worked out their scheme and put it into play. A spur of the Austrian railways crossed the border into Switzerland at a place called Buchs. Van Arkel's man from Zurich was to travel to an inn near Buchs, ostensibly to go skiing. At the inn, he would take his meals in his room. The Austrian track inspector would also be at the inn and dine alone in his room. The waiter, who would serve them both, was part of the arrangement. He would tend first to the track inspector, taking mental note of all the intelligence the man passed to him. Then, he would relay what he had learned to the man in the other room. The arrangement at Buchs proved one of the most productive connections of all OSS Bern operations.

After the Socialist's return from his ski excursions to Buchs, he and Van Arkel would meet in hotel rooms where the American would spread out his maps. The Austrian would then indicate the last-known headquarters of the army staff moving along the Danube, the location of ammunition dumps, the expected passage of troops and armaments along key rail lines.

Van Arkel would race back to Bern and the information was then relayed to the Fifteenth Air Force in Italy. Van Arkel's reports put bombers into the skies. In the next meeting at Buchs the track inspector would provide his Socialist colleague with new targets and report how well the last bombings had gone.

Still Van Arkel's man asked for nothing more than a few of the modest luxuries of wartime, some cigarettes, coffee, and a little cash. He seemed disappointed that Van Arkel could not always provide American cigarettes. The chain from the track inspector to the agent, to Van Arkel, and to the Fifteenth Air Force functioned, unbroken, to the end of the war.

On a day in March 1945 Allen Dulles's valet called Gary Van Arkel at the latter's office in Bern. The servant was agitated. Mr. Dulles had gone to Paris and a gentleman had appeared at the apartment demanding to see someone. Van Arkel said that he would be right over.

At the Dulles apartment, Van Arkel met a suave German who spoke perfect English, and introduced himself as the former German consul general in Los Angeles. The man was disarmingly direct. He came, he said, from the headquarters of General Wolff and he had information which must be conveyed to Mr. Dulles.

It was not Van Arkel's province, but he knew instantly the potential significance of this visit. Since February, Allen Dulles had been in secret negotiations with General Karl Wolff, the commander of the SS in Italy, negotiating the early surrender of German forces in that sector. Just days before, under the heaviest secrecy, Dulles had met with General Wolff in Zurich. Van Arkel, while not a direct party to the negotiations, knew the status of the peace talks from reading the cables.

The German visitor dropped a bombshell. General Wolff was prepared to say that the Germans would accept the terms discussed for the surrender, contingent upon one military courtesy. Officers must be allowed to retain their sidearms.

If what the man said were true, it would mean the cessation of fighting in northern Italy and, most likely, the end of the war. As they talked, Van Arkel dared not reveal, even by the movement of a facial muscle, that he had any knowledge whatever of the negotiations.

But, obviously, he had to get through immediately to Dulles. He excused himself. Soon, the cables began to fly between Bern and Paris. Who was this man? How trustworthy was he? Dulles had to know. Van Arkel gambled on his instincts. He advised his chief against trusting the highly persuasive visitor.

It had been a clever feint. The head of the SS, Heinrich Himmler, suspected that his subordinate, General Wolff, was in secret communication with the Allies. Himmler entertained the wild delusion that if he could dump Hitler and assume power, the western Allies would eagerly embrace him as a new partner in a holy war against the Bolsheviks. Himmler had a fair idea of where the peace negotiations between Wolff and the Americans stood. But he had to be sure to advance his own game.

Leagued with Himmler in this scheme was the Gauleiter of Tirol-Vorarlberg, Franz Hofer, and the man sent by Himmler to try to bluff the Americans into revealing the state of negotiations was an associate of Hofer's from Innsbruck. Van Arkel, his sensitivities honed by constant suspicion, had given away nothing.

Allen Dulles had heard no more from Fritz Kolbe after the twentieth of July plot because the Foreign Office official had been caught up in the Gestapo's dragnet of suspected conspirators.

The fussy little man who bootlegged stacks of top secrets from von Ribbentrop's office to OSS Bern was, evidently, not judged a serious threat to the Third Reich. Kolbe had been interrogated by a part-time Nazi block leader whose regular job was driving a bus. At the close of a stunningly inept questioning, the man asked Kolbe to declare his political convictions. He answered, "I confess my belief in final victory." This unelaborated response apparently satisfied his inquisitor and Kolbe was set free. He was nevertheless sufficiently frightened to shut down his clandestine activities for six months.

Early in 1945, Kolbe was drawn to a new conspiracy. As Allied air raids began to break the regime's grip over Berlin, a small band of anti-Nazi civilians hatched a scheme for taking over the city. The core of this group was the Reichsbanner, a World War I veterans organization whose members were mostly Social Democrats.

They had scouted possible sites for landing American paratroops and settled on an area between Berlin and Potsdam identified by two lakes, the Wannsee and the Schlachtensee. A cadre of guides and scouts was formed who were to lead the American invaders around Nazi defenses and into the heart of the city. They had planned the operation meticulously, down to a temporary American headquarters, which was to be set up in an office at 28 Unter den Linden, belonging to a Herr Bauer, a member of the conspiracy.

The plan's transparent political purpose was to get the Americans into Berlin before the Russians. Kolbe believed it could succeed. He schemed his way to Bern in February to win the support of the Americans.

If Allen Dulles was disappointed with what Kolbe delivered on this trip, in contrast to the rich yields of the past, he said nothing. He heard Kolbe out and loyally relayed the plan to higher authority. Its fate was preordained, as were all stratagems which might provoke that ever-suspicious ally, the Soviet Union.

This time, Dulles urged Kolbe to remain safely in Switzerland. But the spy insisted that his usefulness had not yet ended. He told Dulles that he could be particularly helpful in ferreting out Nazi plans for the National Redoubt, which he knew deeply concerned the Americans. He returned to Berlin.

Fritz Kolbe was handed his last opportunity to escape Germany two months later. His chief, the rough old infighter, Karl Ritter, had an unexpectedly lovely young concert singer as his mistress. Ritter wanted the woman and her two-year-old daughter out of Berlin and into the safety of southern Bavaria. It was precisely the kind of job that one assigned to an unquestioning subordinate. Ritter chose Fritz Kolbe to take the woman, the child, and a doctor's wife to Bavaria in Ritter's official limousine, a long black Mercedes-Benz.

The party set out on April 1 for the village of Ottobeuren, southeast of Ulm. The skies were a dull pewter, the roads ice-covered, and the weather biting cold. The concert singer spent much of the trip weeping hysterically as the car repeatedly broke down and Allied planes threatened overhead. Their progress was frequently blocked by military convoys and ragged ranks of retreating Wehrmacht units. Kolbe felt the hard, accusing stare of exhausted soldiers and refugee civilians as the limousine inched through the crowds.

He deposited the singer and child at Ottobeuren and went on with the doctor's wife to the nearest railway junction in Memmingen. There, Kolbe was arrested in the train station by Gestapo officials suspicious of a professed diplomatic courier carrying no pouch. Kolbe managed to bluff his way out and boarded a freight train headed toward Switzerland, which broke down twelve miles from the town of Weiler.

Fortunately, Kolbe had a politically sympathetic friend living in a lodge near Weiler. He proceeded there on foot, and on his arrival was unnerved to find, among his friend's guests, two army staff officers. In the course of a wary conversation, the officers told Kolbe that they had left Berlin with truckloads of important but unspecified material. Kolbe mentally pieced together fragments of information he had gleaned in Berlin and made a cool guess. "Of course, the intelligence files on Russia."

"You know?"

"Yes, I was informed before leaving Berlin," he lied.

The officers then gradually opened up to him, and Kolbe recognized that what they possessed was clearly an intelligence trove. The two men were members of an army intelligence unit serving on the Russian front, independent of Himmler's espionage apparatus. The unit's commander, a youthful forty-year-old general, Reinhard Gehlen, had hatched the idea of using the unit's Soviet files to bargain his way into a special arrangement with the Americans.

Kolbe learned that the two officers had with them in the vicinity five of eleven original trucks. The others had been lost or destroyed in air attacks. He wangled from them the location of the trucks, before borrowing a bicycle and departing his friend's lodge for Bregenz on Lake Constance, virtually on the Swiss border. Kolbe left, convinced that he had one more gem to lay at the feet of Allen Dulles.

But the new atmosphere in Bern clearly excluded Fritz Kolbe. American armies had turned away from Berlin and Kolbe's latest intelligence on conditions in that collapsing capital were now of little interest to Bern. Allen Dulles was wholly absorbed in negotiations for the surrender of six hundred thousand German troops in northern Italy.

Even Kolbe's hole card had failed to impress. Dulles already knew of the truck convoy of Russian intelligence files being offered by General Gehlen to the Americans. He was moderately appreciative to Kolbe for the additional details. But Fritz Kolbe's secret war had ended.

Jack Taylor, chief of the captured DUPONT Mission, arrived at Mauthausen concentration camp on Easter morning, April 1, 1945, among a draft of thirty-eight prisoners condemned to death. They were prodded off a barge and herded up a hill by SS guards. Below him stretched the dark beauty of the Danube, and above, to one side, an avenue of handsome homes. On the other side was a rock quarry. From it, Taylor saw skeletal figures staggering up a long stone stairway, bent under the burden of huge rocks on their backs. Some of Taylor's fellow new arrivals attempted feeble jests. This is the way they would all look in a few days. Most were struck cold with terror.

They were lined up before a building bearing a legend painted in heavy black letters, *"Arbeit Macht Frei,"* "Work Shall Make You Free." Hans Prellberg, an SS officer, came before them and eyed the new arrivals wordlessly. He grabbed a cane from a crippled man and began randomly striking the prisoners, grunting with the force of each blow. He threw aside the cane and turned his attention to the camp's regulations. The punishment for most infractions, however trifling, was death. Taylor struggled with his meager German to stay abreast of Prellberg's commands. Two Russians could not understand the SS officer and Prellberg punched and kicked them almost unconscious.

Prellberg reached the end of his introduction to Mauthausen. "If you attempt to escape"—he drew his pistol—"you will be shot like this." He then fired into a prisoner standing nearby who had attempted to get away earlier that day.

They were then marched through the main gate. Here, relays of SS men beat them for three hours. One guard, Hans Bruckner, took special pleasure in working over Taylor, calling him, with each blow, an "American swine." The beatings over, the men were shaved of all bodily hair and given a shower. They were issued striped uniforms, little better than rags. Jack Taylor became Mauthausen inmate #138070 and was assigned to Cell Block 13. Since the block was filled to triple its intended capacity, three men were required to sleep in a wooden bunk two feet wide.

Mauthausen was designated a Class III camp, a *Vernichtungslager,* or extermination facility. Its population shifted between ten thousand and fifteen thousand inmates. Shoftly after Austria had become part of the Third Reich, Heinrich Himmler had visited the stone quarries at Mauthausen and decided it had model attributes for a concentration camp. The camp was the center of a constellation of satellite camps totaling over ninety thousand prisoners.

Jack Taylor was assigned to a gang constructing a new crematorium. He hauled sand, cement, and water to a crew of Spanish tile setters, Communist veterans of Spain's civil war. The new crematorium had been planned to break a troublesome bottleneck. Camp officials could not execute more prisoners than they could cremate. Burying prisoners was out of the question since their graves would provide evidence of what was occurring at Mauthausen. But as soon as the new crematorium was completed, they could double the number of executions. The prisoners worked as slowly as they dared without arousing the guards' suspicion.

While laboring on the crematorium, Taylor absorbed the tenor of life at Mauthausen. When guards took a dislike to a prisoner, they would taunt him, bait him, all the while driving the man against the electrified barbed wire. Or they might throw a man's cap against the wire fence and order him to retrieve it. The fence carried a three-phase 380-volt current. Armed guards lined it at fifty-foot intervals. Prisoners driven against the fence and killed were recorded as shot while attempting to escape. The guards received a special bonus for working at the fence. For killing an escaping prisoner, a guard received twenty extra cigarettes or eight days' leave.

Prisoners would sometimes fling themselves against the wire seeking their escape from Mauthausen in death. In one suicide attempt, too many prisoners struck the fence at once. The current was too weak to kill; the guards had to machine-gun them. Camp officials had photographers film the lifeless bodies strung from the barbed wire.

At the stone quarry, guards occasionally relieved the monotony by playing "parachutist," dropping prisoners 150 feet to the quarry's rocky bottom. If victims survived, they were hauled up the 186 "Steps of Death" and dropped again.

Two classes of privileged prisoners provided the first level of supervision at Mauthausen: block leaders who ran the barracks and Kapos, who ran the work details. Camp officials liked to appoint common criminals, murderers, and thieves as block leaders: men who reveled in tormenting the intellectual and often cultivated political prisoners entrusted to their mercies. The Kapos were mostly Spanish Communist prisoners who maintained their status by rivaling their masters in brutality.

Shortly after Taylor's arrival, German and Austrian prisoners were given the opportunity to join the Waffen SS. Of about one thousand who volunteered, three hundred were selected, given old Afrika Korps uniforms, regular German Army rations, trained for combat, and then assigned to guard the prisoners. Overnight, former inmates made the leap from the oppressed to oppressors. To Taylor the rapid adjustment seemed to confirm an ingrained love of authority in the German character.

A few months before Taylor arrived, the SS had terminated what amounted to the Mauthausen recreation program. Until January, they had maintained a camp brothel and allowed each inmate one visit a week. The SS maintained its own brothel recruited from among attractive female prisoners in other camps. The women assigned to service the prisoners were all diseased.

Thievery was as natural as breathing at Mauthausen, and as necessary. Prisoners were deliberately fed a starvation diet. Jack Taylor was part of a nutrition experiment to see how much sawdust could be substituted for flour in bread. Prisoners stole clothing and personal belongings to trade for food. In the argot of Mauthausen, a man "organized" a pair of shoes, or he "organized" someone else's blanket, so that he could "organize" more to eat. The inmates, therefore, slept in their clothes, including shoes, with their few possessions tucked under their bodies.

When they were awakened in the morning, the prisoners were rushed through showers. If they came out too wet, they were beaten for being wasteful. If they came out too dry, they were beaten for being dirty. In the evening they were fed a slice of bread and jam with black, ersatz coffee. They were not allowed to bring food into the barracks, nor to linger outside eating their supper. The solution was to gulp down bread and coffee while trotting from the mess line to the barracks.

Jack Taylor observed that though the men stole from each other and had no room in their lives for the simplest kindness, the prisoners seemed less brutalized by the experience of Mauthausen than their jailers.

Mauthausen was located in an area near several war industries, and its more fortunate inmates were farmed out to work in these plants. Here, the camp commandant, SS Standartenführer Franz Ziereis, revealed an enterprising character. He formed a company called "Deutsche Erd und Steinwerke," "German Earth and Stoneworks," and turned a private profit of over 5 million reichsmarks a month by hiring out workers. The workweek for prisoners was seven days. Ziereis was marvelously well cast in his role as concentration-camp commandant. He was a strutting, powerful man of forty-three with blue eyes, a shining pate fringed with blond hair, and a face, quite simply, that was brutal.

What the prisoners endured at Mauthausen was merely a prelude to their ultimate reason for being sent there. Executions were performed by hanging, shooting, or gassing in a building called the "Death House." Gassings took place at 9:00 A.M. and 5:00 P.M. daily in a chamber accommodating 120 prisoners at a time. The gas used was cyclone cyanide. On an occasion when 220 prisoners were packed into the gas chamber, SS men fought each other for places in front of the small window in the door so that they could watch the final agony.

In another room prisoners were taken presumably to be photographed. They were told to stand facing a camera resting on a tripod. An SS man standing behind them would then shoot the prisoners in the back of the head with a small carbine. Franz Ziereis frequently enjoyed taking over this responsibility himself and had killed some four hundred men. It was in this room, three months before Jack Taylor arrived at Mauthausen, that OSS agents of the DAWES and HOUSEBOAT missions, whom Taylor had tried to contact, were shot by SS Hauptsturmführer Georg Bachmayer on orders signed personally by Ernst Kaltenbrunner, the RSHA chief.

The caliber of his fellow inmates in Block 13 deeply impressed Taylor. The range of their talents suggested to him what it might be like in America if one political party upon coming to power could automatically imprison the writers, lawyers, scientists, businessmen, and professional elite who belonged to the opposition party.

These men pressed a heavy obligation on Jack Taylor. They were sorry that an American had fallen into this hell. But if he survived, he could be highly useful. If they were to describe the truth of Mauthausen, it might be dismissed as propaganda; but if an American experienced these horrors and lived to tell, he would be believed. Thus, they unburdened their most painful memories on him, a litany of men torn to pieces by trained dogs, injected with magnesium chlorate in the heart, tossed into concrete mixers, and given hot showers followed by naked exposure in subzero temperatures while having hoses turned on them. For each story, Taylor insisted upon two eyewitnesses. Then he committed the accounts to memory.

One morning, SS officers Roth and Prellberg marched to the site of the new crematorium and angrily told the prisoners that they were not satisfied with the pace of the work. They knew, Roth shouted at the Spanish Kapo, that the crew was stalling. If this oven was not finished and ready for operation by the next morning, the Kapo and his crew would be the first to test it.

The following morning, 367 Czech Jews came through the entrance gate after a long overland march to the camp. As they were driven along, they dropped diamond rings, gold watches, coins, bills, jewelry, all valuables which they were not supposed to possess. They were stripped and led directly into the gas chamber. Later, when their bodies were placed in the new crematorium, Taylor noticed something unusual. The old, emaciated prisoners usually emitted a pale, yellow smoke. These younger, healthier victims produced black, oily fumes and flames which shot from the stack.

XVII

The Spy Who Saved a City

✝ ✝ ✝

Fred Mayer, of the GREENUP Mission, had begun to feel that his pose as a German officer living at the *Offizierskasino* was wearing thin. At the beginning of April, he learned that foreign laborers were fleeing into Innsbruck before the Russian advance from the east. Most lacked papers. Mayer discarded the Wehrmacht uniform and acquired some plain work-clothes through the sisters of his Austrian partner, Franz Weber. He joined a line of displaced conscript workers reregistering at the Labor Office in Innsbruck. While there, he observed that the common impression of vast armies of workers dragooned to slave in Germany was not wholly accurate. Most of the Frenchmen he met had volunteered to work in the Reich.

Mayer registered as a Frenchman, again using the happily flexible name of Frederick Mayer. He listed his occupation as "electrician." He told the labor registrar that he had been employed at the Boehler Werke in Saint Marienat, but had left when the Russians approached.

He used the work card he was issued at the Labor Office to register with the police as a legal alien worker, and, now properly documented, took lodgings at Innstrasse 21. Through his resistance connections, he found a job working for Robert Moser, a forty-year-old anti-Nazi who ran a radio shop and who did contract work for the Messerschmitt plant at Kematen.

Life for foreign workers, Mayer found, was not particularly onerous. They worked an eight-hour day, were reasonably well paid, and allotted an extra food-ration card. In Oberperfuss, where Mayer spent his free time, fresh farm produce, eggs, and meat were never short. On Easter Sunday, 1945, he enjoyed in that village a memorable holiday feast.

During that period, Mayer saw that Innsbruck was becoming a strangely ambivalent world. It was the rallying ground for a final stand by unregenerate Nazis and the center of an awakening Austrian resistance. The potential for an Armageddon looked promising.

The man was small fish, a black marketeer arrested in a routine Gestapo dragnet in Innsbruck on April 20. Leo broke down immediately, after the first few routine slaps, and blurted out that he would tell everything. The startled policemen stopped the interrogation and notified their superior, Kriminalrat Busch, the local Gestapo chief. They had, they said, picked up a *"Gauner,"* a little punk who claimed he knew something about an American spy in Innsbruck.

Alois Kuen, the anti-Nazi policeman, got word to Fred Mayer that Leo had been arrested. Mayer had little faith in the black marketeer's staying power. He decided against returning to his room at Innstrasse 21. He went instead to the home of the Weber sisters. There, he began to prepare the pouch containing the names of all important Nazis in the Tirol-Vorarlberg for the courier to take to Vaduz in Liechtenstein the next day.

Someone was pounding on the door downstairs. Fred could hear Genoveva responding garrulously, obviously stalling. Mayer shoved his papers under the bed and tried unsuccessfully to open the bedroom window. Yet he felt unaccountably calm. He had probably been spotted as a French foreign worker who had strayed off limits. The story he and Genoveva had prepared was that she had met Mayer after a movie and brought him home. Six days at hard labor at most, Mayer estimated.

Three plainclothesmen and five uniformed SS armed with pistols came into the room. "Frederick Mayer?" *"Oui."* They ordered him into a car and took him to the Gestapo headquarters.

What befell Fred Mayer after his arrest was later recounted in a deposition by Walter Guttner, Kriminalsekretär of the Innsbruck Gestapo.

"Everyone was quite jubilant over the capture of Mayer, and it was to my regret that I was given the assignment from Busch [Guttner's superior] to interrogate the prisoner immediately. The following questions were to be answered by the prisoner: nationality, pinpoint, persons who accompanied him, the place where the [radio] sender was stationed, and contacts with OWB [Austrian resistance]. . . . I warned Mayer the same as Moser that he would not be mishandled if he answered all the questions truthfully."

The Moser to whom Guttner referred was Robert Moser, the radio contractor for whom Fred had worked, who was also arrested that night.

Guttner's statement went on: "I have to mention the fact that I had several schnapps before the interview as I did not think that it would be necessary to question anyone that night."

For four hours, under Guttner's questioning, Mayer stuck by the story that he was a French laborer. Guttner had to use a French interpreter to question him. The translation time gave Mayer a valuable interval in which to invent his answers. The Nazis grew impatient. His interrogators began to punch and kick him, and Mayer's face began to swell.

Guttner finally tired of the game. He had Leo, the black marketeer, brought in. Leo entered, head averted, sobbing. "It's no use. I've told them everything."

But Mayer knew that Leo did not know everything. He did not know the whereabouts of Hans Wynberg, his radioman, and Franz Weber, his Austrian accomplice. Mayer refused to be bluffed and made only a tactical retreat. He admitted to being an American agent and that Frederick Mayer was his true name.

Guttner's statement continued:

"He spoke fluent German, however. I noticed that he had a Schwabian dialect. I told him I did not believe that he was an American, but that, because of his dialect, I took him for a German. . . . If this had not been the case, I would have tried to prevent force during the interrogation, since I have a great deal more respect for a foreign soldier who fights for his country than one who betrays his fatherland."

Guttner was trying to be a man of principle, but Mayer would not cooperate. The American insisted that he had entered Austria alone, overland by way of Switzerland. But through Leo, Guttner knew that Fred had parachuted into Austria, accompanied by others and carrying a radio. His patience was wearing thin. He was further infuriated by Mayer's stoic tolerance of the blows and shouted accusations.

"Since I had no further ambitions to continue the interrogation, and since I was very tired—I had slept a few hours in several days—I gave the belt to Busch and made my report. Busch, however, insisted that I continue the questioning, and in a more severe manner, as Mayer had to tell the location of his accomplices, so that they could be arrested and the radio taken from them. . . . Busch's answer to my question was, 'Naturally, use extreme measures in your questioning.' "

Guttner had his problems, too. He had recently served seven months in jail for, as he put it, "an extended furlough which I took in Bad Schallerbach, as well as several minor incidents which probably caused me to lose the respect of the SS and the Gestapo." Guttner was on probation and needed to regain the confidence of his boss, Kriminalrat Busch.

"Since Busch had already told me that he would try to take favorable steps in connection with my arrest—of which I have told nothing to my wife—I decided to use severe measures in the interrogation. I told myself that any objection would have caused harm to my family because of my arrest. Usually, anyone arrested would be sent to a dangerous front, or on partisan missions. . . . I had, however, no desire to be shot so shortly before the end of the war so that four helpless children would be left behind."

The "severe measures" unelaborated in Guttner's statement involved stripping Mayer and forcing him to sit on the floor with his knees bent. Guttner then looped his handcuffed arms over his knees. The policemen then placed a rifle through the triangle now formed by his arms and legs and suspended him between two tables, head downward.

In this position they bull-whipped him. They poured water into his nose and ears, one of which by now had been punctured. Mayer began to choke and prayed to pass out, but he remained conscious. He spent six hours on this improvised rack. At dawn, his exhausted interrogators dumped him, naked, on a straw bed crawling with vermin. He lay there for the next twenty-four hours with his hands tied behind his back, too uncomfortable to fall asleep. He was fed once—a bowl of foul soup and a piece of stale bread.

Robert Moser did not fare as well. The Austrian resistance leader had been bull-whipped for almost an entire day. His screams rang throughout the Gestapo jail. But he did not talk. At midnight on April 22, his screams ceased. A Gestapo man announced, "The pig Moser is gone."

Kriminalsekretär Guttner had an idea. Lodged nearby in Brugriesen was another agent of the Americans whom the Gestapo had recently snared. The man was Hermann Pfluger, the same small, unsavory character whom Fritz Molden had rejected in Bari when he had selected Lothar Koenigsreuter for the latter's fatal mission, with Joseph Franckenstein.

Hermann Pfluger set something of a minimum standard for OSS recruitment in Italy. He was a deserter from the German Army and had quit, he said, out of anti-Nazi convictions. This explanation struck Dyno Lowenstein, his recruiter, as odd, since one would not have suspected

Pfluger capable of any convictions. His paybook, however, did indicate a nine-month sentence served for the curious offense of "lowering morale of troops."

Pfluger was a stunted, oily fellow, with a smudgy black mustache and long lank hair drooping over his ears. The sharpness of his features, his furtive movements, and beady eyes suggested a rodent. OSS staffers at Bari variously described Pfluger as a "wharf rat," "a guttersnipe," "a thug." Lowenstein and Ulmer were convinced that the man was a petty criminal.

Lowenstein had recruited him because he believed that, in the context of espionage, Pfluger had redeeming qualities. He was cunning, quick-minded, a plausible liar, and unfettered by principle. "He's a hustler," Lowenstein told Ulmer. "If he wants to do a mission, let him hustle for OSS."

Pfluger had to be sent into the Reich alone, since no other agent would go with him. He was to parachute near Innsbruck and then make his way to Munich. His mission was code-named DEADWOOD.

On the flight into the Reich, Walter Haass, acting as dispatcher, waited until the last possible moment before giving DEADWOOD his radio set and pistol. As he was about to jump, DEADWOOD announced with fierce pride, "I know you bastards don't trust me, but I am going to prove you are wrong." He then bailed out of the plane with seeming unconcern.

How rigorously Pfluger stuck by his good intentions was difficult to know. According to the OSS *War Report:* "He was arrested on the train from Innsbruck, having aroused the suspicions of a German soldier by expressing the apparently unorthodox view that the prospects of the war were unfavorable to Germany, by taking undue interest in military installations, and, finally, by the use of American matches to light a cigarette."

After his capture, Pfluger had quickly agreed to operate his radio under Nazi control. His messages were classics of ambiguity, confusing both the Germans and OSS.

On the afternoon of April 21, Guttner visited Pfluger in his cell and showed him a photograph of Fred Mayer. Pfluger studied the picture and said that the Gestapo had snared a high-ranking American intelligence officer out of Bari, whom Pfluger knew as "Lieutenant Fred." The Gestapo already had considerable knowledge of the Bari operation wrung from the DAWES and HOUSEBOAT team members before they had been executed at Mauthausen. DEADWOOD filled in the gaps.

Guttner confidentially returned to Mayer's cell and was immediately put off by his prisoner's cheery greeting and the smile Mayer managed through his battered face. Guttner was not to be outplayed.

"Good afternoon, Lieutenant Fred." His voice had a preening self-assurance. Mayer denied Guttner the satisfaction of reacting. But he became troubled as the German unveiled a detailed knowledge of OSS activities in Bari. Guttner spoke knowledgeably of the Villa Pasqua and Villa Suppa. He dropped the names of agents who had trained with Mayer. Guttner's later formal report stated that his approach had the desired effect:

"Mayer then gave exact statements about the information that we wanted, so that immediately the next morning a patrol could be sent out to Oberperfuss to arrest his accomplices. . . . Everyone was quite satisfied with the information and I was sorry that I didn't think of Pfluger before this, and thus could have prevented the severe questioning.

"After the protocol had been taken the night of 21 to 22 April 45, the patrol was prepared, which at 0530 left for Oberperfuss, where the companions of the American—one American radioman and an Austrian as a guide—were said to be. Mayer accompanied the group and pointed out the houses in which the men were quartered, but when the patrol entered, the companions of the American had left."

Fred Mayer later convincingly rebutted that he ever talked, whether under Guttner's torture or his blandishments. OSS records of the GREENUP Mission support him. They show that the Gestapo had picked up several KRIPO men as a result of Leo's confession. An OSS debriefing report stated: "One of the policemen broke under pressure and said that Hans Wynberg was at Oberperfuss. Therefore, they began to beat Fred again. Since he did not talk, they took him to the village to begin a house-to-house search. The village had been alerted by a woman [Franz Weber's sister] in sufficient time for Frank [Franz Weber's code name] and Hans to make their getaway."

However the Gestapo obtained its information about the rest of the team, the key consideration, as Guttner admitted in his statement, was that "Mayer, by the time he had wasted in telling his lies, was able to warn his comrades and make it possible for them to escape."

When the Gestapo did arrive at Oberperfuss, a frightened farmboy revealed that he had seen Maria Tomas, a woman who had earlier befriended Mayer, slip out of the village two days before with Hans Wynberg and Franz Weber. The Gestapo told Maria to lead them to the two men or else see Mayer shot on the spot. She then led a search party on a deliberate alpine goose chase that added six more hours to the fugitives' lead time.

Dr. Max Primbs was a puzzling man, a decent, intelligent, civilized Nazi. Primbs was Kreisleiter of Innsbruck, the city's Nazi party leader. He was a surgeon by profession and an early, ardent, and unshakable believer in Adolf Hitler as the godhead of Germany. As a student, Primbs had belonged to the Storm Troopers. He was practicing medicine in Innsbruck in 1937 when he was called upon by the Gauleiter, Franz Hofer, to resolve a party leadership problem.

The current Kreisleiter was thoroughly despised by the people of Innsbruck. Primbs, on the other hand, while an equally fervent Nazi, was a man of tact and charm. Hofer had persuaded Primbs to take over the Kreisleiter post. Primbs had been a wise choice. He was admired by the party faithful and tolerated as the best of a bad lot, even by anti-Nazis in Innsbruck.

Primbs had been present the night that Fred Mayer was arrested. He had seen Guttner slap Mayer around early in the latter's interrogation and had urged Guttner to go easy on the prisoner. Later, Primbs would claim that this experience was the first time he had ever set foot in the Innsbruck Gestapo office, though he had been Kreisleiter for seven years. He was, he said, appalled that a prisoner should be so brutally abused.

When Guttner informed Primbs that the other prisoner, Hermann Pfluger, had identified Fred Mayer as a potentially important American intelligence officer, Primbs acted quickly. He instructed Guttner to prepare Mayer for a trip to the home of Primbs's superior, Gauleiter Franz Hofer.

Mayer, Dr. Primbs, and Guttner arrived on April 24 at a large farm owned by the Gauleiter located south of Hall. Mayer and Primbs went in to meet Hofer. Guttner was left waiting outside. They were greeted by a heavily handsome, civil man, who tactfully ignored his guest's battered appearance. Also present was an SS intelligence officer, the man who had once been the German consul general in Los Angeles and who recently had tried to trick Gary Van Arkel into revealing the status of Allen Dulles's peace negotiation with SS General Wolff.

Gauleiter Franz Hofer was the Nazi party chief for the Tirol-Vorarlberg province, and thus the most powerful figure in the region. As the area's supreme Nazi, Hofer dealt directly with Hitler, or with the Führer's deputy, Martin Bormann. Hofer was not only the party chief but the Reichskommissar in charge of the Tirol-Vorarlberg defenses. His region embraced much of the suspected National Redoubt. Indeed, Hofer might well be considered the father of the Redoubt.

In order to collect intelligence from inside Switzerland, the SD maintained a wireless monitoring post at Bregenz, near the border. The post intercepted Allied radio traffic coming out of Switzerland and passed it on to Kaltenbrunner's RSHA headquarters in Berlin.

In the fall of 1944, this listening post relayed to Major Gontard, the SD chief in Innsbruck, a message from OSS Bern to Washington reporting that the Germans were believed to be building a vast fortification network in the Alps to hold out after German armies were defeated in the field. It was news to Gontard who, as a member of the SD, was privy to most secrets and who was then sitting practically in the center of this alleged alpine fortress.

Gontard took the information intercepted on the Redoubt directly to Gauleiter Hofer. The idea of fortifying the Alps for a last-ditch defense struck Hofer as inspired. He mulled the prospect over for two months, possibly not wanting to be thought a crackpot, but, in the end, decided that here was a plan worthy of the Führer's attention.

Hofer sent the American dispatches with a covering letter to Hitler through Martin Bormann. In his letter, Hofer urged Hitler to order the construction of an *Alpenfestung,* an Alpine fortress. His detailed proposal followed faithfully what the Americans had said the Germans were already doing.

Early in 1945, perhaps in response to the failed initiative of the Bulge, and having learned that the Allies dreaded the prospect of the war being continued from a mountain redoubt, Hitler authorized the preparation of defenses in the Alps. He made the project the responsibility of the man who had lobbied for it, Gauleiter Hofer. However, months had passed before Hofer received authority to begin actual construction and by the time of Fred Mayer's arrest little had been done.

That mendacious genius, Joseph Goebbels, however, grasped immediately the propaganda uses of the Redoubt. After the Battle of the Bulge, he organized a unit in his ministry to concoct stories of elite troops occupying impregnable positions supplied by vast underground stores and hidden factories carved out of bomb-proof caves. To the neutral press, Goebbels leaked choice items of progress in turning the mountains into an invincible fortress. The Americans had created their own nemesis and, in using the term "National Redoubt," had christened it as well.

Another Nazi who seriously considered the potential of a redoubt was the RSHA chief, Ernst Kaltenbrunner. The idea of his Austrian homeland serving as the unvanquished heart of the Reich had a special appeal for Kaltenbrunner. He complained to Hitler at the end of March that no serious preparations had yet been made for the mountain defenses. Kaltenbrunner himself had taken admirable initiatives and had secured promises from leading industrialists in the Tirol-Vorarlberg to begin installing underground facilities. The managing director of the Steyrer industry, Austria's largest munitions-maker, was supposedly already installing machinery in Tirolean caves and was expected to be producing by May 1.

Kaltenbrunner also had planned a system through which essential raw materials could be channeled into the Redoubt through smuggler trails maintained by hardy mountaineers. He had dispatched an agent to Madrid to sound out Spanish leaders on an air-supply and communications link as well.

It could be a costly business, but Kaltenbrunner had thought that problem through, too. He proposed to use the same counterfeit pound notes produced by Project Bernhard and used to pay off Cicero to finance the supplying of the Redoubt. In fact, he informed his agent in Spain, they might soon possess even greater monetary flexibility, since the reproduction of the American dollar was well along and expected to be as fine a piece of work as the British notes.

OSS continued to feed a belief in the probability of the Redoubt. On March 15, OSS reported: "Art objects and archives have arrived by train in the Zillertal, 90 km. south-southeast of Munich . . . maneuvers simulating Allied parachute landings near the Berghof, Hitler's mountain retreat in the neighborhood of Berchtesgaden, were staged during December. First of the war."

Later that month, OSS reported: "The entire SS-Führer Division was transferred to the Obersalzberg area at the beginning of March 1945. It is believed that eventually the Redoubt will hold 15–25 divisions composed chiefly of SS Storm Troop detachments, Hitler Jugend, and the special OKW Führer Reserve created for service in the Redoubt."

OSS spies in the Austrian resistance provided practical confirmation. They reported increasing arrivals in alpine villages of automobiles from northern Germany burdened with the women, children, and the luggage of high Nazi officials.

The accretion of evidence had its impact on an epic decision of the war. On April 11, American armies were only sixty miles from Berlin and separated from the capital by weak, disorganized German divisions. Instead of brushing aside this flimsy defense and seizing the capital, General Eisenhower set a different priority. He drove instead toward the Russian lines to bisect Germany below Berlin, then turned his armies south to overpower the National Redoubt. "The evidence was clear that the Nazi intended to make the attempt, and I decided to give him no opportunity to carry it out."

The Redoubt had never existed. A few fortifications had been half-heartedly dug. Some matériel and troops were sent south. Nothing more. Eisenhower's armies broke through a hollow shell. The National Redoubt had been a self-fulfilling delusion, the fear becoming father to the thought. OSS had, nevertheless, satisfied the army's determination to have the phantom fortress penetrated and had thirty secret agents in the region.

By the time Fred Mayer had been brought before him, Gauleiter Hofer was suffering an acute ambivalence. His devotion to the party and to Hitler was pure. The idea of a *Götterdämmerung* here in the Alps appealed to the mystical and the romantic in every true Nazi. But Hofer was no fool. The morning after the Twilight of the Gods, ordinary mortals would have to pick up the pieces. Hofer was well aware of the discussions going on over an early surrender in northern Italy, which bordered his jurisdiction. He had taken an interest in this issue. But Allen Dulles wanted no truck with Hofer, and regarded the Gauleiter as a "dangerous intriguer, interested solely in protecting his position in the Tirol."

Still, Hofer raised with Fred Mayer the possibility of negotiations for the surrender of his province. Would Mayer be able to put him in touch with the Americans? Mayer said he could. He also seized this opportunity to test Hofer's sincerity. He asked if he could notify OSS of his situation. Hofer agreed. He would have the message delivered personally by his other guest, the former consul general in Los Angeles, who was about to go to Bern again.

Since Hofer was still wavering over whether he should surrender the Tirol-Vorarlberg, Fred Mayer was returned to custody. He went back to Innsbruck and was put in Reichenau, a concentration camp outside the city.

Gary Van Arkel regarded the message he received in Bern as one of the more curious of the war. "Presently in Gestapo hands, but will get out one way or another. Don't worry." Van Arkel was amused. During his service in Bari he had met the impetuous sender of the message, and it seemed completely in character for Fred Mayer. The message had been delivered to Van Arkel by Gauleiter Hofer's representative, the same man who had tried to bluff the state of the secret surrender negotiations from him a few weeks before. Van Arkel informed the German that if anything happened to Mayer, he would be held personally responsible with his life.

At Reichenau prison, Fred Mayer found his cell door left unlocked, and when he wandered out, there was a car nearby with two of his old KRIPO contacts waiting to spirit him away. Mayer assumed that Dr. Primbs had engineered his escape.

Within days, Mayer received dismaying news. Gauleiter Hofer had apparently made up his mind. The Nazi chief intended to make a speech at noon on May 2, consistent with the position which Grand Admiral Karl Dönitz had taken the day following the announcement of Hitler's death. Dönitz, noting that the Führer had fallen to save the nations of Europe from Bolshevism, had indicated that the Reich would surrender to Great Britain and the United States, but not to the Soviet Union. Hofer was going to call upon the people of his region to go on fighting under the same terms.

Fred Mayer went to Hofer's office at the Gauhaus. He argued with the Gauleiter that the Dönitz position was futile, that the Allies would never accept a separate peace excluding the Russians. The sole effect of Hofer's intended stand would be a senseless loss of life and the destruction of Innsbruck on the eve of Allied victory. Further resistance was mad.

The beleaguered Hofer finally agreed to soften his speech after winning one commitment from Mayer. He wanted to be kept under house arrest, under Mayer's protection, until the Americans arrived and thus be shielded from Austrian anti-Nazis. Mayer agreed.

Hofer went on the air. When the Americans crossed the mountains to the west, he urged no further resistance. Innsbruck, once viewed as a potential capital of the Redoubt, should be given over to the enemy without a fight.

Innsbruck that day hung in an uneasy limbo. Resistance groups had surfaced and brazenly roved the city's streets. An uprising had erupted at one of the Wehrmacht barracks.

Mayer threaded his way to Oberperfuss with Primbs in the Kreisleiter's car, where they tracked down Fred's radioman, Hans Wynberg. Mayer exclaimed wildly to Wynberg that they had taken Innsbruck. The two men put on whatever they had available of American army clothing and headed back with Primbs to the Gauhaus.

The place was a maelstrom. The SS men were particularly unnerved by armed Austrian bands roving the streets. Mayer and Wynberg, in American uniform, were paid scant attention. A ringing phone went unanswered. Mayer picked it up. An official wanted to know what he should do with remaining food stocks. Burn them? Mayer confidently ordered that under no circumstances was any food to be destroyed.

That evening, Mayer and Wynberg, with Primbs, went to Gauleiter Hofer's farm, arriving at 11:00 P.M. Mayer was determined to see that the Nazi carried through on his promise of surrender. The house was surrounded by Hofer's personal guard. The Gauleiter had retired early. A half-dozen senior party men sat about morosely. When Mayer and Wynberg entered, the Nazis leaped on them, pouring forth their hurt and anger. They acted not so much as brutes who had terrorized half the world, but misunderstood men, puzzled by the harsh reverses that fate had dealt them. The two Americans sat up until dawn listening to a view of Europe's recent past which stood history on its head.

A deputy Gauleiter named Hauser spoke with passion. "How can you say that we invaded neutral countries? The Poles murdered sixty thousand Germans in August 1939, we have documented proof of that. And when the Führer, with unparalleled vision, destroyed Poland in twenty-eight days and then offered peace to the western powers, they refused and prepared to attack Germany through the back by invading Norway. The Führer waited all winter, hoping for a peaceful settlement. But in the spring of 1940, when it became obvious that England was going to use Norway as a springboard for attacks against Germany, he attacked first. The same applies to the Low Countries."

Their clinging to the rightness of their cause, with the twisted regime they had erected crashing down about their heads, left the Americans dumbstruck. The Germans went on, each in turn picking up the falling banner of Nazism. The Americans, they claimed, didn't understand that when Hitler died, he had died not only for Germany but in the struggle of all peoples against Bolshevism. The Americans had better start worrying now about Communist domination of Europe. It would not be long, they warned, before the western Allies and the Soviets would begin to clash.

They asked if it was true that the Allies would cut Germany back to its 1939 borders. Yes, they were told, and Austria would again become independent. That might not be so bad, the Nazis said, if the West were going to use Austria as a buffer against the Russians. As the dawn came up, they all pledged that they would happily fight alongside the Allies against the Communists. Their utter insensitivity to what Nazism had wrought depressed these two Jewish-refugee Americans. On the other hand, they thought, what a marvelously satisfying enemy to defeat.

On May 3, the American 103rd Infantry Division of the Seventh Army was rolling irresistibly toward the heart of the Redoubt when it stalled about eighteen miles west of Innsbruck. Three days before, the division had been ordered to take the city. The troops had slogged through mud and snow, then encountered roadblocks, minefields, harassing fire, and sporadic air strikes.

The Germans had taken up defenses on the western edge of Innsbruck. They depressed the barrels of antiaircraft guns parallel to the ground to greet the oncoming enemy. The Americans braced for a final assault. The army knew that the price for the city could be high. Wehrmacht and SS troops of undetermined obstinacy had massed in and near the Tirolean capital. Hofer, the Gauleiter of the province, was a known Nazi fanatic.

At four-thirty in the afternoon, the division's intelligence officer, Major Bland West, was summoned to the head of the column. A civilian sedan had emerged from the enemy lines with two German soldiers standing in it holding aloft the staff of an enormous white flag.

Major West returned the salute of the driver, who leaped from the car and introduced himself as "Lieutenant Fred Mayer of OSS." West saw a man with a face marbled with bruises and a hugely swollen ear. The man spoke colloquial GI with a German accent. He was hatless and dressed in a vaguely military outfit.

Fred Mayer throbbed with adrenal vitality. A broad grin never left his battered face as he told the startled West why he had come through the enemy lines. He wanted West to accompany him back to arrange the surrender of Innsbruck and the province. As West absorbed what Mayer was saying, he noticed that the flag of truce was a bed sheet.

In April 1945, Fritz Molden performed his final mission. He had first smuggled Circe and Adriana Del Piano into Switzerland after their operation had become exposed to the Gestapo in Milan. Then, in the last days of the war he returned to Italy, where he learned that the Austrian resistance was about to surface in a bid to seize Innsbruck. He persuaded Al Ulmer that they ought to break through the crumbling German defenses in northern Italy and be in on the kill. They drove a twisting course of back roads to escape the heavy German traffic on the Brenner Pass. Molden, Ulmer, and four other Americans arrived in Innsbruck in time to witness a curious battle, not for a city, but for the laurels of liberating it.

In Innsbruck, a man named Karl Gruber, who just the month before had been elected head of the Tirolean resistance, deployed bands of armed Austrian partisans to subdue the city's four Wehrmacht barracks. His actions eliminated two thousand defenders. Gruber then persuaded the city's police chief to capitulate. His partisans took over the radio station, then the Landhaus, the seat of local government. An SS tank group started fitfully to move on the city, thought better of it, and withdrew. Their retreat signaled the collapse of all remaining resistance in Innsbruck.

Two men, unknown to each other, had been working different avenues toward the same end. Fred Mayer had persuaded the Nazi Gauleiter not to incite a last-ditch bloodletting against the enemy approaching from without; Gruber had disarmed the defenders from within.

Innsbruck was surrendered bloodlessly on May 4 at 10:15 A.M. The streets burst into the red-and-white banners of pre-Nazi Austria. Just hours after the city had been freed, and before the American army arrived, Al Ulmer, Fritz Molden, and their party arrived from Italy. They went to the Landhaus, where Karl Gruber exclaimed, "What do you think? We just took Innsbruck!"

Shortly after, Ulmer and Molden found Fred Mayer beaming. "We just took Innsbruck!" Mayer was annoyed to learn that people he saw as eleventh-hour anti-Nazi Austrians had shared in his triumph.

Karl Gruber had indeed arrived late to the Austrian resistance. He had spent most of the war in Berlin working for the Telefunken company, until the ceaseless Allied bombing had dispersed the firm and sent Gruber back to his native Austria. Once there, however belatedly, he plunged into resistance work and led the only Austrian military insurrection of any magnitude against Nazi rule. For his role, the Americans named Gruber civil governor of the Tirol, much to Fred Mayer's annoyance.

Mayer had gone without sleep the last three days before Innsbruck's capture and barely cared. He had had in those months undercover, he said later, "one hell of a time." He felt he had one last duty in Innsbruck, a matter of honor. Mayer had found an old-fashioned gentleman in the devout Nazi Gauleiter. He had promised Hofer that if the German tried to avoid a fight for Innsbruck, he would keep him under house arrest until he could explain Hofer's cooperation to the Americans. Hofer had kept his word and Mayer intended to keep his.

Unfortunately for Hofer, a U.S. Army combat intelligence team, led by members of the Austrian resistance, got to the Gauleiter before Mayer did. They asked Hofer if he had any weapons. He responded, "On my word of honor, I have none." A search of his house produced three high-powered rifles, three pistols, and ammunition. He was placed under arrest, and as he left his home, Hofer paused, gave the Nazi salute and muttered, *"Heil Hitler."*

The Gauleiter was taken to an Allied interrogation center from which he eventually managed to escape. When the most powerful Nazi in the southern Reich was recaptured, he was disguised as a chimney sweep. Hofer later faced capital charges as a war criminal.

Two weeks after Innsbruck fell, army counterintelligence officers notified Fred Mayer that they had captured Walter Guttner, the Gestapo officer who had tortured Mayer. They asked if he wanted to see the prisoner. "I can't wait," Mayer answered.

Mayer found Guttner cowering in the corner of a cell. He yanked the small, huddled figure to his feet and looked into a face as battered as his own had been. Guttner spoke to Mayer in a dull, dead voice: "Do what you want with me, but do not harm my family."

Mayer flung him to the floor. "What do you think we are, Nazis?" He then left the prison.

On February 21, Julio Prester, the other surviving members of the late Lieutenant Miles Pavlovich's DILLON team, and twenty Austrian civilians were transported by train to the Gestapo prison in Klagenfurt. Viktor Ruthi, the agent who had led the Gestapo to Pavlovich and Martha Frais, had provided the names of all local people who had aided the mission. For the following two weeks, Prester was placed in a cell and ignored. Nine of the civilian accomplices were sentenced to death.

After the team was captured, Johann Sanitzer, the Gestapo radio expert for the region, was notified by his subordinate in Klagenfurt, Luftwaffe Oberleutnant Rudi Pienitz, that Pienitz was going to try to get Prester to transmit under control.

Pienitz and another Gestapo official, Helmuth Helfricht, pressured Prester to save himself by agreeing to work for them. Prester at first refused. But as they persisted over several weeks, he finally asked what it was that they expected him to do. They informed the stunned Prester that they wanted an air drop arranged of American cigarettes and chocolates. Here, Prester thought, was an opportunity to tip off OSS Italy to the DILLON Mission's fate, while causing no more harm than reducing the inventory at the PX. He agreed.

On March 24, Prester was led from his cell and taken by Helfricht and Pienitz to a villa on the banks of the Wörthersee, outside Klagenfurt. From there, OSS received its first communication since the DILLON team had departed three months before, a message of baffling incongruities. Prester reported that Karl Lippe was dead, Lieutenant Pavlovich was "missing in action," and that the team needed a drop of cigarettes and chocolates. Somehow, the OSS radio operator in Italy had missed, within Prester's message, the danger signal that he was operating under control.

Believing that he had warned home base of his situation, Julio Prester was stunned when he received the base's reply. OSS wanted to know what intelligence contacts he had made, and were suggesting leads that he might follow, thus revealing American military intentions to the Germans. Worse still, knowing that the team had lost two men, the base wanted to drop reinforcements.

In a later message, Prester tried again to reveal his situation. He managed to include, amid the coded text, in plain language, "Miles dead" and "Klagenfurt Jail." These words, unaccountably, were not included by the OSS radio operators in typing up the decoded message for the OSS staff.

The base went forward relentlessly with the drop plan, informing Prester of the time and place at which he should be prepared to receive the supplies and the two unrequested agents. Altogether, Prester sent fourteen messages containing the danger signal, which was never detected.

Shortly after 1:00 A.M. on April 16, Bernd Steinitz, an OSS corporal posing as an aviator who had been shot down, and an Austrian deserter volunteer were parachuted near Klagenfurt. Within fifteen minutes after hitting the ground, the two agents and the cigarettes and chocolate dropped with them were in the hands of the Gestapo.

Though the war's outcome was certain and the end near, Julio Prester observed an unnerving ambivalence in his captors. Some Nazis, like the Gestapo officer, Helmuth Helfricht, were softening and obviously eager to court his favor. Others were unpredictable, wavering between concern for their own skins and a desire to destroy the prisoners in a last vengeful rage. Helfricht confessed to Prester that his superiors had pressed him to move quickly against the DILLON prisoners in order to make an example of them. Execution dates had subsequently been fixed for the agents and the nine local people under death sentences.

Early in May, at the villa from which he transmitted his controlled messages to OSS Italy, Julio Prester was approached, through the intercession of Helfricht, by a prominent anti-Nazi Austrian interested in an early surrender in this region. The man thought that Prester might serve as liaison. Prester set his price. All the DILLON prisoners, both agents and civilians, were to be freed first.

As an initial gesture of good faith, Helfricht formally released Prester, after which the Gestapo officer, the Austrian peace-seeker, and Prester returned to Gestapo headquarters in Klagenfurt. The German in charge now received Prester as an Allied officer and agreed to his demand that the civilian prisoners be freed. He would not, however, consent to the release of any German Army traitors who had gone over to the enemy. They were to be shot the next day, including Viktor Ruthi, whose confessions had resulted in the arrest of DILLON's civilian supporters and the deaths of Miles Pavlovich and Martha Frais.

Prester left the Gestapo office and went to the jail, where he demanded that the warden release all the DILLON prisoners. The warden refused, insisting that he could not violate a lawful order. Prester reminded the jailer that in view of the imminent collapse of the Nazi regime a new order would soon prevail, and that the warden would be held responsible by the Allies for the deaths of these men. The cell doors were hurriedly opened.

XVIII

Final Acts

Of the Belgian teams recruited by Ray Brittenham, CHAUFFEUR had gotten off to the least promising start before the team eventually found its secure bases of operation—in a dairy and a brothel.

Young Michel Dehandtshutter, the one-time Gestapo employee in Brussels, and André Renaix, his older radioman partner, whom Ray Brittenham had warily recruited from Direction Action, thought they had a safe house in Regensburg. But when they arrived at the address, they found that the Belgian worker who was supposed to shelter them had left six months before. The Belgian who gave them this information became suspicious at the line of their conversation and threatened to denounce them to his German superiors if they did not leave the house at once.

They had thereafter tried to travel between two small villages near Regensburg and had been arrested by the Volkssturm. They spent an uneasy night locked in a barn until their forged papers were checked and found in order. They had hoped to encounter among their captors a faltering loyalty to the regime. Instead, they saw only die-hard Nazis or apathetic citizens still terrified of the police. They met no German anti-Nazis. They spent the first fifteen days living in the open woods, subsisting on eight days' worth of rations brought from England.

In the small town of Abensberg, about eighteen miles southwest of

Regensburg, the CHAUFFEUR agents asked the driver of a dairy truck to sell them some milk. The man turned out to be a Belgian POW assigned to work in a nearby dairy. His name was Raoul. The two agents were hungry and tired. The batteries on their radio had failed and they had not been able to reach London. Raoul appeared approachable, and they staked their all on him. They revealed their true identities, explained their mission, and asked for his help.

Raoul was one of ten Belgian and French prisoners of war working in the dairy. The manager was usually absent and the prisoners were under the control of a gullible German sergeant. Raoul slipped the two men into the dairy and presented them to the other workers. André Renaix showed them some radio equipment and reminded them what could happen if the gear was found in their quarters. Michel Dehandtshutter promised that if even one of them had any concern about their presence, the team would leave at once, with no hard feelings. The workers unanimously chose to help. They moved the rest of the team's equipment into the cellar of the dairy, fed the two men, and made them comfortable.

It would have been difficult to invent a better vantage point from which to spy on Regensburg. Early every morning the trucks rolled out of the dairy to collect milk from farms which virtually formed a circle around the city. Michel Dehandtshutter rode the trucks, and gathered military intelligence for André Renaix to radio back to London.

The CHAUFFEUR team was pioneering a new communications strategy. Joan-Eleanor, for all its advantages, had one failing. The rendezvous had to be set up in advance. No way existed for the agents on the ground to notify London if they had something urgent and needed to talk. Wireless radio, for all its limitations, allowed a team to call the home base at any time. CHAUFFEUR was equipped, as an experiment, with both systems.

André Renaix set up his radio in a loft from which he talked to London, using electrical power from the dairy. CHAUFFEUR thus became the first clandestine wireless radio to communicate directly out of Germany. Renaix reported that while regular Wehrmacht units appeared to be crumbling, crack SS troops were digging in on a perimeter around Regensburg. The mission also reported the location of petroleum supply depots for the forces defending the city and pinpointed antiaircraft emplacements standing guard over Danube River bridges on the approaches to town.

One evening, while discussing women, the POWs told the CHAUF-

FEUR agents of two French girls who had been forced into a German brothel in Regensburg as a disciplinary measure. Dehandtshutter went to the city and managed to find the girls. He was candid. Would they work for the Allies? They would help in any way, but they did not want money. They insisted that they had been coerced into this life. All that they asked for was to have Dehandtshutter put in a good word for them with the Americans after the war and to help them get repatriated. He then told them how to steer conversations with their clients in a way that would produce valuable intelligence.

Dehandtshutter passed up the milk runs for the next four days and spent most of the time in the girls' closet with a flashlight and note pad. The women proved to have a rewarding clientele. They enticed the grand strategy for the defense of Regensburg from a highly placed and frequent visitor, a Colonel Kluger. Complementing details came from the enlisted customers who manned Regensburg's defenses.

The girls' loyalty to the Nazis was apparently unquestioned by their masters. Another client, a police official, told them that he counted on them to report any deserters or political unreliables coming around the place.

On the night of April 23, Dehandtshutter returned to the dairy. He and his partner, Renaix, talked for forty-five minutes to a French-speaking OSS officer via Joan-Eleanor. The postcoital boasts of Colonel Kluger and his comrades were duly repeated to a recording machine in an American airplane circling miles above the city:

Ground: ". . . the general staff is at Regensburg, Hôtel du Parc, Maximilianstrasse. The street facing the station, first house on the left. In permanent residence there are at least four to six generals."

Plane: "Understood . . . continue."

Ground: "All the Russian, Rumanian, and Bulgarian soldiers who were in the German Army at Regensburg left on the twentieth and twenty-first for Augsburg. . . . The SS teams break into houses . . . take everything, pillage everything . . . they kill twenty to thirty persons every day. . . ."

The operator asked them about the fate of prisoners of war in the area. Renaix answered: "Here in Regensburg there were columns of British, American, and French POWs and political prisoners which left every night for eight days. Corpses are found all along the road. We think that they attack them at the slightest sign of fatigue. . . ." The transmission closed with Renaix asking the operator to tell his wife and Michel's fiancée that they were safe and well. They were, he said, being eaten alive by bedbugs and lice, but that did not matter. They were content. They also sent their regards to Major Bill Grell, who had looked after them in London.

Joan-Eleanor had provided a dividend not contemplated when Stephen Simpson first designed his system. To men isolated in a hostile world, the sound of a friendly voice produced a warm rush of excitement. For Renaix and Dehandtshutter the frustration, the fear, the hardship they had undergone dissolved when they talked to their unseen ally in the sky.

With the fall of Regensburg, the CHAUFFEUR agents made contact with OSS field officers and were transported back to London well before the war ended. For the risks they had taken and the quality of intelligence they had produced, the CHAUFFEUR team was recommended for the Distinguished Service Cross.

In terms of sheer output the Belgian DOCTOR Mission had been the most productive of all those parachuted. Jean Smets and Lucien Blonttrock filed over fifty messages to London from the Kufstein area.

DOCTOR's intelligence was not acquired without a price. Rudolf Steiner, the resistance leader who had placed the Austrian flag on the mountaintop just as the DOCTOR team had coincidentally landed, disappeared after a police dragnet of Kufstein on about April 20 and was believed killed. Another Austrian supporter was shot and killed by the SS while trying to slip through no-man's-land between the approaching Americans troops and German defenders.

Smets and Blonttrock continued to shift their radio between their mountain shack and safe houses in Scheffau and Ellmau. While transmitting from Ellmau, they learned that three direction-finding trucks were criss-crossing the surrounding mountain roads searching for them. On a modest level their partisan band got the military action it craved. The Austrians put the three gonio vehicles out of action with hand grenades.

The greatest danger to the team actually originated in Hitler's bunker hundreds of miles to the north in Berlin. Two of the last people to see Hitler alive were Luftwaffe General Robert Ritter von Greim and his girl friend, Hanna Reitsch, an outstanding test pilot. Both were fanatic loyalists. Von Greim, then head of the Sixth Air Force, had been summoned by Hitler from Munich on April 26 to succeed the traitor Hermann Göring as chief of the Luftwaffe. Von Greim, with Hanna Reitsch, had piloted a small aircraft through a rain of Russian antiaircraft fire and crash-landed on a Berlin boulevard.

He suffered a painful leg wound from the Russian guns and spent two days with Hanna resting in Hitler's bunker. But they were denied their most ardent wish—to die with the Führer in this tomb. Instead, Hitler ordered von Greim and Hanna to leave for the Rechlin Air Field, where the new field marshal was to rally nonexistent units of the shattered Luftwaffe for a last blow against Soviet troops approaching the chancellery. Von Greim was also supposed to arrest Himmler who, like Göring, had betrayed the Führer. Hitler personally presented von Greim and Hanna Reitsch with suicide capsules and, as they left, said, "God protect you."

However little von Greim succeeded in carrying out Hitler's deluded last commands, he did move quickly to get himself established in a new headquarters in the Redoubt.

Early in May, Lucien Blonttrock was transmitting from the house of an undercover supporter in Ellmau when he heard strange voices. Field Marshal von Greim's staff had chosen Ellmau as the new headquarters of the Luftwaffe, and the chief of staff was commandeering houses in the village for quarters. The officer strode into the handsome home where Blonttrock was hiding and demanded to see all the rooms. The owner took the officer through the house, but when he reached the upstairs room where Blonttrock was trapped, he put his finger to pursed lips and whispered that his small children were sleeping there.

The house was selected as suitable for von Greim's quarters, and the chief of staff told the owner to have the large room opposite Blonttrock's prepared for the field marshal's arrival.

In the last days of the war, the DOCTOR agents, through local resistance leaders, had available a force of over two thousand armed men. Their resistance chiefs in Kufstein and Kitzbühel were able to talk local military commanders out of making a defense, thus allowing American troops to take over the area without bloodshed.

The commanding officers of the American Twenty-sixth and Forty-second divisions testified that the operating area of the DOCTOR team was the most thoroughly purged of Nazis of any place that they had conquered. The region had been completely neutralized and offered a reliable nucleus of trusted anti-Nazis available for implanting democratic government.

The DOCTOR team led the American troops in a roundup of remaining Nazis. The first arrest occurred at the house in Ellmau from which Blonttrock had barely escaped with his radio. There, Field Marshal von

Greim was seized. The Belgians and the Austrian partisans were disappointed, however, to find most Americans more concerned with collecting souvenirs than fugitive Nazis.

Orpha Gresham, the WAC sergeant, did not see her fiancé, Emil Van Dyck, of the PAINTER Mission, for eighteen months after he had left England for Germany in March 1945. Only then did she learn fully what had befallen him and his partner, François Flour.

PAINTER was one of the grander failures of the German campaign. This Belgian team had managed to penetrate the most sensitive nerve center of the SS in Munich. Yet they had never been able to raise London on their radio and report their coup.

On their arrival, the PAINTER agents had located a Belgian who worked as a mechanic in a garage used by the SS. This man managed to get Van Dyck and Flour hired also as mechanics. Whatever decisions were made on high seemed to be translated ultimately into somebody moving somewhere out of the SS garage. Thus, the agents were well positioned to gather intelligence.

From the laborers' shack where they lived the two agents tried unsuccessfully, after ten-hour days at the garage, to transmit the information they had to London, amid an incessant rain of Allied bombs.

Late in March, American planes struck Munich with a force which Emil Van Dyck described as "the most terrifying experience in my life." After spending four hours in an SS shelter with protective concrete walls seven feet thick, he emerged. "Finally the explosions stopped, and we cautiously crept out into the open. The destruction was indescribable. About a hundred and fifty yards from our garage a foreign workers' camp had gotten it. . . . Several hundred slave laborers had been killed . . . those who had been injured presented a ghastly appearance with their faces completely black from the concussion, which had broken all surface blood vessels. . . .

"One makeshift shelter constructed of huge concrete slabs had received a direct hit. About twenty workers were crushed to death inside, but two unfortunates, one French and the other Dutch, were trapped half in, half out by the very concrete walls. They were being slowly squeezed to death and it would have taken a derrick to lift the concrete . . . in answer to their pitiful pleas, a German officer shot them through the head."

One evening after work, the PAINTER agents were confronted at the laborers' shack by two Gestapo officers who had been on their trail since the Belgians had landed six weeks before. The Nazis were looking for a bargain. They turned over to Van Dyck and Flour the payroll of the entire Gestapo organization in the Munich area: all officers, undercover agents, and informants, including actual and code names and addresses. In return, the Belgians blithely promised to deliver what the two Germans wanted. On the arrival of the Americans, they would arrange for OSS to ship the Gestapo officers and their families to South America with enough money to start a new life.

With the Gestapo pay list and information gathered at the SS garage, the PAINTER agents were key figures in a roundup of over sixty major Bavarian Nazis after Munich was taken. During this sweep, their two Gestapo informants eagerly fingered their former colleagues and filed affidavits against them. Now it was time for the PAINTER agents to fulfill their end of the deal.

Two years before, François Flour had been captured by the Gestapo while working in Belgium as an agent of the British SOE. He had been brutally tortured, then put on a train for a concentration camp in Germany. Flour escaped only after a resistance group attacked the train. Flour and Van Dyck squared their debt with their Gestapo informants by turning them in to American counterintelligence and telling the Americans that the two Nazis were war criminals.

After the Allies overran Munich, Orpha Gresham learned that Emil Van Dyck was alive. Several months later, after she had been mustered out of the WACs and returned home, she began to receive letters from him. Van Dyck, with the help of former OSS officials, arrived as an immigrant to the United States in December 1947. He and Orpha were married five months later.

Ferdi Appenzell and Leon Lindau, the LUXE Mission, lived out the rest of their operation in the safety of their church steeple in Unterstillern. After having ordered the bombing of Weilheim, Ferdi continued to bully intelligence from local people by threatening raids on their villages if they did not cooperate, or death before an American firing squad after their towns were captured if they dared give him false information. On Sundays, the LUXE team enjoyed listening to the church services and hymn-singing below them. They continued their Joan-Eleanor communications with Calhoun Ancrum—six successful contacts in all—and reported military information from in and around Munich, including the intriguing arrival of Heinrich Himmler's armored train.

They learned that Himmler's train was shuttled between stations near Wessling and that during the air raids it was parked in a forest between towns. In these woods, there was a villa where, resentful villagers said, high SS officials and their women carried on a nightly bacchanal. Ferdi reported, erroneously, that Himmler was soon expected to join the train.

On April 29, the LUXE team was overrun by a column of American tanks. Ferdi gave the unit G-2 the tactical information the team possessed. He then led army intelligence officers to Camp IV, a satellite of Dachau. On their arrival, they found the camp afire and a stack of some four hundred bodies burning. As they passed a group of former German guards, now prisoners themselves, these men thrust out from their ranks a cringing figure in civilian clothes. The prisoners eagerly identified him as the commandant of Camp IV.

American soldiers then went into Landsberg and rounded up all the male civilians they could find and marched them out to the camp. The former commandant was forced to lie amidst a pile of corpses. The male population of Landsberg was then ordered to walk by, and ordered to spit on the commandant as they passed. The commandant was then turned over to a group of liberated camp survivors.

Ferdi and Leon later took a CIC team on a search of Himmler's armored train then parked at Steinbach on the Wörthersee. It was fruitless. The once most terrifying figure in the Reich was then far to the north, near the Danish border where he had fled.

Appenzell took another unit of troops from the 103d Division to a fortress in Landsberg which held a special place in the legend of Nazism. Over one cell they found a plaque: "Here a system without honor kept Germany's greatest son a prisoner from 11 November 1923 to 20 December 1924. In this cell Adolf Hitler wrote the book of the national socialist revolution, *Mein Kampf.*"

After the grueling months of Joan-Eleanor missions and with the war over, Calhoun Ancrum had been assigned soft duty supervising a London town house where recovered agents were lodged. He was awakened one night from a deep sleep by someone shouting, *"Vic! Vic! Ich bin Ferdi!"* Ancrum opened his eyes to a man grinning wildly at him. He pulled his thoughts together sufficiently to summon this voice from a far-off world. He groggily told Ferdi Appenzell to see him the next day, and fell back asleep.

The next night, three German-speaking men stirred a small wake of curiosity in a London restaurant. Calhoun Ancrum studied Ferdi Appenzell and Leon Lindau, once only disembodied voices that had reached up to him in the rear of an airplane on desperately cold nights. He found

Ferdi bombastic, filled with himself, much as he had sounded with his "Take it *avay*, New York!" Leon spoke little. Appenzell related gleefully to Ancrum his successes in intimidating people into helping them in Germany and the story of the bombing of Sergeant Sommer's house in Weilheim.

The evening grew uncomfortable as Ancrum failed to match Ferdi's beer-hall camaraderie. Toward the end, sensing a last opportunity slipping by, Ferdi reminded the American of his understanding that the LUXE Mission had earned him entry into the United States. Ancrum said nothing, but shuddered inwardly.

Ancrum's superior officer later learned that the LUXE agents had been in contact with the former Joan-Eleanor operator. The man instructed Ancrum not to say a word to anyone about the mission. It was the officer's plan, Ancrum knew, to use the LUXE Mission as the basis for a screenplay. Ancrum reacted as he usually did when confronted by foolishness in his superiors. He filed a report denouncing the man.

Willi Drucker, who had been slipped over the Swiss border on New Year's Eve, had spent January through April in the Gestapo prison in Innsbruck, after Kriner, the duplicitous Gestapo official, had betrayed him. On his arrest Drucker had been stripped naked and left standing in a room where a secretary calmly continued her typing. Other Gestapo officials ignored him as they ate their lunch. For two months, he was alternately beaten and questioned. He stuck by a story that, though German-born, he had become a French citizen years before, and had returned to Germany working for French intelligence. He gave his name as Marcel Dusellier. His deepest dread was that if they learned his true identity, they would find out that he was a long-time fugitive from the Gestapo. The Germans maintained a list of deserters and suspected spies which they updated monthly.

On April 13, Willi Drucker went on trial before a military tribunal in Innsbruck. His court-appointed attorney offered a brief, and, to Drucker, surprisingly impassioned defense. Yes, the man deserved life in prison, his lawyer agreed. But his experience in living among so degenerate a race as the French had inevitably corrupted him. For this, he did not deserve to die. The judge answered that the defendant was, nevertheless, born of German blood and had defiled his precious birthright.

Drucker was asked if he had anything to say. He remained silent. He was sentenced to death. The trial had lasted three minutes. Drucker was moved from his regular cell to death row, where each morning he was awakened by clanging doors followed shortly thereafter by shots from the prison courtyard.

Among the OSS officers coming to Innsbruck in the days immediately following the German surrender was Gary Van Arkel from Allen Dulles's operation in Switzerland. Van Arkel had arrived at his hotel and was about to enter when he thought he heard his name being called. He looked down to the basement level and saw a cadaverous face grinning up at him through barred windows. He studied the hollowed features. "It's me, Willi Drucker!" Van Arkel thought he must be mad. This crazed, shriveled figure was a man he had thought to be dead for five months.

During his imprisonment, Drucker had been deliberately starved. He had for a time been put to work labeling bottles and would lick the glue from the labels for nourishment. After he had been transferred to death row, his only shaft of hope was a kindly old guard who reported to him daily the progress of the Allied armies. Still the cell doors clanged each morning and the shots rang out from the courtyard.

On the first day of May, the prison director, who had always abused Drucker, opened his cell, smiled broadly, and tried to shake the prisoner's hand. "You are free," he said. The Americans had arrived. Drucker reported to G-2 of the 103d Division and had been temporarily housed in the basement of the hotel when Van Arkel found him.

The American offered to take Drucker back to Switzerland. En route they stopped at an office of the French Deuxième Bureau. The French had under arrest in their occupation zone several former Nazis, including some of Drucker's jailers. Van Arkel wanted Drucker to get his story into the record so that his tormentors could be prosecuted as war criminals.

The long drive had exhausted Drucker physically. The repetition to the French of what he had endured in captivity drained him emotionally. Van Arkel regretted putting the man through the ordeal. As he watched Drucker give his testimony, he could not help notice that the man's thighs were about the same size as his own wrists. After they had returned to Switzerland, he arranged for Drucker to be admitted to a sanatorium. There, the man's basically robust constitution quickly revived.

After the war, Willi Drucker returned to police work in Germany. But his dream while exiled in England of a rebirth of the police system was never realized. Too many of the old guard remained in place. He remembered once submitting his papers to a new police chief. The officer, after reviewing his record, said: "To be in the resistance was a good thing. But to serve one's country is also a good thing. I myself served the fatherland. I fought for Germany, not against her."

On May 20, 1945, Jules Konig, an OSS army captain, drove up the gently rising road of Austria's Lieser Valley to the old city of Gmünd. His orders were to tie up the still loose ends of an OSS mission that had cost three lives. There he met Julio Prester, who was to guide him as Konig sought to help those who had aided the DILLON team and to initiate legal action against its persecutors.

The war had deeply riven the people of the town. Konig noted in his report: "It is symptomatic of the spirit of the present population of Gmünd that they consider our people traitors of the fatherland and as scum because they helped the Americans."

The owner of a small vegetable market pleaded with Konig to see if OSS might help him relocate. He had been boycotted by his neighbors for aiding the DILLON Mission and could no longer make a living in Gmünd. Still, other villagers placed fresh flowers on the crude grave of Lieutenant Miles Pavlovich every day.

Konig informed British army officials who had liberated the area as to which Austrians the Americans wanted arrested: Wegscheider, the peasant who had betrayed the team; Hartlieb, the policeman who had shot Miles Pavlovich; Oberlechner, the mayor of Gmünd who had buried Pavlovich and Martha Frais like dogs; and the OSS agent, now a fugitive, Viktor Ruthi, who had informed on his fellow team members and their civilian supporters.

One by one, in the privacy of his hotel room, Konig listened to the claims of those who had risked themselves for the American mission. To Bertha Krabatt and her daughter Maria Winkler, the first people to aid the team in their modest home in Treffenboden and who had been sentenced to death for their role, Konig proposed settlements of $500 each. Johann Fichomer, who had occasionally hidden team members, asked that he be allowed to keep the Volkswagen that the German Army had left behind. For the father of the late Martha Frais, Konig proposed a payment of $405. Martha's sister, Leni, who walked ten miles to her job every day, asked for a bicycle, which Konig said she would have. Konig sent Julio Prester to Eisentratten to see if Frau Lippe needed any help. She was the mother of the feckless Karl, whom Prester had executed.

The final act of DILLON was left to Prester as well. He ordered several Nazis who had abused the DILLON team to exhume the bodies of Miles Pavlovich and Martha Frais from their shallow graves. At the request of her father, the woman's body was returned for burial in the family plot. Lieutenant Pavlovich was placed in a coffin and reburied at a formal funeral service attended by villagers who had gambled their lives for his mission. His grave was adorned with flowers and marked by a cross and an American flag.

Sergeant Albert Koziek and seven other men of General Patton's Third Army had been sent ahead to reconnoiter roadblocks and bridges along the Danube west of Linz. They had pulled up their jeep and half-track to the gate of some sort of encampment. Immediately, they were engulfed by a sea of gaunt, foul-smelling, hollow-eyed figures clothed in rags, grinning from skull-tight faces, clutching at them, and cheering hoarsely in a dozen languages. One man clawed his way to the jeep and waved a pair of dog tags in the sergeant's face. "God bless America." The man's voice was cracked and faint. He told the incredulous sergeant that he was Jack Taylor, a lieutenant in the United States Navy. He also informed Koziek and his men that they had just liberated a concentration camp.

The last days before the Americans arrived at Mauthausen had been a cruel commingling of hope and despair. The camp was swept daily by fresh waves of rumor. The Russian army was known to be bearing down from the east. If the Soviets arrived soon enough they might be freed. Then, word raced through the camp that the panicky SS were going to kill them all before the Russians could arrive. A report had circulated that Churchill or some other British leader had seen Buchenwald and had vowed that if similar death camps were found, the Germans would pay. This report had galvanized the SS to step up executions and the cremation of sick and starving prisoners. In effect, they were burning the evidence.

On April 25, representatives of the International Red Cross were allowed to evacuate French, Dutch, and Belgian prisoners from Mauthausen. The hopes of the remaining prisoners rose. The next day, 1167 of them were gassed, shot, clubbed, or died of starvation. A few days later a squadron of P-38s buzzed the camp at rooftop altitude. The prisoners cheered wildly at the possible portent of these American aircraft. Then, on May 1, the SS contingent pulled out of Mauthausen and turned the camp over to the Vienna fire-police. From that moment, the atrocities and executions ceased. Four days later, Sergeant Koziek and his men arrived.

As Third Army personnel drove Jack Taylor away to an army hospital at Regensburg, he could see the liberated prisoners impaling block leaders and Kapos on the fence posts which supported the once electrified barbed wire.

Taylor arrived at Regensburg weighing 112 pounds and suffering from dysentery and fever. His back and legs were a mass of sores. He could not stand long without fainting. But as soon as his strength began to return, he forced himself to a task which he knew he could not escape. He returned to Mauthausen.

In one respect, the operation of the camp had not changed. The Communist prisoners, with their talent for organization and unity, had held the key trustee positions under the Nazis. Much of the daily administration of the camp was in their hands. Communists drew up the execution lists and were thus in a position to spare their own. Now, after liberation, they were in full command of Mauthausen. When Taylor arrived, with several U.S. Army officers, the Communists were holding trials of the more vicious Kapos and block leaders and putting them to death.

American officials took over the camp and stopped the executions. Among the Communist camp leaders was a man named Heinrich Duermayer. Taylor knew him well and had, in fact, fought with Duermayer to be first to welcome the liberating Americans. The American military government was now recruiting trustworthy, talented people to replace deposed Nazi civil leaders. Taylor overcame his profound aversion to the man's politics to recommend Duermayer. "He's a Communist," he said, "but he's an able man." Duermayer eventually became the chief of the Austrian internal security police in Vienna.

Jack Taylor spent three weeks collecting documents and talking to prisoners who could be helpful in prosecuting Nazi camp officials as war criminals. His most valuable find was a set of eighteen *Totenbücher*, death books. These journals constituted something of a double-entry system of Mauthausen barbarity. They contained the official cause of death, which the Nazis insisted on recording with meticulous care for every Mauthausen victim. Clerks were provided with a list of fifty legitimate causes of death from which to choose. The death books also contained the actual cause of death, recorded through simple codes which the clerks had devised. In one set of books, for example, a dot after the place of birth meant that the victim had received the lethal injection in the heart. "Zellenbau," the name of one of the prison buildings, written in the fourth column signified a gas-chamber death.

Taylor was spurred on in his painful task by continuing evidence of what Mauthausen had done to its victims. After three weeks of American medical care and healthful food, liberated prisoners were still dying at a rate of over fifty a day. As a reminder of what he himself had been spared, Taylor found in Commandant Ziereis's desk a pair of U.S. Navy lieutenant insignia. They had belonged to Holt Green, the executed leader of the DAWES Mission whom he had once hoped to contact.

During this final inventory Jack Taylor learned how he had survived. His execution order had been signed for April 28, along with twenty-six other prisoners from Block 13. On that date, six days before liberation, all but two of the men were gassed. Milos Stransky, a Czech trustee, had spotted the names of Taylor and another Czech friend. Stransky had burned their execution orders.

Taylor learned that the other members of his team, all sentenced to be beheaded as traitors, were still alive. In the crumbling last hours of the Reich, Ernst Ebbing, Anton Graf, and Felix Huppmann had managed to escape from a temporary prisoner cage and had eventually found their separate routes back to OSS Italy.

Nine months passed after Jack Taylor completed his dossier on Mauthausen, a documentation described by military lawyers as "the outstanding report" on the death camp and "the best war-crimes evidence" produced in that theater of operations. He returned to California, a homecoming hero, to complete his recuperation.

The intelligence virus had apparently infected him, however, since he soon wrote to Washington and asked to be reassigned to OSS duties in Europe. Al Ulmer, who had tried originally to talk Taylor out of the DUPONT Mission, was then with the OSS office in Vienna and assigned to handle Taylor's request. Jack Taylor had been a fearless, dedicated officer. But all his missions, however courageous, had been stillborn. Furthermore, he knew no foreign languages. Ulmer was under instructions to retrench. With the war over, there was no place in America's shrinking intelligence service for Jack Taylor. The man accepted his fate, not without a tinge of bitterness, took his navy discharge in October 1945, and returned again to California and to dentistry.

But Taylor was not yet free of Mauthausen. On a raw March morning in 1946, in Dachau, the case of *The United States* vs. *Hans Altfuldisch et al.* opened. Altfuldisch was alphabetically first among the sixty-one Mauthausen officials indicted for crimes against humanity. The first prosecution witness was Jack Taylor, lieutenant commander, U.S. Navy.

Against his strong disinclination, the navy had temporarily recalled Taylor to active duty at a new rank, and sent him as the star prosecution witness against the Mauthausen gang. He began his testimony by apologizing for having to refer to notes. "I have tried to forget most of these things for the past year."

Along one wall of the courtroom sat the defendants, each with a numbered placard hanging from his neck. They had operated a hell to which Nazi justice consigned 206,000 human beings, of which 110,000 died. Among these wan, defeated figures Taylor did not see those most deserving of a place in the docket. Franz Ziereis, the gleefully cruel commandant, was not there, nor was Hans Prellberg, Taylor's first tormentor, nor Roth, who had goaded them to complete the crematorium, nor SS Hauptsturmführer Georg Bachmayer, who had shot the DAWES and HOUSEBOAT men. These Mauthausen figures were known dead, believed dead, or missing. Ziereis had been mortally wounded by one of General Patton's men in a shootout the day after the war in Europe ended.

Taylor saw again the eighteen *Totenbücher* that he had helped preserve as evidence. He saw photographs of the dead, suspended from the barbed-wire fences, introduced as evidence. He gave his testimony and it was instrumental in the verdicts. The major surviving officials of Mauthausen were convicted and executed. Jack Taylor again returned to his dental practice in southern California.

The industrialist, the priest, and the pianist who had aided Allen Dulles and who had been betrayed in Istanbul, shared the same Viennese Gestapo prison as Jack Taylor for a time. In the fall of 1944, Franz Josef Messner and Dr. Heinrich Maier were tried by a federal court in Vienna and charged with fomenting a separatist movement and providing intelligence to the enemy on the location of vital wartime industries. They were convicted of treason and sentenced to death.

Barbara Issikides underwent a rigorous, protracted interrogation, but found an unbending determination within herself to tell the Nazis nothing. During one grilling her inquisitor had slapped a special pencil in front of her which the group had used to conceal secret messages. "Of course, you know what this is!" At that moment she spied two pigeons mating on the windowsill and concentrated a fierce attention on them. After several minutes of silence, the pencil was angrily snatched away. She was not tortured, perhaps because of her celebrity as a pianist. But she endured an unrelenting assault on her will through months of alternating interrogation and isolation in the Gestapo prison. She lost weight, became ill, but did not break.

Working from Bern, Kurt Grimm tried, through connections with influential lawyers he had known in Vienna, to have the pianist released, but without success. In the case of Franz Josef Messner, he worked on a slender thread. Messner was technically a Brazilian citizen. At Grimm's urging, OSS Bern proposed that Messner be freed in exchange for a German in Brazil. Grimm tried to enlist the Papal Nuncio in Bern in the scheme. He asked the Swiss embassy in Berlin to intervene. To a degree, his efforts succeeded. Messner's death sentence was postponed for a time. For Dr. Maier, the priest, he could do nothing.

In its death throes the regime's unregenerate Nazis exacted what came to be known as "revenge in advance." The priest was beheaded in Vienna on March 22, 1945. Messner was one of the last victims gassed at Mauthausen on April 24, eleven days before the camp was liberated. His body was cremated in the oven that Jack Taylor had been forced to help construct.

After months of incarceration, Barbara Issikides complained of severe stomach pains. She could eat nothing, she said. She was taken, under the surveillance of a Gestapo official, from her cell in the Metropol Hotel to Dr. Franke, a Viennese physician. Franke knew the prisoner as a distinguished musician and recognized, as he questioned her about her symptoms, a fairly accomplished actress. He helpfully diagnosed a duodenal ulcer and had the patient assigned to a prison hospital. It was enough to delay her trial a critical four weeks.

Lieutenant Alfred Ulmer, who had known of the ring during his service in Istanbul before his transfer to Bari, was sent to Vienna in the summer of 1945. There, during that first harsh summer of peace, he and other OSS Americans sought to help those who had aided the Allies. As they entered the city, the Viennese were flying red-and-white Austrian flags. Ulmer could still see the outlines on them where the swastikas had been cut away.

He paid a call on the mother of Dr. Maier. Ulmer found the old woman living modestly, but reluctant to take any help. He pressed on her a payment in Austrian money worth $2500. It was not overly generous, since the Americans had confiscated large sums of currency from their recent foes.

Ulmer located Barbara Issikides, whose life had been spared by the delay of her trial. He found a fierce, gaunt beauty still illuminating this extraordinary woman. As soon as her strength returned, she gave a concert in Vienna. OSS arranged a lavish reception afterward.

She had been strong when others were weak. But the strength that had sustained Barbara Issikides through her ordeal seemed to have consumed something within her. She became ill and succumbed to a long siege of nervous exhaustion. In time, she left her musical career for marriage.

Dyno Lowenstein was sent to tend to the needs of the widow of Lothar Koenigsreuter, the agent whom Dyno had located for Fritz Molden in the prisoner cages of Italy, and who was subsequently killed on the HOME-SPUN Mission with Joseph Franckenstein near Innsbruck.

Apart from whatever she might have needed, what Frau Koenigsreuter seemed to welcome most was another man, although—from what Lowenstein observed in her busy apartment—she hardly appeared to be lonely. She was a pert, attractive woman in her mid-thirties, utterly incredulous that the Americans wanted to give her money. Her memory of Koenigsreuter had already dimmed, except that she remembered him as that "crazy man." Frau Koenigsreuter was, nevertheless, the slain man's designated beneficiary and was paid the equivalent of $2500 in Austrian schillings.

Lowenstein showed a partiality for the political kin of his Social Democrat father, who had been driven from Germany by the Nazis. After he had delivered several truckloads of food to the headquarters of the Vienna Social Democrats, Al Ulmer reminded him gently, "This has to stop. We aren't here to subsidize political organizations."

The Metropol Hotel, the Vienna Gestapo prison that had once housed Dr. Heinrich Maier, Franz Josef Messner, Jack Taylor, and his DUPONT team, had been destroyed during the Russian attack on the city. Later, a small stone monument was placed on its site, inscribed:

> Hier stand das Haus der Gestapo.
> Es war für die Bekenner Österreichs die Hölle.
> Es war für viele von ihnen der Vorhof des Todes.
> Es ist in Trümmer gesunken wie das 1000-jährige Reich.
> Österreich aber ist wieder auferstanden.
> Und mit ihm unsere Toten, die unsterblichen Opfer.*

Their recent liberators, the Russians, appeared to have won little gratitude from the Viennese. The catch phrase then making the rounds was: "The new state. The old pigsty. New pigs."

While so much of the effort out of OSS Bari had ended in disaster, with DUPONT, DILLON, and DEADWOOD, all failing, the GREENUP Mission had been an intelligence triumph, even with Fred Mayer captured at the end. Sergeant Mayer's pose as an officer was soon legitimized.

---

*Here stood the Gestapo house.
For the Austrians, it was hell.
For many, it was the vestibule to death.
Like the Thousand-year Reich, it has sunk into ruins.
But Austria has risen again,
And with her our dead, the immortal victims.

After the mission, he and Hans Wynberg were both commissioned second lieutenants in the U.S. Army. For his accomplishments, particularly for helping to spare a battle for Innsbruck, Fred Mayer was later recommended for the Congressional Medal of Honor.

Karl Gruber parlayed his role in freeing Innsbruck into a distinguished career in the Austrian government, serving ultimately as ambassador to the United States and later as his nation's foreign minister.

OSS agents had also been intruded into Germany from Sweden. This neutral country should have been almost as favorable a vantage point as Switzerland for piercing Germany, but it never was. A constant stream of travelers, sailors, businessmen, officials, and refugees moved between the Reich and Sweden. North German ports could be easily reached from Sweden by boat or via Denmark. But infiltration of the Reich from that neutral country hardly matched the potential.

The venture had started off badly. In March 1942, Bruce Hopper, a Harvard professor of government, arrived in Stockholm to establish an American intelligence office. The Department of State had complete control over the entry of American personnel into Sweden, and Hopper's reception by the U.S. minister suggested the environment of innocence in which he was expected to conduct espionage. The minister, Herschel V. Johnson, equated spying with sin. On Hopper's arrival, Johnson warned him that any intelligence activities in which he engaged would lead to Hopper's immediate recall.

The Passport Division of the State Department, in a stunning example of diplomatic candor, insisted upon stamping the passports of intelligence officers going to Stockholm "OSS," boldly and clearly. When the OSS operation did break through its own government's obstructionism, it ran into other obstacles. Its path was also blocked by British intelligence officers in Sweden who refused to let their lines be used for infiltrating "leftist" agents into Germany.

The Labor desk in Stockholm had to develop an independent contact for its only attempted penetration. Its agent was Herbert, a Social Democrat who was landed in Denmark, then escorted to the German border by the Danish resistance. Herbert was to make contact with trade unionists in the Hamburg area. Months passed, and no word was heard from Herbert.

Four other attempts were hazarded to penetrate Germany out of Stockholm of which only two succeeded.

Eric Siegfried Erikson was a late bloomer in life and also came late to

316

espionage. Erikson had not graduated from Cornell until he was thirty-three, yet had played varsity football and baseball there. He then went to work for Standard Oil of New Jersey, and by the time the war came along, he had his own oil business in Sweden. Erikson eventually became a Swedish citizen, for business reasons, thus returning full circle to his Nordic roots.

Early in the war Erikson incurred the displeasure of U.S. officials who suspected him of trading with the Germans. He protested his innocence and was offered the opportunity to redeem himself by spying for the Allies. Erikson was instructed to cultivate German business and government figures in Stockholm and to try to gain permission to travel inside Germany. He plunged into the work wholeheartedly, bad-mouthing the Allies, spouting Aryan nonsense, even cutting dead old Jewish friends. He invited German businessmen into profitable deals and joined the German Chamber of Commerce in Sweden.

Erikson told his new-found associates that he was planning to build a synthetic oil plant in Sweden—an interesting prospect to the fuel-hungry Germans. To help him study the necessary technology, project the volume of production, and explore the market potential, they passed along to Erikson valuable information on the state of the synthetic fuel industry inside Germany.

Erikson was grateful, but asked if he might take a closer look. In October 1944, he was granted permission to make a one-week tour of German synthetic-oil facilities. On his return, he provided a comprehensive report which the British Ministry of Economic Warfare and American oil experts found highly valuable. But he apparently had pushed too far. After his return to Sweden, the Germans grew suspicious and dropped him.

The second OSS mission to penetrate Berlin out of Stockholm arrived two weeks before the HAMMER team had flown out of London. In the fall of 1944, a Dane approached the OSS Stockholm staff bearing impressive credentials. His name was Hennings Jensen-Schmidt, and he was a member of the Danish underground. The Germans had smashed his ring, putting his father into a Danish prison, his brother into a concentration camp, and sending Jensen-Schmidt flying into exile in Sweden.

Jensen-Schmidt had a Swedish friend named Carl Wiberg who lived in Berlin. The Swedish businessman's apartment had become an unofficial retreat for anti-Nazi Germans and Swedes. OSS developed a plan for Jensen-Schmidt to go to Germany under the cover of a businessman buying electrical equipment. In Berlin, he was to make contact with Carl

Wiberg and would be followed later by a radioman and an explosives expert. He was provided with a false passport and the letterhead of an imaginary electrical-equipment firm, prepared by the BACH Section in London.

In the months preceding Jensen-Schmidt's departure, a courier chain was established through which radios, arms, and explosives were delivered to Carl Wiberg, who stored the equipment in several safe houses around Berlin. This underground channel also delivered cigarettes and coffee for the black market, now the primary economy of the city.

The Jensen-Schmidt mission differed from other OSS missions sent into Germany. It was an SO operation and, like IRON CROSS, had sabotage as well as espionage as its objective. Jensen-Schmidt's SO sponsors in Stockholm believed that saboteurs might be recruited from the thousands of foreign workers in Berlin. One of his instructions was to get weapons and explosives into their hands.

In March 1945, Jensen-Schmidt traveled from Göteborg, Sweden, to Skagen in Denmark on a Swedish trawler. He was then smuggled across the Danish border on the night of March 13 in the back of an enclosed truck, wedged among crates of fish and live lobster. By March 15, he was in Berlin and in touch with his contact, Carl Wiberg.

Including Jensen-Schmidt, OSS had five functioning agents in Berlin: Fritz Kolbe in the Foreign Office; Youri, the White Russian, inside the SD; and the two HAMMER agents in successful Joan-Eleanor contact.

In April, the radioman and explosives expert left Stockholm to join Jensen-Schmidt, carrying what were evidently regarded as essential accessories for their mission—false documents, cigarettes, and pornographic pictures.

Like the HAMMER team, Jensen-Schmidt lived through the ironies of Berlin in the spring of 1945. The intelligence network that he had created needed transportation. With the Allies bombing the city into a coarse-grained powder, with Russian troops hammering at the Berlin gates, Jensen-Schmidt found himself in a used-car lot dickering with a salesman over a battered Mercedes-Benz. As they haggled, he could hear the fire of heavy guns around the city. The sound was not supposed to alarm Berliners. The Nazi-controlled press had informed its readers that Wehrmacht batteries were practicing nearby.

Jensen-Schmidt was a rather effective agent until the bombing swelled to an intensity which forced him to spend most of his time in air-raid shelters. He had managed to recruit into his network a distinguished physician whose patients included Ribbentrop and Goebbels. He had smuggled out the intelligence obtained from the doctor and other sources in three successful courier runs to OSS Stockholm. As for the high explosives he had stashed away around Berlin, Allied bombers had made sabotage rather superfluous.

During the months in which he watched Berlin being relentlessly leveled, Jensen-Schmidt had once asked a Berliner: "Why does an entire nation choose to commit suicide for the sake of one lunatic?"

The man threw up his hands. "It's difficult to get the lunatic certified. He happens to be director of the asylum."

The last information which Jensen-Schmidt passed on to OSS was that SS Reichsführer Heinrich Himmler, whom Hitler had deposed as a traitor in the final days of the regime, and a pack of Himmler's minions had fled northwest toward Güstrow. Himmler, in disguise, was caught not far away at a British control point east of Hamburg. He committed suicide a few days later. Jensen-Schmidt also provided information on the whereabouts of Dr. Robert Ley, the drunkard chief of the German Labor Front, who had done so much to destroy the authentic trade-union movement in Germany.

Jensen-Schmidt hoped to be allowed to join in pursuit of these war criminals. Instead, he was advised to move west and get himself into American hands as quickly as possible before the Russians arrived. He was unaware that Allied armies had turned away from Berlin and headed south. He had rather looked forward to welcoming the Americans as their successful agent in the Nazi capital.

Jensen-Schmidt's long-awaited radioman and explosives expert never got farther than Kiel before they were overrun by the Allies, still carrying, presumably, their false papers, cigarettes, and pornography.

The only other attempted penetration out of Stockholm had been the Labor desk's Social Democrat, Herbert, who had never been heard from after being left at the German border. The British found Herbert, after V-E Day, in a Hamburg prison, awaiting execution.

Joe Gould had fielded five teams for the London Labor Division. HAMMER had reached the farthest in penetrating Germany, with an audacious drop into the enemy capital. The team had also proved the extraordinary worth of Joan-Eleanor as an instrument for clandestine communication. The agents' rewards were to be far off and few.

Paul Land and Toni Ruh had felt the anxiety and confusion of any Berliner in the last days of April 1945. They had been nearly overrun by tanks on April 21 while trying a Joan-Eleanor contact from the suburbs.

They were stunned to discover that the tanks were Russian. The civilian population moved about the city in dull resignation. No attempt was made at a mass exodus. Flight, even if attempted, was virtually impossible: tank barriers formed a steel ring around Berlin; rigid controls prevailed at every exit. Women and children, earlier evacuated to Silesia and Saxony, had returned as the Allies pressed in from east and west. People gathered on the outer rim of the city to escape the heaviest concentration of bombing at the core. Here they waited out the end.

The day after they had emptied their laundry bag for the Hermann Göring officer who had stopped them, the HAMMER agents received their last instructions from London. A coded message over the BBC directed one of them to remain in Berlin. The other was to cross the lines to the Americans. Paul, because his papers were stronger, particularly the Nazi party membership, was to break through. He reached the defense perimeter, but was turned back. He quickly returned to the city, since every available able body was being impressed into the defenses on Berlin's outskirts.

Two days later, Paul and Toni left their hideaway to check on the activities of an SS Panzer division posted in a vital part of town. They were accompanied by Paul's father; his brother-in-law, the war hero Otto; and two trusted neighbors. En route, they approached a bridge in the Neukölln area. A platoon of German soldiers was attempting to prevent some Russians from reaching the bridge. Paul and Toni tried to talk the Germans, mostly young fanatics, out of defending it. They refused and withdrew to the far end. But two men who deliberately tarried were easily overpowered and gratefully became prisoners.

The two HAMMER agents took the rifles from these two soldiers and began to fire on the Germans defending the far end of the bridge. Russian infantry circled around them and assumed that they too were defenders. They waved and yelled to the Russians to stop firing. The Russians finally understood and joined them.

An artillery blast heaved the bridge into the sky and chunks of it splashed into the water. The Russians cursed at their enemies, now safely insulated on the far side. But they were warm in their gratitude toward the six unexpected allies. A Russian captain wrote their names on a slip of paper with a notation that they had assisted the Red Army. He gave this document to Paul's father. The officer's men then relieved their new-found comrades of their weapons, their watches, and any other valuables. The following day, April 25, Paul Land and Toni Ruh turned themselves in to a Russian commander, telling him they were American intelligence officers.

They were sent to a Soviet counterespionage detachment where they were subjected to a harassing interrogation at the hands of a Captain Martov. Martov haughtily rejected their offer to provide information on the defenses of Berlin. He informed them that Soviet intelligence was quite capable of handling the Red Army's needs. The only thing they could tell the Russians of any value, he said, was if they knew where Hitler was.

Captain Martov then demanded to know how much the Americans were paying them. They answered that they received the salary of an American military man of equivalent rank, but that they had become involved to help destroy fascism, not for profit.

Captain Martov became enraged when they asked that he guarantee their safety from other Russians until they could be delivered into American hands. Didn't they understand that the Soviets were an army of liberation for all peoples, even Germans? Yes, they answered tactfully, they understood. But they had, in fact, seen Russian soldiers abusing Germans. Of course, they could understand why. Martov launched a blistering harangue against those who falsely accused the Red Army of misconduct, even outrageous charges of rape. If this vilification did not stop, he threatened, they would be treated as enemies of the Soviet Union.

Two months passed and the HAMMER agents were still in Russian captivity. During their confinement, they became friendly with a thirty-six-year-old Berliner named Kurt. He had returned to Berlin during the same moon period as they had and under highly similar circumstances. Kurt had been parachuted into Berlin after two years of agent training by the Russians. What troubled Land and Ruh most was how they were going to escape the Russian grip, when Kurt, who had served the Soviets, seemed to have equal difficulty in clearing himself.

At last, on June 16, they were driven over a bridge on the Mulde River near Leipzig and turned over to the U.S. Army's Sixty-ninth Division, and eventually reached the bosom of OSS. Ten days later, they were at the Saint-Germain Base D, outside Paris, being interrogated by the same Henry Sutton who had helped construct their cover stories in London.

Sutton seemed incredulous at seeing them again. The questioning was pointed and not entirely amicable. Sutton was particularly skeptical at their eagerness to return to England, though that was where their wives and children waited for them. They were, at bottom, still Communists,

Sutton knew. They had spent two unaccountable months with the Russians. How could Sutton be sure that they had not become double agents? One of them, he recalled later, "had the low cunning of a Czech." He referred to Toni Ruh, a native Berliner, for whom Sutton had helped invent the cover story of a Czech worker.

The two men had further difficulty obtaining re-entry visas from the British. Their return to England was delayed until the end of July 1945, six weeks after they had been recovered. Something had changed, a shift in tone that was unspoken but unmistakable. The unity born of common purpose, with which Joe Gould had appealed to them nine months before, had since evaporated. Ever since their return to the west, the treatment of their case seemed invariably to bog down in the issue of communism.

By the end of July, all of Joe Gould's agents had been accounted for except BUZZSAW and MALLET. The disappearance of MALLET particularly troubled Gould. Adolf Buchholz had been a favorite. At age thirty-one, the youngest of the Gould group, Buchholz was a man of enormous physical vitality and human warmth. His buoyant good humor had won the affection of all the OSS staff who had worked with him in London.

Before the Nazi takeover Buchholz had been a well-known physical-culture enthusiast in Berlin and sports director of the German metalworkers' union. He had long since won his anti-Nazi credentials in Germany by serving two and a half years at hard labor during the 1930s for treason. After his escape to England, he became the leader of the youth wing of the Free Germany Committee.

Buchholz was the last of Gould's agents to be dispatched. On April 10, he parachuted alone into a huge suburban park at Wannsee, about five miles southwest of Berlin, equipped with a Joan-Eleanor radio. Buchholz had been deliberately dropped during an air raid to draw attention from his arrival.

Two Joan-Eleanor flights had failed to contact Buchholz, and the war in Europe had ended with no word from him. After the German collapse, Calhoun Ancrum toured hospitals in Berlin looking for Buchholz, but to no avail. He was presumed dead.

Joe Gould was assigned, after V-E Day, to work with the Allied Military Government in Berlin. In August 1945, Gould was eating in a mess hall when a soldier informed him that some Russians wanted to see him in the foyer. There, between two Soviet soldiers, was a thin, drawn figure who nevertheless greeted Gould with sunny enthusiasm. One of the Russians gave Gould a slip to sign which read, "I have received Adolf Buchholz."

The man was easily seventy pounds lighter, but his spirit remained undaunted since Gould had last seen him. Gould fed Buchholz while the agent recounted his fate since bailing out of an A-26, more than four months before. He had fought with a ragtag local resistance group in Berlin, but had never found an opportunity to make his Joan-Eleanor rendezvous.

His true ordeal had begun after the war, because of a stroke of bad luck. Buchholz had entered Germany under cover as a Gestapo agent. As the Russians approached, he decided that a Gestapo medallion might be a hard item to explain. The Russians had seized Buchholz as he was trying to dispose of the medallion. He was taken to a prison camp a hundred miles to the east of Berlin. It had required nearly three months to talk his way back into American hands. After delays similar to those experienced by other OSS Communist agents, Adolf Buchholz eventually was returned to London.

The reluctance of the British to allow the HAMMER team, Adolf Buchholz, and other Communists to return to England was explained to OSS. The British complained that during their internment in England, some of these people had drawn up lists in their camps showing which prisoners were or were not Communists. This, the British contended, represented a form of reprehensible blacklisting. It was on these grounds, they said, that they resisted readmitting the Communists to their country.

OSS officers took the matter to the highest levels in England, arguing that the agents had been assured that they would be returned to the same conditions from which they had been recruited. The British retorted, in effect, that it was their decision as to who would or would not enter Great Britain. The matter dragged on for weeks, until the British, in the end, grudgingly allowed the Germans to return.

Though many of them hoped to continue serving OSS, the Communists were by now untouchables. An OSS officer writing on the final disposition of their case said: ". . . these men did render extremely valuable service to our organization during the hostilities period when they were dropped blind into enemy territory to accomplish secret intelligence missions. . . . Because of the political background of these men, there is serious doubt as to whether they could fit into our [postwar] German operations."

Bert Jolis, who had worked with anti-Communist labor leaders while Joe Gould had handled the Communists, still had one agent unaccounted for, when, on April 15, he received a message from a Ninth Army unit at Maastricht in Holland. They were holding a man who claimed to belong to Jolis's operation.

Youri Vinogradov's luck had held, but barely. After he had helped Michel Kedia and the other ethnic Russian leaders to meet Jolis in Switzerland, he had left Berlin himself. He had managed to travel to the western front and reached the American lines, where he faced the greatest danger since he had first penetrated Germany over six months before. He had to cross over as edgy GIs blazed away at him, ignoring his frantically shouted password. When he was finally allowed to surrender, army intelligence people refused to accept his story. Youri was clapped into an open prisoner-of-war cage, where he spent two days in the rain and without food.

When Youri did manage to convince the army to turn him over to the OSS detachment in Paris, Jolis met a man he barely recognized. Gone was the cocky intriguer. He now saw a frightened, haggard figure. Jolis gave the White Russian time to rest, eat well, and collect himself at the Saint-Germain villa.

Over the next few weeks, he found Youri obsessed with the idea of going to the United States. He had earned it, he pleaded. The Americans owed him this much. Jolis told Youri that it was not possible immediately. He should be patient and remain in Paris until something could be arranged.

For all his earlier suspicions of this once brash, faintly dishonorable fellow, Jolis now thought, here is a brave man who penetrated the inner sanctum of German intelligence. With the war coming to a close, Youri's intimate knowledge of the SD, particularly his association with Nazi operations against the Soviets, had priceless postwar value. He had performed a perilous, highly valuable function for the United States. And now, Jolis thought, he deserved to have his wish fulfilled. He also nominated Youri Vinogradov for the Silver Star.

Perhaps because he knew that he had never inspired complete trust in the Americans, Youri did not feel that he could now trust them. He hung on at the OSS compound for two months after the war's end. Then Youri melted into the Paris scene and no one at OSS ever heard from him again.

The agent who had parachuted first and stayed longest was Jupp Kappius, who had gone into Bochum in the Ruhr. Kappius's secret life ended on April 9, 1945. He was walking down a road toward Essen to keep a rendezvous with an agent when he found his way blocked by Volkssturm. They told him the road had been cut by the Americans. If he had to get through, the only safe way was via footpaths. He followed the paths until he was out of sight, then cut back to the main road. It was ominously empty. He reached a point where the road dipped under a railroad via-duct. There, he saw a parked tank. Kappius walked toward it, head erect, making as much noise as possible with his steel-tipped heels. A soldier peered out from behind the tank. Jupp Kappius heard his first American voice in eight months.

The G-2 officer to whom he was taken asked how long Kappius had been in Germany. The answer startled the man. When he learned how Kappius had arrived, his skepticism grew. Kappius was taken to the regi-mental commanding officer and told the American of the flimsy Volks-sturm roadblock up ahead, the location of nearby Panzer units, machine-gun emplacements, and bridges still intact. Kappius also provided an extensive list of anti-Nazis in the cities of the Ruhr whom the Americans could trust. Within days, Jupp Kappius was flown back to England.

In London, he was called on for one last service to OSS. There was, at war's end, an annoyed disbelief among the Allies that so many Germans claimed no knowledge of the Nazi death camps. Ten million had died in them, including nearly 6 million Jews. These German professions of ignorance were preposterous, nakedly self-serving, even insulting. The logistics alone of slaughter on so vast a scale ruled out secrecy.

Jupp Kappius was a fervent anti-Nazi, a man of reflexive honesty who had just returned after an extensive stay in the Reich. He could give OSS an objective account of what the ordinary German knew of Nazi atroci-ties.

Kappius pointed out that there had never been any mention of the concentration camps in the press or radio, the only legal sources of infor-mation available to the German people. Those who operated the camps were sworn to secrecy. Inmates who returned were few. Those who did come back were not in contact with the vast preponderance of obedient Germans.

Kappius noted that what people did hear about the death camps origi-nated with Allied propaganda organs. This information was regarded skeptically. The Germans had been through it all before—the atrocity stories of World War I, the lurid tales of the kaiser's soldiers bayoneting Belgian infants. It had all been proved a gross fabrication then. Allied reports of what went on in the camps won about the same credence in

Germany that similar stories would have received in the United States had German radio announced that Americans were systematically gassing millions of men, women, and children.

"People who wanted to know about the Nazi terror system could know and did know," he reported. But people would have to search out the truth. And it was asking too much of ordinary people, Kappius observed, to "really want to do or to know something which makes . . . them unhappy." Kappius concluded: ". . . only a few people in Germany were fully informed about concentration camps and Nazi atrocities, while quite a large proportion did not seem to know much about them, if anything at all."

Of course, none of the major Nazi slaughterhouses were located in the Ruhr, where Kappius had operated. These people would, therefore, not have been directly exposed to the camps. But the same would have been true for the majority of Germans.

Gary Van Arkel had investigated the question too. He left Switzerland after the fighting and drove to the Ruhr with a load of food to relieve the hardship of ISK people who had aided Jupp Kappius. He took the opportunity to question these anti-Nazi Socialists on the matter of the camps. Of each of them, the American asked, "Did you know what went on in the concentration camps?" In every instance these confirmed foes of the system gave virtually identical answers. They knew the camps existed, but assumed they were places of confinement and not of extermination.

Jupp Kappius and his wife, Anne, who had served as his courier, returned to live in Germany after the war. He continued his involvement in Socialist politics and was eventually looked upon as a true enough German patriot to be elected to the state legislature of North Rhine–Westphalia.

When Mary Bancroft again saw Hans Gisevius, his hair had turned white. He would sweat profusely whenever he talked of the conspiracy of July 20. But in those first weeks after his escape to Switzerland in January 1945, it was important that he talk. Dulles wanted it all down. The cables to Washington were burdened for days with the details of the plot, its members, and their fate, the catharsis of Gisevius's memory.

Then it was over. He was to be treated with fairness and consideration. Mary Bancroft was again conscripted to keep him happy with the English translation of his book, though its anticipated ending had to be painfully altered. But Gisevius was puzzled that he no longer enjoyed his former entrée at Herrengasse 23. Allen Dulles, who at his peak was running one hundred agents from Switzerland, had moved on.

Mary Bancroft told Dr. Jung that she and Gisevius had somehow lost their capacity for psychic communication. "He goes to the wrong place," she complained, "phones at the wrong time." Jung suggested that conspiring against the Third Reich had given Hans Gisevius his direction. When the plot failed, he had lost his psychological bearings, just as bees become disoriented when the queen dies.

The psychiatrist had a long session with Gisevius and formed an opinion which doubtless would have saddened the German. Jung concluded that it was just as well the plot had failed. Men like Gisevius and Count Schenk von Stauffenberg, the officer who planted the bomb at Rastenburg, were, in Jung's view, only after what Hitler had: power. "They were," he said, "like a couple of lions fighting over a hunk of raw meat."

After the war, Hans Bernd Gisevius performed his final service for his fellow conspirators, an obligation which he felt he owed to those who had lost their lives. At the war-crimes trials, it began to appear that the ring of conspirators was far wider than anyone had expected. One Nazi defendant after another sought to link himself to the anti-Hitler resistance. Hans Gisevius spent days on the stand as a prosecution witness, identifying those who had or had not been actual parties to the plot. It was a fairly simple issue, as Gisevius well knew. Virtually all of the true conspirators were dead.

After the war, his book was published, including an edition in English entitled *To the Bitter End*. He lived in the United States for a time, hoping to establish himself in research and writing with one of the American foundations. Things never seemed to work out. "He always got the runaround," his friend Mary Bancroft noted. He was, it seemed, still a suspect figure. He returned to Europe, where he lived in Switzerland and Germany and continued to write until his death.

Fritz Molden's association with Allen Dulles was to continue on an unanticipated level. In that first summer of peace in Europe in six years, Molden had been invited to the home of a Swiss publisher, a friend also of Allen Dulles. There he met Joan Dulles, the daughter of the American intelligence chief. The young woman, just out of college, had brought two young cousins to Europe, children of Dulles's sister, Eleanor. Eleanor Dulles was then en route to Vienna to join the staff of the U.S. Commission for Austria. Fritz was returning home to Vienna, too. It was congenial that they all travel together.

Joan Dulles became Fritz Molden's first wife. Back in Vienna, he went to work as secretary to Karl Gruber, who, with Fred Mayer, had liberated Innsbruck, and who had been named Austria's foreign minister. Later, Molden went into journalism. Later still, he established one of the eminent publishing houses in the German-speaking world. His partner on the mission to Vienna, Ernst Lemberger, pursued a distinguished diplomatic career, during which he served as Austrian ambassador to the United States.

Fritz Kolbe's last journey from the Foreign Office in Berlin to Allen Dulles in Bern had ended on a minor key. Dulles had been wrapped up in negotiations for the surrender of German troops in northern Italy. Kolbe's reports from the Nazi capital were suddenly passé. Still, the passage of time would place his achievements in correct perspective. For over eighteen months, beginning in August 1943, Fritz Kolbe passed over sixteen hundred secret documents to OSS. He made five trips from Berlin to Bern and was never detected. The extraordinary range, quantity, and quality of his material led Allen Dulles to declare Fritz Kolbe an "intelligence officer's dream . . . undoubtedly, one of the best secret agents any intelligence service ever had."

Kolbe's services had initially been turned down by the British in Bern. His work for Dulles was long viewed by British intelligence officers with both scorn and anxiety. These naïve Americans, they feared, had probably been taken in by a double agent who could threaten Britain's operations in Switzerland. James Angleton, as a young OSS counterintelligence officer, remembered seeing stacks of Kolbe's material treated with casual disregard in London because it came from so spurious a source. The sheer volume of the material, it seemed to the British, taxed one's credulity. In the end, MI-6 recanted and graciously rated Fritz Kolbe the best single intelligence agent of the war.

With the war over, Dulles became concerned about the reception which the Germans might accord a man who had devoted himself so wholly to his country's defeat. Still, Fritz Kolbe insisted on returning home. He was determined to be a witness against his old Foreign Office chief, Karl Ritter, at the war crimes trials. He felt deeply that if Germany were to cleanse herself of the disease of Nazism, its people would have to learn the full depravity of those by whom they had been led. The trials, in Kolbe's judgment, were just and necessary.

What Kolbe learned about Ritter during this process must have been a revelation. Ritter told his interrogators of his intense dislike for his boss, Joachim von Ribbentrop. That man was truly a war criminal, Ritter agreed. As for himself, he had repeatedly requested permission to retire, but Ribbentrop had refused. Indeed, he had been plotting his escape in order to join the Allies since September 1944. "I am," he pleaded, "not a war criminal. I am a harmless old man of sixty-three, who is now anxious to help the Americans." He complained bitterly of his confinement. Though he dearly loved to play bridge, all the Nazi prisoners had only one deck of cards among them, worn and soiled with use, and he was not even given any socks.

After the trials, OSS decided that it owed something special to the centerpiece of Dulles's crown jewels. Peter Sichel, the young Seventh Army OSS Detachment finance officer, was charged with looking after Kolbe's well-being. To lure him out of Germany, for his own sake, Kolbe was offered an undisclosed but substantial sum of money to establish himself in the United States. Kolbe balked at first at the idea of material reward for what he had done, but finally yielded and went to live in New York.

At the tag end of the war, Peter Sichel had tended his own family interests as well. He had watched with mingled pleasure and anxiety as American forces approached the German city of Mainz. The ancient river port had been, since 1857, the seat of the Sichel wine business, which the family had abandoned when life under Hitler became untenable for German Jews. Anticipating the potential fate of a quarter of a million bottles of wine as the Germans fled and the victors took over, Sichel asked for permission to proceed to Mainz to protect the warehouses. His object was to get the Sichel property under the trusteeship of the Allied Military Government.

Sichel was granted permission and enlisted his fellow German-American, Carl Muecke, and another Seventh Army OSS officer to drive with him to Mainz soon after the city was taken. They found the property, with a sign on it still reading "H. Sichel Söhne." The Nazis had shown enough business acumen to continue trading on a good name. Another sign ordered trespassers to keep out. An old German watchman tried to bar them from entering, belligerently pointing to the warning. "It says Sichel and Sons, doesn't it?" Sichel asked, looking out over the property with a serene possessiveness. "Well, *Ich bin ein Sohn.* Open the Goddamned gate!"

Months after Sichel had set up Fritz Kolbe in New York City, the German contacted the OSS official and said that he wanted to return to Germany. While in New York, Kolbe had run across an old acquaintance from his diplomatic career who interested him in a business venture. The secret agent who had outwitted the world's most thoroughgoing police state, who had stolen some of the hottest secrets of the war from under the Nazis' noses, and who had schemed his way across foreign borders to freedom, had been promptly bilked of all his money in America.

Kolbe was embarrassed but uncomplaining. He told Sichel that he should not have accepted the money in the first place. It was silly to believe that anyone was going to harm him in Germany. His conscience was clear. He wanted to go home. OSS agreed. Sichel again helped him, this time, to obtain a German dealership in powered hand saws.

Fritz Kolbe earned a decent living in Germany, but forever felt a subtle ostracism. He took comfort in some favorite lines by Rudolf Pechel, a fellow German foe of Nazism: "It remains unimportant that the resistance failed to reach its goal and that the surviving members of the resistance are today as lonely as they were under Hitler. Each great idea and each courageous deed bears the fruit in itself. We did not expect any thanks."

XIX

Debriefing

✛ ✛ ✛

At 2:41 A.M., May 7, 1945, in a small schoolhouse in Rheims, General Alfred Jodl, a whole-souled Hitler loyalist, rose to speak. "With this signature the German people and the German armed forces are, for better or worse, delivered into the hands of the victors. . . ." Jodl had signed the instrument of surrender, 2076 days after the Germans first rolled across the Polish frontier.

OSS agents who had penetrated Germany enjoyed a brief final flurry of influence. They were eagerly sought out to help Allied military governments find worthy Germans to help rebuild the country and to track down Nazis and possible war criminals. A curious shift in the attitude of the Americans toward their erstwhile enemies complicated the task. The change was particularly apparent and disquieting to two American Jews with roots in Europe.

Long months before, when Peter Viertel and Peter Sichel had been recruiting German agents from the POW cages for the Seventh Army, they had encountered strong skepticism among regular army people. A simplistic "kill-them-Krauts" mentality left little room for making political distinctions among German prisoners. The two Americans, with their personal knowledge of Germany, had argued that not all Germans should be judged alike. They were dealing with good and bad people, and to condemn all indiscriminately would be shortsighted.

Then, with Germany conquered, they found their American comrades quickly seduced. The conventional wisdom now ran: these people are clean, hard-working, efficient, respectful. The Germans are just like us, unlike the French, or Italians, or British, or Poles, or whatever other people had offended American standards of hygiene or industry. Viertel and Sichel now found themselves arguing against the assumption that every fawning German could be trusted.

The attitudes of the vanquished disturbed some of the recovered agents as well. Two men from Joe Gould's group of Communist recruits reported after months inside Germany:

> . . . we have made observations which in our opinion may not be without importance for the further treatment of the German people. The first is that the tendency exists in the largest part of the population to shift all the guilt onto the Nazis, while they consider themselves guiltless, or even in case they recognize themselves as guilty in part, yet they think that this has been already atoned for by all the misfortune which has come upon them. As a further observation we believe that we can show that a large part of the population, although it has cut itself loose from Nazism as a political leading force, is very far from having freed itself from the ideology of Nazism and militarism. We consider this observation important because the danger of a Nazi underground movement still exists, and can create a certain basis for itself by joining on to the Nazi ideology in the minds of the population.

Then the postwar value of the agents ended, and it was time to demobilize spies along with soldiers. The fear among OSS officers that their homeward-bound German agents might suffer retaliation proved exaggerated. It was true after World War I that Germans who had collaborated with the Allies were treated as pariahs. But the Nazis had so debased German values that concepts of patriotism and decency had become twisted almost beyond recognition.

OSS officers went into the Reich to pay off a remaining debt of honor to those agents who had risked not only their lives but their reputations by their cooperation with the Americans. Al Ulmer in Austria, Peter Sichel in Germany, Gary Van Arkel from Switzerland, and others saw that former agents did not lack for food or housing; they pressed occupation officials to find work for agents and looked after the wives and children of those killed or missing.

Some agents did collect on the unauthorized pledge which had lured them to accept the risks in Germany. Belgians recruited by Ray Brittenham who wanted to emigrate to the United States were allowed to do so with a little assistance from their former employers. A few were given funds for an American education, in something of an unofficial GI Bill.

In England, Lieutenant Commander Steve Simpson continued to work with his RCA associates to improve the Joan-Eleanor system for possible use in the Pacific war. Simpson noted, "It would have been a great blow to the Japs—if they hadn't been atomized first."

The redoubtable privates who had devised the agents' cover stories in the BACH Section, Lazare Teper and his assistant, Henry Sutton, were both rewarded near the end of the conflict by elevation to the rank of second lieutenant.

When the European fighting was over, Mike Burke, Rob Thompson, Hans Tofte, and others who had directed London operations drafted Tomsen, the Norwegian chef of Claridge's, for a farewell party. They had him prepare a list of necessities and gave it to that *nonpareil* of unofficial procurement, Captain Eddy Miller, the OSS London supply officer. At the top of a long list was "100 eggs." Miller disappeared for two days. When he returned with the order fulfilled, the officers threw themselves a party which some were still recalling fondly over thirty years later.

Five months after the last agent had been dropped into Germany, a rough cycle of justice was completed. In the docket of war criminals at Nuremberg stood the strange and saturnine chief of Nazi security, Dr. Ernst Kaltenbrunner, whose domains of terror had included the Gestapo. The case against Kaltenbrunner had been developed under General Donovan, who served for a time as chief of prosecution at the trials. Kaltenbrunner was hanged on October 16, 1946. The blood of hundreds of thousands was on his hands, but among the evidence which most firmly condemned him was Kaltenbrunner's personal order for the execution of OSS agents at Mauthausen.

During World War II, OSS had nearly two hundred secret agents inside the Third Reich. Its operatives were infiltrated into most militarily significant cities: Berlin, Munich, Bremen, Mainz, Düsseldorf, Mannheim, Stuttgart, Essen, Regensburg, Kassel, Karlsruhe, Vienna, and over sixty other cities. Casualties had been heavy, but not inordinate. Of the total, thirty-six agents were killed, captured, or missing. The region of the Redoubt, however imaginary as a battleground, proved a treacherous snare for spies. Over half of the agents infiltrated there were lost.

Whether the secret penetration of Germany shortened the war by a day or an hour cannot be separated out from the myriad ingredients of victory.

Through an agent like Fritz Kolbe, the Allies had a pipeline to the highest German secrets, second only to Ultra. In Hans Bernd Gisevius, the Allies had a virtual day-by-day knowledge of the progress of the conspiracy against Hitler. In failing to exploit the anti-Nazism which Gisevius and his co-conspirators represented, the Allies may have let slip the best hope for an earlier ending of the war.

The reports of OSS agents inside the Reich contributed to the mosaic of information which enabled decisive attacks on V-weapons sites, oil fields, and synthetic-fuel plants. Their intelligence-gathering led to the destruction of German jets on the ground before they could extend the war in the skies. When Allied bombers moved, artillery spoke, or troops marched, it was often toward objectives revealed by the heroism and craft of American spies operating within Germany.

These agents exploited Austria's growing discomfort at being part of Germany, and were responsible for reducing the potential for extended bloodletting in that uneasy province of the Reich. They persuaded local military commanders in Austria that surrender was an act of humanity and sense and that to fight on was madness.

The rounding up of key Nazis and their replacement by decent democratic leaders proceeded far more effectively where OSS agents had operated than where Allied military governments lacked reliable, first-hand knowledge of local personalities.

The development of Joan-Eleanor alone stood as a giant stride in clandestine communication and bore the seeds of the incredibly sensitive electronic devices that would dominate much of the intelligence field in the next generation.

In the beginning, it had seemed near suicidal to pit an intrepid handful against the institutionalized terror of the Third Reich. Years later, remembering their farewells to agents departing for Germany, OSS veterans would repeatedly voice a common refrain: "Of course, we never expected to see them again."

America's entrance into secret warfare had been a late but brilliant flowering. The United States achieved in less than four years what other nations had developed over centuries. The recruitment, training, documentation, and dispatch of nearly two hundred agents into the most terrifying police state ever known marked the highest peak of proficiency achieved by OSS during the war and demonstrated a capacity for secret warfare equal to that of any other nation. The performance was acknowledged by British intelligence—never sanguine about penetrating Germany—as remarkable. OSS had infiltrated three times as many agents out of England alone into the Reich as had the British. The American architects of the German operations later regretted only that they had not started earlier, when the harvest of intelligence could have been even richer. The piercing of Nazi Germany clearly ranks among the great espionage triumphs of World War II.

The German operations also provided intimations of the coming cold war. The Russians had balked at allowing A-26s to land on territory under their control, which would have vastly increased OSS's capacity to penetrate deeply into the Reich. The Soviets had only grudgingly yielded up American agents recovered by their side. OSS, for its part, had vacillated over the use of Communist agents, finally used them, then immediately after the war became uncomfortable with them.

In Berlin, Dick Helms recalled that as OSS officers helped prepare evidence for the war crimes trials, they were already keeping one eye on the Soviets. This preoccupation with communism would become virtually the full-time function of the American intelligence agency which Helms would one day head.

After Germany surrendered, Allen Dulles struck a bargain with General Reinhard Gehlen, former chief of the Wehrmacht anti-Soviet espionage operation, under which the United States acquired Gehlen, his staff, and his valuable Russian files.

Colonel Howard Chapin, who had overseen OSS operations from Italy, had gone back to Washington temporarily after V-E Day. When he rejoined the 2677th OSS Regiment at Salzburg, in the summer of 1945, one of his subordinates recalled the group's astonishment when Chapin told them that their next target was the Russians. In Vienna, soon after V-E Day, agents who had served OSS were directed to help the Americans find out what the Russians were up to in the Soviet zone.

This nascent hostility of East against West plucked General Donovan's child from the brink of extinction. It had been close. On September 20, 1945, barely a month after World War II ended, President Harry S. Truman recognized OSS's achievements in a letter to General Donovan of glacial impersonality: "I want to take this occasion to thank you for the capable leadership you have brought to a vital wartime activity in your capacity as Director of Strategic Services. You may well find satisfaction in the achievements of the Office and take pride in your own contribution to them."

Truman, wanting no part of a peacetime "Gestapo," then proceeded to abolish the OSS, scattering its few remaining functions between the departments of State and War. These orphaned activities and a handful of OSS alumni held on like spores, dormant but alive, awaiting a climate in which they might germinate again.

They did not have long to wait. By 1947, President Truman felt the chill winds blowing from the east and created the Central Intelligence Agency. At its heart were former officers of the OSS, many of whom had matured as intelligence professionals through the operations to penetrate Nazi Germany.

In August 1945, a young man and woman set out with two guides to climb a glacial massif in the Stubaier Alps, southwest of Innsbruck. The man knew where in the mountains he could find a valuable cache. He was Franz Weber, the Austrian who had led Fred Mayer and Hans Wynberg down from the Sulztaler Ferner seven months before on a madly careening sled. The woman was Annie Liederkirche, his fiancée. Weber had been able to lead the GREENUP Mission down the mountain slopes, but he needed the guides to find his way back among the icy peaks to his objective.

They started out in a scarred, prewar Volkswagen from the village of Oberperfuss, where Annie's mother had hidden the GREENUP agents in the attic of her inn. They went by the site of the Messerschmitt plant at Kematen, where Fred Mayer had posed as a French conscript worker, then past Zirl, where the American 103d Division exchanged its last fire with the enemy before Innsbruck fell.

They turned south and felt the ancient engine strain as they climbed the Ötz Valley road to Längenfeld. There, Weber turned onto the unpaved road that wound steeply up to Greis, the village where the team had successfully deceived the first civilians they had encountered and had borrowed the sled from the Bürgermeister. Beyond Greis the dirt road narrowed to a trail twisting up into the slopes. They left the car.

The weather at this time of year in the mountains was curiously ambivalent. Where they walked in the sun, the air was warm and the ground soft and wet from melting snows. When they turned into the shadows of the mountainsides, the snow became crusted and the chill air intimated the alpine winter.

Weber squinted up into the skies from which he had parachuted the February before. He scanned the mountain crags and tried to orient himself. He conferred from time to time with the guides, and within less than an hour of their arrival atop the Sulztaler Ferner, Weber had found what he sought, a treasure of pure silk in the parachutes they had hidden.

In September 1945, Franz Weber and Annie Liederkirche were married in the mosque-domed church of Oberperfuss. The bride's gown was silk, cut from the parachutes they had recovered from the alpine snows.

Missions

✠ ✠ ✠

Bruce, David: Commanding Officer, OSS European Theater of Operations
Casey, William J.: Chief, Secret Intelligence, ETO
Pratt, George O.: Director, Division of Intelligence Procurement

CHAUFFEUR
Dehandtshutter, Michel*
Renaix, André*

CHISEL
Macht, Karl*

CROCUS
Meisel, Hilde

DOCTOR
Blonttrock, Lucien
Smets, Jean

DOWNEND
Kappius, Anne
Kappius, Jupp

*An asterisk indicates a pseudonym.

HAMMER
Land, Paul
Ruh, Toni

LUXE
Appenzell, Ferdi*
Lindau, Leon*

MALLET
Buchholz, Adolf

MARTINI
Adrian*

PAINTER
Flour, François
Van Dyck, Emil

RAGWEED
Drucker, Willi*

OUT OF FRANCE

IRON CROSS
Bank, Aaron (leader)

RUPPERT
Vinogradov, Youri*

SEVENTH ARMY DETACHMENT
Hyde, Henry B.: Chief, Secret Intelligence
Ada*
Emily*
Maria*

OUT OF ITALY

Chapin, Howard: Chief, Secret Intelligence, Central Europe
McCulloch, John B.: German-Austrian Desk, Bari
Ulmer, Alfred C.: German-Austrian Desk

DEADWOOD
Pfluger, Hermann*

DILLON
Fiechter, Ernst
Lippe, Karl*

Pavlovich, Miles (leader)
Prester, Julio
Ruthi, Viktor*

DUPONT
Ebbing, Ernst*
Graf, Anton*
Huppmann, Felix*
Taylor, John H. (leader)

GREENUP
Mayer, Frederick (leader)
Weber, Franz
Wynberg, Hans

OUT OF SWEDEN

Erickson, Eric
Jensen-Schmidt, Hennings
Herbert*

OUT OF SWITZERLAND

Dulles, Allen: Chief, OSS Switzerland
Van Arkel, Gerhard (Gary): Labor Desk, Bern

Gisevius, Hans Bernd

HOMESPUN
Franckenstein, Joseph
Koenigsreuter, Lothar*

Kolbe, Fritz

MAIER RING
Issikides, Barbara
Maier, Heinrich (leader)
Messner, Franz Josef

Molden, Fritz

Interviews

✛ ✛ ✛

(With OSS affiliation and present occupation)

Allen, Harper, B-24 pilot: insurance executive.

Ancrum, Calhoun, Joan-Eleanor operator: clergyman.

Angleton, James, OSS Counterintelligence Branch, London: CIA officer; retired.

Balaguer, Romeo, Seventh Army OSS Detachment: banker; retired.

Bancroft, Mary, OSS Bern: journalist, author.

Bank, Aaron, leader IRON CROSS Mission: founder, Green Berets, U.S. Army; retired.

*Becu, Omar, secretary, International Transport Workers Federation.

Boyd, Ann Willets, Seventh Army OSS Detachment: novelist.

Brittenham, Raymond, leader, ESPINETTE Missions: senior vice-president, International Telephone and Telegraph Company.

*Bross, John, OSS London: CIA officer; retired.

Bruce, David, commanding officer, OSS European Theater of Operations: diplomat; deceased.

Burke, Michael, deputy operations officer, Division of Intelligence Procurement, OSS London: former president, New York Yankees; president, Madison Square Garden.

*An asterisk indicates a telephone interview.

Cannoot, Ferdinand, chief, ATHOS, Belgian Secret Service: engineer, industrialist.

Casey, William J., chief, Secret Intelligence, OSS London: former chairman, Securities and Exchange Commission; attorney.

*Circe (pseudonym), secret agent, Milan: retired.

Cline, Ray S., Research and Analysis, OSS Washington: former deputy director, CIA; director of Studies, Center for Strategic and International Studies.

Colby, William E., OSS Operational Group Command: former CIA director; attorney.

Copeland, Miles, OSS Counterintelligence Branch: former CIA officer; private consultant.

*Doering, Otto C., Jr., OSS executive officer: attorney.

Drucker, Willi (pseudonym), member, DOWNEND Mission: former municipal police chief, West Germany; retired.

Ebbing, Ernst (pseudonym), member, DUPONT Mission: journalist.

Eidlitz, Johannes, Austrian resistance movement: chief editor, Verlag Molden, Vienna.

Fellinger, Barbara Issikides, Austrian resistance movement: pianist; retired.

Fleischer, Henry, 2677th Regiment, OSS Bari: labor public relations.

*Gold, Jay, Research and Analysis, OSS London: writer.

Goldberg, Arthur J., chief, OSS Labor Branch: former secretary of labor; former associate justice, U.S. Supreme Court; former U.S. ambassador to the U.N.; attorney.

Gould, Joseph, Labor Division, OSS London: public relations.

Grell, William, Belgian desk, OSS London: hotel manager; retired.

Grimm, Kurt, Austrian resistance movement: banker, Vienna.

Gruber, Karl, Austrian resistance movement: former Austrian ambassador to the United States; former Austrian foreign minister; retired.

Haass, Walter, 2677th Regiment, OSS Bari: lighting industry executive.

*Hayden, Sterling, OSS Italy: actor; author.

Helms, Richard M., OSS London: former CIA director; business consultant.

Hoguet, Peter, Seventh Army OSS Detachment: executive, Marcona Company.

Hood, Cordelia, OSS Switzerland: CIA.

Houston, Lawrence, OSS Cairo: former CIA general counsel; retired.

Hyde, Henry B., chief, Secret Intelligence, Seventh Army OSS Detachment: attorney.

Jolis, Albert, Labor Desk, OSS Paris: diamond merchant.

Jungk, Robert, journalist, Switzerland: author.

Karlow, Peter, Oral Intelligence unit, OSS New York: former CIA officer; private consultant.

Käs, Ferdinand, Austrian resistance movement: colonel of Gendarmerie, Austrian Ministry of the Interior.

Katz, Milton, deputy chief, Secret Intelligence, OSS London: director, International Legal Studies, Harvard.

Kurz, Edmund, Labor Division, OSS London: former professor, Queens College; retired.

Laverge, Jan, OSS, Holland: tobacco company executive.

Legradi, Helene, Austrian resistance movement: director, Austrian Bureau of East West Trade.

Lowenstein, Dyno, 2677th Regiment, OSS Bari: Pictograph Corporation, New York City.

Mayer, Frederick, leader, GREENUP Mission: former official, Voice of America; retired.

*McCulloch, John, German-Austrian section, 2677th Regiment, OSS Bari: president, English Speaking Union.

Miller, Gerald, chief, Secret Operations, OSS London: former CIA official; retired.

Molden, Fritz, Austrian resistance movement and OSS agent: publisher, Verlag Molden, Vienna.

*Morgan, Edward, journalist, commentator.

Morgan, Henry, S. chief, Censorship and Documentation Section, OSS Washington: financier, Morgan Stanley and Company.

Muecke, Carl, Seventh Army OSS Detachment: federal judge.

*Murphy, James, chief, OSS Counterintelligence Branch; attorney.

Oakes, John B., OSS Counterintelligence Branch: senior editor, *New York Times*.

Pauley, Albert, member, RUBENS Mission: Sabena Air Lines executive; retired.

Perry, Hart, 2677th Regiment, OSS Bari: president, SoGen-Swiss International Corporation.

Pratt, George, chief, Division of Intelligence Procurement, OSS London: international public-works developer; retired.

Primbs, Dr. Max, Kreisleiter, Innsbruck, Austria: surgeon, Munich.

Reddick, Willis, Research and Development Section, OSS London: printer, retired.

Roman, Howard, OSS Counterintelligence Branch: former CIA officer; author.

Roosevelt, Kermit, chief historian of the *War Report*, OSS: former CIA officer; public relations.

Sichel, Peter, finance officer, Seventh Army OSS Detachment: former CIA officer; H. Sichel Sons, wines.

Simpson, Stephen H., Jr., Communications Branch, OSS London: president, Southwest Sound and Electronics, Inc., San Antonio, Texas.

Steiner, Herbert, Austrian resistance movement: director, Archives Center of the Austrian Resistance, Vienna.

Strahle, Carl, Cover and Documentation Section, OSS London: printer.

Sutton, Henry, BACH Section, OSS London: former CIA officer; deceased.

Teper, Lazare, chief, BACH Section, OSS London: director of research, International Ladies' Garment Workers' Union.

Thalberg, Hans, Austrian resistance movement: Austrian ambassador to Switzerland.

Thompson, Robert E. S., Operations Office, Division of Intelligence Procurement, OSS London: environmental consultant.

Tofte, Hans, deputy chief, Division of Intelligence Procurement, OSS London: former CIA officer; retired.

Turano, Anthony, Air Dispatch Section, OSS London: photographer.

Turnbull, William, Cover and Documentation Section, OSS London: real-estate consultant.

Ulmer, Alfred C., Jr., German-Austrian section, OSS Bari: former CIA officer; Lombard, Odier et Cie., Geneva.

Van Arkel, Gerhard P., Labor Desk, OSS Bern: attorney.

Van Dyck, Orpha Gresham, WAC sergeant, OSS London; retired.

Vanwelkenhuyzen, Jean, director, Centre de Recherches et d'Etudes Historiques de la Seconde Guerre Mondiale.

Viertel, Peter, Seventh Army OSS Detachment: screenwriter; novelist.

Vujnovich, George, 2677th Regiment, OSS Bari: aircraft-parts manufacturer.

Watt, Richard, OSS Labor Division: attorney.

Weber, Franz, member GREENUP Mission: agricultural association representative, Innsbruck, Austria.

*Wilson, Thomas, Labor Division, OSS London: administrative law judge, National Labor Relations Board; retired.

Wolf, David, Mauthausen inmate: restaurateur, New York City.

*Work, J. R., Cover and Documentation Section, OSS London: commercial artist; retired.

CORRESPONDENCE RECEIVED

Bell, Dana, 1361 Audiovisual Squadron, U.S. Air Force.

de Caumont, Madeleine Sada, French resistance movement.

Foot, M. R. D., historian, former officer, Special Air Service.

Hanauer, Bernard, Resistance and Psyops Committee, The Reserve Forces Association, London.

Hinsley, F. H., Faculty of History, Cambridge.

Joll, James, The London School of Economics and Political Science.

Lockhart, John Bruce, British Secret Intelligence Service.

Roselli, Jean-Pierre, French resistance movement.
Templer, Sir Gerald, Secret Operations, executive.
Trevor-Roper, Hugh, Regius Professor of Modern History, Oxford.
Wynberg, Hans, member, GREENUP Mission.

Glossary

✠ ✠ ✠

Abwehr: secret intelligence, counterintelligence, and sabotage service of the
    German General Staff.
Anschluss: political union, particularly of Germany and Austria in 1938.
BACH: Cover-story section of OSS London.
Belgian Sûreté: Belgian intelligence service.
COI: Coordinator of Information, original designation of OSS.
DGER: Direction Générale des Etudes et Recherches, a French intelligence
    unit.
DIP: Division of Intelligence Procurement, unit of OSS London in charge of
    German penetration.
ETO: European Theater of Operations.
Feldwebel: German army sergeant.
Führerhauptquartier: Hitler's headquarters.
Gauleiter: highest Nazi party official in a "Gau," in effect, a provincial governor.
Gestapo: "Geheime Staatspolizei," the secret police, under the SS.
G-2: intelligence section of U.S. army units.
ISK: Internationalen Sozialistischen Kampfbundes, an offshoot of the German
    Socialist Party.
ITWF: International Transport Workers Federation.
Maquis: the French resistance, named for a thorny bush found in Corsica.
MI-5: British domestic counterintelligence service.

MI-6: British secret intelligence service.

MO: Morale Operations, OSS propaganda branch.

O5: Austrian military resistance organization.

OWI: Office of War Information, conducted U.S. propaganda operations.

POEN: Provisorische Oesterreichische Nationalkomite, Austrian Provisional National Committee, Austrian resistance organization.

R and A: OSS Research and Analysis Branch.

RSHA: Reichssicherheitshauptamt, the Nazi state security service, incorporating the Gestapo and SD.

SA: Sturmabteilung, Nazi assault detachment, or storm troopers.

SD: Sicherheitsdienst, the intelligence and counterintelligence wing of the SS.

SHAEF: Supreme Headquarters Allied Expeditionary Forces.

SI: OSS Secret Intelligence branch.

SIS: British Secret Intelligence Service, same as MI-6.

SO: OSS Secret Operations branch.

SOE: Special Operations, Executive; British organization to aid resistance organizations.

SS: Schutzstaffel, guard detachment; the military, political, and police organs of the Nazi party.

Totenkopfverbände: death's head detachments; SS element which ran the concentration camps.

Ultra: Code name for messages obtained by decoding the German Enigma ciphers.

Volkssturm: the German home guard.

Waffen SS: military units of the SS.

Wehrmacht: the German armed forces.

X-2: OSS counterintelligence branch.

XX Committee: MI-5 group controlling double agents.

Bibliography

✣ ✣ ✣

GENERAL WORKS

Alcorn, Robert Hayden. *No Banner, No Bands.* New York: David McKay Co., 1965.

———.*No Bugles for Spies.* New York: David McKay Co., 1962.

Alsop, Stewart, and Braden, Thomas. *Sub Rosa: The OSS and American Espionage.* New York: Reynal & Hitchcock Co., 1946.

Ambrose, Stephen E. *Eisenhower and Berlin, 1945: The Decision to Halt at the Elbe.* New York: W. Norton & Co., 1967.

Andersen Hartvig. *The Dark City.* New York: Rinehart Press, 1954.

Bazna, Elyesa, and Nogly, Hans. *I Was Cicero.* New York: Harper & Row, 1962.

Best, S. Payne. *The Venlo Incident.* London: Hutchinson Publishing Group, 1949.

Borsdorf, Ulrich, and Niethammer, Lutz. *Zwischen Befreiung und Besatzung.* Wuppertal, Federal Republic of Germany: Peter Hammer Verlag, 1976.

Bowyer, Michael J. F., and Sharp, C. Martin. *Mosquito.* London: Faber & Faber Ltd., 1967.

Brook-Shepherd, Gordon. *The Anschluss.* Philadelphia and New York: J. B. Lippincott Co., 1963.

———. *The Austrian Odyssey.* London: Macmillan Publishers, 1957.

Brown, Anthony Cave. *Bodyguard of Lies.* New York: Harper & Row, 1975.

Brown, Anthony Cave, ed. *The Secret War Report of the OSS.* New York: Berkley Publishing Corp., 1976.

Burns, James MacGregor. *Roosevelt: The Soldier of Freedom.* New York: Harcourt Brace Jovanovich, 1970.

Churchill, Winston S. *Memoirs of the Second World War.* Boston: Houghton Mifflin Co., 1959.

Cline, Ray S. *Secrets, Spies and Scholars.* Washington, D.C.: Acropolis Books Ltd., 1976.

Collier, Basil. *The Battle of the V-Weapons.* New York: William Morrow & Co., 1965.

Crankshaw, Edward. *Gestapo.* London: Putnam & Co., 1956.

Downes, Donald. *The Scarlet Thread.* New York: British Book Centre, 1953.

Dulles, Allen W. *Germany's Underground.* New York: Macmillan Publishing Co., 1947.

————. *The Secret Surrender.* London: George Weidenfeld & Nicolson Ltd., 1967.

Foot, M. R. D. *SOE in France.* London: Her Majesty's Stationery Office, 1966.

————. *Resistance.* New York: McGraw-Hill Book Co., 1977.

Ford, Corey, and MacBain, Alastair. *Cloak and Dagger.* New York: Random House, Inc., 1945.

Frischauer, Willi. *The Man Who Came Back: The Story of Otto John.* London: Frederick Muller Ltd., 1958.

Gisevius, Hans. *To the Bitter End.* Boston: Houghton Mifflin Co., 1947.

Höttl, Wilhelm. *Hitler's Paper Weapon.* St. Albans, England: Hart-Davis, MacGibbon, 1955.

Howe, George. *Call It Treason.* New York: The Viking Press, 1949.

Hymoff, Edward. *The OSS in World War II.* New York: Ballantine Books, 1972.

Irving, David. *Hitler's War.* New York: The Viking Press, 1977.

————. *The Mare's Nest.* London: William Kimber & Co., 1964.

Kirkpatrick, Lyman, Jr. *The Real CIA.* New York: Macmillan Publishing Co., 1968.

Klein, Alexander. *The Counterfeit Traitor.* New York: Holt, Rinehart & Winston Co., 1958.

Landman, Isaac, ed. *The Universal Jewish Encyclopedia.* New York: Ktav Publishing House, Inc., 1969.

Link, Werner. *Die Geschichte des Internationalen Jugen-Bundes (IJB) und des Internationalen Sozialistischen Kampfbundes (ISK).* Meisenheim-am-Glan, Federal Republic of Germany: Verlag Anton Hain, 1964.

Lovell, Stanley P. *Of Spies and Stratagems.* Englewood Cliffs, N.J.: Prentice-Hall Inc., 1963.

MacCloskey, Monro. *Secret Air Missions.* New York: Rosen, Richards Press, 1966.

MacDonald, Charles B. *The Mighty Endeavor.* New York: Oxford University Press, 1969.

Maršálek, Hans. *Mauthausen.* Mauthausen, Austria, undated. Österreichische Lagergemeinschaft.

Masterman, J. C. *The Double-Cross System in the War of 1939 to 1945.* New Haven and London: Yale University Press, 1972.

Maurer, Maurer. *Air Force Combat Units of World War II.* Washington, D.C.: U.S. Government Printing Office, 1961.

———. *Combat Squadrons of the Air Force, World War II.* Washington, D.C.: U.S. Government Printing Office, 1969.

Minott, Rodney G. *The Fortress That Never Was.* New York: Holt, Rinehart & Winston Co., 1964.

Molden, Fritz. *Fepolinski und Waschlapski.* Vienna, Austria: Verlag Fritz Molden, 1976.

Moyzisch, L. C. *Operation Cicero.* London: Allan Wingate Ltd., 1969.

Pia, Jack. *Nazi Regalia.* New York: Ballantine Books, 1971.

Pick, Franz, and Sedillot, René. *All the Moneys of the World: A Chronicle of Currency Values.* New York: Pick Publishing Corp., 1971.

Reitlinger, Gerald. *The Final Solution.* London: Vallentine, Mitchell and Co., Ltd., 1953.

Roberts, Walter R. *Tito, Mihailović and the Allies, 1941–1945.* New Brunswick, N.J.: Rutgers University Press, 1973.

Roosevelt, Kermit, ed. *The Overseas Targets: War Report of the OSS,* Vol. II. New York: Walker & Co.; Arlington, Va.: Carrollton-Clark, 1976.

Ryan, Cornelius. *The Last Battle.* New York: Simon & Schuster, 1966.

Shirer, William L. *The Rise and Fall of the Third Reich.* New York: Simon & Schuster, 1960.

Smith, R. Harris. *OSS: The Secret History of America's First Central Intelligence Agency.* Berkeley, Cal.: University of California Press, 1972.

Stevenson, William. *A Man Called Intrepid.* New York: Harcourt Brace Jovanovich, 1976.

Swanberg, W. P. *Luce and His Empire.* New York: Charles Scribner's Sons, 1972.

Swanborough, F. G. *United States Military Aircraft Since 1909.* London and New York: Putnam & Co., 1963.

Toland, John. *Adolf Hitler.* Garden City, N.Y.: Doubleday & Co., 1976.

Whiting, Charles. *Hitler's Werewolves.* New York: Stein & Day Publishers, 1972.

———. *The Spymasters.* New York: Saturday Review Press/E. P. Dutton & Co., Inc., 1976.

Wiskemann, Elizabeth. *The Europe I Saw.* London: William Collins & Co., Ltd., 1968.

Ziemke, Earl F. *The U.S. Army in the Occupation of Germany*. Washington, D.C.: Center of Military History, U.S. Army, 1975.

DOCUMENTARY MATERIAL

Assessment of Men. The OSS Assessment Staff. New York: Rinehart Press, 1948.

Casualties to the Imperial and Allied Forces in Western Europe. Reported from 6 June 44 to 15 November 44, Supreme Headquarters Allied Expeditionary Force.

Complete List of War Crimes Trials. Headquarters, European Command, Office of the Judge Advocate, 10 June 1950.

Die Devisen Bestimmungen in Deutschland. Bank für Internationalen Zahlungausgleich, Basel, 1944.

"Erlebnisbericht." Jupp Kappius, cited in "Diary Report" by Werner Link, unpublished manuscript copy number 348, University of Marburg, Federal Republic of Germany.

Final Report on SI Operations into Germany. William J. Casey, 24 July 1945.

G-1 Division Daily Casualty Report. 4 January 45, 30 November 44, 31 October 44, 30 September 44, Supreme Headquarters, Allied Expeditionary Force.

"Histoire du Centre Syndical Belge à Londres," 1941–1944. Dore Smets and Jef Rens (unpublished, undated monograph).

History of the Carpetbagger Project. 492d Bombardment Group (H) vol. October 1943.

History of the Eighth Air Force. Second Bombardment Division, Fourteenth Combat Bombardment Wing, 492d Bombardment Group, 856th Bombardment Squadron. 1 October 43 to 1 June 44, 1 September 44 to 1 April 45.

International Military Tribunal. Nuremberg, vol. D626.

Military Government Court. Vol. 1, U.S. v. Hans Altfuldish et al. 29, 30 March 46, Dachau, Germany, 1946.

Oesterreichische Widerstandsbewegung. An das Bundes Ministerium für Ausseres (undated bulletin).

Prisoners of War, Convention between the United States of America and Other Powers, Treaty Series no. 846. Washington, D.C.: U.S. Government Printing Office, 1932.

Statistical Story of the Fifteenth Air Force. Record of operations from activation, 1 November 43 to 8 May 45.

Supreme Headquarters Allied Expeditionary Force, G-1 Casualty Reports. August 1944 through January 1945.

The Public Papers and Addresses of Franklin D. Roosevelt, 1944–45. New York: Harper & Brothers Publishers, 1950.

"*The 20th of July: A View from Without.*" Mary Bancroft (undated script of radio broadcast).

354

2641st Special Group Unit History (Provisional). For months of February, March, April 1945.

U.S. Armed Forces in Austria. War Crimes Section Progress Report, 31 August 45.

War Crimes Trials, RG 38: Nuremberg. U.S. National Archives.

War Report, Office of Strategic Services (OSS). Volume 2, prepared by History Project Strategic Services Unit, Office of the Assistant Secretary of War, War Department, Washington, D.C.: September 1947, U.S. Government Printing Office, July 1949.

World War II Operations Reports, 1940–48. 103d Infantry Division, The War Department Records Branch.

CIA DECLASSIFIED DOCUMENTS

"Cover Stories." OSS Training Manual (untitled, undated).

"Fabricated Documents." OSS Training Manual (untitled, undated).

"German Military Police, German Military Security Police, German Intelligence Service." OSS Training Document. July 1943.

"History of the Swiss Desk, SI Branch, MEDTO." Headquarters 2677th Regiment OSS (provisional, undated).

"Joan-Eleanor Logbook." Stephen H. Simpson, Lieutenant Commander, USNR, October 1, 1944–May 3, 1945.

"Memorandum of Information for the Joint U.S. Chiefs of Staff: OSS Operations in Switzerland, 1942–45." Washington, D.C.: Office of Strategic Services, June 1945.

"Memorandum of Information for the Joint U.S. Chiefs of Staff: OSS Penetration of Nazi Germany." Washington, D.C.: Office of Strategic Services, June 1945.

Missions: CHAUFFEUR (25 documents).
CHISEL (4 documents).
CROCUS (2 documents).
DARTMOUTH (1 document).
DAWES (3 documents).
DEADWOOD (3 documents).
DILLON (5 documents).
DOCTOR (25 documents).
DOWNEND (3 documents).
DUPONT (120 documents).
GEORGIA (4 documents).
GREENUP (201 documents).
HAMMER (38 documents).
HOUSEBOAT (5 documents).

LUXE I (3 documents).
LUXE II (3 documents).
MALLET (3 documents).
MARTINI (3 documents).
MIMI (7 documents).
PAINTER (7 documents).
RUBENS (3 documents).
RUPPERT (7 documents).
TROY (6 documents).
VIRGINIA (3 documents).

"Organization of the German Police Services." May 1943.
"Recruiting." OSS Training Manual (untitled, undated).
"The Nazi Party and Its Organization." OSS Training Document, May 1943.
"Training." OSS Training Manual (untitled), 14 February 44.
"War Diary of the OSS," volumes 6 and 12 (undated).

PERIODICALS

"Development of Law Relative to Treatment of Prisoners of War." J. V. Dillon, *Miami Law Quarterly,* December 1950.
"Hitler and Mars, Inc." Richard Helms, *The Indianapolis Times,* 15 March 1938.
"Jung and His Circle." Mary Bancroft, *Psychological Perspectives,* Jung Centenary Issue II. Vol. 6, no. 2, Fall 1975. C. G. Jung Institute of Los Angeles, Inc.
"A Marine with OSS." Captain William F. Grell, *Marine Corps Gazette,* vol. 29, no. 12, December 1945.

SPEECHES

Bruce, David. Annual Dinner, Veterans of OSS, 26 May 1971.
Casey, William J. "The Clandestine War in Europe," on receipt of the William J. Donovan Award, 5 December 1974.

Index

✠ ✠ ✠

Donovan, General William J. *(cont.)*
labor movement as intelligence source,
18–20, 22; and Kolbe connection, 67; and
London documents operation, 25, 28–29,
33–34; and OSS employment of German
Communists, 166–67, 255; prosecutes
Kaltenbrunner at Nuremberg, 333; and
psychology of refugee recruits, 38; recruits
Bruce, 12; recruits Dulles, 46; sees
permanent necessity of secret intelligence,
15–16; sends safecrackers, 214–15; and
Seventh Army OSS Detachment, 109;
Truman letter to, 335
Dornier aircraft factory (Weilheim), 242, 243
Doroski, Captain, 164
Dortmund, 74, 84, 149, 150, 151, 152
DOWNEND Mission, of OSS, 1–3, 5, 74–78,
83–89, 157, 324–26. *See also* RAGWEED
Mission
Dresden, 113
Dreyfuss, Paul, 64
Drucker, Willi, 74–75, 84; as "Marcel
Dusellier," imprisonment of, 307–308; OSS
evaluation of, 150; policeman, 74, 308;
RAGWEED Mission of, 149–52
Duermayer, Heinrich, 311
Dulles, Allen W.: 47, 49, 93; and Austrian
anti-Nazis, 54–58, 96, 225, 227–28, 231,
232, 269, 313, 327; in Bern, 45–57, 58–59,
62, 64–66, 186, 308, 326–27; and British re
"Cicero," 70; communication problems of,
91–92; and German Communists, 166–67;
and German Foreign Office, 62–72,
273–74, 275, 318, 328–29; and German
generals, 61–62; and Gisevius, 49–54,
56–57, 58–59, 61, 96, 152, 153, 196, 326;
and Mary Bancroft, 48–49; in New York
office of OSS, 19; and Seventh Army OSS
Detachment, 109; and V-Weapons
intelligence, 56–57; and Wehrmacht files
on Russia, 355; and Wolff peace
negotiations, 272–73, 275, 287, 290
Dulles, Eleanor, 327
Dulles, Joan, 327
Dulles, John Foster, 46
DUPONT Mission, of OSS, 219, 221;
personnel of, 122–25; progress of in Austria,
125–36, 141, 146–47; team arrested by
Gestapo, 136–40, 222, 223–25, 276–80,
310–12, 315
"Dusellier, Marcel": *see* Drucker, Willi
Düsseldorf, 333

EAGLE Project, 249–52
Eaker, Lieutenant General Ira C., 146
East Prussia, 8, 68

Ebbing, Captain, 134–36, 224, 225
Ebbing, Ernst, 120–21, 122, 123–24, 125,
127–29, 131–37, 224, 225, 312; as
"Underwood," 138
Ebbing, Frau, 132, 134, 141, 224
Ebreichsdorf, 57
Eichler, Willi, 74–75
Eichmann, Karl Adolf, 93
885th Heavy Bomber Squadron: *see* Fifteenth
Air Force, U.S.
Eighth Air Force, U.S., 162, 171; 492d
Bombardment Group of, 157–60, 180, 182,
190–91, 195–202, 263. *See also* 492d
Bombardment Group; Joan-Eleanor
communication system; missions: CHISEL,
HAMMER
Eindhoven, 248
Eisenhower, General Dwight D., 8, 20, 267,
268; and German Redoubt, 11, 289–90
Eisentratten, 141, 142, 309
Elbe River, 200
Elder, Sergeant Lawrence N., 172, 177
Ellmau, 302, 303
Emily (OSS agent), 261, 264
Emmel, Lieutenant Oliver, 183
Ems Canal (Leeuwarden), 164
"Engelke, Ewald": *see* Land, Paul
Engraving and Printing, Federal Bureau of,
24, 27
"Enigma" machine, 14
Epinal, 105, 107
Erfurt, 266
Erikson, Eric Siegfried, 316–17
ESPINETTE: objectives of, 186, 189;
recruiting by, 187–88. *See also* Belgium
Essen, 74, 84, 325, 333
European Theater of Operations (ETO), 195,
259
Evacuation permit, 251, 252
Extermination policy, Nazi, 22, 57, 276–80,
306, 310–13; Jupp Kappius on German
unawareness of, 325–26

Fairbairn, W. E. ("Delicate Dan"), 246
Farben, I. G., 88
"Fatherland Front," 120
Feldkirch, 151, 152
Fichomer, Johann, 309
Fiechter, Ernst, 141–45
Field, Noel, 166
Fifteenth Air Force, U.S.: bombing of Reich,
57, 130, 139–40, 220, 235, 236, 243–45,
269, 272; 885th Heavy Bomber Squadron
of, 146, 147, 222; Molden protests civilian
bombing to, 269. *See also* missions:
GREENUP, LUXE
Fifth Army, U.S., 2677th OSS Regiment of,

Germany, Nazi *(cont.)*
13, 93, 189, 190, 223, 235, 255, 258, 259,
270, 274, 287–89, 290, 291, 293, 303, 333;
refugees from 4–5, 13, 19, 20, 21, 22, 31,
32, 38–39, 73–74, 118, 166–68, 173,
219–20; Russia, pact with, 102; security in,
13, 41, 79–81, 325; security precautions
with documents, 26, 43; slave laborers in,
131, 276–78, 304; SO guerrilla operations
unpromising in, 254; Soviet ethnic
collaborators with, 264–68; spies, execution
of, 82, 140, 222, 279, 285, 296, 307,
311–12, 313, 314, 319, 333; surrender of,
331; surrender terms excluding Soviet
Union, 291; and Swiss neutrality, 46; trade
unions, suppression of, 18–19, 319;
V-Weapons of, 29, 56–57, 115, 139, 167,
214, 334. *See also* Austria; Kolbe, Fritz;
missions: DOWNEND, HAMMER,
LUXE, RAGWEED, RUPPERT
Gestapo (Geheime Staatspolizei), 2, 13, 59,
71, 76, 130, 133, 135, 136, 149, 173, 179,
203, 207, 218, 246, 255, 262, 263, 271,
275, 290, 293, 299, 304, 333; arrests
Adrian, 251, 252; arrests Austrian contacts
of OSS, 58, 313, 314; arrests DILLON
team, 145, 295–97; arrests Drucker, 152,
307; arrests DUPONT team, 136–40,
223–25, 276–80, 310–12; arrests following
July 20 plot, 61, 82, 84, 152, 273; arrests
Mayer, 282–87, 290, 295; block wardens of,
80, 273; Communist Party, infiltration of,
84; and Dehandshutter, 192, 299;
documents forged by OSS, 28, 152–55;
evolution of, 78, 79; Gisevius in, 50, 53,
196; GREENUP intelligence in Tirol,
236–37; interrogation practices of, 81–82,
282–86; interrogations simulated by OSS,
150; Jewish Section of, 93; and Jupp
Kappius, 88; Munich payroll of, 305; and
OSS cover stories, 40, 42–43, 150–51, 152,
153, 154, 155, 323; responsibilities of, 79;
and Vinogradov, 264. *See also* RSHA, SS
Gevrey-Chambertin, 200
Gisevius, Hans Bernd, 47, 96; and Bancroft,
Mary, 52–54, 326–27; book by, 49, 52, 59,
326, 327; and British intelligence, 50–51,
64, 97; on conspiracy, 327; as "Dr.
Bernhard," 48–49; as "Dr. Hoffmann," 153,
154; and Dulles, 49, 51, 58–60, 61, 186,
326, 334; Jung on, 327; rescue of, 152–55;
returns to Germany, 60–61, 62, 152; and
V-Weapons intelligence, 56–57
Glavin (OSS officer), 235
Gleiwitz, 135
Gmünd: DILLON Mission in, 142, 143,
144–46; postliberation inquiry in, 309–10

Goddard, DeWitt R., 161–62
Goddard, Eleanor, 162
Goebbels, Joseph, 28, 258, 318
Gold, Jay, 215
Goldbeck, Sergeant, 258
Goldberg, Arthur J.: and OSS recruitment
from trade unions, 19–21, 22–23, 35, 83,
89, 102–103, 118, 167, 168; recruits Jolis,
20, 101, 102, 103; reports death camps, 22
"Gonio" vans, 160, 302
Gontard, Major, 288
Göring, Reichsmarschall Hermann, 258, 265;
creates Gestapo, 50, 78, 80; replaced as
chief of Luftwaffe, 302
Göteborg, 318
Göttingen, 84, 88
Gould, Lieutenant Joseph: with Allied
Military Government in Berlin, 322–23;
recruits and trains German Communists,
167–69, 171, 173–74, 177–78, 182, 319,
322, 324, 332
Goums, 105
Goverts (German publisher), 154
Graf, Anton, 123, 127–29, 130–38, 140, 312;
compromises mission, 133, 136–37, 224,
225
Graz, 100
Greece, 11, 240
Green, Lieutenant Holt, 129–30, 132, 139,
222, 311
GREENUP Mission, of OSS, 217–23,
232–37, 281–87, 336; and Fritz Molden,
236–37, 294; paramilitary ambitions of, 236;
and surrender of Innsbruck, 290–95;
triumph of, 315–16
Greim, General Robert Ritter von, 302–304
Greis, 233, 236
Grell, Leon, 209–10
Grell, Major William F., 188–89, 190, 209,
302
Gresham, Orpha, 206–208, 304
Grimm, Kurt, 54–55; links Austrian anti-Nazis
and Dulles, 56–57, 96, 313–14
Grinzing, 230
Gruber, Karl, and liberation of Innsbruck,
293–94, 316, 328
Güstrow, 319
Guttner, Walter: captured by U.S., 295; and
Fred Mayer, 282–84, 285–86, 287; sees
Pfluger, 284–85

Haass, Walter, 118, 146, 219–20, 221, 223,
285
Hachselberger (German Army deserter), 204
Hahn, Private Gerard, 243
Hall, 235, 236
Halle, 251

London *(cont.)*
  Section; Britain; London Labor Division;
  Meisel, Hilde; missions: CHAUFFEUR,
  CHISEL, DOCTOR, DOWNEND,
  HAMMER, LUXE, MALLET, PAINTER,
  RAGWEED; OSS
London Labor Division, of OSS: absorbed by
  DIP, 35; contributes strategic-bombing
  intelligence, 22; formation of, 20; and labor
  refugees, 2, 21–23, 31, 32, 33, 74, 167,
  168–69, 239–40, 249; recruits German
  Communists, 167–69, 182, 319, 322–23;
  research of, 31–34; role in penetration of
  Reich, 18, 23, 35, 74, 88, 167–69, 215, 319
Los Angeles, 121, 272, 287, 290
Louis (Belgian agent), 188
Low Countries, 292
Lowenstein, Dyno, 118, 147, 219–20, 221,
  269–70, 284–85, 314–15
Loyalists, Spanish, 21, 255
Lubbe, Marinus van der, 52
Lublin, 250
Luftkuehler A. G. (Bochum), 88
Luftwaffe, 62, 110, 120, 123, 134, 135, 218,
  240, 295; von Greim appointed chief of,
  302–303
Lugano, 95
Lunéville, 260
LUXE Mission, of OSS, 241–45, 305–307
Luxembourg, 40, 186
Lyons, 160, 190, 195, 198, 199, 201, 208,
  241, 259

Maastricht, 250, 324
MacArthur, General Douglas, 6
MacCloskey, Colonel Monro, 146, 147, 222
Macht, Karl, 182–83
Madrid, 64, 289
Magnesium chlorate, 279
Mährisch-Ostrau, 176
Maier, Dr. Heinrich, 56, 58, 225, 313–14, 315
Mainz, 329, 333
Malines, 206
MALLET Mission, of OSS, 322–23
Malta (Austrian village), 144
Malzer, Otto, 212–13
Manila, 3
Mannheim, 333
Maquis, 187, 228
March, Juan, 49
"Marchand, Henri": *See* Bank, Aaron
Margulies, Daniel, 153–54
Maria (OSS agent), 261–63
Marine Corps, U.S., 109, 172, 188, 209, 218
Marseilles, 187
Martinique, 118, 256–58
Martov, Captain, 321

Marxism, 73
Mauthausen concentration camp, 222, 225,
  285, 314; conditions in, 276–80; liberation
  of, 310–12; and war-crimes trials, 312–13,
  333
Mayer, Frederick, 217–23, 232–37, 281, 336;
  and Innsbruck surrender, 291–95, 316, 328;
  interrogation of, 282–84; as "Lieutenant
  Fred," 285, 286; in Reichenau camp,
  290–91; reward to, 315–16; taken to
  Gauleiter Hofer, 287, 288, 290
Mayer, Gerald, 64–66, 69
McCulloch, Major John B., 118, 121, 122–23,
  125–26, 127, 137
Mediterranean Allied Air Forces, 146
Mediterranean Theater of Operations, 195
Mein Kampf, 306
Meisel, Hilde, 74; as "Crocus," 83; death of,
  89; 196
MELANIE recruitment operation, 248
Mellon, Paul, 266
Memmingen, 275
Menzies, Stewart, 64, 70
Messerschmitt ME-109, 192
Messerschmitt production, 57, 192, 234, 242,
  281, 336
Messner, Franz Josef, 315; arrested, 58, 313;
  gassed at Mauthausen, 314; and
  V-Weapons intelligence, 56–57
Metropol Hotel (Vienna), 138, 223–25, 314,
  315
Metz, 9
MI-5, 209
MI-6 (Military Intelligence), 14–15, 36, 232;
  and Canaris overture, 64; and "Cicero,"
  70–71; and Gisevius, 50; and Kolbe, 328.
  See also Intelligence, British
MI-6(v), and OSS counterintelligence, 15
Milan, 82, 95, 97, 99, 226, 229, 293
Miller, Captain Edward C., 170–71, 333
Miller, Gerald: heads SO, 254, 259
"Milwaukee," 33
Ministry of Economic Warfare, British, 317;
  and SOE, 15
Mishko, Lieutenant, 164, 177
MO (Morale Operations), of OSS, 7, 121
Molden, Ernst, 94, 98
Molden, Fritz: in Austria, 98–100, 157,
  225–27, 229–32, 236–37; dual objectives of,
  99–100, 227; and French intelligence,
  227–28; and GREENUP agents, 236–37,
  294; as "Hans Steinhauser," 97, 229; and
  HOMESPUN Mission, 269–70, 284,
  314–15; and Innsbruck liberation, 293–94;
  in Italy, 94, 226, 269, 293; as "Luigi
  Brentini," 95; marries Joan Dulles, 327;
  postwar career of, 328; problems with OSS,

226; protests bombing of Austria, 269; represents POEN, 227–28, 229–30, 236–37; in Switzerland, 95–97, 100, 225–26; X-2 questions, 232
Molden, Paula, 97–98
Molotov, V. M., 102
Montecassino, 94
Montgomery, General Sir Bernard Law, 9
Morale Operations: see MO
Morgan, Henry S., 5, 24–25
Morgan, J. Pierpont, 5, 24
Morocco, 105
Moscow, 224, 231
Moscow Declaration, 98
Moselle River, 9, 107
Moser, Robert, 281, 283, 284
Mosquito (aircraft), 162–65, 171, 172, 180, 181, 211, 242, 243
Moyzisch, L. C., 70
Muecke, Carl, 110, 111, 261, 329
Muggeridge, Malcolm, 16
Mulde River, 321
Müller, SS Gruppenführer Heinrich, 80
Munich, 32, 71, 115, 159, 189, 289, 302, 333; and DEADWOOD Mission, 285; LUXE Mission, 241, 244, 305; PAINTER Mission in, 208, 304–305
Munich-Garmisch-Partenkirchen railway, 245
Munich Pact, 205
Murphy, James, 19
Murray, Dr. Henry, 38
Muslims, 264
Mussolini, Benito, 63, 93, 99, 235, 258

Namur, 199–200
Nancy, 107, 187
Naples, 220
National Georgian Government (in Germany), 264
National Labor Relations Board (NLRB), 19, 20, 21, 103
National Lawyers Guild, 19
National Redoubt: Eisenhower on, 11, 290; Hofer as father of, 287–88; and Innsbruck surrender, 291, 293; intelligence objective of Belgian OSS teams, 189, 190, 199; intelligence objective of GREENUP Mission, 223, 235; intelligence objective of HOMESPUN Mission, 270–71; Kolbe intelligence on, 274; OSS losses in area of, 333; propaganda use by Goebbels, 288; sabotage objective of IRON CROSS Mission, 255, 258, 259; security precautions in area of, 13; U. S. intelligence reports on, 10–11, 12, 93, 288, 289; von Greim headquarters and, 303–304

National Socialist German Workers' Party: see Nazi Party
National Union of Scottish Mine Workers, 182
Nationalism, of Soviet ethnic collaborators, 264–68
Navigation, 121, 173, 200
Navy, Italian, 37
Navy, Japanese, 69
Navy, U. S., 121, 310, 311, 312
Nazi Party: in Innsbruck, 287; police apparatus of, 78–80. See Germany, Nazi
Nazi Party (Swiss), 51
Nazi Security Service: see SD
Nebe, Artur, 60
Neue Freie Presse, 94
Neukölln (Berlin), 320
Neusiedlersee, 125, 127–28, 129, 138
New Deal, 18, 19
New York, 3, 5, 17, 24, 31, 36, 46, 102, 141, 188, 215, 329; OSS Labor Branch in, 19–20
New York Times, The, 232
Ninth Army, U. S., 107, 324
Normandy landings, 6, 7, 57; "Cicero" intelligence on, 70; and OSS intelligence, 11, 13. See also D day
North Africa, 26, 46, 65; OSS operations in, 15, 19, 21–22, 23, 74, 93, 103, 150, 169, 195
North Rhine-Westphalia, 326
Norway, 11, 292
"Nowatny, Private": see Lemberger, Ernst
Nuremberg, 152, 192, 239
Nuremberg trials, 333
Nyle, Jack, 104–105

O5, 99, 230, 231, 270
Oakes, John B., 232
Oberlechner, Josef, 146, 309
Oberperfuss, 218, 221, 222, 233–34, 282, 286, 291, 336–37
Obersalzberg, 10, 218, 289
Office of Censorship and Documentation, of COI, 5, 24
Office of Special Funds, of OSS, 193
Office of Strategic Services: see OSS
Ohrdruf (Thuringia), 218
OKW (Oberkommando der Wehrmacht, High Command of the Armed Forces), 62. See also Abwehr
OKW Führer Reserve, 289
103rd Infantry Division (of U. S. Seventh Army), 293, 306, 308, 336
106th High Alpine Troops, 234–35
Operation MARKET GARDEN, 9
Oppeln, 135
Oral Intelligence section, of COI, 3–5

prospects of, 8–9, 60–61; separate peace
with western Allies, 291
Pearl Harbor, 3, 15, 17, 46, 139, 162
Pechel, Rudolf, 330
Peenemünde, 56–57, 225
Perpignan, 255
Perry, Lieutenant Hart, 142, 147, 222, 270
Perugia, 123
Pétain, Marshal Henri Philippe, 260
Pfluger, Hermann, 270, 284–85, 287
Pforzheim, 115
Philadelphia, 107
Philadelphia Inquirer, 36
Pienitz, Oberleutnant Rudi, 295
Pigments, German, 30
Pills, to OSS agents, 210
Pine Camp, 102, 103
Pinpoints, of OSS agent drops, 196–97, 200,
203, 205, 222, 259, 282
Pistols, to OSS agents, 210
PITT Mission, of OSS, 197–98
PLANTER'S PUNCH Mission, of OSS, 200
Ploesti oil fields, 230
POEN (Provisorische Oesterreichische
Nationalkomite, Provisional Austrian
National Committee), 227–30, 231–32, 236
Poison gas, 115, 279, 310, 311, 312
Poland, 3, 8, 22, 35, 57, 58, 231, 292, 331;
government-in-exile, 249–50; supplies OSS
agents in England, 249–52; supplies RAF
crews, 146
Portugal, 32
"Post-Collapse Personnel," 208
Potomac River, 121
Potsdam, 274
Pottendorf, 57
POWs, American, 301
POWs, Belgian, 300
POWs, English, 134, 301
POWs, French, 300, 301
POWs, German: agents pose as, 182;
authority on documents, 42; and BACH
Section procedures, 39–41; camps of,
conflict within, 229; enlisted by OSS in
North Africa, 21–22; moral problems of,
111; parachute training of, 119; recruited by
DGER, 210–11; recruited by Fifth Army
OSS Regiment, 118–20, 122–23, 220,
269–70; recruited for IRON CROSS
Mission, 255, 259; recruited by Seventh
Army OSS Detachment, 107, 109–15, 261,
331; rejected as OSS recruits, 13–14, 239;
as source of clothing, 170; three classes of,
110
POWs, Russian, 129
Poznan, 251

Prague, 123, 176
Pratt, George O.: heads DIP, 35, 36, 157,
190, 203, 215; heads London Labor
Division, 2, 20, 22, 23, 31–32, 35, 74, 103,
167–68; in OSS Labor Branch, 19, 102;
recruits Jupp Kappius, 2, 74–75
Preiler, Angela, 140
Preiler, Josef, 133, 140
Prellberg, Hans, 276, 279, 313
Prester, Julio, 140–45, 295–97; executes Lippe,
143–44, 309; and Gmünd inquiry, 309; and
surrender negotiations in Klagenfurt,
296–97
Primbs, Dr. Max, 287, 291–92
Printing operations, of OSS, 24–31, 42, 174
Pripet Swamps, 95
Privacy Act (1974), x
Provisional government: Austrian, 98, 227–29;
Polish, 250
Provisorische Oesterreichische Nationalkomite:
see POEN
Prussia, 8, 49, 68, 78
Prussian Ministry of the Interior, 78
Psychological Club (Zurich), 48

R and A (Research and Analysis), of OSS, 7,
215
Radar, 162, 165, 199, 200
Radiogoniometry, 160
RAF, 162, 172; and OSS missions, 1, 85, 126,
146, 222; 334th Wing, 146, 222
RAGWEED Mission, of OSS, 149–52,
307–308
Raoul (Belgian POW), 300
Rastenburg, 60–61, 68, 327
Ration stamps, 179
Rax Werke (Wiener Neustadt), 122, 133
RCA, 161, 333
Rechlin Air Field, 303
Red Army: *see* Army, Russian
Red Cross, 4, 12, 83, 201, 268, 310
Reddick, Willis: heads COI printshop, 23–24;
procures diamonds, 193; sets up documents
operation in London, 25–27, 37, 153, 169
Refugees: Austrian, 228; character of OSS
recruits from, 38, 168, 219–20; clothing of,
4, 24, 169–70; and COI, 4–5, 24;
Communist, 13, 166–69, 173, 255; and
OSS Labor Division, 19, 20, 21, 22, 31, 32,
33, 73, 118, 167–68
Regensburg, 192, 299–301, 310, 333
Rehbrücke, 218
Reichenau concentration camp, 290–91
Reichsbanner conspiracy, 274
Reichskanzlerei, 218
Reichstag, 52, 173
Reisting, 241–44